SPIES, LIES, AND CITIZENSHIP

SPIES, LIES, and CITIZENSHIP
THE HUNT FOR NAZI CRIMINALS

MARY KATHRYN BARBIER

Foreword by DENNIS SHOWALTER

Potomac Books
AN IMPRINT OF THE UNIVERSITY OF NEBRASKA PRESS

CONTENTS

ILLUSTRATIONS

FOREWORD

French novelist and philosopher George Bernanos once defined realism as "the good sense of bastards."[1] That cynical phrase seldom finds more frequent application than in accounts of one of the greatest surprises after World War II: the revelation that literally thousands of former Nazis had not only escaped punishment for their crimes but were living peacefully and prosperously in the United States under the sponsorship and protection of various government agencies, with their files comprehensively sanitized. Not only that, but hundreds of others, now relocated to Germany, were receiving social security payments!

On one level Americans should have been little more surprised than Casablanca's police chief, who is "shocked" to learn that gambling is going on in Rick's American Bar. German scientists and technicians had been high-profile figures in the U.S. space program from its inception. The West German Bundeswehr initially depended heavily at all levels on Wehrmacht veterans. American occupiers found it impossible to administer their conquest effectively without at least tacit cooperation from locals whose recent pasts were unlikely to withstand close questioning. But there was the Fulda Gap to screen, Europe to rebuild, and a Cold War to wage.

By the 1970s, however, times were changing. The Cold War seemed little more than a ritualized game played by the rules of John le Carré. A quarter century of research and memory had exposed the Third Reich as a comprehensive experience that had left "good Germans" thin on the ground. Under growing public and congressional pressure in 1979, the Office of Special Investigations was established in the Department of Justice. Its mission was to find and prosecute war criminals living in the United States, and it had comprehensive powers of investigation, litigation, and negotiation.

Most accounts use this as the framework for an international detective story—succeeding or failing depending on the author's perspective. Prof. Mary Kathryn Barbier has mined printed and archival sources from a fresh perspective. Using case studies ranging from near anonymous figures to familiar names like Josef Mengele and Kurt Waldheim, Barbier demonstrates and unravels the complexity both of the unique origins of each situation and the problems a democracy faces when investigating crimes backward: starting with the offender and seeking the offenses.

Arguably, Professor Barbier's major contribution to the story of the hunt for Nazi Germany's second-string criminals is her sophisticated analyses of their characters and careers. Those who achieved enough to interest American recruiters were uniformly cunning, connected—and unscrupulous. All three were requisites for securing and maintaining one's position on the slippery poles of power in the Third Reich. Some, like Klaus Barbie, had a fingertip sense of when and where to report himself ready to serve new masters. Some, like Mengele, depended on friends and family. Others, like ex-Wehrmacht lieutenant Kurt Waldheim, burrowed into emerging political systems—in his case Austria's—and developed carapaces against awkward questions, especially those raised by foreigners. It is no disrespect to their American opposite numbers to say the Germans were often able to play them like gaffed fish.

Circumstances disproportionately favored the survivors of the broken Reich. The challenge began with the greatest surprise that the postwar U.S. security system faced: the outbreak of the Cold War. Until as late as 1944, Britain had been considered, especially by the armed services, as America's primary postwar antagonist and competitor. Files on the Soviet Union were correspondingly episodic, and emergency measures seldom create coherent systems. The United States was beginning from scratch, and from a dozen start lines.

The problem of who to let in and who to shut out was further exacerbated by the sheer chaos of postwar Germany. Records were destroyed; people were scattered at random. Basic administrative problems like providing basic food and medicine overshadowed the issue of seeking what seemed at the time the small fry of the Nazi regime. Overlooked as well was a consequence of the Occupation's most pleasant surprise: the absence of overt resistance in any significant form, in any zone. By every conceivable standard the Third Reich no longer represented any reasonable threat—at least from the West's perspective. In that context making use of some of its detritus was a reasonable prospect. Few of the intelligence types who made the arrangements were likely to have read Thomas Aquinas, but they were familiar enough with his principle of "double effect": an action that can cause harm as a side effect of generating a good result.[2] With the Reich destroyed and its leaders facing trial for their lives, it required some imagination to conceive of what autonomous harm this human flotsam, bought and paid for with U.S. dollars, could generate in any case. And if it took prevarication here and there to evade President Harry Truman's ban on importing deeply involved Nazis—well, some lies can be noble lies.

All seemed well, with files left to molder, secrets mutually kept, and the dead left to bury the dead—until the creation of the Office of Special Investigations. Yet as Barbier shows, the wide-ranging powers granted to the OSI in theory proved far less sweeping in practice. Agencies competing for funding and influence shouldered the newcomer to the margin whenever possible. Immigration laws and regulations limited effective domestic sanctions to deprivation of citizenship and deportation—the Construction's ex post facto clause forbade prosecution for war crimes. And even those sentences were subject to a complicated appeals system favoring the defendant. Internationally, extradition treaties were a continuing obstacle, especially in Latin America, where enforcing their terms was a useful way to assert freedom from American control. Actuarial statistics also complicated investigations. More and more of the designated targets were dying off. Too many of the remainder had been low-ranking, menial, or marginal participants, whose advanced age could generate not necessarily sympathy but a question whether in such cases the quest was for justice or vengeance. And from the beginning the OSI was challenged for working too closely with Jewish organizations having similar objectives and with the USSR to obtain information whose accuracy was often dubious.

In 2010 the OSI was merged into a new Human Rights and Special Prosecutions Section, with what amounts to a global mandate. Statistically, its record was arguably unimpressive: around a hundred deportations all told. But it was by far the most persistent, the most systematic, and the most successful of any of the national or international organizations, outside of Israel, at exposing and at least partially cleaning up a particularly noxious legacy of Adolf Hitler's world.

Dennis Showalter

ACKNOWLEDGMENTS

This project would not have been successful had it not been for the help and support of so many people. First, let me thank Prof. Dennis Showalter, who has mentored me in every stage of my career. He called one night and said that he had a great idea for a project for me—one related to a recently released Office of Special Investigations report. As he has done so many times in the past, Dennis nudged me to explore topics, such as this one, that are on the periphery of my normal research focus. I was not initially sure that I could do justice to an analysis of the work completed by the Office of Special Investigations with regard to possible Nazi war criminals living in the United States or in the employ of a government agency, but as I delved deeper into the material, I was hooked. The result was this book—*Spies, Lies, and Citizenship*. Dennis did more than just suggest this topic. He provided advice throughout my research and writing. Furthermore, as I completed each chapter, I sent it to him for an assessment. Dennis always came through, and his encouragement paid off. This manuscript would not have seen the light of day without Dennis Showalter.

I would like to thank my editors at University of Nebraska Press/ Potomac Books—first Kristen Elias Rowley and then Thomas Swanson—who believed in me and in this project. Without their support and a contract, I might have let this research simmer on the backburner indefinitely. I would also like to thank Jonathan Fennell and the Defence Studies Department at the Joint Services Command and Staff College in Shrivenham, who invited me to the college to give a talk based on this research. Not only did Jonathan and his colleagues give me positive feedback, but presenting my research also fueled the momentum that has enabled me to write much of this book in the past year.

ACKNOWLEDGMENTS

I would like to thank my colleagues at Mississippi State University for their support and advice as I worked on this project. I also gratefully acknowledge my family, who believed in me. Without them, I could not have accomplished all that I have. Special thanks to Dr. David I. Hall, who supported me as I researched and wrote this manuscript. His faith in me and my abilities gave me the confidence that I needed to complete this project.

TERMS AND ABBREVIATIONS

AICE	American-Israeli Cooperative Enterprise
BIA	Board of Immigration Appeals
BND	Bundesnachrichtendienst, or Germany's Federal Intelligence Service
CIA	Central Intelligence Agency
CIC	Counter Intelligence Corps
CIG	Central Intelligence Group
DOJ	Department of Justice
DP	Displaced Persons
DPA	Displaced Persons Act
FBI	Federal Bureau of Investigation
GAO	General Accounting Office
Gehlen Organization	West German intelligence service
HEART	Holocaust Education & Archive Research Team
INS	Immigration and Naturalization Service
IRO	International Refugee Organization
Iron Guard	Romanian fascist group
JCS	Joint Chiefs of Staff
JDL	Jewish Defense League
JDO	Jewish Defense Organization
JIOA	Joint Intelligence Objectives Agency
MSFC	Marshall Space Flight Center
NASA	National Aeronautics and Space Administration
OMGUS	Office of the Military Government of the United States
OSI	Office of Special Investigations

RSHA	Reichssicherheitshauptamt, or Reich Headquarters of the Security Service and Security Police
SA	Sturmabeilung, or Stormtroopers
SD	Sicherheitsdienst, or SS Intelligence Agency
SLU	Special Litigation Unit
SS	Schutzstaffel, or Protective Corps
SSA	Social Security Administration
SWC	Simon Wiesenthal Center
UN	United Nations
USAO	U.S. Attorney's Office
USHMM	United States Holocaust Memorial Museum
WDGS	War Department, General Staff
WJC	World Jewish Congress

SPIES, LIES, AND CITIZENSHIP

Introduction

Why was part of a human scalp found in a Department of Justice official's desk? To whom did it belong? Did government officials put a
target on the back of a man they mistakenly identified as Nazi concentration camp Treblinka guard Ivan Demjanjuk, also known as
"Ivan the Terrible"? And did a vigilante actually murder a former
SS soldier in New Jersey? Is it possible that the government wrongfully accused naturalized citizens of being notorious Nazi war criminals? The government learned, however, that it could keep its Cold
War activities related to former Nazis a secret only for so long. Once
things began to unravel, it was only a matter of time before someone
found the thread, pulled it, and then ran with it.

In November 2010 the *New York Times* obtained a copy of, and
released to the public, a previously confidential report written by the
Department of Justice (DOJ), which held shocking secrets regarding
the government's botched attempts to hunt down and prosecute Nazis
in the United States, as well as abroad, and its willingness to harbor
and even employ some of these criminals after World War II.[1] This
exhaustive six-hundred-page report, "The Office of Special Investigations: Striving for Accountability in the Aftermath of the Holocaust," was written in 2006 by Judy Feigin, edited by Mark M. Richard
(former assistant attorney general, Department of Justice, Criminal
Division), and released four years later, after the DOJ's unsuccessful
attempt to keep it strictly under wraps. How had these alleged criminals operated under the radar for so long?

In the 1970s news broke that former Nazis had escaped prosecution and were living the good life in the United States. While some
details of the investigations into these people's pasts have slowly
trickled down to the public over the years, much more has remained

shrouded in secrecy by the U.S. government—until now. More than thirty-five years ago, Americans first learned that former Nazis who persecuted Jews and other groups resided in the United States. This enlightenment came as a result of publicity from a court case involving Hermine Braunsteiner Ryan, who was ultimately stripped of her citizenship and deported. The government based its case on evidence that demonstrated that Braunsteiner Ryan, a housewife, had been a guard supervisor at the Majdanek Nazi death camp in Lublin, Poland, and that she had lied about never being convicted of a crime, although she had served three years in prison after her conviction in 1948 for her brutal treatment of internees at the Ravensbrück concentration camp.

Although Hermine Braunsteiner Ryan's case was not included in the Office of Special Investigations (OSI) 2006 report, several of its investigations deserve special note because they provide examples of government overreach or of investigatory mistakes that had dire consequences. The cases in question concern Frank Walus, a Pole; John Demjanjuk, a Ukrainian; and Tscherim Soobzokov, a Russian. Whether due to mistaken identity or efforts to mask mistaken prosecutions, each of these cases is scandalous in its own way and demand brief illumination. In addition they illustrate, in some ways, that popular myth does not quite hold up. Accusations of being a war criminal does not make it so, but the ramifications of those charges could still have long-term consequences.

First is the case of Frank Walus, the start of which actually predated the creation of the OSI by the Department of Justice. Although he was born in Germany of Polish parents, Walus was very young when his father died, and he returned to Poland with his family. Where he was and what he did during the war has been the subject of much debate. After the war Walus resided in Kielce, Poland, for seven years. In 1959 he came to the United States under the 1952 Immigration and Nationality Act but returned to Poland a short time later. Walus reentered the United States in 1963, set up residence in Chicago, and received naturalization status in 1970.

In 1974 Walus came to the attention of the Immigration and Naturalization Service (INS) thanks to a letter from Simon Wiesenthal of the Jewish Documentation Center. According to Wiesenthal, Walus had betrayed Jews to the Gestapo in the Polish towns of Czestochowa and Kielce. The INS investigation initially failed to locate substantiating evidence. In addition, Walus claimed to have been a forced laborer in Germany during the war. Not willing to abandon the inquiry, the INS requested that Israel advertise for camp survivors who knew Walus to come forward. Of the six witnesses who provided testimony, five swore affidavits claiming to have witnessed atrocities committed by Walus. The INS subsequently located additional witnesses in the United States and decided to move forward with a case against him. The U.S. attorney filed suit. "In January 1977 Walus was charged with procuring his citizenship illegally, both because he concealed material facts (wartime atrocities and his membership in the 'Gestapo, SS or other similar organization') and because he lacked the good moral character required (as evidenced by his having committed war crimes and having concealed his membership in the Gestapo)."[2]

Eighty-two-year-old judge Julius Hoffman presided over the trial, which began in March 1978. During the trial the judge's rulings made his bias against the defense clear: "At times the court was so antagonistic to defense counsel that the government joined with the defense in an effort to salvage the record."[3] Walus's testimony remained consistent with what he told INS during its investigation—that the Germans forced him to work on farms in Germany during the war. While Walus was able to provide documentation to verify his testimony, the U.S. government was unable to demonstrate definitively the version of events that it had the burden to prove: "The Germans had no record of Walus having served in the military and the Polish war crimes commissions in Kielce and Czestochowa had no record of him either." After a seventeen day trial Judge Hoffman "revoked Walus' citizenship."[4] Following the trial Walus and his attorney uncovered additional evidence that provided further documentary and eyewitness proof that he had indeed been a forced farm laborer in Germany during the war. Consequently, they filed a series of motions requesting that the verdict be vacated. Unconvinced, the judge denied the motions, claiming that much of the testimony could not be considered "newly discovered," and he failed to give any credence to the newly discovered documents.[5] In each case—even when the Polish War Crimes Commission offered to provide corroborating evidence if ordered by the court—Judge Hoffman remained consistent and denied the motions.

A week before the creation of the OSI, the Seventh Circuit Court heard the appeal, in which Walus cited bias in both his trial and pretrial motions. The court rendered its verdict seven months later. Although the court decided not to reverse the earlier verdict based on bias, it did rule that the government's case was weak. It had not presented enough evidence to support the verdict. The court ruled that it could not affirm Judge Hoffman's decision and ordered a new trial in a different court. At this point OSI deputy director Allan A. Ryan Jr. recommended reopening the investigation before proceeding to a new trial. The OSI conducted an exhaustive seven-month investigation in Germany and Poland. In addition, Israel was asked to review the evidence and weigh in on its authenticity. Two OSI attorneys—Jerry Scanlan and Robin Boylan—reviewed the case and concluded that only one of the original government witnesses was reliable. The evidence overwhelmingly supported Walus's claims, not the government's. Although Boylan was convinced that there was no case and the government should not pursue Walus, there was debate over whether or not the government should admit its mistake. Boylan admitted that if the government acknowledged that it was wrong about Walus, it would be opening a Pandora's box, and it would be difficult to replace the lid. Doing nothing, as some advised, was not a good option either, according to Boylan. He "believed Walus was innocent, and that 'no reasonable person who has examined the file could conclude otherwise.' A failure to admit the government's error would therefore create the false impression that Walus was a war criminal. This would be particularly egregious since the government had the evidence in hand, before trial, to realize that the case against Walus could not stand."[6]

Ryan concurred with Boylan's recommendation and consulted with the U.S. attorney. They agreed to release a joint statement, which they did on 26 November 1980. They did not, however, let Walus off the hook. In fact, they blamed him for confusion caused by the embellished "stories" that he had told family, friends, and neighbors over the years. On that same November day the U.S. attorney, supported by the DOJ Criminal Division, moved to dismiss the case against Frank Walus. The court agreed and dismissed the case. In Walus's case the OSI and the U.S. Attorney's Office (USAO) made the honorable decision. They recognized that without the eyewitness testimony (proven unreliable) and corroborating documentary evidence (nonexistent) they had no real case and that pursuit of one could lead to a miscarriage of justice. As other cases would demonstrate, however, they would not always choose the honorable path. For Frank Walus, the nightmare was finally over—or was it? Despite the final result, there would be those who would not believe that he was innocent and would remain suspicious of him. Once the label of "war criminal and murderer" had been applied to Frank Walus, it was difficult to completely erase it, and to some extent it would haunt him for the rest of his life.

John Demjanjuk would learn that same lesson when he was accused of being "Ivan the Terrible." John Demjanjuk—also known as Ivan Demjanjuk—was born in the Ukrainian village of Dubovi Makharintsi on 3 April 1920. Two years later the Soviet Union incorporated the Ukraine and extended its policies to its new Soviet state. Growing up in the Ukraine exposed Demjanjuk to much hardship and horror—millions dying because of famine or Stalinist purges. In fact, because of his family's dire circumstances, they came very close to succumbing to the famine as well. As might be expected, Demjanjuk received little schooling—only four years of formal education. Before the war he got a job driving a tractor on a collective farm, but the outbreak of war earned him an invitation to join the Soviet Red Army. Demjanjuk's career as a soldier was short-lived. He was wounded, recovered, returned to the front, and was captured by the Germans in May 1942.

There is some question about what Demjanjuk did for the rest of the war. Following the war he was sent to a displaced persons camp, where he met and married his wife Vera Bulochnik in 1950 and where he worked as a driver for the U.S. Army for a short time. Two years later Demjanjuk came to the United States under the Displaced Persons Act, settled in Cleveland, and got a job as a mechanic at Ford

Motor Company. Six years after landing in Cleveland—in 1958—he became a U.S. citizen and changed his name from Ivan to John. It was not until 1975 that Demjanjuk came on the INS's radar. The INS received a communication from the New York editor of *Soviet Weekly*. The editor claimed that Demjanjuk, who had received guard training at Trawniki, Poland, had subsequently worked as a guard at the Sobibór death camp. In 1977 the *Soviet Weekly* publicly outed the Ukrainian in an article that included Demjanjuk's Trawniki identification card. The card noted the Ukrainian's posting to Sobibór. The article also included an interview with a fellow guard who claimed to have served with Demjanjuk at Sobibór and Flossenbürg. Based on these factors, the INS determined that an inquiry was warranted.

As part of its investigation into Demjanjuk and other Ukrainians accused of war crimes, the INS sent a photograph bank to Israeli investigators. The Israelis compiled a photograph album, which they showed to survivors of the Treblinka concentration camp. Unfortunately for Demjanjuk, his photograph was on the same page as Feodor Fedorenko, another Ukrainian, who was under investigation for his participation at Treblinka. When viewing the album, several Treblinka survivors, as well as witnesses in Germany and the United States, identified Demjanjuk as "Ivan the Terrible," a Treblinka guard who had committed unspeakable atrocities. If true, this was even worse than INS had imagined and demanded immediate action.[7]

In 1977, based on the eyewitness identifications, the USAO in Cleveland filed a denaturalization suit against Demjanjuk. According to the suit, the government accused Demjanjuk of entering the United States and obtaining citizenship under false pretenses—unlawfully—by concealing his connection to Treblinka. Although the government stopped short of calling Demjanjuk "Ivan the Terrible," the attorneys leveled serious charges against him: "'cruel, inhumane and bestial treatment of Jewish prisoners and laborers' at Treblinka. And while there was no allegation that he had served at Trawniki, Sobibor or Flossenbürg, the complaint charged him with falsely listing Sobibor on his visa application as a place of residence during the war."[8]

Because these events occurred at the same time that the DOJ created a new division—the Special Litigation Unit (SLU)—the decision was made that the USAO and the SLU would combine their resources and try the case together, although the DOJ appointed the SLU as lead counsel. Before the case came to trial, however, the OSI replaced the SLU. As part of their investigation, the OSI requested information about Demjanjuk from the Soviets, who had interviewed Treblinka guards and survivors, and from Poland. The Poles provided a partial guard list for Treblinka. While the name Ivan Marchenko appeared on the list, Demjanjuk's did not. Despite that, two factors convinced one OSI attorney that Demjanjuk was Ivan the Terrible. First, the Ukrainian had listed "Marchenko" as his mother's maiden name. Second, eighteen survivors and a medical aide from Treblinka had all identified Demjanjuk's photograph as Ivan the Terrible. Another OSI attorney, however, remained unconvinced, particularly since evidence seemed to suggest that the time when Demjanjuk was supposedly at Sobibór and at Treblinka overlapped and witnesses testified that Ivan the Terrible rarely left the camp. Despite the attorney's appeal to the OSI director, the government chose to move forward with the case against Demjanjuk, after amending the complaint to include his guard service at Trawniki and Sobibór.

The DOJ proved—yet again—not to be deterred by contradictory evidence. Bringing a Nazi war criminal to trial and gaining a conviction was more important than a possible miscarriage of justice. The case went to trial in 1981. Demjanjuk denied the charges, but his nightmare continued. Although the government's case was not rock solid, Demjanjuk's defense was even weaker. According to the defense, following his capture, Demjanjuk was compelled to become a member of a "German-sponsored anti-Soviet army."[9] In addition, the defense claimed a case of mistaken identity and argued that the Trawniki identification card had been forged. Although it hurt his case, Demjanjuk admitted that he had lied on his immigration documents. He had feared that honesty would have resulted in his return to the Soviet Union, where he would have paid the ultimate price for fighting against the Soviet army—his life. Because the court felt that the government's contention that the Ukrainian was in fact Ivan the Terrible was compelling, the judgment went against Demjanjuk, and the judge ordered his citizenship revoked. Vehemently denying that he was Ivan the Terrible—the guard in charge of the Treblinka gas chamber—Demjanjuk filed several appeals, all of which were rejected by November 1982. The handwriting was on the wall. Next step: deportation. In July 1982, even before Demjanjuk's appeals had been exhausted, the government filed a deportation action against him. For almost two years Demjanjuk fought deportation to the Soviet Union, but his efforts ended in failure in May 1984, when he received a notification for his deportation to the USSR.

During this same time, however, the DOJ had another ace up its sleeve. It had been negotiating Demjanjuk's extradition to Israel, where he would face additional, more serious charges. While his deportation to the Soviet Union was under appeal, the court ordered the Ukrainian extradited to Israel to stand trial for murder. Things went from bad to worse for Demjanjek, or so he thought. Still he chose to fight extradition. Losing his final appeal in February 1986, Demjanjuk found himself bound for Israel. Based on the premise that he was Ivan the Terrible, Demjanjuk was "charged with crimes against the Jewish people, crimes against humanity, war crimes and crimes against persecuted people."[10] For the next fourteen months the case against Demjanjuk played out. The Israelis presented much of the same evidence that the OSI had used in its case against him, but the defense, which had acquired discarded OSI notes that undercut some of its case, argued that the OSI had concealed and falsified information in the U.S. litigation. Unconvinced, the Israeli court found Demjanjuk guilty and sentenced him to death. He spent the next five years in solitary confinement while his conviction was under appeal. Then fate intervened.

The collapse of the Soviet Union resulted in access to new evidence that Ivan Marchenko—not Ivan Demjanjuk—had operated the gas chambers at Treblinka. There was also corroborating eyewitness testimony. This time the eyewitness testimony benefited the defense. By July 1993, following a review of all available evidence, the Israeli Supreme Court had concluded that Demjanjuk was not Ivan the Terrible. This opened the door to his return to the United States, but the nightmare was not yet over. He would soon face new charges. Although the courts vacated the 1981 deportation order in 1998, the

U.S. government didn't waste much time in filing a new denaturalization suit in 1999, citing the fact that Demjanjuk had been a guard at several concentration camps—Majdanek, Sobibór, and Flossenbürg. He lost his citizenship for the second time in 2002. In April 2004 the ruling was upheld, and in November 2004 the U.S. Supreme Court declined to review the case. The government initiated deportation proceedings a month later. In June 2005, when Demjanjuk again received notice of deportation, he petitioned the court to take the Ukraine off the table. Because he believed that the Ukrainians would both prosecute and torture him, he argued that sending him there would be in violation of the Convention against Torture. Although the court denied his motion, Demjanjuk appealed. In 2009 he both won and lost. He was deported, not to the Ukraine but to Germany, where he was convicted in 2011 of "28,060 counts of being an accessory to murder" and received a five-year prison sentence. Demjanjuk died at the age of ninety-one while awaiting the outcome of his appeal. For John Demjanjuk, the nightmare that began with a case of mistaken identity was finally over, but only because he was no longer around for the accusations to affect him. The questions about his identity and his culpability, however, remain. Unlike in the Walus case, the DOJ and OSI did not give up when their first efforts failed. They just tried again. While the initial judgment against Demjanjuk was a false start, the subsequent litigation resulted in a slam dunk. At the end of the day, the DOJ got its man even though he wasn't the horrible monster Ivan the Terrible.[11]

As the case of Tscherim Soobzokov proves, however, even when the OSI and DOJ do not get their man, unintended consequences and unanswered questions can result from an investigation and litigation. Much uncertainty surrounds Soobzokov—who he was, what he did during the war, what work he did for the U.S. Central Intelligence Agency (CIA), and who killed him. Tscherim Soobzokov was born in Tachtamukai, Russia, in 1918 (according to the 2006 OSI report). Tachtamukai, like Circassia, was in the North Caucasus region.[12] Like Demjanjuk, Soobzokov grew up in Russia during a difficult time, when new agricultural and industrial programs, purges, and efforts to eliminate opposition to the Communist Party made life quite difficult, if not disastrous, for many Russians. With the German invasion of Russia in 1941, Soobzokov had a choice to make—fight or join the invaders. There is no indication if he willingly made a choice, but by August 1942 he was recruited by an SS (Schutzstaffel, or Protective Corps) or an SD (Sicherheitsdienst, or SS Intelligence Agency) officer. As reward for his enlistment, Soobzokov received appointment as police chief of Tachtamukai, and he became a member of the Field Gendarmerie. Attached to the SS, he admitted, during a CIA polygraph, his role with an execution commando that scoured the area for Jews and communists. The rewards continued—recruitment into an SS-sponsored Caucasian Legion and promotion to first lieutenant in the Waffen-SS in 1945.

After the war Soobzokov's life took an interesting turn. In 1947 Soobzokov and a group of Circassians took advantage of help from the International Refugee Organization to emigrate from Italy to Jordan, where he initially worked for the Iraq Petroleum Company as an agricultural engineer before gaining employment with the city of Amman. During the 1950s Soobzokov was recruited by the CIA and worked under the code name "Nostril." His role for the CIA was primarily informant and spotter. As a spotter, he was to recommend Circassians who might conceivably go on CIA-sponsored missions into the Soviet Caucasus. In 1955—after submitting the appropriate applications to the INS—he immigrated to the United States with his family. The CIA denied helping Soobzokov obtain his visa, although, apparently, after his arrival in the United States, his connection with the CIA continued on a part-time basis, and within three years the Federal Bureau of Investigations (FBI) also employed him as a source. While Soobzokov and the CIA had a parting of the ways a few years later, the intelligence organization would play a role in the final hand that the Russian was dealt—or so it would seem.

Soobzokov settled into life in the United States. He became a citizen in 1961; lived in Paterson, New Jersey; joined the Democratic Party; and became active in the local Circassian community. Although he established himself as a leader in the Circassian community, he was a controversial one and made many enemies. Soobzokov had achieved what many immigrants, like most Americans, wanted. He was living the American dream, but he would soon learn that his dream life would not last.

All was not peaceful and happy between Soobzokov and his fellow compatriots. This contentious relationship chipped away at Soobzokov's American dream and, eventually, helped turn the dream into a nightmare. In fact, beginning in the 1960s several Circassians decided to contact different government offices, suggesting that they take a closer look at the Russian. The first agency to receive such a notification was the INS. A brief inquiry did not, however, convince the INS that a deeper investigation was warranted. In 1972 things took a different turn. The Social Security Administration (SSA) was contacted by Soobzokov's rivals, who made allegations of falsified birth certificates, bribery, and fraudulent government subsidies, which the government agency could not ignore. During the inquiry, rumors drew the SSA's attention to Soobzokov's wartime record. The accusation was that "Soobzokov had been in the SS and was involved in the killing of three Soviet officers" during the war. Because of these serious allegations, the SSA contacted the Berlin Document Center for information about the Russian. According to the director of the center, in 1945 Soobzokov had transferred to the Waffen-SS from a foreign army. Then came the damning bit. Although she admitted that there were no more records related to the Russian, the director was willing to make certain assumptions— "'based on similar cases' that Soobzokov transferred from a group that had either worked with SS partisan-hunting units or SS mobile killing units."[13] The SSA concluded that it had no choice but to turn the case over to the INS, which it did.

It was not long before Soobzokov learned that he was under investigation. His name was on the 1974 published DOJ list of people under scrutiny "for alleged war crimes." In addition, the INS launched a "full-scale" inquiry that lasted approximately two years.[14] What was quickly apparent was a power struggle in the Circassian community, which made it virtually impossible for the agency to acquire all of the facts and which, perhaps, should have sounded alarm bells. Frustrated, the INS announced in March 1976 that it was no longer scrutinizing Soobzokov, and the agency closed its file officially in January 1977.

While Soobzokov hoped that this was the end of the matter, life does not always work that way. This was not going to be the case. That same month Howard Blum's book—*Wanted: Nazi War Criminals in America*—hit bookstores around the country. Although the author targeted several naturalized Americans, he focused on four in particular—one of whom was Soobzokov—all of whom he labeled war criminals. Blum specifically alleged that Soobzokov had "served as a first lieutenant in a mobile killing unit that had participated in the murder of 1,400,000 Jews on the Eastern Front."[15] The Jewish Defense League (JDL) joined the fray and organized protests outside the homes of Soobzokov and his attorney. Soobzokov vigorously fought against these claims and filed a series of lawsuits against government officials and members of the media. Although he won his libel suit against Blum, the media attention did not end and persuaded the USAO for the Southern District of New York to commence a criminal investigation of Soobzokov in May 1977. Investigating a number of allegations, including charges that he had lied to the INS, the USAO requested that the State Department approach the Soviet government for information about Soobzokov, whose nightmare had returned—with a vengeance. The death threats began, making life difficult for Soobzokov and his family.

Both the Soviets and Soobzokov provided conflicted affidavits regarding his wartime record. In 1979, the same year that the OSI acquired the case, the first assassination attempt occurred, when a pipe bomb in a cigar box was delivered to Soobzokov's house. The attached note read, "Buddy. You didn't kill enough of them. Have a smoke on me. Fedorenko."[16] Although the bomb brought the FBI to the case, the agency does not seem to have agreed to Soobzokov's requests for protection. Consequently, Soobzokov's life and those of his family members remained in danger.[17]

Meanwhile the OSI investigation continued. The OSI failed to substantiate Soobzokov's claim that he had informed the U.S. vice consul in Amman about his SS connection when he applied for a visa to the United States, but they were able to corroborate his assertion that he had informed the CIA. Despite unwillingness to rely on the affidavits provided by the Soviets, the OSI was under pressure to proceed quickly against Soobzokov. The OSI needed to justify its existence, and achieving a victory in the Soobzokov case would go a long way in doing so. Other factors increased the pressure on the OSI. Not only did the DOJ expect immediate results from the OSI, but Soobzokov was also the only one of the four Blum targets who had not yet been charged—a situation that was quickly remedied.

In December 1979 the OSI made its move and filed charges against Soobzokov. In its suit the OSI claimed that Soobzokov had "unlawfully" received a visa and citizenship because he had not been honest about his complete military and criminal history on his applications. "The complaint also charged that Soobzokov lacked the good moral character necessary for citizenship; the lack of good moral character was based on his misrepresentations." Weighing in on the case, the media suggested that, because of his work for them, the CIA had helped the Russian obtain "asylum secretly."[18]

The case was not a slam dunk for either side. Soobzokov was able to supply a copy of a document from 1952—State Department Personal Data Form V-30—that detailed all of the "supposedly" omitted information, which provided the basis of the OSI suit against him. According to Soobzokov, he had provided the completed form to the vice consul when he applied for his visa. While the State Department could not produce this document because some of their records had been destroyed, the CIA did so, along with other crucial documents. Here is where things get really interesting. These documents—all of which were Department of State generated—were not in the original file supplied by the CIA to the OSI when it commenced its investigation. When questioned about the discrepancy, the intelligence agency had a curious response. According to the CIA, because of the terms of the "third party rule," the agency could not provide classified information to another agency. In its 2006 report, however, the OSI verified that Soobzokov "had been a CIA agent in Jordan and that the agency had misled the United States Immigration and Naturalization Service on Soobzokov's Nazi past."[19]

Although there seemed to have been some sleight-of-hand CIA action, the documents had to be entered into the record, and the OSI had to ascertain their authenticity. Once the OSI had done so, half of its case had gone out the window. There was no longer a "lack of moral character" case. The only thing left was Soobzokov's failure to disclose his criminal past. According to the Soviets, he had been incarcerated for five years on the charges of "hooliganism and arbitrariness"—charges generally leveled against those who had a beef with the communist state. Despite OSI requests, the Soviets declined to provide additional information about Soobzokov's "alleged criminal activity."[20] There went the rest of the OSI case. Consequently, in July 1980 the government filed a motion, which included a litany of information about inquiries made by the OSI to verify the facts of the case, requesting dismissal of the complaint against the defendant.

Although he had achieved victory with the dismissal of the government suit, Soobzokov did not see an end to the nightmare. The Jewish Defense Organization (JDO), an offshoot of the JDL, was unwilling to let it go and publicly continued to advocate a violent resolution. Multiple responses to the JDO's rally cry occurred on 14 August 1985. According to police, Soobzokov reported that a car containing two people had tried to run him down. A few hours after he phoned the police, Soobzokov's car, which was in front of his house, burst into flames. When a neighbor saw the burning car, he went to warn Soobzokov. When the beleaguered man opened the door, a bomb that had been wired to it went off and fatally injured Soobzokov, who died three weeks later. Three other people in the house—Soobzokov's wife, his daughter, and his four-year-old grandchild—were also injured in the blast.

Who was responsible for the bomb that killed Soobzokov and injured three members of his family? The obvious culprit was the JDO. While the JDO and the JDL "denied responsibility," neither group expressed sorrow regarding the tragedy. In fact, "the JDL applaud[ed] the action," while the JDO claimed that the bombing was a "righteous act."[21] No one has yet been brought to justice. While the OSI did not have enough evidence to convict Soobzokov, at the end of the day, that did not matter. People like Blum, the media, and groups like JDO decided that he was guilty. Once the target was drawn on his back, it was only a matter of time before someone hit the bull's eye. One could argue that the ultimate outcome was unforeseen by the OSI.

It was an unintended consequence of the OSI's mission—to root out and prosecute Nazi criminals, those who had persecuted Jewish and other disadvantaged groups before and during World War II. It was the OSI's job to achieve justice for the millions of victims. Unfortunately, the OSI target made Soobzokov a victim as well.

Since the Braunsteiner Ryan case broke, numerous books on the hunt for Nazis have been published. Some of the more recent publications include *Hunting Eichmann: How a Band of Survivors and a Young Spy Agency Chased Down the World's Most Notorious Nazi*, by Neal Bascomb; Guy Walters's *Hunting Evil: The Nazi War Criminals Who Escaped and the Quest to Bring Them to Justice*; and *Operation Paperclip: The Secret Intelligence Program That Brought Nazi Scientists to America*, by Annie Jacobsen. *Spies, Lies, and Citizenship* answers questions like those articulated earlier and exposes scandalous new information about Nazi fugitives—such as Josef Mengele, Andrija Artuković, Arthur Rudolph, Kurt Waldheim, and Klaus Barbie—sheltered and protected in the United States or relentlessly pursued by criminal investigators.

In each of these cases, the OSI had to decide whether or not to rely on eyewitnesses, either through affidavits or in direct courtroom testimony. Eyewitness testimony can frequently be unreliable. In some cases the witnesses deliberately mislead investigators because they have a specific agenda. In the case of Tscherim Soobzokov, rivals in the Circassia community had an axe to grind and did their best to spark investigation of their Russian neighbor. In other cases, such as in the case of John Demjanjuk, the witnesses made honest mistakes. The placement of his picture next to that of another Treblinka guard in a photo array influenced eyewitness identification of Demjanjuk as Ivan the Terrible. Although the evidence proved that Demjanjuk was not Ivan the Terrible, the government vigorously pursued other charges against the Ukrainian and succeeded in stripping him of his citizenship and deporting him. Finally, in the case of Frank Walus, while eyewitness testimony initially bolstered the government case against him, subsequent investigation undercut the validity of that testimony. As a result, the case against him was dismissed. Unlike Demjanjuk and Soobzokov, Walus did not face further government inquiry or litigation. The Walus, Demjanjuk, and Soobzokov cases seem to establish a pattern of behavior by the government agencies in question—INS, USAO, DOJ, and OSI—and their pursuit of high-profile cases whether there was substantiating evidence or not. It is possible, however, that, as the OSI settled down to business and the dust settled, there was less government overreach or investigatory mistakes.

1

Office of Special Investigations, Department of Justice

In the wake of 11 September 2001, the terrorist attacks in the subsequent decades, and most recently the refugee crisis caused by multiple conflicts in the Middle East and Africa, states have grappled with issues of security. These are, however, not unique. The United States faced similar issues in the aftermath of World War II, as displaced Europeans, particularly from Eastern Europe, sought new homelands in an environment of conflict. The sticking point in the twenty-first century is the possibility of terrorists crossing borders with legitimate refugees. As the Cold War unfolded, the possibility of Soviet spies infiltrating the United States created similar issues of exclusion and screening. Similar to the contemporary refugee-terrorist debate, the intellectual and moral fault line after 1945 developed between concern for America's security and a compassionate, humanitarian desire to help victims of Nazi and Soviet crimes against humanity. True to its democratic roots, the nation turned to Congress to solve the problem by passing the appropriate legislation—particularly legislation that identified who would be barred from entering the United States.

Otherwise known as the McCarran-Walter Act, the Immigration and Nationality Act of 1952 was meant to exclude certain immigrants from immigrating to America, post World War II and in the early Cold War. The McCarran-Walter Act moved away from excluding immigrants based simply upon country of origin. Instead it focused upon denying immigrants who were unlawful, immortal, diseased in any way, politically radical etc. and accepting those who were willing and able to assimilate into the U.S. economic, social, and political structures, which restructured how immigration law was handled. Furthermore, the most notable exclusions were anyone even remotely associated with communism which in the early days of the Cold War was seen as a serious threat to U.S. democracy. The main objective of this was to block any spread of communism from outside post WWII countries, as well as deny any enemies of the U.S. during WWII such as Japan and favor "good Asian" countries such as China. The McCarran-Walter Act was a strong reinforcement in immigration selection, which was labeled the best way to preserve national security and national interests.[1]

Truman indicated his disagreement by vetoing the McCarran-Walter Act, but to no avail. Congress had enough votes to override the president, and the bill became law. Passing the law was the first step; enforcing it was the next.

Based on the terms of the Immigration and Nationality Act of 1952, or the McCarran-Walter Act, Nazis who persecuted, abused, or executed Jews, gypsies, and other groups targeted by the Third Reich should not have been allowed to immigrate to the United States. In reality, it was difficult to vet all those who requested admission to the United States under the terms of the Displaced Persons Act, which Congress passed in 1948, or the 1953 Refugee Relief Act. Between 1948 and 1953 more than six hundred thousand Europeans emigrated to the United States. They sought asylum primarily for two reasons. Either they were victims of Nazi persecution or they were "political refugees from Communism." The sheer numbers requesting admission under the Displaced Persons Act, and later under the Refugee Relief Act, overwhelmed consular offices. Consequently, it was very difficult for officials who reviewed the applications and interviewed applicants to identify the ex-Nazis attempting to pull a fast one. Those hoping to "sneak" into the United States either presented false identification papers or lied about their wartime activities in their applications for asylum. Many former Nazis succeeded in obtaining the documentation necessary for them to gain entry to the United States. The 1952 McCarran-Walter Act was an effort by Congress to close the loophole in the 1948 immigration law.[2]

Over the next few decades, however, news would occasionally emerge that would suggest otherwise. Apparently, some Europeans of questionable character, who were possibly guilty of committing war crimes, had succeeded in immigrating to the United States and, in some cases, had even become naturalized citizens. Many refugees to the United States—survivors of Nazi atrocities—found the trickle of news about possible Nazi criminals living in their adopted country disturbing and distressing on many different levels. Was the U.S. government guilty of harboring these criminals? Surely, only a few had slipped through the cracks and found asylum in the United States. The country would not have willingly admitted these monsters—or would it?

In the 1970s the dam burst wide open. The news broke that a large number of former Nazis who had persecuted Jews and other groups were living in the United States. Outrage swept across the nation. The public outcry put extreme pressure on the U.S. government to investigate these claims and, when warranted, to deport the offenders. The number of cases that came to light demanded the establishment of a special division within the Department of Justice that would be devoted solely to investigating possible Nazi criminals, to building cases against them, and to wielding the gavel of justice against them. The result was the creation in 1979 of the Office of Special Investigations. For the next few decades the OSI was kept incredibly busy.

Prior to the establishment of the OSI, however, both the Department of Justice and the Immigration and Naturalization Service had taken seriously the possibility of Nazi criminals living in the United States, openly or under assumed identities, and had instigated numerous investigations and court cases against several alleged perpetrators of wartime atrocities. In some cases investigation of alleged wartime criminals began relatively early in the Cold War era. In 1951, for example, Andrija Artuković, the suspected "Butcher of the Balkans," first came to the attention of authorities. Pursuing an investigation of and legal action against Artuković, who had entered the country under a fictitious name, the Department of Justice spent over three decades trying to deport him. Shortly after the OSI was established in 1979, it took up the case. It was not until 1986, over three decades after the commencement of the initial DOJ investigation, however, that the case against Artuković was finally resolved; it resulted in his deportation.[3]

Similarly, Karl Linnas, who became a naturalized U.S. citizen in 1959, came to the attention of the DOJ in 1961. An article in the *New York Times* outed him. A DOJ investigation confirmed the war crimes allegations lodged against Linnas, but, despite its strenuous efforts, the government agency found itself unable to achieve deportation until the OSI took on the case in November 1979. It still took until 1987, however, for the OSI and the DOJ to achieve the desired outcome in the Linnas case—denaturalization and deportation.[4]

Finally, there was the case of the Romanian Otto von Bolschwing, who found employment in Europe for the CIA in 1949. Five years later the CIA facilitated his immigration to the United States. He achieved citizenship by the end of the decade. Von Bolschwing avoided a DOJ investigation until 1977. The OSI became involved in the investigation, but the CIA continued to stonewall for a time. Although the OSI ultimately succeeded in proving its case against the Romanian, the agency declined to pursue deportation for humanitarian reasons.[5]

What brought the issue to public attention? What caused the floodgates to open? Although cracks had appeared over the years, a number of events occurring in the 1970s combined to burst the dam. The events included

1. The denaturalization and extradition of Hermine Braunsteiner Ryan, a German-born New York City housewife who had served as a guard supervisor at a Nazi death camp.

2. Public denunciation of the INS by the investigator and prosecutor in the Braunsteiner Ryan trial, each of whom left the agency after accusing it of foot-dragging and coverup in other Nazi investigations.

3. Publicity attendant the simultaneous filing of three deportation actions against alleged war criminals in 1976.

4. Congressional oversight hearings in 1974, 1977 and 1978 which highlighted deficiencies in the INS procedures for investigating Nazi cases.

5. A GAO [General Accounting Office] study that concluded that the INS investigations of Nazis were "deficient or perfunctory."

6. Publicity surrounding the prosecution of a denaturalization case against the Romanian Orthodox Bishop of America for his alleged involvement in atrocities during World War II.

7. The 1977 bestseller *Wanted! The Search for Nazis in America.*

8. NBC's 1978 broadcast of a powerful four-part miniseries titled *Holocaust.*[6]

Once the floodgates were opened, there was no going back. The public demanded justice—and accountability.

At the end of the day, in each of these cases—Artuković, Linnas, von Bolschwing, and Braunsteiner Ryan—and in others initiated prior to the creation of the Office of Special Investigations, the Department of Justice lacked the legal recourse to prosecute and deport these and other alleged Nazi criminals. Most of the cases involving alleged Nazis were handled by the INS, which was the practice in any disputed immigration situation. Unfortunately, because each district was responsible for cases raised locally, there was no central coordination through the Washington DC or New York offices, which resulted in poor results and suggested a lack of seriousness on the part of the INS. That situation would remain unchanged until Congress got involved and passed legislation that increased the DOJ's powers in cases such as these. Congress remained uninvolved, however, until one of its members led the charge and proposed legislation. Initially, however, congressional leaders dragged their feet until pressure dictated oversight hearings. They seemed unwilling to jump into the fray and take the bull by the horns.

What changed? Or rather, who convinced Congress to provide the muscle that the 1952 Immigration and Nationality Act lacked when it came to expelling former Nazis of questionable character who had not only gained entry into the United States but had also, in some instances, acquired citizenship. It is impossible to tell this story without acknowledging, and emphasizing, the roles that Simon Wiesenthal and Elizabeth Holtzman played. Both were dedicated to finding justice for the millions who suffered and died—or in some cases survived—at the hands of the Nazis during World War II. To understand their dedication and what drove them to advocate for the victims and to push for the persecution of Nazi criminals, one has to know more about who Wiesenthal and Holtzman were.

Key Players

Born in 1908 in Buczacz, Galicia (in what today is the Ukraine), Simon Wiesenthal survived internment in not one, but five, concentration camps. Wiesenthal and his family were not strangers to prejudice and persecution. As Jews, they had been targets for decades before World War II, but the Nazis took persecution to a new level. While life under the Soviets was not easy, the situation became much worse with the 1941 German occupation of Galicia. Initially, the Germans forced both Wiesenthal and his wife, Cyla, to work "at the German Eastern Railway plants." Although an "underground movement" smuggled his wife out of the area, Wiesenthal remained behind.[7] His life was a living hell. For the next several years he found himself moved from camp to camp. He tried to escape, but freedom did not last. Recapture meant return to the camp and harsher treatment. He also tried suicide—twice—but was equally unsuccessful.

In 1944 Wiesenthal was transferred again. His new residence was the Janowska concentration camp. Located in the suburbs of Lvov, Poland, the camp complex included both a ss-run armaments factory and housing for the forced laborers. Established in 1941, Janowska also served as a transit camp for Polish Jews being sent to extermination camps. As the Soviet steamroller pushed German troops out of the Soviet Union and through Poland and other eastern European countries, the ss guards liquidated a large number of camp internees and evacuated with the rest. Of the hundred thousand who inhabited the camp, fewer than forty, including Wiesenthal, accompanied the fleeing ss guards. A short time later Wiesenthal and the others joined the population in a new camp—Mauthausen—in Austria. Wiesenthal would not be moved again by the Germans. In May 1945 he was liberated from Mauthausen by American soldiers.

The ordeal had taken a mental and physical toll on Wiesenthal, who "at 6 feet tall, weighed less than 100 lbs" at the time of his liberation. By late 1945 he had found his wife, Cyla, who had also survived the war. Both had, however, lost family and friends in the camps. Once he had recovered, Wiesenthal quickly determined his life's mission: justice for those who suffered at the hands of the Nazis, both those who had survived and those who had not. To obtain justice, he had to identify, locate, and facilitate the prosecution of the responsible Nazis—those responsible for the laws that denied Jews, gypsies, and other groups their rights, jobs, property, freedom, and lives; those who set the "Final Solution" policy; those who carried out the policies, the guards at the camps, the torturers, and executors; those who had committed atrocities; those who carried out medical experiments on concentration camp inmates.[8]

Wiesenthal was also dedicated to educating the world about the realities of the Jewish wartime experience under German control. One of the ways in which he combined both goals was by being director of the Linz Jewish Documentation Center, a position that he held from 1947 until 1954. In 1961 he became the director of the Vienna Jewish Documentation Center, and in 1977 he founded the Simon Wiesenthal Center in Los Angeles, California. Throughout this time he worked tirelessly to locate numerous former Nazis; he and others felt these individuals should be held accountable for their wartime actions. In addition to his detective role of trying to track down persecutors, Wiesenthal focused a spotlight on the worst of the offenders. He made efforts to locate the perpetrators publicly. Furthermore, he kept attention focused on them. Although at times his methods were controversial and he was accused of being a loose cannon who got it wrong, Wiesenthal contributed to the capture of the likes of Adolf Eichmann, Franz Stangl, and Karl Silberbauer. Eichmann worked with top Nazi officials in designing and implementing the Final Solution for the eradication of the Jewish population in German territory and eventually worldwide. The Austrian Stangl joined the ss and had the dubious distinction of being the commandant of two extermination camps: Sobibór and Treblinka. Silberbauer, a member of the Gestapo, was credited with arresting Anne Frank and her family, who were sent to a concentration camp.[9] Of the four members of the Frank family, only the father, Otto Frank, survived.

Wiesenthal kept attention on the fight through his many publications. Included among them were *The Murderers among Us: The*

Simon Wiesenthal Memoirs (1967), *The Sunflower: On the Possibilities and Limits of Forgiveness* (1969), and *Justice Not Vengeance: Recollections* (1989). Although at times controversial, Wiesenthal received recognition of his life's work from several governments. During his lifetime he was awarded the Dutch Medal of Freedom, the Luxembourg Medal of Freedom, and the U.S. Congressional Medal of Honor. Through his postwar work Wiesenthal accomplished two goals. He "shed light on the injustices and horrors of the Holocaust." Furthermore, he challenged governments, including the U.S. government, to intervene "in the capture of war criminals" and to bring them to justice. Ever the activist, Simon Wiesenthal did not make it easy for the U.S. Congress to remain outside of the fray.[10]

Although Wiesenthal could only indirectly pressure the U.S. Congress and DOJ to get involved in the location and prosecution of alleged Nazi war criminals, Elizabeth Holtzman, on the other hand, was positioned to affect change in the U.S. government's ability to prosecute identified persecutors to achieve denaturalization and deportation and to facilitate court cases filed against them in other countries—France, Germany, the Soviet Union, and Israel. Born with a twin brother in 1941 to Russian immigrant parents, Holtzman followed in her lawyer father's footsteps. In 1965 she graduated from Harvard Law School. Out of the five hundred in the 1965 graduating class, there were fifteen women, one of whom was Holtzman.

With her graduation behind her, she returned to New York, where she engaged in activities that would define her career and her future—the law and state politics in the Democratic Party. It did not take Holtzman long to obtain a political position. As one of Mayor John Lindsay's assistants (1967-70), her job was to oversee parks and recreation. Holtzman was on the road to great things in politics. Following her position as Lindsay's assistant, she worked as a state Democratic committee member. She was also a Flatbush "district leader." During this time, not one to let the grass grow under her feet, Holtzman also championed feminist causes. She was one of the founders of the Brooklyn Women's Political Caucus.[11] Then she set her sights on a bigger political prize—one that would allow her to make a difference on a national level.

In 1972 Holtzman decided to take on the establishment in a bid to win a congressional seat. To do so, she had to challenge the incumbent—Rep. Emanuel Celler. At eighty-four, Celler, who was the chair of the House Judiciary Committee, had represented his central Brooklyn district for over half a century. Defeating both Celler and her Republican opponent, Holtzman joined the Ninety-Third Congress (1973–75). She was only thirty-one. While serving in Congress for four terms, Holtzman received assignments to several important committees. For the eight years in which she was in Congress, she was on the House Judiciary Committee. It was in that capacity that Holtzman became involved in the INS-Nazi criminal controversy.[12]

Times They Are a Changin'

Newly elected to Congress, Holtzman received an assignment to the House Subcommittee on Immigration, Citizenship, and International Law. This subcommittee had the task of holding INS oversight hearings. INS commissioner L. F. Chapman Jr. immediately found himself pressed for answers by the young representative from Brooklyn. When Chapman acknowledged the presence of former Nazis in the United States, Holtzman found a cause into which she could sink her teeth. Holtzman did not lose time bringing the ineptitude of the INS to public attention in a press conference, where she also advocated for the creation of an INS War Crimes Strike Force. Taking things a step further, Holtzman approached the INS for a list of all individuals under investigation. The INS submitted a list of seventy-three names. In addition, the DOJ acknowledged investigation of thirty-seven individuals.[13] Holtzman proceeded to conduct her own assessment of the INS. She also took the secretary of state's office to task for not cooperating with INS investigations of alleged Nazi criminals. When the Department of State failed to respond to her satisfaction, Holtzman went public, again. The pressure worked—the State Department agreed to process INS requests in a more timely fashion.[14]

The spotlight was not just on the INS and the Department of State. In January 1977 Congress requested a GAO investigation, which resulted in the release of a report, *Widespread Conspiracy to Obstruct Probes of Alleged Nazi War Criminals Not Supported by Avail-*

able Evidence—Controversy May Continue, in May 1978. Part of the report focused on the role of the Central Intelligence Agency in the investigations of alleged Nazi criminals. The CIA did not emerge from the investigation unscathed. According to the report,

> the GAO found that in its search for information on 111 alleged Nazi war criminals, the Agency had no records on 54. Of the remaining 57, CIA had references, such as newspaper articles and general correspondence with other Federal agencies, on 35. That left 22 individuals with whom CIA admitted to GAO investigators that it had a more substantial relationship. In an unnamed case, CIA sponsored the immigration of a "senior official of the German Foreign Ministry during the Nazi era" to the United States. The remaining 21 had contact with CIA either overseas or after their immigration to America; some were paid, while the Agency declined to use others.[15]

The GAO report sparked heated reactions in Congress. Rep. Joshua Eilberg directed his response to "the Federal Government because 'this report makes clear that the CIA and FBI were more interested in using these people and getting information from them than in conducting any background investigation as to their wartime activities or pursuing allegations that they were war criminals.'"[16] An implied challenge had been issued. The CIA, FBI, and INS had to clean up their acts, focus on the task at hand, and take investigation of questionable individuals who potentially committed atrocities seriously.

The GAO investigation was not the only one initiated in 1977. Holtzman and a colleague approached the chair of the House Subcommittee—Representative Eilberg—to request new oversight hearings that focused exclusively on Nazi criminals. Holtzman found an ally in Eilberg, who was equally outraged at the situation.[17] In an effort to stop the flow of bad press, another bad subcommittee assessment, and the possibility of congressional interference in investigations, however, the INS announced a procedural overhaul related to investigations of alleged Nazis—the creation of a task force consisting of five attorneys who would be devoted specifically to these cases. Washington DC attorney Martin Mendelsohn would lead the newly created Special Litigation Unit (SLU). Mendelsohn answered to the INS general counsel David Crosland, who "ordered all closed cases involving alleged Nazi war criminals still alive and in the United States reopened for investigation." Mendelsohn and the SLU also had to assess all open cases to determine the unit's role in each moving forward, but the wheels of justice moved at a snail's pace. It was late summer 1978 before the SLU was fully staffed and ready to get to work.[18] It appeared, however, that INS had gotten the message and that things were beginning to move in the right direction, albeit slowly.

From the beginning Mendelsohn established a working relationship with Representative Holtzman, which did not please his boss, Crosland. He also met with U.S. attorneys already involved with litigating cases against alleged Nazis. Because of funding and other issues, both Holtzman and Mendelsohn recommended relocating the SLU to the Department of Justice building. Opposing the move, both the DOJ and the INS tried to convince Holtzman to embrace their position. Not only was she unconvinced, but she also "threatened to legislate the move if the Department did not accede." Justice reluctantly agreed but registered its reticence with the subcommittee. Holtzman was not finished. She advocated for placement of the unit in the Criminal Division of Justice. Justifying her position, Holtzman "felt that this would be the most appropriate fit since 'the cases involve murder' with an order of proof almost as high as that required in a criminal trial."[19]

Justice would comply. In March 1979, when testifying before the House Immigration Subcommittee, Associate Attorney General Michael J. Egan, who had early that year provided notification of the transfer of the SLU from INS to Justice, admitted that the Special Litigation Unit "had 'not worked out as we had hoped.'"[20] The transfer became official on 4 September 1979, when "Attorney General Benjamin Civiletti signed" the authorization. Civiletti tasked the Criminal Division with "primary responsibility for detecting, investigating, and, where appropriate, taking legal action to deport, denaturalize, or prosecute any individual who was admitted as an alien into or became a naturalized citizen of the United States and who had assisted the Nazis by persecuting any person because of race, religion, national origin, or political opinion."[21] Although this was what she wanted,

Holtzman was not satisfied that it was going to be enough, and she took steps to ensure the establishment of specific protocols—before the formal transfer of the SLU to Justice had occurred.

On 2 May 1978, along with Eilberg, her cosponsor, Holtzman introduced a bill into the House: "H.R. 12509—An Act to amend the Immigration and Nationality Act to exclude into, and to deport from, the United States all aliens who persecuted any person on the basis of race, religion, national origin, or political opinion, under the direction of the Nazi government of Germany, and for other purposes." While the DOJ was organizing the transfer of the SLU, first the House of Representatives and then the Senate discussed and voted on Holtzman's bill. Before the final vote, which occurred on 10 October 1978, the Senate amended it by adding two provisions: Title I and Title II. The former is most germane to the issue at hand. Title I "amends the Immigration and Nationality Act to exclude from admission into, and provide for the deportation from, the United States of any alien who between March 23, 1933 and May 8, 1945, under the direction or in association with the Nazi government of Germany, or any government allied or collaborating with the Nazi government of Germany, engaged or assisted in, or incited or directed others to engage in, the persecution of others on the basis of religion, race, national origin, or political opinion."[22] With the passage of H.R. 12509 by both houses of Congress, the bill went to President James (Jimmy) Carter's desk. The president signed the bill into law.

In the meantime, the transfer of the SLU resulted in an overhaul and a name change. Recrafted as the Office of Special Investigations, or OSI, the unit was under the oversight of Philip Heymann, the assistant attorney general of the Criminal Division, and his deputy Mark M. Richard. Determined to establish credibility for the OSI, Heymann convinced a former U.S. prosecutor at Nuremberg— Walter Rockler—to be the unit's interim director until it was firmly established with a permanent director. The majority of the lawyers who had worked at the SLU, including Mendelsohn, transferred to the OSI. Mendelsohn, as Rockler's second in command, was the OSI deputy director. While Mendelsohn assumed responsibility for the litigation section, Rockler focused on new case assessment and getting the OSI on a firm footing. He also reaffirmed connections with his counterparts in Israel and the Soviet Union that had been established by Mendelsohn.

Not one to take a hands-off approach, Holtzman kept a close watch on the newly established OSI. She expected—and received—regular briefings from Rockler, who recognized what Holtzman brought to the table. While OSI and DOJ had to work through the Department of State, Holtzman did not. She had tools that she could use to apply pressure and get results, and she was not afraid to use them. For example, Holtzman, "along with Rep. Hamilton Fish (the ranking Republican on her immigration subcommittee) was able to gather 120 cosponsors on a 1979 resolution urging the West German government to extend or abolish its statute of limitations governing the prosecution of Nazi war crimes." The statute of limitations was eliminated as a result of their actions. This made prosecution for war crimes possible even thirty years after the war.[23]

Early Years of the OSI Pursuing Its Mandate

In the beginning Rockler and others believed that the OSI would have served its usefulness in a half a dozen years because, surely, they would have exhausted all of the possible cases that fell under the unit's jurisdiction. That would prove not to be the case. In 1980, when Rockler stepped down as director of OSI, his replacement was Allan A. Ryan Jr., who served as director until 1983, when he was succeeded first by Neal M. Sher (1983–94) and then by Eli M. Rosenbaum (1994–2010).

Recognizing the need for transparency and good public relations, Ryan reached out, with help from DOJ, to the "Jewish and ethnic communities," with varying degrees of success. He also understood the importance of establishing a good relationship with Representative Holtzman, who was unhappy that Rockler's successor was not Mendelsohn. According to Ryan, Holtzman "had the reputation in OSI . . . of being . . . Ghengis Khan incarnate. . . . I had to speak with [her] because she was the key person on the Hill. . . . It was the beginning of a very mutually respectful relationship."[24]

To some extent, the congresswoman continued to live up to her reputation. Holtzman "remained vigilant about OSI matters, issuing press releases to announce OSI filings and victories, exhorting the State Department to work with OSI to update its Watchlist (they did), demanding that State modify its visa application form to take into account new legislation precluding the entry of Nazi persecutors (also done), and notifying OSI when she learned of a potential subject."[25] Despite Holtzman's oversight and help in opening doors, OSI faced many challenges from the beginning, not the least of which was the age and availability of witnesses and access to Nazi documentation—some of which had been destroyed, some of which was behind the Iron Curtain.

These factors complicated matters. To pursue any case that came to the OSI, witnesses and documentation were crucial. What documentation did the OSI need? Beginning in the early 1980s, the OSI focused on locating "surviving Axis records. These include, but are not limited to, SS concentration camp guard rosters, postwar wanted lists, and other documents from which the unit's investigative staff might gather names of individuals who could be reasonably suspected of having participated in wartime crimes."[26] While many of these records had been destroyed, others—"including German military and administrative records, newspapers and magazines published or supported by German occupation authorities, post-war trials and transcripts"—did survive. Because many of them were housed in Germany and the Soviet Union, acquiring access was complicated to say the least—and in some cases, particularly with regard to records controlled by the Soviets, virtually impossible.[27]

In an effort to gain access to materials held behind the Iron Curtain, particularly in the Soviet Union, members of Congress (Holtzman and Eilberg) and the OSI (Mendelsohn, Rickler, Richard, and Ryan) traveled to the USSR for meetings with Soviet officials. Attorney General Civiletti met with the chief justice of the Soviet Supreme Court to discuss the matter. Efforts at outreach paid off. "The U.S. would be allowed to take videotaped depositions of Soviet witnesses and to have increased archival access." Although this was a positive step forward, the lack of indices to archival material slowed down the acquisition of pertinent documents. The lack of Soviet personnel to process information requests and equipment to photocopy documents also hindered swift progress.[28]

Not all of the delays came from impediments to international cooperation. Others resulted from inefficiencies within the United States. Repositories in the United States, such as the Library of Congress, the National Archives and Records Administration, and private institutions, did not always catalog or physically maintain the integrity of materials that had appeared to be unimportant at the time of acquisition. Access to materials held in private collections was also difficult. Furthermore, as noted in the GAO report *Widespread Conspiracy to Obstruct Probes of Alleged Nazi War Criminals Not Supported by Available Evidence—Controversy May Continue*, government agencies, including the CIA, frequently complied with OSI requests for information, but the documents that they submitted were often heavily redacted, which made them less useful. Restrictions on interagency information sharing also complicated an already difficult situation and impeded OSI investigations and litigations. Deputy Assistant Attorney General Richard worked hard to facilitate the sharing of information between government agencies.[29] The longer that it took for the OSI to accumulate the information required to move forward with a case, the more likely it was that fewer witnesses—that is, camp survivors—would be able to testify credibly when the case reached the courts. All of these factors made OSI's work more difficult, but the unit remained determined to carry out its mandate.

Case Protocols

As might be expected, the OSI established protocols for the cases that it handled. Decisions had to be made about which cases did not have merit and which ones should be pursued, what steps to take moving forward in the investigative and litigation stages, and what outcomes were most desired. While each case was unique, there had to be a template to follow. One of the first steps was to identify potential suspects. By 2006 more than seventy thousand had been identified.

The next step was to verify the authenticity of these individuals "by methodically checking all of these names against U.S. immigration records and other domestic records." Generally, the OSI moved forward with an investigation of target individuals only if they were still alive, although there was at least one notable exception to that rule—Josef Mengele. An OSI investigation was unlike a "traditional law enforcement investigation." Instead of starting with crimes and working backward to identify the guilty parties, the OSI began with suspects and worked forward to identify what, if any, crimes they committed, which was not always easy to determine definitively decades later. At the end of the day, the OSI found evidence proving wartime crimes in only the minority of the cases that the unit investigated. Although it might seek some assistance from other government agencies—"in forensic document examination, DNA analysis, and other technical specialties"—the OSI generally handled all aspects of the investigation. Unlike other law enforcement agencies, the OSI relied on its in-house historians "to conduct the bulk of the investigative work."[30]

Was Litigation the Only Option?

Tasked with "detecting, investigating, and taking legal action to denaturalize and/or deport individuals who, in association with the Nazi Government of Germany and its allies, ordered, incited, assisted, or otherwise participated in the persecution of civilians because of race, religion, national origin, or political opinion," OSI had three avenues of action:

1. Suits are brought in federal district courts seeking to revoke the United States citizenship of individuals implicated in the Nazis' persecution of civilians, such as the mass murder of Jews and other crimes against humanity.

2. Removal actions are commenced in United States immigration courts to remove noncitizens or former citizens from the United States because of their assistance or participation in persecution of civilians during World War II.

3. A border control "watchlist" is maintained and enforced to prevent suspected Axis persecutors from entering the country.[31]

Between its establishment in 1979 and 31 December 2005, OSI had compiled the evidence necessary to undertake successful action against approximately one hundred identified as persecutors. Furthermore, "over 170 suspected European and Japanese World War II perpetrators," who were on OSI's "watchlist," had been barred from entry into the United States.[32]

Before initiating any legal proceedings, OSI conducted an extensive investigation on the suspected persecutor. OSI historians located and combed through "wartime documents and postwar investigative records." The goal was to lay the ground work for "civil prosecution." Although the focus was primarily on suspected individuals who had entered and remained in the United States, the OSI also investigated individuals who had briefly worked in Europe for the CIA or its predecessor in the first decade after the war and notorious Nazis who had immigrated to South America—such as Klaus Barbie and Josef Mengele.[33] The bulk of the cases that OSI prosecuted resulted from "allegations made by European governments" or a comparison of "names of Axis personnel with U.S. immigration and other government documents."[34] By January 2006 OSI had conducted comparisons of more than seventy thousand names.

Finding a name on both lists was just the beginning. If the person lived in the United States or was a U.S. citizen living abroad, OSI followed the paper trail and interviewed Holocaust survivors who could provide information about specific people and events. Witness testimony could be a powerful component of a case moving forward. Compiling the data and witness testimony was only the first step in a process that could be a lengthy one. If the alleged criminal had acquired citizenship, then the next step was to seek denaturalization by filing "suit in federal court to obtain an order revoking citizenship." Weight was given to the suit because it would be brought by OSI and the U.S. attorney jointly. A denaturalization case was heard by a federal judge only; this was not a jury trial. It was up to the government to "meet a 'heavy burden' in order to establish the conditions necessary for denaturalization." Government attorneys had to dot all of the i's and cross all of the t's. There could be no doubt that the defendant had acquired citizenship illegally—by concealing or misrepresenting the truth—or had not met the "good moral character requirement." If OSI and the U.S. attorney convinced the judge of the legitimacy of their suit, then the judgment would go against the defendant. Because "denaturalization is a civil proceeding," either side could appeal an unfavorable decision to a "federal court of appeals."[35] On a rare occasion, an appeal could eventually be heard by the U.S. Supreme Court.

Denaturalization, if achieved, was generally not the OSI endgame. The next step was deportation. In cases where the alleged persecutor was not a citizen, denaturalization was unnecessary, and OSI could move immediately to deportation. An effort to remove someone from the United States required "filing a civil complaint" in U.S. District Court. The OSI filed jointly with the Bureau of Immigration and Customs Enforcement in the Department of Homeland Security. As was the case for denaturalization hearings, deportation hearings were adjudicated by a judge. A jury was not involved. A defendant had recourse to appeal to the U.S. Board of Immigration Appeals, or BIA, if the judge ruled in favor of deportation. If the appeals ruling supported the district court ruling, the defendant could "seek review of the removal order in the appropriate federal circuit court, and ultimately, the Supreme Court." Once all appeals were exhausted, the government could deport the defendant after it had found a country willing to accept the individual.[36] The entire process could be a lengthy one, as some of the chapters in this book demonstrate.

Additional OSI Functions

Although the OSI's primary mandate was "investigating and prosecuting denaturalization and removal cases involving World War II–era Axis persecutors," other responsibilities fell within the unit's job description. For example, since its inception, the OSI has engaged in a "Watch List" program. It compiled a list of identified war criminals who did not live in the United States but who might at some point try to gain entry to the country. Consequently, the Department of State and, more recently, the Department of Homeland Security have turned to the OSI for help "in screening applicants for entrance to the United States and petitioners for naturalization as U.S. citizens." OSI has also responded to requests for information from DHS Customs and Border Protection immigration inspectors. As a result of information provided by OSI, approximately 170 individuals from the Watch List have been prevented from entering the United States. Included in that number are Franz Doppelreiter and Kurt Waldheim.[37]

Who were Doppelreiter and Waldheimer and why were their names on the Watch List? Doppelreiter was a SS guard in Mauthausen who allegedly tortured prisoners. While the exact number of victims was unknown, some suspected the number to be more than two hundred. In May 1946 Doppelreiter went on trial for "crimes of torture and ill-treatment, sometimes resulting in death" in a Viennese court. At the trial's conclusion in August 1946, he was convicted and received a sentence of "death by hanging." In a retrial three years later, the penalty was amended to a life sentence. In 2004 Doppelreiter, who had been released from prison, tried to enter the United States via Atlanta's Hartsfield-Jackson International Airport. A Customs and Border Protection immigration inspector stopped and questioned Doppelreiter, who was denied entry into the United States because he was a "convicted Nazi criminal."[38]

Unlike Doppelreiter, who was relatively unknown in the United States, Kurt Waldheim was well known. Entering the Austrian diplomatic service in 1945, he was posted to Paris from 1948 until 1951 as "First Secretary of the Legation." After serving in a number of diplomatic positions, Waldheim became "Permanent Representative of Austria to the United Nations" in 1964. He served in that capacity for four years and, after six years during which he had other assignments, received reassignment to the United Nations in the same position. Waldheim served as secretary-general of the United Nations from 1972 to 1982. In 1986, when he ran for president of Austria, questions about his past emerged. The OSI conducted an investigation and issued a lengthy report in 1987. As a result of the OSI report, Waldheim's name was added to the Watch List, and he was subsequently denied entry into the United States—even in his capacity as Austrian president.[39]

In addition to cooperating with other federal agencies, such as U.S. Customs and Border Protection, the OSI worked with foreign governments. The multifaceted assistance that the OSI provided was generally a coordinated effort with the State Department. The OSI facilitated the investigation and prosecution of individuals accused—by foreign governments—of committing Nazi war crimes. The OSI also provided encouragement to foreign governments contemplating such actions. According to Eli M. Rosenbaum, "This has involved undertaking extensive efforts to persuade foreign governments to take law enforcement action despite initial reluctance to prosecute, or even to investigate, any Nazi cases."[40] OSI efforts have come to fruition abroad in several instances.

OSI went public with some of its investigations of notorious Nazis who did not live in or work for the United States—such as Klaus Barbie and Josef Mengele—and worked with other agencies to make "information on Nazi crimes and their aftermath" available to scholars, researchers, and the public. During the past couple of decades, OSI also participated in several interagency initiatives. In 1996, for example, OSI took the lead in an investigation ordered by President William Clinton "to trace the fate of victim assets looted by the Nazis, including gold that had been ripped from the mouths of civilians murdered in the concentration camps." OSI research provided evidence of the transfer of Holocaust gold from Germany to Switzerland and resulted in the liquidation of gold and "distribution of the proceeds to needy Holocaust survivors." OSI research also revealed the Nazi plan to ship "Jewish jewelry" to the German legation in Switzerland via diplomatic pouch. The jewelry subsequently funded the acquisition of "industrial diamonds essential for the German war effort." OSI investigation expanded to include other items, such as artwork, that had been stolen from Jews by the Nazis. In December 1998 the unit concluded that four works held by the National Gallery of Art in Washington DC had been "looted by the Nazis." Almost two years later, after an extensive inquiry, the National Gallery of Art returned a painting—*Still Life with Fruit and Game*—to the French Jewish family from which it was stolen by the Nazis. In October 1998 the Nazi War Crimes Disclosure Act, which created the Nazi War Criminal Records Interagency Working Group, went into effect, and OSI received a new task. The unit "was to assist in the unprecedented government-wide effort to locate, declassify, and disclose to the public, classified documents pertaining to Nazi criminals and to transactions in plundered assets of Holocaust victims." In an era in which "transparency" is a buzz word, OSI helped set a bar that current politicians have difficulty reaching.[41]

New Days—New Mission?

On 11 September 2001, a date forever etched into the annals of U.S. history, a horrific event changed the lives of thousands of people—Americans and non-Americans, individuals and families directly and indirectly affected, first responders—when Al Qaeda carried out multiple attacks in New York and Washington DC. The attacks changed the ways in which nations, particularly the United States, approached issues of security. They also raised questions about how the perpetrators entered the country, acquired the skills that they needed, and carried out the mission that cost thousands of lives and left scars that will never heal. Of those questions, one stands out. How were the men who carried out the attacks able to enter the United States? Did they enter on legitimate visas? Did they overstay their approved visit?

These and other questions shone a spotlight on the Immigration and Naturalization Service, its policies, its enforcement capabilities, and its exchange of information with other government agencies. Studies focused on all aspects of the attacks, including interagency cooperation, as lawmakers scrambled to take steps to secure the borders and prevent future assaults against innocent civilians. President George W. Bush and his advisers, when possible, rapidly initiated measures to accomplish these goals and investigations to identify and bring to justice those responsible for the attacks. Congress took steps as well. Members crafted legislation designed to make the nation safer by granting broad powers to investigative departments, such as the FBI. Congress "nearly unanimously" passed the USA PATRIOT Act: Preserving Life and Liberty, which it sent to the president for his signature. President Bush signed the bill into law.[42]

Although some decisions and actions were taken in the months immediately after the 9/11 attacks, others came a bit later. Three years later Congress passed the Intelligence Reform and Terrorism Prevention Act of 2004, and President Bush signed it into law on 17 December. This piece of legislation increased the responsibilities of the OSI, which received the "authority . . . to investigate and take legal action to denaturalize any naturalized U.S. citizen who participated abroad in acts of genocide or, acting under color of foreign law, participated in acts of torture or extrajudicial killing." The act "also mandates the exclusion and removal of such persons, which will be handled by the Department of State (State) and the Department of Homeland Security (DHS)."[43]

As a result of this new law, the OSI's mandate was greatly expanded. This expansion was not just an accident or the result of a congressional whim. For several years various congressional committees had undertaken investigation of human rights violations and "state-sponsored atrocities." In November 2003 the Senate Judiciary Committee issued a report that provided "the justification for the legislative provisions that were ultimately enacted as part of IRTPA." The report gave kudos to OSI for its work and credited it with "demonstrat[ing] the effectiveness of centralized resources and expertise in these cases," that is, cases against alleged Nazi war criminals. The committee argued that OSI could bring its "centralized resources and expertise" to investigating cases of alleged human rights violations.[44]

For the next seven years OSI focused on its new mandate, but not at the expense of its original one. It resolved several cases related to World War II war crimes committed by ex-Nazis, including those concerning Elfriede Rinkel and John Kalymon. Although not a U.S. citizen, Rinkel, married to a German Jew for forty-two years, resided in San Francisco in May 2006 when "OSI filed a deportation action." Rinkel had kept her husband in the dark about her real past. OSI argued that Rinkel had been a guard at a notorious concentration camp for women—Ravensbrück. A settlement was reached a month later, and the judge ordered Rinkel deported. She departed the United States for Germany in August 2006.[45]

A year later OSI won a case against eighty-eight-year-old Kalymon. A resident of Michigan, Kalymon was a "former Ukrainian auxiliary policeman and suspected Nazi collaborator." According to Ralph Blumenthal, author of "The Last Nazi Hunter," Kalymon had kept incriminating documentation that investigators found and that was ultimately used against him. In the Ukrainian documents

Kalymon noted that he had "'fired four shots while on duty,' killing one Jew and wounding another." The documents chronicled other incriminating details about his wartime activities. OSI not only won the denaturalization case against Kalymon but also initiated deportation proceedings. Kalymon's deteriorating health due to cancer put the deportation proceedings on permanent hiatus. He died in 2014 at the age of ninety-three.[46]

With each passing year the possibility of successfully locating and prosecuting Nazi war criminals decreased. Although OSI had a new mandate, it would not last. In March 2010 the Department of Justice announced a change in the Criminal Division: the establishment of a new section, which was the culmination of a decision made in agreement with the president. In December 2009 President Barack Obama had approved the merger of OSI and the Domestic Security Section. This new section, called the Human Rights and Special Prosecutions Section, would "prosecute torture, genocide, child soldiers and war crimes that are committed by any person who is in the United States."[47] With the creation of this new section, OSI ceased to exist. Over thirty years after receiving its first mandate to pursue alleged Nazi criminals, OSI's usefulness had ended, but the legacy of its work, which is explored in this volume, remains.

2

Klaus Barbie—"Butcher of Lyon"

While some called him the "Barber of Lyon," Klaus Barbie also received the label "Butcher of Lyon" from others. Whichever characterization is chosen, each indicates that Barbie had the distinction of being viewed as a horrible torturer and executioner by those who fell under his control. A member of the SS, Barbie served in France from 1942 to 1944, at which time he was head of the Gestapo in Lyon. During his tenure thousands of Jews and resistance fighters were tortured by the Gestapo and sent to concentration camps, resulting in the death of most of them. After the war a French military tribunal tried Barbie in absentia and sentenced him to death. In 1963, when he was discovered in Bolivia, the French government began efforts to have Barbie deported to France. They finally succeeded in 1983, but then the allegations that Barbie had provided postwar intelligence information to the United States surfaced—complicating the story and extradition efforts. This prompted an investigation by the Office of Special Investigations. How did Barbie become a U.S. employee, albeit briefly? How could the United States employ such a horrible person? Who was Klaus Barbie?

Early Years

On 25 October 1913 Nikolaus and Anna (née Hees) Barbie had their first child—Nikolaus Klaus—who was born in Bad Godesberg. The German town is located on the Rhine River south of Bonn. The family belonged to the local Roman Catholic Church. Although his early profession was as an office worker, Nikolaus Barbie—the elder—switched careers and became a teacher, like his wife. He taught at Noder Primary School, where his son became a pupil when he reached school age. The elder Barbie, a veteran of World War I, fought in the Battle of Verdun. The battle would have a life-altering effect on him, on his wife, and on his young son, who was only four years old when his father left for war. Wounded when a bullet struck him in the neck, a bitter Barbie returned from the war. In his dejection he turned to the bottle, to the detriment of the family. Alcohol quickly contributed to the abuse that the elder Barbie directed toward those dependent on him. Apparently, young Klaus Barbie became a victim, and a student, of his father's methods of abuse.

In 1923 multiple events affected Klaus Barbie's life, when he was an impressionable nine years old. First, the small town where the Barbie family lived in the Saarland became occupied by the French. In addition, "a German Freikorps leader was captured and shot."[1] If Barbie had not harbored hatred for the French before 1923, the seed for his hatred became planted that day. Second, the young Barbie left the Noder School because he was ready to commence the next phase of his education—and to escape from his abusive father. He was accepted by a boarding school, the Friedrich-Wilhelm Grammar School, located in Trier, approximately a hundred miles from Bad Godesberg. In his new school the focus of his education was the classics, especially Latin and Greek. Unfortunately, Barbie was only briefly removed from interaction with his family—particularly his father. Two years after he enrolled in the boarding school, Nikolaus Barbie retired and moved his family to Trier. Less than a decade later, the family faced great challenges.

The year 1933 was another watershed year for Barbie. He graduated, which meant the beginning of the next phase of his life, but 1933 also brought with it much tragedy that would send him down a different path than he had intended. Barbie's younger brother, who suffered from a chronic illness, died of heart failure, as did their father, who succumbed to a neck tumor that resulted from the wound he suffered during World War I. Barbie wanted to attend university and focus his studies on the law, archaeology, or theology, but his father's passing had left him without the financial resources to pursue his preferred career choice. Barbie's grandfather, who controlled his father's estate, refused to give the surviving son his rightful share.[2] The ironies of fate played on his frustration and his building anger against his father—

and now his grandfather. He would find a way to redirect his feelings of dissatisfaction with the hand that life had dealt him. Swept up in enthusiasm for Adolf Hitler and the Nazi Party, Barbie made a life-changing decision in 1933. He joined Hitler Youth. Demonstrating his leadership capabilities, he quickly became a patrol chief—or Fahnenführer—tasked with supervising 120 boys.

The lack of the money that would have allowed him to attend university meant that Barbie could not delay fulfilling mandatory service. He signed up for a "six-month work detail" under a "compulsory labor service" requirement and departed for his assignment in Schleswig-Holstein. At the same time his work with the Nazi Party took shape. By February 1935 he had a new position within the party in the town of Trier. Barbie became "personal adjutant to the head of the local Nazi party office." It was at this same time that his work with the SD—Sicherheitsdienst, or SS Intelligence Agency, of the Nazi Party—began, although he was not officially a member of the group. That changed, however, on 26 September 1935, when, following the advice of an older party member, he signed on the dotted line and thus officially joined the SS and was posted "to the central office of the SD—the IV-D." Barbie's SS membership number was 272,284.[3] His associations with the SS and SD would afford Barbie with an avenue for advancement, particularly since he lacked the funds necessary to pursue a higher education. It would not take long for him to realize that he had found his calling.

A few months after his induction into the SS, Barbie spent a year furthering his education—but it was not an academic one. He attended the SS school in Bernau, approximately twenty miles from Berlin, where he received SS training, which consisted of lectures on Hitler's life and the "doctrine of racial selection" and physical and military exercises. Among those who lectured on the "Jewish question" to the new SS recruits was Adolf Eichmann. By the time he graduated from the SS school in 1937, Barbie was truly representative of the German Nazi, who would follow Hitler to the end. He embraced the führer's antisemitic and anticommunist ideology. "He believed in the crusade against Jews and Bolsheviks. He believed that his mission in life was to serve the goals of his Führer. He was ready to do the bidding of his superiors." Furthermore, Barbie understood that the rules of engagement were changing and that civilian targets were no longer off-limits. "There had once been a concept of honor in war. You didn't kill civilians, or torture suspects, or take hostages in reprisal. But that concept was not taught at Bernau."[4] Not a stranger to violence growing up, Barbie took to the training at Bernau like a duck drawn to water. He found peace in a system that allowed him to unleash his internal demons.

On 1 May 1937 Barbie became a "full-fledged" Nazi Party member. In addition to completing training at Bernau, he also participated in an "elite leadership course" in Berlin. Upon graduation Barbie's first posting was to Düsseldorf, where he was attached to an SD unit. After his arrival in Düsseldorf, he registered with the local Nazi Party. For three months in 1938, he completed military service with an infantry unit, the Thirty-Ninth Infantry Regiment.[5]

As Barbie rose in the Nazi Party, there were changes in his personal life as well. He met and courted Regina Margareta Maria Willms, whose father was a postal clerk. Unlike Barbie, she had not completed high school, but, after finishing a cooking course, she initially found domestic work in Berlin. In 1937, however, she moved to Düsseldorf, where her path would cross that of Barbie's. In addition to working at a Nazi Women's Organization day care, Willms joined the Nazi Party that year. In April 1939, on the eve of the outbreak of war, the couple became engaged. As Nazi Party members, however, the next step was not a foregone conclusion: "In order to marry, Klaus and Regina had to present evidence of their racial purity. Regina submitted character references as well, and both passed medical examinations, replied to questions about family medical history and supplied pictures of themselves in bathing suits so they could be scrutinized for possible racial defects."[6]

A year later, on 25 April 1940, five days after Barbie's promotion to SS-Untersturmführer, or SS second lieutenant, the couple married in a "special SS ceremony" performed by Barbie's unit commander. "The symbolism of Nazi weddings was Teutonic. Traditional wedding flowers were replaced by sunflowers and fir twigs representing natural earth. The couple exchanged rings and received a gift of bread and salt representing the fruitfulness and purity of the earth. An eternal flame burned in an urn before them." The newly married couple, although Catholic, embraced a new religion—that of the ss of the Nazi Party.[7]

Events in Europe guaranteed that Klaus and Regina Barbie would have only a short honeymoon. The storm clouds that were gathering as they became engaged erupted with the outbreak of war on 1 September 1939. It was only a matter of time before Barbie would receive orders to proceed to the front. The lull that occurred after Poland succumbed to pressure from both Germany and the Soviet Union had given the young couple time to become joined in an ss ceremony. Their lives changed, however, as the German offensive in western Europe began. It would not take long for Barbie to receive new orders.

War Years

The expected orders arrived. Barbie's SD unit was already in the Low Countries, attached to an invading army. Following his 29 May 1940 orders, Barbie traveled to Holland to join his unit, which was under the direct control of the SD commander in the Hague—Willy Lages. Barbie's unit soon received a new directive: to proceed to Amsterdam for attachment to the Central Bureau for Jewish Emigration, or the Zentralstelle. There Barbie's task was to facilitate the removal of Jews and other groups, including freemasons and German émigrés. He carried out his orders enthusiastically. His promotion to Obersturmführer (first lieutenant) soon followed. Before long events would occur that would enable Barbie to facilitate the mass deportation of Jews from Amsterdam.[8]

On 12 February 1941 Dutch Nazi Party military formations unleashed attacks against homes and businesses owned by Jews. The Nazis were surprised to meet resistance from Jews—and non-Jews. The expectation that the containment and deportation of Jews would be a walk in the park did not materialize. During a fight with Dutch dockworkers, Hendrik Koot, a Dutch Nazi, lost his life. German officials seized on Koot's death to take drastic steps against Jews in Amsterdam. First, Hans Rauter, of the Dutch ss high command, ordered retaliation that resulted in the death of six defenders, the physical removal of "non-Jewish inhabitants," and the isolation of the "Jewish Quarter." "Canals leading into the quarter were closed, with the exception of one that could be closely monitored. The fighting went on for weeks, and when calm was finally restored, the Jews of the old quarter of Amsterdam found themselves living in a permanently sealed ghetto."[9] Jews in the ghetto received orders to relinquish all weapons. This was not a new SS tactic. It had worked in Warsaw—why not in Amsterdam?

In addition to helping close off the Jewish Quarter, Barbie led an SD raid against Jews on 19 February. One of the targets was the Koco—an ice cream parlor owned and run by Ernst Cahn and Alfred Kohn, German Jewish refugees. The two men resisted the Dutch Nazi attack during which a previously installed "protective device" activated and doused the attackers with ammonia.[10] There was an immediate reaction from Barbie, who had orders to arrest—not kill—Cahn and Kohn, when he arrived on the scene. How dare the Jews resist and use weapons against his men? This required harsh punishment! Using an ashtray, Barbie personally struck one of the men in the head. Both Cahn and Kohn received death sentences for their resistance. Ernst Cahn's execution occurred on 3 March 1941 on the Waalsdorpervlakte. The firing squad was under the command of Barbie. Although he escaped execution at the same time as his partner, Kohn did not survive the concentration camp. Barbie would subsequently receive an award for his zealous actions in the Jewish Quarter—the Iron Cross, second class.[11]

Barbie would not let the grass grow under his feet. Three days later further retaliation occurred. Under Barbie's direction, the SS launched a raid against Amsterdam's Jewish Quarter. The targets were primarily young men. The SS arrested approximately 425 Jews between the ages of twenty and thirty-five. Deportation to Mauthausen followed immediately. None of these men would survive their incarceration there. Outraged, the Dutch population initiated a general strike in protest—an action that virtually paralyzed the nation, an action that the Germans could not and would not tolerate. The Germans acted swiftly in the face of Dutch defiance. They imposed martial law and harshly restored order. Thus, they quenched Dutch resistance—virtually, for good.

Once the Amsterdam ghetto had been firmly established and general Dutch resistance derailed, Barbie set his sights on Jews living under the radar in Amsterdam. On 11 June 1941 he presented himself to Abraham Ascher and David Cohen, who administered the Jewish Council. Underneath his calm exterior, Barbie had a definite agenda. He acknowledged that approximately 300 young Jews, who had formerly lived on a farm colony outside Amsterdam, had received sanctuary within the city from ordinary Dutch citizens. Claiming a German command decision to allow these young men to return to the colony, Barbie requested information about their current locations. Aware of the official notification, Ascher and Cohen complied with his request. Ever the polite gentleman, Barbie thanked the men and took his leave—giving the impression of a peaceful relocation in the offing. On 13 June, however, more than 230 young men were arrested and deported to the Mauthausen concentration camp—none to return. Afterward, Ascher and Cohen received a summons to SD headquarters, where they learned that the Jewish boys had in fact been arrested in reprisal for a 14 May 1941 bomb attack on the German officers' club.[12]

Barbie was well on the way to establishing a name for himself—at the very time when his family was expanding. On 30 June his daughter, Ute Regina, was born. The Barbies' life was also about change in other ways. The Germans found themselves battling resistance throughout their occupation zones. Key Germans, such as Barbie, received orders to proceed to Germany to undergo "counterinsurgency techniques" training. As his daughter neared her first birthday, Barbie received a mission that would enable him to implement his new counterinsurgency training. In June 1942, traveling to Gex in the German-occupied zone on the French-Swiss border, Barbie prepared to carry out his orders—the capture of three spies. He had some flexibility for successfully completing his mission. He believed that he was up to the task and anticipated a successful outcome. Little did he know, however, that things would not go as planned: "Barbie devised an intriguing, rather comical scheme to make his arrests by actually living in a house that stood on the border and had doors into either country; but his quarry escaped, and Barbie returned empty-handed."[13] Luckily for him, Barbie's failure did not derail his mete-oric rise within the SD and SS—or within the Nazi Party writ large.

As 1942 wound down, the German war effort, which had been achieving one victory after another, suffered a series of setbacks. First, in October Gen. Bernard Montgomery and the British Eighth Army gained the upper hand over Field Marshal Erwin Rommel and the Afrika Korps at El Alamein. Then, on 8 November Allied forces landed in North Africa—at Oran, Algiers, and Casablanca. A couple of weeks later German troops attacking Stalingrad found themselves surrounded by Soviet forces. As the Soviets tightened the noose at Stalingrad, German armed forces moved into Vichy, and the German occupation of France was completed. By occupying southern France, the Germans hoped to close and bar the backdoor, which would pre-vent an Allied leap from North Africa into France. Occupation also opened the door to Barbie's next posting, in Lyon.

Barbie's next position—chief of Section IV, Intelligence, or head of the Gestapo, Lyon—was a real feather in his cap. He would have unprecedented authority to carry out the wishes of his party, particu-larly with regard to the elimination of the Jewish and the French Resis-tance presence. November 1942 brought not only occupation and a new Gestapo chief to southern France but also a dramatic increase in the French Resistance footprint in the region—a footprint that Bar-bie hoped to erase. When he arrived in Lyon, Barbie believed that a "hundred years of German history and the whole of his lifetime had prepared him for this moment." The time had come to fulfill his des-tiny, and he would use every resource at hand to do so.[14]

Although initially based in Hôtel Terminus—adjacent to Per-rache railway station—Barbie established new headquarters in June 1943 in the École (du Service) de Santé Militaire on Avenue Berthelot. This was a more spacious facility that could accommo-date the torture chambers that Barbie had built. While in Lyon, Barbie brought torture, deportation, and execution to a new level. Numerous documented cases bear witness to his cruelty—to his psychotic behavior. The horror, which will unfold in these pages, is not for the faint of heart.

On 6 June 1944—the day that Allied forces landed on the Normandy beaches and the liberation of France had begun—a French neighbor denounced Simone Lagrange and her parents as Jews. The Gestapo arrested the family and brought them to headquarters, where Mlle Lagrange met Klaus Barbie for the first time. He was a well-dressed man, who did not immediately strike her as someone to fear. According to Lagrange, who later testified against the "Butcher," "He was caressing the cat. And me, a kid 13 years old, I could not imagine that he could be evil because he loved animals. I was tortured by him for eight days." Lagrange rarely found relief during that time, as Barbie used beatings to loosen her tongue. He sought information that he could use in his efforts to eliminate resistance and the existence of "undesirables."[15]

Another victim, who lived to give testimony to Barbie's atrocities, was Lise Lesevre, who was working with the Resistance at the time of her capture. Mlle Lesevre endured nine days of torture in 1944. Not only did Barbie beat her, but he also almost drowned her in a bathtub. According to Lesevre, "she was hung up by hand cuffs with spikes inside them and beaten with a rubber bar. She was ordered to strip naked and get into a tub filled with freezing water. Her legs were tied to a bar across the tub and Barbie yanked a chain attached to the bar to pull her underwater. During her final session with him, Barbie ordered her to lie flat on a chair and struck her on the back with a spiked ball attached to a chain. It broke a vertebrae, and she suffered the rest of her life."[16]

Barbie's cruelty and sadistic treatment of the captured earned him multiple nicknames, not the least of which was the Butcher of Lyon. Those who fell victim to him learned to fear him. According to Ennat Leger, who lived to testify against him, Barbie "had the eyes of a monster. He was savage. My God, he was savage! It was unimaginable. He broke my teeth, he pulled my hair back. He put a bottle in my mouth and pushed it until the lips split from the pressure."[17] Sent to Ravensbrück when Barbie finished torturing her, Leger lost her eyesight, which she never regained.

The more Barbie abused his captives, the greater his reputation became, and so did his stature. The reality of his appearance was somewhat different—and unexpected. He was short and stocky with dark hair and "piercing blue eyes." As Leger articulated, the way that Barbie stared at his victims was forever etched in their minds. His eyes were the first feature that many survivors mentioned when asked to describe their tormentor. The way that he carried himself reflected his confident arrogance. It was all part of the process—humiliation and physical destruction.

> He kicked heads, injected acid into human bladders and hung almost lifeless people upside down from ceiling hooks while he took a break from business to play a little love song on the piano. "Parlez-moi d'amour" was one of his favorites. Women were always tortured naked, to the deep enjoyment of their torturers. Barbie kept two German shepherd dogs. One was trained to lunge and bite. The other was trained to mount naked women who had first been ordered on their hands and knees, a humiliation that could cut deeper than the whip, than having one's fingernails pulled out, or one's nipples burned with cigarettes. He threatened the lives of his victims' families, sometimes presenting them in person, or pretending they were just downstairs about to be tortured. He led his victims to understand he was just about to shoot them.[18]

Barbie had learned how to torture—at the hands of his father and in his SS training—but he took it to new levels. When the torture ended, deportation guaranteed that the nightmare would continue. Not all of Barbie's victims survived long enough to be deported to a concentration camp. The captives who suffered at Barbie's own hands number in the thousands. The capture of forty-four Jewish children, whom the citizens of the village of Izieu had hidden, and their deportation to Auschwitz falls squarely at Barbie's door.[19] He had no sympathy for them. He was just doing his job—a job that he embraced wholeheartedly.

The most famous Frenchman to fall into Barbie's hands and not survive was one of the highest-ranking members of the French Resistance—Jean Moulin, who was credited with uniting the numerous resistance groups that had sprung up spontaneously around France into an organized unit. Under his guidance the newly organized French Resistance became an effective movement that resisted the German occupier and one that worked as much as possible with allies based outside of France. Moulin was the epitome of the French Resistance leadership that Barbie was determined to eradicate.

Born on 20 June 1899, Jean Moulin enlisted in the army in 1918, but the war had ended before he had a chance to do his part. After World War I he decided to devote himself to public service. Joining the civil service, Moulin worked hard and rose quickly through the ranks. He earned the distinction of becoming the youngest prefect, or regional administrator, of Chartres. Because of his extreme left-leaning politics, however, Moulin quickly came to the Germans' attention following their occupation of northern France. In June 1940 the Gestapo arrested him and applied their unique methods to him because they suspected that he was a communist. Moulin's effort to commit suicide by slitting his own throat while in custody was thwarted by a German guard. After recovering in a hospital, Moulin returned to his job, where he took a stand against an order mandated by the Vichy government in November 1940. Ordered to fire "all elected left-wing officials," Moulin refused and, as a result, lost his own government position.[20]

Moulin, determined to fight against treasonous laws issued by the Vichy government and against the German occupiers, had a new focus in life—resistance. He realized, however, that crucial to success was connection with resistance outside of France. In September 1941, with help from his friends, Moulin left France and traveled to London, where he made a connection with the Free French. He met with Gen. Charles De Gaulle and "other exiled French leaders." Four months later, armed with the code name Max, Moulin returned to his homeland, via parachute, and proceeded to organize the various resistance groups from around France into one unified movement.[21]

Moulin organized the French Resistance movement and orchestrated various actions against the Germans for over a year before falling victim to the Gestapo again—and to Klaus Barbie more specifically. In a May report Moulin acknowledged that while he was on the Gestapo and Vichy police radar, they did not know what he looked like. He hoped to use that to his advantage to avoid capture while continuing his work. Little did Moulin know that his days of freedom were, in fact, limited. On 7 June 1943 Barbie arrested René Hardy, a member of the Resistance, and proceeded to apply his tried-and-true methods at information extraction on him. Although he initially endeavored to resist, Hardy eventually gave Barbie the information that he needed to capture other members of the movement, including Pierre Brossolette, Charles Delestraint, and Jean Moulin. Two weeks after the arrest of Hardy, on 21 June, Barbie arrested Jean Moulin and Raymond Aubrac, who claimed to be "Claude Ermelin" from Tunisia. Moulin, Aubrac, and others, including the newly freed Hardy, had assembled for a meeting. In the ensuing chaos of the arrest, Hardy was slightly wounded but escaped. He would later face charges of treason.

Initially, Barbie did not know which of the captured Resistance members was the highly sought after "Max." It did not take him long, however, to figure out that Jean Moulin and Max were one and the same. Soon the torture began. By all accounts, Moulin's torture was merciless, as Barbie and his men unleashed their worst on the Resistance leader. "Hot needles were shoved under his fingernails. His fingers were forced through the narrow space between the hinges of a door and a wall and then the door was repeatedly slammed until the knuckles broke. Screw-levered handcuffs were placed on Moulin and tightened until they bit through his flesh and broke through the bones of his wrists."[22] Despite repeated beatings on his head and whippings, Moulin refused to talk. While Barbie admired Moulin's strength and unwillingness to break, the Frenchman's resilience fueled the fire within the German and drove him to increase the torture. The beatings continued until Moulin fell into a coma.

Although Moulin was unresponsive, the "Butcher" was not yet finished with him. He ordered the prison barber—Christian Pineau—to shave the unconscious man. According to Pineau,

> *Moulin was unconscious, his eyes pushed into his skull as though they had been punched through his head. A horrible blue wound scarred his temple. A rattling sound came out of his swollen lips.* Pineau asked the guard for soap and water, and while he was waiting he felt Moulin's face and hands. His skin was cold. Suddenly Moulin opened his eyes. Pineau wasn't sure he had recognized him. "Water," Moulin whispered. Pineau asked the guard for water. The latter, clearly compassionate, took the shaving bowl to rinse it.

A few words in English escaped Moulin's mouth. Pineau did not understand what he was saying. Pineau held the water to Moulin's lips; Moulin sipped a few drops, then fell into unconsciousness again.[23]

He was put on display at Gestapo headquarters, and Barbie forced other captured Resistance members to view their physically broken leader. On 7 July Moulin's unconscious body was carried away to be sent to Germany, but he died on the way. The dead Moulin was returned to Paris, cremated, and buried in the Père Lachaise Cemetery.[24]

With the capture of Moulin, Barbie had hit the mother load! He was aptly rewarded for his work in Lyon, particularly for his capture and torture of Jean Moulin. Hitler awarded him the "First Class Iron Cross with Swords." Despite Hitler's appreciation, circumstances of the war caused a change in Barbie's situation in the summer of 1944. The Allies' successful landing in Normandy and deeper drive into France made Barbie's position untenable. With Allied troops breathing down his back, he returned to Germany, reported for duty, and received new orders. Following his new orders, he traveled to Halle, but when it came to reporting for front-line service, Barbie baulked. His training had not prepared him to fight on the front lines. He was at his best hunting down, arresting, and torturing Jews and members of the French Resistance—not carrying a weapon into the fray. His arrogance let him down, and he fled. After a brief visit to Berlin, where it was not exactly safe since he had abandoned his post, Barbie decided to wait for the end in Düsseldorf. Barbie's own words condemn his final actions as the war ended:

My war ended in Wuppertal. We turned a garage into a stronghold. Nearby were two trucks loaded with civilian clothes for the Werewolf's [sic] (the abortive German resistance movement). But no one had made any plans to continue the fight underground, probably because no one thought that we would lose the war. So I buried my gun.

The four youngsters I was with and myself changed our clothes, got some false papers from the police headquarters and headed off through the forests and pastures towards the Sauerland. It was very hard. From one day to the next, I'd become a beggar.[25]

Postwar Work

How the mighty have fallen! At the end of the war, Barbie was on the run. In his own words, he had "become a beggar." His efforts to escape capture and punishment for his actions were only partially successful. He certainly avoided punishment for decades. Capture was a different story, but the outcome of his initial detention was unexpected. In a stroke of bad luck, Barbie was stopped near Hohenlimburg, in Westphalia, Germany. He failed to navigate an American roadblock successfully. Although he was arrested and placed with other prisoners in a school, Barbie's incarceration was short lived, a brief setback on the road to freedom. Ultimately, his luck would hold. Because he was traveling with false papers, the Americans had no idea that the Butcher of Lyon was in their hands. In fact, had they known his real name, it is possible that the Americans would still have not held him. Word of who he was and what he had done had not yet begun to spread—or at least it had not yet spread far enough for Barbie to be on the right Watch List to result in his permanent detention. It would not take long, however, for the Barbie name to become better known, but would it make a difference to the postwar Americans tasked with making Europe safe from the new threat to the east?

What Barbie did immediately after the war in Europe ended is not completely clear. What is known is that at some point the Western Allies recruited him, and he found himself in the employ of the British until 1947. How the notorious Butcher of Lyon came to be recruited is a mystery, but the story becomes even more bizarre as things got even murkier. By April 1947 the U.S. Counter Intelligence Corps (CIC) had set up shop in Memmingen, which is located in Bavaria, Germany. On a spring day in April, Robert Taylor, who was an operations officer in the Memmingen CIC Field Office, was working the desk when Kurt Merk approached him. During the war Merk had been an Abwehr lieutenant. During the course of their conversation, Merk mentioned a couple of things that Taylor found interesting. Merk had recently reconnected with an old friend who had been posted to France during the war. This friend, Klaus Barbie, was at loose ends and was seeking employment. Barbie was willing to work for the Americans—for a price. While he recognized the benefits from hiring Merk's friend, who might provide useful, actionable intelligence, Taylor quickly made the connection between the friend's name and "two Allied lists of wanted war criminals."[26] Taylor knew that Barbie's name was on both lists. Unwilling to make a decision about Barbie on his own, Taylor contacted Lt. Col. Dale Garvey, his superior, who was based in Munich.

Taylor and Garvey discussed the pros and cons of hiring Barbie. On the definite con side of the ledger was the German's status as a "wanted war criminal." The two men concluded, however, that the plus side—Barbie as a "valuable asset"—far outweighed the negative. With Garvey's approval in hand, Taylor arranged to meet Barbie in Merk's Memmingen apartment. Barbie, who turned on the charm, made a "favourable impression" on Taylor, who knew nothing of the German's history as the Butcher of Lyon. Barbie did not enlighten the American because it served his best interests to be hired by the other side. Negotiations commenced between Barbie and Taylor, and they reached agreement. According to an American intelligence officer, in addition to protection, the United States paid Barbie "$1,700 a month for intelligence information."[27]

Despite the agreement negotiated between Taylor and Barbie, Taylor's superiors had to approve Barbie's recruitment. That process would not prove smooth sailing. When the paperwork hit his desk at CIC's Frankfurt headquarters, Operations Officer Earl Browning could not believe his eyes. Shocked and appalled, Browning sent a directive to the Munich CIC in October. He ordered the arrest of Barbie and his transfer to Frankfurt for "detailed interrogation."[28] Thus began a two-month struggle between Browning and Garvey over Barbie. Garvey argued that Barbie's arrest would have an unintended consequence—CIC informants would lose trust in them. By December Browning achieved victory of sorts with Barbie's arrest. For the next six months Barbie underwent extensive questioning. By the time his interrogation ended in May 1948, Barbie had revealed little, and none of it was new. He basically just confirmed his SS membership.

Following Barbie's interrogation, the CIC issued a report. According to the report, the impediment to turning Barbie over for trial was his knowledge about the CIC's operations—information that could potentially be damaging if released during a public trial. Basically, the report's recommendation was that the CIC not prosecute or facilitate the prosecution of Barbie for war crimes. Browning was not pleased with the report or the requirement to comply with it. Like a dog with a bone, Browning continued to press his colleagues to "drop" Barbie from their list of assets, but he was ignored. Upon his release, Barbie resumed his "intelligence activities" for the CIC at the very time that more information about his tenure in Lyon found its way into the public realm.[29]

Merk soon learned that working with his old friend was not a picnic. By early 1949 the relationship between the two men hit a major snag. Because the rift seemed irreparable, Merk decided to approach his CIC employers and come clean about Barbie's role in Lyon during the war; therefore, he sought out Barbie's handler, Erhard Dabringhaus. In 1948 Dabringhaus, emeritus professor at Wright State University, was a civilian employee of the CIC. Merk told Dabringhaus, "If the Americans found out what Barbie did in France, the atrocities he committed—not even your General Eisenhower could protect him." Merk also admitted that he had personally seen "some French Resistance fighters hanging by their thumbs, day after day, until they died." Although what he revealed about Barbie was damning, the CIC decided to part ways with Merk, the whistle-blower—not with Barbie. Barbie continued to work for the CIC. He provided weekly reports that included information about specific groups of interest. Targeted groups included "other missing Nazis, the Communists in East Germany and Eastern Europe as well as French Communists."[30]

Soon, however, the CIC had to deal with other troublesome information about Barbie and to make a decision about how to proceed. A Paris newspaper published an article—"Arrest Barbie Our Torturer"—in May 1949. When the headline grabbed his attention, Browning continued reading. According to the article, "During the occupation, he [Barbie] burned his victims with an acetylene torch to make them confess during interrogations that lasted more than 48 hours." The situation was worse than Browning had originally imagined. There was no denying Barbie's liabilities. When he brought the article to his superior, Browning did not receive the response he had expected. Instead, Col. David Erskine claimed that the article, which was based on the testimony of "former Resistance fighters," was unreliable. After all, most of them, according to Erskine, were "communists" and, therefore, could not be trusted to tell the truth.[31]

Although still unwilling to part ways with Barbie or to turn him over to "war crimes" authorities, the CIC recognized the prudence in removing his name from their records. That would give them "plausible deniability." Erasing his name from their records did not mean, however, that the CIC was giving Barbie the boot. Unfortunately, the situation did not improve with time. By early 1950 Browning had returned to the United States. With the troublemaker no longer in Germany, CIC officials prepared for the dust to settle and to get back to work as normal. That did not happen because actions by the French complicated matters further. The French government decided to begin extradition proceedings and submitted a formal request. An extradition request was not so easy to ignore. How would the CIC officials respond? What were their options?

Colonel Erskine decided decisive action was required, and he took it on 4 May 1950. Citing an alleged strong connection between the French intelligence services and the Soviet Union, Erskine refused the French request. He thwarted French efforts to get their hands on Barbie, but he went further than that. In addition to arguing that acquiescing to the French was impossible on intelligence grounds, Erskine and the CIC also claimed not to know where Barbie was. Luckily for Erskine and the CIC, who would have been outed, Barbie evaded capture. Although a disaster had been—albeit briefly—avoided, the CIC acknowledged that Barbie had become a liability—a "difficult disposal case." Consequently, the CIC decided to eliminate the problem by helping Barbie and his family relocate. Out of sight, out of mind. Right?[32]

Relocation

Relocation could be a tricky business—unless the right channels were known and available. After World War II the International Red Cross was in the relocation business. The organization provided ethnic

Germans with the necessary travel papers. It did not take Nazis and war criminals long to figure out how to exploit the system, particularly since the vetting process was superficial at best. The International Committee of the Red Cross, in all likelihood overwhelmed by the sheer number of applicants, earned the reputation for providing travel documents to "ethnic Germans" without investigating claims of "ethnic German" status. As a result, dubious characters succeeded in obtaining the travel documents necessary for relocation, even though the name on the materials was frequently a fictitious one. With some help, Barbie took advantage of this committee.[33]

CIC headquarters in Germany recognized that the first thing that Barbie needed for relocation was a new identity for himself and his family. By this time the Barbie family numbered four. In addition to Barbie; his wife, Regina; and daughter, Ute, there was a son, Klaus-Georg. Once travel documents in their new names were available, the next step would be to help the family travel to Italy. From there the Barbie family would proceed to their final destination, in South America. Surely that would get Barbie far enough away to avoid damage to the CIC's—and by extension to the United States'—reputation. What would the family's new identity be? Interestingly, Barbie was involved in the process of choosing a new identity. Deciding that it was necessary only to change his last name and his ethnicity, Klaus Barbie became Klaus Altmann, an "ethnic German from Romania," which meant that he was "officially deemed to be stateless." But, in reality, he needed more than a name change. He needed a way out. For that, he and the CIC turned to a "rat line."[34]

A rat line was an escape route established in 1947. It was initially designed to help people employed by the United States in Soviet-occupied Europe who needed to relocate because they had been compromised and their lives were in danger. Generally, they found temporary accommodation in a safe house and received "false identification documents" and transportation to a safer location, frequently in South America. Initially, people sent along the rat line were not war criminals, but people who had provided a useful service, such as spying, for the Americans. That changed over time, and the rat line came to be a vehicle "to smuggle senior Nazis" and war criminals "into the U.S. along 'illegal routes.'" To be fair, the United States did not help just any dubious character. They focused on helping those who had helped the United States in the past or who could perform a useful service in the future. The CIC turned to the rat line in the Barbie case only when it became expedient to help him "disappear." The final destination was not, however, the United States, but a South American country, which made using the rat line to relocate Barbie an acceptable move.[35]

March 1951 was a big month for the Barbie—or Altmann—family. Their arrival in Genoa marked the completion of the first leg of their relocation. While in Genoa, they received important documentation, including a visa for Bolivia and travel documents from the International Committee of the Red Cross, made out to Klaus, Regina, Ute, and Klaus-Georg Altmann. On 23 March the family began the next phase of their relocation trip via a boat, the *Corrientes*. The ship set sail for Bolivia on that momentous day. According to U.S. intelligence files that justified CIC efforts to facilitate Barbie's relocation, "In 1951 because of the French and German efforts to apprehend subject, the 66th Detachment resettled him in South America. Subject was documented in the name of Klaus Altmann and routed through Austria and Italy to Bolivia. Since that time, Army has had no contact with Subject."[36] The final sentence indicated that the U.S. Army was washing its hands of Barbie. The hope was that Barbie would fade into the sunset, that there would be no fallout from his employment by the CIC, and that Barbie would be forgotten. Only time would tell if the U.S. Army's wish list would be fulfilled.

By the time the family arrived in Bolivia, Barbie had fully embraced his new identity—and his new life. He was no longer the Butcher of Lyon. He was now Klaus Altmann, businessman, but he was no ordinary businessman, although it was essential that he establish himself as such. As he became integrated into La Paz society, no one could know that he was really Klaus Barbie, the man whom the French had tried and convicted of war crimes in absentia—not once, but twice—in 1952 and 1954. No one could know that he had a death sentence hanging over his head. He had to become Altmann and put his past behind him. Under certain circumstances, however, that would prove difficult, particularly when he created "brutal internment camps" for Hugo Banzer (Suárez).[37]

Over the next three decades Barbie, or Altmann, had his finger in numerous pies, both legitimate and illegitimate. In addition to his "businessman" persona, Barbie became an integral member of the "German colony" in La Paz, Bolivia. In addition to opening a lumber business and becoming director of Transmarítima Boliviana, which was a shipping company, he quickly established relationships with various generals and government officials. As a "legitimate" businessman, he traveled to the United States and several European countries without anyone being the wiser that Klaus Barbie was in town.[38]

Unfortunately for Barbie, his business ventures were not all smooth sailing, but lucky for him, he had reestablished contact with an old friend, Fritz Schwend. In fact, Barbie recorded the benefit of this reconnection:

> We, Herr Schwend, you and I now have every reason to team up together, as we have become the victim[s] of a particular race where hatred for us will probably never end.
>
> I regret to an extraordinary degree what happened.... You can depend all the more on my and Herr Schwend's help and comradeship. I too have lately, after a long-prepared action by the German embassy, been removed from the German Club here, on the basis of a committee decision, for supposed "anti-Semitic statements."[39]

As Barbie noted, sometimes his views were not well received, but his connections to people like Schwend would serve him in good stead. In 1970 he suffered a temporary business setback that forced him to leave La Paz for a time under a cloud of the "fraudulent collapse of his country." He turned to Schwend, who not only arranged a Peruvian "resident permit" for him but also introduced him to certain "Peruvian businessmen." These connections helped Barbie get back on his feet, which allowed him to return to La Paz.[40] But Barbie did not rely just on business connections and overt activities to provide support for himself and his family.

There is some evidence to suggest that not only were the ties between the United States and Barbie not severed, but that he also did intelligence work for the Bundesnachrichtendienst (BND; Germany's Federal Intelligence Service). When the Barbie family set sail for Bolivia on the *Corrientes* on 23 March 1951, there was a collective sigh of relief in the CIC that Barbie was no longer their problem. Apparently, however, Barbie just moved from one American intelligence agency to another—the Central Intelligence Agency—but his work included more than gathering information. Barbie made contact with another member of the German colony: Col. Hugo Banzer. Trained in the United States, Banzer served as Bolivian education and culture minister from 1964 to 1966. By the early 1970s not only had Banzer been promoted to general, but he had also seized dictatorial powers in Bolivia. At some point between 1966 and 1970, Banzer turned to Barbie for help in acquiring weapons. Believing that Banzer was a staunch opponent of communism, Barbie willingly helped him. The connection between the two men became more than arms dealing. Barbie provided some of the muscle behind Banzer's efforts to stamp out opposition to his leadership. As a result of Banzer's repressive measures during his tenure as dictator, many Bolivians lost their lives. In many cases Barbie was responsible. His old tried-and-true methods found new targets: "Barbie was in charge of the murders of many Bolivian citizens, including priests and members of the opposition."[41]

Old habits die hard. Before he became Banzer's enforcer, Barbie was engaged in several intelligence ventures. Sometime between the early 1950s and the mid-1960s, the connection between Barbie and the CIA, which had been established, faded. By 1964 the CIA wanted to reconnect with Barbie and other former agents operating in South America in order to determine which remained "valuable." The CIA knew, however, that they had to tread carefully where Barbie was concerned. France still wanted him back to face punishment for his war crimes. Because it was possible that a CIA-Barbie connection might not remain secret, "U.S. authorities" were aware of the potential negative press that could result from exposure. On 5 April 1967 the CIA formally weighed in when it issued a memorandum intended to remain secret: "The war criminal charges against Altmann require serious consideration, since exposure of CIC's role in evacuating him from Germany to avoid prosecution would have serious consequences for the U.S. government; these would be still graver if a current operational relationship could be claimed (or demonstrated)."[42] While the CIA mulled over the pros and cons of employing Barbie/Altmann again, another opportunity opened up which allowed Barbie to pursue another intelligence avenue.

Never one to miss a beneficial opportunity, Barbie expanded his intelligence work to include another organization. Wilhelm Holm's job for the BND was to scout out new talent and notify headquarters in Pullach, a municipality near Munich. In 1965 Holm spent four weeks in La Paz interacting with members of the German colony. There he met a "staunch German patriot," who was a "committed anti-communist." Both were useful Cold War attributes. In a late November meeting between the two men, Holm admitted that he was "looking for an agent for a Hamburg company."[43] When asked if he was interested, Barbie responded positively. Holm raved about the transplanted German to his superiors. Within a few weeks the new man had been hired as an agent by the BND, given a code name (Adler [eagle]) and a registration number (V-43118). The new man was all set. Who was "Adler"? He was Klaus Barbie. As far as Holm knew, however, the new man was Klaus Altmann. Obviously, Barbie could not apprise Holm of his real identity. After all, he was a wanted man, but it is possible that Holm's superiors who approved hiring Barbie knew the truth about his identity and hired him anyway. After all, fighting the communist threat to the east was what was most important during the Cold War.

According to BND files, Pullach sent Barbie his first payment of 500 deutsche marks in May 1966. They subsequently paid him "performance bonuses." All moneys were paid through the wire transfer of funds to a Chartered Bank of London account in San Francisco. The BND assigned "Solinger" as Barbie's handler.[44] Barbie traveled to Santiago, Chile, in May 1966 to meet Solinger. During that meeting Solinger "officially" hired Barbie, gave him "intensive" training, and worked out arrangements for the transfer of information collected by Barbie. "The two men agreed that important information would be disguised as economic news from the lumber industry" and sent "to a teacher in Bad Bevensen in northern Germany, who would then forward the letters, unopened, to a post office box in Hamburg."[45]

Interestingly, Barbie received a "political source" classification from his new employers. A short time after signing on the dotted line with BND, Barbie "became the Bolivian representative for Merex AG, a Bonn-based company that sold Bundeswehr military surplus materials worldwide on behalf of the BND." It was Barbie's responsibility to contact Merex whenever Bolivia suffered a weapons or ammunition shortfall. Apparently, the BND was more than satisfied with the information provided by Barbie in the thirty-five reports that he submitted. They applied words such as "intelligent," "very receptive and adaptable," and "discreet and reliable" to Barbie, also known as Altmann or "Agent 43118." All did not, however, prove to be smooth sailing in the relationship between Barbie and the BND.[46]

During their first meeting Solinger asked Barbie for details about his background—and he kept a record of that information. It did not take much digging to ascertain Barbie's true identity and information about this past, including the fact that he was wanted in France to face war crimes charges. Even if they knew the truth about Barbie, the powers that be in the BND initially chose not to act. Furthermore, they kept that information close to their chests. Red flags were raised, however, "when agent V-43118 refused to travel to Germany for training." Uninformed BND intelligence officials began to ask questions. On 13 September 1966 one official raised the possibility about an SS past. Within weeks the word was out. The Wiesbaden "public prosecutor's office" had initiated a search for Barbie "on the basis of a preliminary investigation by the Central Office for the Investigation of Nazi Crimes in Ludwigsburg." Things were about to get hot. News of the investigation, coupled with information of a "run-in" between the German ambassador to Bolivia and Barbie, forced the BND's hand. By the fall of 1966 the BND had decided to sever ties with Barbie "to avoid later complications and difficulties." Unfortunately, as the BND would learn, that was not exactly possible, even though they had closed the book on Adler. In an effort to keep the lid on a situation that could potential blow up in their faces, the BND made the decision to keep Barbie's whereabouts a secret, even though he was a "person of interest" to the "German judicial authorities" and he faced charges for murder and war crimes. Barbie's cover remained secure until the early 1970s. It helped that he had government protection.[47]

OSI Investigation

As long as Banzer was dictator, Barbie was safe from extradition to France, even once he was outed. In 1972 a series of events began that eventually led to Barbie's extradition and to the OSI investigation.[48] At some point between 1954 and 1971, the French and German governments abandoned the search for Barbie. When the official search was suspended, husband-and-wife Nazi-hunting team—Beate and Serge Klarsfeld—took up the mantle. They were determined to bring Barbie to justice. In late December 1971 the couple received a tip from Herbert John, the "manager of a publishing company owned by . . . Peruvian industrialist, Luis Banchero Rossi," who had business connections with Altmann and Schwend. According to the tip, Altmann and Barbie were one and the same. Based on the details about Altmann's background provided by John, the Klarsfelds believed that they had found Barbie, but they needed proof—photographic proof. Within weeks they had that proof. Beate Klarsfeld traveled to Bolivia and made a public statement on 28 January 1972. In her statement Klarsfeld dropped two bombshells. First, she claimed that Klaus Altman was in fact Klaus Barbie, the Butcher of Lyon. Then, she laid blame at the door of the United States when she asserted that the United States could have turned Barbie over to French authorities in 1950 but had refused to do so.[49]

With Klarsfeld's announcement, the cat was out of the bag. The French government immediately issued an extradition request to the Bolivian government. There is some suggestion that the French government knew as early as 1963 that Barbie, or Altmann, resided in Bolivia but chose not to act on extradition until forced to do so by Beate Klarsfeld. Once the French officially requested extradition, however, there was a question about whether or not the Bolivian government would turn Barbie over to the French. It was quickly apparent that Banzer would not be supportive. Extensive reports in the French press and pressure from various French groups demanding justice just made the Bolivians dig in their heels. Beate Klarsfeld did not help matters by publicly criticizing Banzer's government for shielding Barbie and by organizing a protest demonstration in La Paz. Even the U.S. government weighed in on the matter. On 8 March the U.S. secretary of state, William Rogers, contacted his counterpart in La Paz.[50] He said, "While we recognize that Bolivia's disposition in the Altmann case is an internal Bolivian matter, the hope of the U.S. government is that justice will be done in this matter."[51]

Despite pressure from all sides, including from the U.S. government, the Bolivians denied the French extradition request both in 1972 and in 1975. In addition to the protection Banzer gave Barbie, who had been his supporter on multiple levels, the Bolivian government justified its refusal on the lack of an extradition treaty between France and Bolivia. The French government had no recourse but to accept the Bolivian decision—at least in the short term. It seemed apparent that as long as Banzer remained dictator a stalemate would exist. One could only hope for a miracle, and one seemed in the offing in 1978, when Banzer was forced from office. Recognizing that he could regain power only if he changed, Banzer worked to "establish his democratic credentials," which he accomplished by 1985. In the meantime France decided to push for Barbie's extradition again.[52]

Issuing new charges of "crimes against humanity" against Barbie, the French again petitioned for the criminal's return for trial. While the sticking point again was the lack of an extradition treaty between France and Bolivia, the new government found a creative solution that allowed compliance with the French request and kept the French in the loop as the plan was put in motion. Charging him "with making a fraudulent loan" to the government, the Bolivians put Barbie on a plane and shipped him to French Guyana, where French officials were waiting as he stepped off the plane. Barbie was immediately arrested and put on a plane to France. On 6 February 1983 Barbie arrived back to the place where he had perpetrated his most egregious crimes—Lyon. Although he had been tried and convicted in absentia, "the statute of limitations had expired." The French courts would have to retry Barbie.[53]

Barbie's return to French soil opened the whistle-blower floodgates. All the secrets about Barbie's employment by the CIC, about the refusal of Americans to tell the French about Barbie's whereabouts, and about Barbie's trips to the United States in the 1960s and 1970s became public. As a result, the media demanded a government investigation to determine the exact nature of the relationship between the United States and Barbie, if one indeed existed. The question then became which government agency—the "Justice Department, the State Department, the CIA, [or] the Defense Department"—would receive the task. The chair of the House Judiciary Committee contacted Attorney General William French Smith and made a recommendation. According to the chair, the OSI

> could play a unique and valuable role in any investigation conducted by the Executive Branch. Given the expertise of OSI's staff, and the fact that attorneys and investigators there have the necessary security clearances, it would seem that the office would be ideally suited to coordinate such an inquiry. More importantly, OSI, with no direct ties to the intelligence community and no vested interest in any predetermined outcome, is sufficiently detached to assure its findings would be viewed as complete and honest. . . . While the primary function of the OSI must remain the prosecution of denaturalization and deportation actions involving suspected Nazi criminals in this country, the case of Klaus Barbie is potentially too important a part of the historical record to be left unattended.[54]

Although he acknowledged that the assignment would be outside their mandate, the chair made a compelling case for assigning the investigation to the fledgling division within the Department of Justice.

Despite the chair's recommendation, there was resistance to the idea. Various groups voiced their support or opposition to the OSI conducting the investigation. Initially, the attorney general resisted the chair's recommendation, but one phone call changed the dynamic. An ABC reporter, who had pursued the story in Bolivia, telephoned Allan Ryan, the director of OSI. According to the reporter, he had proof not only that Barbie had been employed by U.S. intelligence but also that the United States had facilitated his relocation to Bolivia even though he was wanted by the French. The reporter guaranteed that his story would air that night. Dismayed, Ryan informed the attorney general, who within hours "authorized the Department to conduct an inquiry" into the matter.[55]

Assistant Attorney General D. Lowell Jensen placed Ryan in charge of the investigation. Furthermore, Ryan became "AAG [Assistant Attorney General] Jensen's Special Assistant for the duration." Ryan and his team completed the investigation and released a report in five months. According to the "218 page report (with over 600 pages of attachments)," not only had

> the Army used Barbie as an informant after the war, but it had ignored several requests by the French for extradition, had misled the State Department (which then passed on this misinformation to the French) as to Barbie's whereabouts, and had used the services of a shady intermediary to help Barbie escape to Bolivia in 1951 under the name Klaus Altmann. Once he was there, the U.S. no longer protected or used him. He obtained Bolivian citizenship and twice made business trips to the United States under his new name; the visits were not connected to any agency or activity of the U.S. government.[56]

The report, in addition to containing minute details about Barbie, rendered certain conclusions that ultimately reflected Ryan's evaluation of the facts, particularly with regard to the decisions made by army officials "to use and protect Barbie, even after they had reason to suspect he was a war criminal." According to Ryan, they were motivated by "two reasons: (1) surrender of Barbie would "embarrass" the U.S. by revealing it had worked with a former Gestapo official, and (2) it would risk compromising procedures, sources, and information." A further extenuating circumstance was the American belief "that French intelligence had been penetrated by Communists." The end result would be the compromising of U.S. assets.[57]

In his final assessment Ryan did not condemn or condone the decisions made at the time. In addition to demonstrating an understanding about why they were made, he suggested alternative ways in which the situation could have been handled:

> I cannot conclude that those who made the decision to employ and rely on Klaus Barbie ought now to be vilified for the decision. Any one of us,

had we been there, might have made the opposite decision. But one must recognize that those who did in fact make a decision made a defensible one, even if it was not the only defensible one. No one to whom I spoke in this investigation was insensitive to the horrors perpetrated by Nazi Germany, nor entirely comfortable with the irony of using a Gestapo officer in the service of the United States. They were, on the whole, conscientious and patriotic men faced with a difficult assignment. Under the circumstances, I believe that their choice to enlist Barbie's assistance was neither cynical nor corrupt.[58]

Ryan did not, however, completely exonerate the army officials involved from actions taken after Barbie's war crimes had become known. The decision to lie to the Department of State compromised the assessment of France's extradition request; therefore, Ryan concluded that "the Army's actions amounted to a criminal obstruction of justice."[59]

Ryan's condemnation suggested the need for punishment and the implementation of steps to prevent an occurrence of actions similar to those taken by the army. He admitted, however, that the "statute of limitations" on the "obstruction of justice" charge had run out. He also lacked confidence that "legislative or regulatory reforms would be effective." He did believe that U.S. intelligence agencies, over the thirty years since Barbie had been employed, had acquired a "greater sense of accountability"; therefore, there was hope for the future. At the end of the day, Ryan did not give the army a complete pass on the actions that it took with regard to Barbie between 1947 and 1951.[60]

Ryan made one final recommendation, which although originally in the report, was eventually sent as a "separate memorandum to the Attorney General." He recommended that the United States apologize to France publicly. Because there was some resistance from the Department of State, Deputy Assistant Attorney General Mark M. Richard stepped in to negotiate a solution with the Department of State. At the end of the day, those involved recognized that Ryan was correct about the need for an official apology. On 12 August 1983 a meeting between the Department of State and the French chargé d'affaires occurred. During that meeting the Department of State submitted two documents to the French representative: the complete OSI report, "along with a note expressing the United States' 'deep regret over the actions taken in Germany . . . to conceal Barbie.'" Less than a week later both documents were made public. The cat was completely out of the bag.[61]

The OSI investigation and the subsequent report did not affect Barbie's situation—his trial or its outcome. Although Barbie and his French escorts arrived in Lyon on 7 February 1983, a legal battle between groups representing the victims delayed the actual trial for over four years. On 11 May 1987 the trial began. Barbie, the sole defendant, faced charges of "crimes against humanity." Numerous survivors, including Simone Lagrange, Lise Lesevre, Ennat Leger, and Christian Pineau, bore witness against the Butcher of Lyon, while he sat and smiled. Otherwise he displayed little emotion throughout the trial, which lasted for eight weeks. On 4 July 1987 the court rendered its verdict—guilty. By the time the trial occurred and the verdict was rendered, Barbie was seventy-three years old. He received "France's highest punishment"—life in prison. Unlike the outcome of his previous two trials in the 1950s, Barbie avoided the death penalty because it had been abolished in 1981. Barbie would have been eligible for parole in 2002 at the age of eighty-eight had he survived that long, but he died of cancer in the Lyon prison hospital on 25 September 1991.[62]

Even at the end, as he awaited his trial for "crimes against humanity," Barbie remained unrepentant. In an interview with Agence France-Presse in 1985, he suggested that his actions were nothing more than wartime acts. According to Barbie, "In times of war there are no goods and no bads. I am a convinced Nazi. I admire the Nazi discipline. I am proud of having commanded one of the best corps of the Third Reich. If I should be born 1,000 times I would be 1,000 times what I have been. I am not a fanatic. I am an idealist."[63] Sadly, Barbie's victims would not agree with his personal assessment; neither does history. He learned violence at the hands of his father. He honed those skills during SS training. He took torture and sadism to new levels in Lyon—and then again in Bolivia. Nikolaus "Klaus" Barbie earned the Butcher of Lyon moniker, and he seemed to wear it proudly to the end.

3

Josef Mengele—"Angel of Death"

Why was part of a human scalp found in a Department of Justice official's desk? Rumor had it that the piece of skull in the OSI director's possession belonged to a man who was hunted for decades—a man whom Holocaust survivors wanted to stand trial for war crimes and brought to justice. At the end of the day, once the OSI became involved, the question was this. Did the bone fragment in the director's desk really belong to Josef Mengele?

Referred to as the "Angel of Death," Josef Mengele was one of the most notorious Nazis to escape prosecution. Assigned to Auschwitz, he determined which inmates were gassed upon arrival, which were suitable for forced labor, and which were identified as "research subjects." Mengele gained notoriety for the scientific experiments that he and his staff conducted on Jewish, gypsy, and other prisoners at Auschwitz. The Angel of Death dropped out of sight after the war, but, according to urban legend, he was living in Paraguay. It wasn't until four decades after the war that a manhunt for Mengele bore fruit. Under the Freedom of Information Act, the Simon Wiesenthal Center, an international Jewish human rights organization, applied for and received documents related to Mengele from the Department of Defense. The center released this information to the public in early 1985. Public outcry ensued. Consequently, the OSI began an investigation of claims that Mengele had been captured and released by U.S. forces at the end of the war, that he had applied for a visa to Canada, and that he had traveled to the United States. These outrageous claims forced the OSI's hand. They had to investigate to confirm or refute these allegations. If true, how had Mengele duped his U.S. captors? Who was the Angel of Death? Was he born a sociopath or was he taught to engage in horrific behavior? Did his early life breed a man who delighted in torture or in experimenting on children and dwarfs?

Early Years

Josef Rudolf Mengele was born on 16 March 1911 in the picturesque German town of Günzburg, which is the current home of Legoland Deutschland. His parents, Karl and Walburga Mengele, had three sons: Josef (1911–79), Karl Jr. (1912–49), and Alois (1914–74). Josef was the oldest of the three. Karl Mengele Sr., an engineer, was a successful businessman, a producer of farming implements. He owned his own business—eventually called Frima Karl Mengele & Sohne—by the time his oldest son was born. Known as a "shirt-sleeve boss," the elder Mengele had thirty employees working in his farm-machinery factory by the time World War I erupted.[1]

Raised Catholic, the Mengele boys grew up in quite comfortable— that is, wealthy—circumstances. Their father spent long hours at the factory. He was rarely at home. The outbreak of World War I, as might be expected, brought change to the Mengele family. When Karl Sr. went off to war, the running of the family company fell to his wife, Walburga, who was not an easygoing boss like her husband.[2] It did not take long for Walburga to prove that she was a "fearsome disciplinarian." Not only did she have to run the business, but she was also tasked with growing the company. In many respects she excelled at the challenge. Walburga landed a "lucrative" government contract to build a "special army vehicle called the *Fouragewagen*." As a result, the family business was in good financial shape during the war. The end of World War I did not diminish the company's prosperity. It quickly retooled and returned to manufacturing farm machinery. A "postwar revival program" provided additional opportunities. Within a few years the Mengele company "had become the third largest threshing production company in Germany."[3]

With the family's continued prosperity, the world was Josef Mengele's oyster. Although his father wanted him to join the family business, he had other ideas, other dreams for his future—a future that did not include Günzburg or the "factory boardroom." Julius Diesbach recognized his school chum's drive for what it was: "Josef was a very ambitious young man with a great need to succeed. He wanted to establish his own fame separate from that already established by his family. He did not want just to succeed but to stand out from the crowd. It was his passion for fame. He once told me that one day I would read his name in the encyclopedia."[4] Decades would pass, but Josef Mengele's prediction would come true. He would make a name for himself. He would stand out apart from the rest of his family. He would gain notoriety, but would the fame that he achieved really be the kind that he sought all those years earlier?

Before the War

Mengele aspired to travel down a different path than the family business. Advanced university studies would help him achieve his dreams, and so he moved to Munich—the hotbed of Hitler and the National Socialist German Workers' Party—in October 1930. His initial field of study, philosophy, introduced him to Alfred Rosenberg's racist theories that emphasized the "innate intellectual and moral superiority of Aryans."[5] As events would later prove, Mengele bought into those theories hook, line, and sinker, and he would continue to demonstrate how committed he was to them for decades after World War II.

Within six months of his arrival in Munich, Mengele had joined the Stahlhelm, or Steel Helmets, a nationalist, right-wing group. Excelling in his studies at the University of Munich, Mengele took courses in anthropology, paleontology, and medicine; successfully defended his thesis, "Racial Morphological Research on the Lower Jaw Section of Four Racial Groups"; and graduated with a PhD in physical anthropology in 1935. He was only twenty-four years old. Step one was completed. In 1937 he continued his medical-degree studies at Frankfurt University, where he became Dr. Otmar von Verschuer's assistant at the Institute for Hereditary Biology and Racial Hygiene. Von Verschuer's research focus was twins. Mengele's appointment as research assistant would be "life changing." It would set him down the path to his own work at Auschwitz, but, at the same time, Mengele would strive to emerge from his mentor's shadow and to gain fame and notoriety for research separate from that which he conducted with von Verschuer.

Mengele's life would change in other ways. He began a relationship with Irene Maria Schöenbein from Leipzig, whose father, Harry Schöenbein, was a university professor. Mengele joined the Nazi Party and, after passing the required background check to verify that he had no Jewish or other non-Aryan ancestors, received acceptance into the Waffen Schutzstaffel (SS) as an officer in 1938. Assignment to the SS as a medical officer did not end Mengele's desire to advance his career academically. He pursued his coveted goal—a professorship in medicine—by continuing his research and by publishing when possible. In fact, prior to his 1943 assignment to Auschwitz, he published three pieces: the dissertation that he wrote in the University of Munich's Anthropological Institute; "Genealogical Studies in the Cases of Cleft Lip-Jaw-Palate," his 1938 published medical dissertation; and "Hereditary Transmission of Fistulae Auris," which was based on research conducted by von Verschuer and others.[6]

Mengele appeared to be on the way to the career and the life that he coveted. In July 1938 he received his medical degree from Frankfurt University; therefore, as a result, he was licensed to practice medicine. A year later he and Irene Schöenbein married, but not before Mengele dealt with a glitch that not only could have derailed the wedding but also could have destroyed his career. To get married, the "Rasse-und Siedlungshauptampt, the Central Office for Race and Resettlement," required that Mengele submit proof that his bride-to-be had no "Jewish blood" in her family. The problem was her "grandfather, who was thought to be illegitimate." Things were complicated because the documentation related to her great-grandfather, American diplomat Harry Lyons Dumler, was lost. Consequently, there was no proof that he had fathered his son, which raised the suspicion that the grandfather's father was someone else—a Jew, perhaps. Acting on a plea from the family, the German consul to the United States conducted an exhaustive search, but to no avail. The Schöenbein family supplied the Central Office for Race and Resettlement with photographs of both Irene and the family's ancestors. Although the Central Office gave the young couple permission to marry, the lack of clarity proved problematic for Mengele. Because he could not prove "that Irene had 'pure Aryan blood,'" Mengele "failed to qualify for the ultimate accolade of racial purity—a place in the hallowed *Sippenbuch*, or Kinship Book, for those who had been able to prove, chapter and verse, that their ancestors were pure Aryan at least since 1750." Ironically, while he focused his research on creating a pure race by focusing on "racial hygiene," Mengele's children could not be "certified as racially clean."[7]

After completing his military training, he returned to Frankfurt University—to the Third Reich Institute for Heredity, Biology, and Racial Purity—and his research with von Verschuer. Mengele's published work demonstrated that he wholeheartedly embraced the Nazi rhetoric on the "supremacy of the German race." He reviewed the work of other scholars and criticized them for not going far enough—for not clearly articulating the threats posed by other races to the Aryan people. The outbreak of war would allow Mengele to put his theories into practice through the research that he conducted on Auschwitz inmates—particularly twins and dwarfs.[8]

War, Auschwitz, and Ultimate Power

Mengele began his military service with a six-month assignment "with a specially trained mountain light-infantry regiment" in 1938–39. When the war in Europe began, Mengele was an SS medical officer. By 1940 he had received his next posting to a Waffen SS unit as part of the "reserve medical corps, where he remained for three years." While serving with the Waffen SS unit, Mengele was wounded. According to a superior officer, Mengele had "proved himself splendidly in front of the enemy," and the Viking divisional medical officer wrote at the time that he was a "specially talented medical officer." His doctor subsequently determined that he was "medically unfit for combat." He was, however, promoted to captain and "awarded the Black Badge for the Wounded and the Medal for the Care of the German People" in recognition of his bravery.[9]

Because he served with such distinction, Heinrich Himmler gave Mengele an additional reward—a prime post as Auschwitz's "chief doctor." Mengele's wife, Irene, would join him at Auschwitz, and his son Rolf would be born there in 1944. Rolf would be too young when his father left the camp in 1945 to remember living at Auschwitz or what his father had done while the family was based at the camp.

Part of Mengele's new position included immediately deciding which of the new inmates would live and which would die. He took that role seriously, especially since it gave him a chance to identify prime candidates for his research projects. He quickly asserted his authority over the process:

> Mengele, in distinctive white gloves, supervised the selection of Auschwitz's incoming prisoners for either torturous labor or immediate extermination, shouting either "Right!" or "Left!" to direct them to their fate. Eager to advance his medical career by publishing "groundbreaking" work, he then began experimenting on live Jewish prisoners. In the guise of medical "treatment," Mengele injected, or ordered others to inject, thousands of inmates with everything from petrol to chloroform to study the chemicals' effects. Among other atrocities, he plucked out the eyes of Gypsy corpses to study eye pigmentation, and conducted numerous gruesome studies of twins.[10]

Mengele viewed his assignment to Auschwitz as an opportunity to continue his work. His subordinates quickly learned to be on the lookout for the kinds of specimens Mengele required. The guards had orders to execute inmates with physical deformities immediately. Mengele would then perform tests on the cadavers.[11]

When he arrived at the camp, Mengele was tasked with addressing a problem in the women's facility—a typhus epidemic. He ruthlessly attacked the problem head on. He quickly ordered the solution that he deemed most appropriate. He issued a directive that resulted in the movement of 498 women to the gas chambers. Problem solved. Mengele then focused his attention on inmate groups that could be exploited for his research. It did not matter if the end result was the death of these inmates. After all, there were lots more from which to choose because new shipments of the "unclean" arrived regularly. Furthermore, for some of his experiments, he needed dead, not living, specimens. For instance, when he decided that he needed eyeballs for his work, Mengele ordered the execution of gypsies and subsequent extraction of their eyeballs.[12]

While at Auschwitz, Mengele conducted experiments to test his theories about heredity and genetics in an effort to discover a way to increase the Aryan gene pool rapidly. Surely, the best way to ensure optimum procreation was to biologically and genetically engineer multiple births—that is, twins—of blond-haired, blue-eyed children to ensure the future of Germany. Consequently, to further his research in this area, he needed the perfect subjects—twins. When Mengele was not present on the ramps to ferret out his prey, his colleagues and subordinates knew that they must single out twins from the other prisoners as they emerged from the cattle cars upon their arrival at Auschwitz or face consequences handed out by the irate doctor. Not trusting them completely, Mengele frequently returned to his position on the ramps even when he was not on duty. He could not afford to miss a single pair of twins. They were too crucial to his research to pass up. Mengele was driven to find them all and bring them to his laboratory. Then the experiments could begin and continue until the twins died or he found the answers that he was seeking—that would give him the notoriety and fame that he craved.[13]

Mengele's obsession with twins was apparent to everyone at the concentration camp—inmates and soldiers alike. In the 1970s some of his colleagues and twins who survived gave testimony about the doctor's behavior. Dr. Martina Puzyna was an anthropologist who worked for Mengele. She was tasked with "measur[ing] the external feature of twins." Dr. Puzyna witnessed Mengele "shrieking in a loud voice, 'Twins, out, twins out,' while running alongside a procession of Hungarian Jews as they streamed off the train."[14] No one dared question Mengele's unusual behavior. Ignoring Mengele's antics, camp personnel identified twins instead.

Irene and René Slotkin were five years old when they arrived at the camp where they were "rescued" by the twin-obsessed doctor. According to René Slotkin, "At one point toward the end of the war I was scheduled to go to the chambers. I knew I was going to lose my life. We were being loaded onto trucks when this car comes up. A convertible. That's when I saw Mengele. We were taken off the truck. He stopped the whole procession because they were going to kill his twins."[15] Mengele's obsession with twins did not fade as the war neared an end. He controlled if and when twins were executed. Being rescued by Mengele was a mixed blessing. Even though they lived separately from the other inmates, ate better food, and wore their own clothes, the twins, thanks to Mengele, did not have it easy in the camp. They endured—and in some cases survived—unspeakable torture.

Kept separate from the rest of the inmate population at Auschwitz, the twins were singled out for special treatment—and experimentation. Five-year-old twins Vera and Olga Kriegel were uprooted from their home in Czechoslovakia and transported via train cattle car to Auschwitz. Mengele personally examined the twins and their mother—who had "perfect Aryan features," including blue eyes—upon their arrival at the concentration camp. He was particularly intrigued by brown-eyed Vera and Olga. Surely, their eye color was an anomaly. According to Vera Kriegel, sometimes the experiments Mengele conducted resulted in the death of one twin. The surviving twin would be killed, which would allow Mengele to dissect both twins at the same time. It was common knowledge among the camp twins that they all faced one of two fates—either both died or both lived—but their fate was ultimately out of their hands. In addition to the trauma of their uncertain future, the twins faced many physical and emotional horrors.[16]

Brought to Mengele's laboratory, Vera saw "a whole wall of human eyes. A wall of blue eyes, brown eyes, green eyes. These eyes they were staring at me like a collection of butterflies and I fell down on the floor." The psychological shock was only part of the horror. The first time that they were part of an experiment, Vera and Olga were placed together in a small wooden cage. Vera received "painful injections in her back." Although she was not certain, she speculated that Mengele hoped that the injections would change her eye color. After all, a true Aryan would have blue, not brown, eyes.[17]

Identical twins, Eva [Mozes Kor] and Miriam Mozes, who were born in Portz, Romania, arrived at Auschwitz in March 1944 and were immediately separated from their family and sent to the twins' section of the camp. Although all of their family, including their parents, grandparents, and two older sisters, perished there, the twins survived the horrors of the concentration camp. Years after the war Eva Mozes Kor described her introduction to Auschwitz: "The first time I went to use the latrine located at the end of the children's barrack, I was greeted by the scattered corpses of several children lying on the ground. I think that image will stay with me forever. It was there that I made a silent pledge—a vow to make sure that Miriam and I didn't end up on that filthy floor."[18]

According to Eva,

> Mengele came in every day after roll call—he wanted to see how many guinea pigs he had. Three times a week both of my arms would be tied to restrict the blood flow, and they took a lot of blood until we fainted. At the same time they were taking blood, they would give me a minimum of five injections into my right arm. After one of these injections I became extremely ill and Dr. Mengele came in the next morning with four other doctors. He looked at my fever chart and he said, laughing sarcastically, "Too bad, she is so young. She has only two weeks to live." I would fade in and out of consciousness, and in a semi-conscious state of mind I would keep telling myself, "I must survive, I must survive." They were waiting for me to die. Would I have died my twin sister, Miriam, would have been rushed immediately to Mengele's lab, killed with an injection to the heart and then Mengele would have done the comparative autopsies.[19]

Her determination paid off. Eva recovered. She saved her own life and that of her sister Miriam.

In addition to experiencing her own horrors, however, she witnessed those of other children. Much of what she saw was forever vividly etched in her mind. She described what happened to a "set of Gypsy twins." They were "brought back from Mengele's lab after they were sewn back to back. Mengele had attempted to create a Siamese twin by connecting blood vessels and organs. The twins screamed day and night until gangrene set in, and after three days, they died."[20] How the creation of Siamese twins would further Mengele's efforts to genetically engineer the procreation of "perfect" Aryan twins is virtually impossible to understand. Perhaps his attempt simply reflected his character flaw—that of a sadistic monster willing to torture children in furtherance of his agenda and his insatiable desire for greatness.

Mengele was not interested just in mass producing twins; he also wanted to eliminate particular genetic traits from the Aryan gene pool. Eradication of the DNA that produced dwarfism would result in a population of tall, strong Germans who could fulfill the Third Reich's destiny. Consequently, in addition to twins, dwarfs found themselves in Mengele's crosshairs. Imagine the doctor's surprise when he learned that a shipment of prisoners that arrived when he was off duty included a rarity—a family of dwarfs. Surprise turned to anger when he learned their location—the gas chamber. This family of dwarfs were luckily saved from death by the doctor at the last minute, but were they really lucky? What did being saved mean? In an interview with the *Guardian*, Perla Ovitz, who survived Auschwitz, described what she and her family experienced at the hands of the Angel of Death.

Residents of Rozavlea, Transylvania, the Ovitz family had achieved notoriety before the war for multiple reasons. Papa Ovitz, a dwarf, and his wife had ten children. Only three were not dwarfs. In 1921 their youngest "little" child, Perla, was born. The seven dwarf children—five girls and two boys—were musically talented and easy on the eyes. Recognizing that they were not suited to traditional rural work, which was the norm where they lived, Mama Ovitz orchestrated the creation of an all-dwarf act—the Lilliput Troupe, which had a successful fifteen-year touring run throughout central Europe. The Ovitz's situation changed, however, with the outbreak of war and Nazi expansion into central Europe. As the Nazis targeted the unwanted for elimination or incarceration and labor, the family had two bull's-eyes on their backs. The German Aktion T-4 euthanasia program ordered the extermination of the "physically and mentally disabled" because they were "unworthy of living." They constituted a "burden on society." Dwarfism translated to "physically disabled." Furthermore, because the Ovitz family was Jewish, they were condemned under the Nazi's Final Solution plan.[21]

Based on these factors, the dwarf family lost their freedom in May 1944. Transported to Auschwitz-Birkenau, they were forced to strip and enter the delousing shower, but instead of water, the chamber began to fill with gas. Before the dwarfs succumbed completely to the gas and died, however, Mengele rescued and claimed them for his research. The Ovitz family thus became "his dwarf family." Although he planned to conduct experiments on "his family of dwarves," Mengele realized that he would probably never find another dwarf family of this size; therefore, he had to be careful if he hoped to preserve them. He had so much to learn from them, but he needed them to be alive to do so. These dwarfs, unlike the rest who arrived at the gates to Auschwitz, were not expendable. Consequently, unlike other dwarfs and Jewish inmates, the Ovitz family received different treatment. Their heads were not shaved, nor were they forced to wear inmate clothing.[22] Generally, all inmates had their hair shaved and wore the same clothes. Not being subjected to either set the Ovitz family apart from other internees. However, their other accommodations—housing and food—were the same as for the rest of the inmates: dwarfs, Jews, and gypsies alike. Not looking like the rest of the inmates denoted the Ovitz family's special status, but did that special status mean they would have an easy time in the camp?

The dwarf family would quickly learn that life under Mengele would not be a bed of roses, but they were grateful to be alive. The first time they were summoned to the laboratory, the dwarfs—who had blood drawn—left with the impression that exchanging a little blood for their lives was not so bad. They rapidly discovered, however, that it was not just a little blood. The technicians frequently drew blood and subjected them to X-rays.[23] According to Perla Ovitz, "The amount of blood they took was enormous and, being feeble from hunger, we often fainted. That didn't stop Mengele: he had us lie down and when we came to our senses they resumed siphoning our blood. They punctured us carelessly and blood spurted. We often felt nauseous and vomited a lot. When we returned to the barrack, we'd slump on the wooden bunks—but before we had time to recover, we'd be summoned for a new cycle."[24] The Ovitz dwarfs also experienced water torture, when "water was poured into their ears"; the extraction of healthy teeth; and eyelash plucking.[25]

If experiencing torture was not enough, the family witnessed the fate of other dwarfs and dreaded that they would face the same end. Following the deaths of a hunchbacked dwarf and his son, Mengele thought that a Berlin museum would benefit from having their skeletons. To prepare them, "Mengele had ordered his staff to boil their bodies over a fire until the flesh separated from the bones." He had another male dwarf killed and his body placed in a vat filled with acid to achieve a clean skeleton.[26] What was a little torture—the loss of blood, teeth, and eyelashes—when compared to boiling in water or acid? It was all about perspective.

By focusing his experiments on the dwarfs, Mengele planned to create his own "research niche" that was separate from the experiments that he and his mentor, von Verschuer, had conducted on twins. Wanting notoriety that would distinguish him from von Verschuer, "Mengele was aiming not only to discover the biological and pathological causes of the birth of dwarves, but to demonstrate the racial theory that in the course of its long history, the Jewish race had degenerated into a people of dwarves and cripples."[27] He would, as a result, be able to provide an even more definitive reason for the extermination of the Jewish race. To accomplish his ultimate goal, Mengele had his assistants repeatedly draw blood from the Ovitz family members. If one of them fainted during the process, he or she was "revived" for the withdrawal of blood to continue. Mengele signed off on blood tests to determine "signs of kidney problems, liver function, typhus, and syphilis." The technicians also took measurements for comparison of the family members, "extracted bone marrow, pulled out healthy teeth, plucked hair and eyelashes, and carried out psychological and gynaecological tests on them all."[28]

Some tests conducted on the dwarfs, however, seemed to have no purpose except to reflect Mengele's depravity. In 1944 Moti Alon became an Auschwitz inmate. He was an unwilling witness to "a dwarf and a Roma woman being made to have sex."[29] It is possible that by forcing conception with a dwarf and a normal woman, Mengele was attempting to determine what percentage of their offspring would be dwarf and what percentage would be normal. Despite the toll of the experiments on them, the Ovitz family was lucky. Unlike many incarcerated at Auschwitz, the entire family survived. At the end of the day, what did Mengele learn from these experiments? That remains unknown. He did not publish the results of his research on dwarfs.

Ultimately, Mengele hoped to achieve academic greatness. He believed that his "research" at Auschwitz would help—particularly if he succeeded in publishing "his *Habilitation*, a second, post-doctoral, dissertation required for admission to a university faculty as a professor in German-speaking lands."[30] In this he did not succeed—much to his everlasting disappointment, as was demonstrated in his repeated efforts later in life to convince his son to pursue a doctorate, but to no avail.

Man on the Run

Outside forces eventually prevented Mengele from achieving research—and, consequently, academic—success. The end to Mengele's research came as a result of the Soviet push to the west and the Western Allies' advance to the east—both of which indicated that the war was coming to a close, but not in the way that would most benefit the Third Reich. In January 1945 word reached Auschwitz that the Red Army, which was on the march across Poland, was getting too close for comfort.

News of the approaching Soviet army made Mengele face reality and make a decision. It was time to get out of "Dodge." He packed up and went on the run to the west. When the Soviet advance team entered "Auschwitz and Birkenau at 3 p.m. on January 27, 1945"—ten days after Mengele had fled—they encountered a horrific scene: "the corpses of the 650 prisoners killed by looting ss-men." By this time Mengele and several of his colleagues had sought sanctuary at another concentration camp—Gross Rosen in Silesia. Two hundred miles stood between Mengele and the Red Army. The reality was, however, that Gross Rosen would be even hotter than Auschwitz when the Soviets arrived. Beginning in early 1942 German doctors at Gross Rosen conducted "bacteriological-warfare experiments on Soviet prisoners." With the Red Army breathing down his neck, Mengele hit the road again on 18 February. Eight days later Soviet troops had reached the gates of Gross Rosen. Mengele had fled not a moment too soon.[31]

If the Soviets were coming from the east, then surely safety lay in the west. It had to be better to be captured by the British or the Americans if he had to fall into enemy hands. Consequently, Mengele headed west until he met up with a Wehrmacht unit in retreat. To blend in with this regular army unit, he shed his SS uniform for a Wehrmacht officer's uniform. Mengele remained with the Wehrmacht unit for two months while they sought refuge in Czechoslovakia, but they were soon on the move again, as the Soviet steamroller steadily headed west. By 2 May Mengele reached Saaz, Sudetenland, where Krieg-slazarett 2/591, a "motorized German field hospital," was located. Dr. Hans Otto Kahler was "one of the chief medical officers" at the hospital—and Mengele's old friend. Mengele's arrival at Kriegslaz-arett 2/591 coincided with another monumental event—the day on which radio commentators announced the suicide of Adolf Hitler.[32]

Although one-eighth Jewish and not a member of the Nazi Party, Kahler had been protected by von Verscheur, who respected his con-tribution to the twins research. It was at von Verscheur's institute where Mengele and Kahler had met and become friends. Kahler, who ignored his friend's uniform, noted that Mengele refused to believe that Hitler was dead. Kahler agreed to let Mengele stay and work at the field hospital. The security of his new location did not last, how-ever. In less than a week, Mengele was on the move again. By 8 May, when Field Marshal Wilhelm Keitel made Germany's unconditional surrender official, approximately fifteen thousand German soldiers faced capture by the Soviets in the east and the Americans in the west. As Kahler's field hospital crossed the border and left Czecho-slovakia behind, the unit separated and the sections fled in differ-ent directions.[33]

When the dust cleared, Mengele realized that he and Kahler were no longer together and that he was in Col. Fritz Ulmann's unit. Ulmann, a senior physician, suspected the truth about Mengele's SS affiliation, but he did not know about the doctor's work at Auschwitz. What gave Mengele away to Ulmann was that he could not remember what name he was using at roll call. Mengele's luck held. Ulmann did not out him. About ten thousand German soldiers became American prisoners on 15 June 1945, but Mengele was not one of him. When his new unit made a break for it, he went with them. Mengele recorded his time on the run in mid-June: "In the end there was less and less food, and the rumors that the Russians would occupy this area became more numerous. So then we decided to act. With several vehicles and a sanitation unit we formed a column, and with some trickery we succeeded in passing through the Americans. We passed their subsequent roadblocks and reached Bavarian territory."[34] A few days later the unit's luck ran out near Hof, where they fell into the Americans' hands, but Mengele's luck was not all bad.

When he arrived at the American prisoner of war camp, he found Kahler there. Although he registered with the Americans under his real name, Mengele successfully concealed his ss affiliation because his blood type was not "tattooed on his chest," even though that was a normal ss practice. Consequently, the Americans did not subject Mengele to close scrutiny, despite the fact that he had already been labeled a "principal war criminal."[35] In fact, he was given that designation prior to his departure from Auschwitz. The following warrant had already been issued: "Mengele, Joseph, Dr., ss-Hauptsturmführer and camp doctor, Auschwitz Concentration Camp, June 1940 until January 1945, mass murder and other crimes."[36] In addition, the Central Registry of War Criminals and Security Suspects, which was "compiled by the Allied High Command in Paris," was aware of his wartime activities. Mengele's name was on the registry list that the Allied High Command circulated to "detention camps throughout Europe," but not all of the detention camps received lists such as this in a timely fashion. Consequently, Mengele succeeded in falling through the cracks, but he had other help as well.[37]

Fearing that someone would discover who he was and the secret of his past at Auschwitz, Mengele appealed to Ulmann for help. Ulmann agreed to keep Mengele's secret and help him get false identification papers, because he realized that Mengele would not be able "to survive in postwar Germany" unless he had an "alias." Ulmann managed to acquire a "second set of release papers in his own name," which he presented to Mengele. Because they remained unaware that he was on a "wanted" list and because they thought that he was a Wehrmacht private, the Americans released Mengele from the camp in August 1945.[38] Finally free, Mengele breathed a small sigh of relief, but he was unsure if he could continue to avoid paying for his past actions—not that he thought, then or later, that he had done anything wrong.

Upon his release, Mengele sought out an old school friend, Albert Miller, and his wife for help. Acting at their friend's request, the Millers got in touch with Karl Mengele Jr. They informed him that his brother was safe. Mengele's brother passed this on to his sister-in-law, his brother Alois, and his parents. In addition, the Millers did not inform the Americans of Mengele's return. Mengele also contacted the brother-in-law of Dr. Fritz Ulmann, who helped him get a job as a farmhand in the Bavarian town of Mongolding. Mengele, who doctored the identity papers given to him by Ulmann, introduced himself as "Fritz Hollmann" to his new bosses—Georg and Maria Fischer. Mengele began work in late October for "10 marks a week." The Fischers were pleased with his work, but they soon realized that Mengele was not who he claimed to be—that he "was really a wanted Nazi." During this time, despite the risk, Mengele and his wife, Irene, occasionally met in Rosenheim, which was approximately ten miles from the farm where he worked.[39]

The longer he went without detection, the more comfortable Mengele felt, and he soon concluded that he was no longer on the Americans' radar. His family was not as confident. They were afraid that Mengele's unrepentant opinion about "the imprisonment of Jews and the conditions in the camps," along with his wartime activities, would result in the ultimate punishment—execution—if he were apprehended. Consequently, they were committed to helping him escape capture; therefore, when Mengele decided in 1948 to start over in Argentina, they were willing to help. Karl Mengele Sr. had business contacts there who could be prevailed on to help Mengele get established. Because Irene Mengele did not want to emigrate to Argentina, she and her husband decided to separate. Their young son, Rolf, who would remain with his mother, grew up thinking that Josef Mengele was his uncle, not his father. When he learned the truth decades later, it was not welcome news.[40]

Mengele could not travel under his own name, nor could he go directly from Germany to Argentina. He still had the travel papers with the name Fritz Hollmann, which he would use for as long as possible. Drawing on his family's wealth to fund his journey, Mengele took a train to Innsbruck. On 15 April 1949 he began the next phase of his trip—Innsbruck to Brenner Pass. Two smugglers—Jakob Strickner and Adolf Steiner—were his guides. They reached Brenner Pass two days later, on Easter Sunday. The next day another guide brought Mengele through Brenner Pass into Italy. From there he took the 5:45 a.m. "workers' train to Vipiteno." Upon his arrival in Vipiteno, he checked into the Goldenes Kreuz (Golden Cross) Inn as Fritz Hollmann. He met two contacts. After providing the first with a passport photograph, Mengele received a German identity card. The second, who was possibly Hans Sedlmeier, gave him a package from his father—money to finance the rest of his trip.[41] This would become a pattern. Periodically for the next thirty years, Mengele's family would both support him financially and help him evade capture by the authorities who wanted to try him for war crimes.

Mengele's stay in Vipiteno was perhaps longer than he would have liked, but it took time to arrange his journey to Argentina. For the next month he and his contact "Erwin" put a plan in place. In early June he took the train to Bosen, where he met another contact, who had been hired to acquire passage to Buenos Aires on the *North King* and new documents for Mengele from the Swiss consul. Mengele successfully received an International Red Cross passport from the Swiss consul under the name Helmut Gregor. The next step was the Argentine consulate, where he applied for the requisite papers for emigration. After supplying a fake "vaccination certificate," he cleared the next hurdle. Only one to go—an Italian exit visa—and he would be home free. The exit visa proved more difficult to acquire because his "friend" in the immigration department "was on holiday." Mengele was naturally nervous because it appeared that he might not be on board the *North King* when it sailed. His situation was further complicated when Mengele was jailed for attempting to bribe an immigration department official. After three weeks in jail, a despondent Mengele obtained his release and the necessary exit visa. His luck held. The *North King* had not sailed on time and was still docked. In mid-July, when the *North King* set sail for Buenos Aires, Mengele was on board.[42]

Mengele initially embraced life in Argentina. He gained employment at the Orbis factory. Its owner—a German-Argentine businessman—welcomed him. His was ready for his new life, but, because his income from his job was not enough to allow him to travel in the circles that he desired, Mengele received financial help from his father, who had begun investing in industry in Argentina. Under his new name—Helmut Gregor—Mengele had the opportunity to meet President Juan Domingo Perón before he was overthrown. Mengele also represented his father's business interests in Argentina, which allowed him to travel around the country and the surrounding countries, including Paraguay and Chile. On one of his trips to Paraguay in 1954, he made a contact who would prove useful in the future—Alejandro von Eckstein, a Paraguayan army captain. Confident that he could avoid capture, Mengele even began to use his own name. The large German community in Argentina knew who he was but did not expose him even though an "international manhunt" for him had begun. The situation for Mengele and other former Nazis in Argentina changed, however, in 1955, when Perón unwillingly left office. No one knew how receptive the new Argentine leader would be to the German community, which had become a refuge for former Nazis.[43]

In addition to making important contacts, Mengele changed his life in other ways. After his divorce from his wife, Irene, was finalized in 1954, he married his brother Karl's widow, Martha. Karl Mengele Jr. had died at a young age in 1949. He left behind a widow and a boy, Karl Heinz, who was probably his son. Karl Mengele Sr. played matchmaker between his son Josef and his daughter-in-law, Martha. In March 1956, traveling under a "120-day" noncitizen Argentine passport, Mengele took a plane to Switzerland—via New York. He met Martha, Karl Heinz, and his son, Rolf—who still thought that he was his "Uncle Fritz"—in Engelberg, where they stayed for ten days, after which Mengele traveled to Günzberg to see his family. To marry Martha, Mengele had to go through certain hoops. Once back in Argentina, he applied for and received a certificate confirming his real identity. He was then able to obtain a "new identity card and a West German passport." In October 1956 Martha and Karl Heinz joined Mengele in Argentina, and Mengele assumed the role of Karl Heinz's father. Their relationship was one that Mengele's son,

Rolf, would later resent when he learned that Mengele was really his father, not his uncle.[44]

Because he was concerned about the uncertainty in Argentina, Mengele decided that it was time to change his residence. He had made connections in Paraguay during his trips for his father's company. In May 1959 he decided to live in Paraguay permanently. As evidence of that decision, he applied for citizenship in Paraguay. Cosponsorship of his application by von Eckstein went a long way, and Mengele received his naturalization notification in November 1959.

Alejandro von Eckstein was useful to Mengele in other ways. Prior to his permanent relocation to Paraguay, Mengele met Alfredo Stroessner, the president, through von Eckstein. Apparently, von Eckstein and president-for-life Stroessner were "close friends." For the first few years of his residence in Paraguay, Mengele lived at a farmhouse in Hohenau that was owned by Alban Krug. Mengele had not moved to Paraguay a moment too soon. A warrant had been issued for his arrest. Because German authorities believed that Mengele was still living in Argentina, they also commenced extradition proceedings with the Argentine government. His move to Paraguay and his application for Paraguayan citizenship were fortuitous. There was no extradition agreement between West Germany and Paraguay. Even if he was discovered in his new country, an extradition battle would be a long, hard one, the outcome of which would not necessarily be what the West Germans sought.[45]

Unfortunately for Mengele, things were becoming more complicated. Various Paraguayan officials—in both the Ministry of the Interior's naturalization section and the police department—had knowledge of the West German extradition request, but that did not delay Mengele's naturalization application. That did not, however, mean smooth sailing into the sunset for Mengele. Premier David Ben-Gurion gave a public speech before the Israeli parliament. He announced that he had authorized efforts to locate a notorious Nazi war criminal—Josef Mengele. This posed a new threat. After all, Israeli agents successfully kidnapped Adolf Eichmann in Buenos Aires. Mengele's picture was plastered all over the place—on front pages of newspapers, on television screens during news reports. The world had become decidedly unsafe for him again. It did not help that Martha was unhappy about his move to Paraguay. Contact with his wife was difficult because she was almost assuredly being watched. The wheels of justice, however, moved slowly. It was not until 30 June 1960 that an Argentine judge—Jorge Luque—received the authority to rule on the West German extradition request, which he would do if Mengele was arrested. Things were getting hotter for Mengele.[46]

Mengele was once again a "man on the run"—both literally and figuratively. He was no longer safe. The capture of Eichmann threw Mengele into a panic, and he decided that Paraguay—the Krug farm—was no longer safe. Where could he go? How would he live? Who would help him? He was alone, without family. The only contact he had with family—with one exception—was in the form of letters. From the time he moved to Paraguay until his death in 1979, he was dependent on other people—friends and contacts to find him a safe place to live, family to supply him with funds—and the tension took a toll on him. His mood and behavior became more erratic over time. His supporters found it difficult to be around him, but they did not abandon him.

Once the international community officially put a target on Mengele's back, stories about Mengele sightings or interaction with him came out of the woodwork. There were multiple reports that Mengele had the protection of armed guards and of President Stroessner. Neither were true. The only protection that Stroessner afforded him was his reluctance to approve the deportation of a Paraguayan citizen. As the hunt for Mengele intensified, however, those who sought him still believed that he was in Argentina and, therefore, concentrated their search there, but some reports suggesting Paraguay as Mengele's place of residence began to emerge. Because he thought that the Argentines were moving too slowly on his country's extradition request, West German chargé d'affaires Peter Bensch began to investigate the Paraguayan end by questioning Alban Krug, who denied helping Mengele.[47]

Despite the apparent incompetence of the Argentines in locating him, the new inquiries in Paraguay were troubling. Occasionally, Martha and Karl Heinz visited Mengele at the Krug farm, but because they were being watched, their efforts to see Mengele were fraught with danger. Mengele became more determined to escape from Paraguay, but to where? By September 1960 he had decided on the location of his new residence—Brazil. It took time, however, to make the arrangements and for Mengele to safely—and secretly—make the journey. It was not until 24 October that his plans were finalized, and Mengele went on the run again.

Depending on a former Nazi—Wolfgang Gerhard—Mengele relocated to São Paulo, Brazil. Mengele made the move without Martha and Karl Heinz for two reasons. The pair were under surveillance by those who hoped they would lead them to Mengele. Furthermore, Martha Mengele decided that a life on the run was not for her or her sixteen-year-old son. Because, at that point, the couple decided to separate, Mengele was truly alone. He would have no more contact with his second wife. There was hope, however, that he would be able to reconnect with his real son—sixteen-year-old Rolf—who learned in 1960 that his Uncle Fritz was really his father—the wanted war criminal Josef Mengele.[48]

Gerhard arranged for Mengele to stay with Geza and Gitta Stammer, but he was not honest with the couple about who Mengele was. According to Gerhard, Mengele was Peter Hochbichler, a Swiss national and suitable manager for a thirty-seven-acre farm in which they were planning to invest. The site for the farm—where "coffee, rice, fruit and dairy cattle" were produced—was approximately two hundred miles from São Paulo in a remote area "near Nova Europa." Gerhard sweetened the pot, as he endeavored to convince the Stammers that they should take on Hochbichler. According to Gerhard, Hochbichler was an "experienced cattle breeder"—which was not close to accurate—and a potential investor in the farm venture. Sold! The Stammers welcomed Hochbichler. This would be the beginning of a long-term but rocky and contentious relationship. As manager, however, Mengele did not play well with others. His subordinates had nothing in common with the German, who "read philosophy and history and loved classical music." Furthermore, he frequently lost his temper when he could not make the workers understand his orders—a problem exacerbated by his inability to speak Portuguese. According to one of the workers, Francisco de Souza, "He loved giving orders and kept saying that we should work more and harder. The worst of it was that he didn't seem to understand much about farming or heavy work."[49]

Mengele's unease and impatience was directly related to the fact that he was forced into a situation—and work—that he did not like. He considered the work beneath him, which made it very difficult for him to adjust when he was first in Brazil. The situation was exacerbated by his fear of capture. Although he did not believe that he had done anything wrong at Auschwitz, Mengele understood that the world did not agree—that he would in all likelihood be executed if he was captured. The fact that the remote location of the Stammer farm provided excellent security did not seem to compute for Mengele.

While he did not necessarily have access to outside news on a regular basis, bits and pieces of the hunt for Mengele would gradually surface in his remote location. The Israelis geared up their apparatus and created a team under Zvi Aharoni, who had located Eichmann in Argentina. The initial Israeli investigation focused on Paraguay. The Israelis hoped to follow the same procedure that had worked in the Eichmann case—locate and extract. By 1965 the West Germans had expanded their search area to include Argentina, Paraguay, and Brazil. In February they sent a formal extradition request to the Brazilian government. In many respects the efforts of both the Israelis and the West Germans suggested that they were looking for a needle in a haystack. By 1970, however, other more pressing matters came to the fore in Israel. As a result, the intensity of their search for Mengele diminished.[50]

For a time, Mengele and the Stammers continued to reside near Nova Europa. Using money that he had made in various business ventures since he had first relocated to South America, Mengele went into partnership with his "landlords." At the end of the day, he owned half of the farm. By the end of a decade or so, the farm had become very prosperous. As a result, the Stammers decided to move. They purchased a house in the state of São Paulo. By this time Mengele's increasingly demanding behavior had caused a rift in his relationship with his partners. There is some suggestion that Mengele had carried on a physical relationship with Gitta Stammer, which—not surprisingly—did not please her husband, Geza. Although strained, the relationship was not completely broken, at least not yet. The three moved to the Stammer's new home in Caieiras—which was much closer to São Paulo than the remote farm.

In 1971 Mengele became emboldened because he had successfully acquired a "priceless Brazilian identity card"—that had belonged to Wolfgang Gerhard. While he was able to have his picture affixed to the card by his friend Wolfram Bossert, he was unable to update the personal information. Therefore, according to his identity card, he was Wolfgang Gerhard, age forty-seven—not sixty, his actual age. As a result, with his new identity card in hand, he bought "a $7,000 apartment in a high-rise building" in the center of São Paulo. He rented it out for the income that it would provide.[51] Life seemed good. Maybe it was time to relax and enjoy it. Unfortunately for Mengele, that was not going to be the case. In the summer of 1972 he became ill—the consequence of his "nervous habit of biting the end of his walrus mustache."[52] The hair that he had swallowed over the years resulted in an intestinal problem that required hospitalization and treatment.

Around the same time that Mengele began his new life in São Paulo, he established contact with his son, Rolf. The two began to exchange letters, in which Mengele frequently found fault with the son he did not really know. For example, his praise for his son's first marriage was accompanied by criticism. Mengele wrote, "I think that I have already shown too much fatherly pride in my newly acquired daughter. Unfortunately, I hardly know her, or rather I only know her as much as the few photographs reveal. But do I know the son better? . . . The description accompanying the photos—you really could have tried a little harder."[53] Over the years, Mengele pushed his son on multiple fronts—including his education and his future career.

Mengele's testiness, apparent in his letters to his son, was increasingly a problem in his relationship with the Stammers, who decided in 1974 that it was time to call it quits. For them, the best way to sever ties with Mengele was to sell the farm and make the move to São Paulo. By December the Stammers had made the move, but they allowed Mengele to remain in their old house until February 1975. The Stammers' decision forced Mengele to make a difficult choice. Knowing that he could not stay in the Caieiras home indefinitely, he explored his options. Because he needed the income from his apartment, he could not live there. While his friendship with Wolfram Bossert and his family had blossomed, they did not have room in their home for a boarder. What would he do? In late January a solution fell into his lap. Feeling sorry for their long-time boarder, the Stammers had agreed to help him. Taking part of their proceeds from the sale of the farm, they purchased a small bungalow—"one gloomy bedroom, an anti-quated bathroom and a tiny kitchen"—that they rented to Mengele. The bungalow, located "in one of the poorer parts of town . . . in the Eldorado suburb of Sao Paulo," allowed Mengele to live near his friends—the Bosserts. As the Stammers withdrew from their relationship with Mengele, the Bosserts stepped up and became his sole emotional support.[54]

In the 1970s things seemed to move quickly—but not necessarily satisfactorily—for Mengele. He lived in a constant state of depression and anxiety. He wrote about ending things in letters to friends and family. In 1977 his son, Rolf, visited him in Brazil. It was not a happy reunion. The unrepentant Mengele was hard on his son, who returned to West Germany ahead of schedule.[55]

The stress under which he lived took a toll on Mengele. In 1976, after an outing with the Stammers' son, Miki, and his friend, Mengele felt unwell. He was incapacitated by a sudden pain in his head. According to Mengele, "fluttering visions, vertigo, tingling sensations in the left half of my face and my left arm (like ants running), and difficulties with my speech and increasing pain in my head were the major symptoms." According to the doctor, he had suffered a stroke.[56]

In the wake of his stroke and the failed visit with his son in 1977, Mengele succumbed again to depression. He became distracted, and, when on rare occasions he left his bungalow, he walked around in a daze. At least once he was almost struck by a car and did not seem to realize that he had had a near miss. Thinking a change in scenery would do him good, the Bosserts invited Mengele to spend a few days with them in a beach house that they rented in Bertioga. On 5 February 1979 he took the bus to Bertioga and joined the Bosserts. At first he remained indoors. On the afternoon of the seventh, however, he took a walk on the beach with Wolfram Bossert. The two men then sat in the sun and talked. Mengele reminisced about Günzburg and talked about returning there to write a history of his hometown. When the burning sun got to be too much for him, Mengele decided to go for a swim. While in the water, he had a massive stroke and drowned before his friends could rescue him. He was quietly buried under a marker that identified him as Wolfgang Gerhard—the name on his Brazilian identity card.

It was over—Mengele was no more. But was it really over? No one outside of his family and a close-knit community of friends knew that he was dead. Mengele's name was still on "most wanted" lists. Investigations by the West German and Israeli governments were ongoing. Soon they would have another partner in the search for Mengele. Ironically, on 5 August 1979 the Paraguayan Supreme Court—citing his absence from Paraguay since 1960—revoked Mengele's citizenship. Extradition from Paraguay was now possible, but Mengele had to be found first. The problem was that no one knew where he was. Was he in Paraguay or had he moved on to another South American country? Brazil was a logical location. Was he there?[57]

osi Investigates

Because his death was kept a secret, the hunt for Mengele continued. Rumors ran rampant. By the early 1980s several Nazi hunters had thrown their hats in the ring as well; they joined the "Mengele-hunt bandwagon." Some of the newcomers were more reputable than others. The man who stirred the pot and pressured the U.S. government to become involved in the investigation was Simon Wiesenthal, the founder of the Jewish Documentation Center in Vienna. Wiesenthal was also a "freelance Nazi hunter." In honor of his efforts on behalf of Jews who suffered as a result of the Holocaust, Rabbi Marvin Hier established the Simon Wiesenthal Center (swc) in 1977. The swc's mission was to expose human rights offenses and to seek justice. Part and parcel of that was to focus the spotlight on the most egregious Nazi war criminals, such as Josef Mengele, who remained unpunished.[58]

Suspecting the U.S. Department of Defense knew more about Mengele than it was letting on, the swc filed a Freedom of Information Act request. After acquiring the requested documents, the SWC chose to release them to the public in January 1985. With the release of the Department of Defense files—particularly those indicating that Mengele had been released from American custody—the floodgates opened. Pressure, demanding government investigation and accountability, mounted from all sides, even from outside of the United States.

The U.S. attorney general tasked the Office of Special Investigations with the investigation. Unlike previous cases—such as the investigation into Klaus Barbie—there was an ongoing manhunt; therefore, the attorney general ordered the U.S. Marshals Service to coordinate with the OSI: "As originally conceived, OSI would focus on the historical issues: had Mengele ever been in the United States? had he worked with U.S. agents?"[59] While the OSI followed its mandate, the U.S. Marshals Service would try to find Mengele. The hunt took on a new life. The public was galvanized. Money, rumors, and offers of assistance poured in from unusual sources. Government agencies received reports of Mengele sightings across the United States and a proposal of help from a psychic.

As the OSI began its investigation, a U.S. Senate panel convened hearings. Under pressure from the Senate panel, the U.S. Army agreed to provide the task force with personnel to help comb records for information about Mengele. While all groups operated under the premise that the Angel of Death was still alive, all leads were old and stale. Suddenly a break came. When German police searched the home of a Frima Karl Mengele & Sohne employee, they hit the jackpot—letters Josef Mengele wrote to his family between 1972 and 1978, letters from the couple who had sheltered Mengele in Brazil, and a 1979 letter informing the family of Mengele's death. They now had a lead. Tipped off by the German police, São Paulo police conducted raids that netted them additional letters and diaries, as well as photographs reportedly of Mengele with his son, Rolf. Caught red-handed, the couple not only informed the police of Mengele's demise but also showed them where he was buried. With great fanfare and press coverage, Brazilian officials exhumed the body that was reportedly Mengele's.[60]

Now the fun could really begin. Was the body really Mengele's? What would the roll of the OSI be moving forward? The exhumation of the body "created two independent strands to the investigation—determining whether (1) the writings, photos and possessions found in Brazil belonged to Mengele; and (2) whether the exhumed body was his." While Brazilian officials agreed to consult foreign experts to help determine the latter issue, the OSI had the task of investigating the former. The OSI consulted experts to analyze the materials. A handwriting analyst received the task of comparing samples of Mengele's handwriting from his SS file with documents found in Brazil. He concluded definitively that documents from both sources were written by the same person. Another expert analyzed the paper and ink and determined that both "had been available in Brazil during the 1970s when the diaries were purportedly written."[61]

The documentary evidence pointed to the presence of Mengele in Brazil in the 1970s. The next step was to analyze the exhumed remains to determine identity. A team of American forensic experts was sent to São Paulo. The U.S. Marshals Service and the SWC each selected three experts for the team. Now the hard work would begin. Identification would prove more difficult than expected. The logical first step was to compare X-rays and fingerprints, which were reliable identifiers. In this case, however, that would not be possible. There were no X-rays—from Germany or Brazil—available. While Mengele's fingerprint records were obtained from his SS file, the decomposed state of the exhumed body rendered accurate fingerprints impossible. Despite these roadblocks, the forensic scientists rendered a judgment two weeks after their initial examination of the body. They concluded "within a reasonable scientific certainty" that the body was Mengele's.[62]

Without accurate fingerprint results or X-rays, how could the team reach this conclusion? Acknowledging that their conclusion would face intense scrutiny, the scientists claimed to have numerous reasons for their certainty. The most persuasive factor was a new technique out of West Germany—"photographic comparison in which pictures of the exhumed skull were matched on a video terminal to known photographs of Mengele in his SS file" and to "photographs found in Brazil." The "24 points of comparison" provided irrefutable proof of identification. Furthermore, there was an additional consistency. The "gender, height and age" of the corpse at the time of death matched Mengele at the time of his drowning. Finally, there were dental consistencies as well. A comparison of Mengele's dental records with the dental work of the corpse demonstrated a match in all areas—filling that were European, not Brazilian; "a gap between the front teeth which matched a known gap in Mengele's jaw"; and "a denture found with the Brazilian belongings."[63]

Numerous groups—including the governments of Brazil and Germany, the SWC, the U.S. Attorney General's Office, and the U.S. Marshals Service—quickly accepted the conclusion of the forensic team. The U.S. attorney general went so far as to announce "that OSI would now focus on the historical portion of the case, determining whether Mengele had ever been in U.S. custody or had any relationships with U.S. officials." A number of loose ends, however, convinced others— the Israelis and some members of the U.S. Army, OSI, and Department of Justice—not to jump immediately on the bandwagon. For example, while Mengele's SS records indicated that he suffered from osteomyelitis, the exhumed skeleton did not display evidence of the disease. There was some concern that the skeletal remains had been somehow compromised during the exhumation. Furthermore, although there was reference in the diaries to dental work performed in Brazil, officials could not locate the records.[64]

According to an OSI report written in 2006, "These unresolved issues raised two disturbing possibilities: (1) assuming Mengele had been living in Brazil, this was an elaborate hoax to connect him to an unrelated dead body in order to end the worldwide manhunt; or (2) the scientists were right, but for insufficient reasons, and the case 'would plague everyone forever.'" Consequently, although officially ended, the OSI investigation continued. Several months after the attorney general's pronouncement, Deputy Assistant Attorney General Mark Richard and OSI director Neal Sher traveled to Jerusalem to meet with officials from Israel and Germany. The main topic of conversation was "the need for more medical evidence" to prove conclusively that the exhumed body was that of Mengele.[65]

The next breakthrough, however, came from an unexpected, non-medical source—"an autobiographical novel" that Mengele had sent to his son, Rolf. OSI historian David Marwell, who read the manuscript, made a startling discovery. The manuscript described events in Mengele's life, beginning with his brief detention by Americans at the end of the war. Following leads provided in the novel, Marwell, with help from the German consulate, located the Nazi doctor who had been in the American prisoner of war camp with Mengele. Although a reluctant witness, the doctor "provided a plethora of previously unknown information about Mengele's post-war aliases and travels."[66]

The OSI then identified and interviewed those whose paths had crossed with Mengele's during this period. Based on this evidence, the OSI was able to complete some of its mandate with regard to Mengele by answering the questions that they had been tasked to investigate. While he had been in U.S. Army custody, no one knew that Mengele was wanted for war crimes, and therefore the army released him. In addition, he had not worked for the CIA or any other U.S. governmental office, nor had he traveled to the United States or neighboring Canada. Consequently, the OSI was able to put some of the rumors to rest.[67]

As the OSI completed the historical investigation, another piece of the puzzle fell into place on the medical side of the identification. The U.S. consul general in São Paulo located the dentist who had done work on Mengele's teeth. The doctor's records of visits and payments matched Mengele's diary exactly. As the result of his interview with the Brazilian dentist, the consul general also located the Japanese dentist who had taken X-rays of Mengele's teeth. The X-rays provided a key piece of evidence. Another came from the dentist's confirmation "that the bridges and crowns in the skull were his own work." Eureka! The OSI only had to locate a few more pieces of the puzzle. They needed medical records from the doctors mentioned in Mengele's diary. When the Brazilian government stonewalled, Marwell, accompanied by a team of German, Israeli, and Brazilian investigators, went to Brazil, located the doctors who treated Mengele, and interviewed them. Marwell also received access to the medical records that confirmed—in his mind—that the exhumed corpse was in fact

Josef Mengele. According to Marwell, "we have removed the basis for any reasonable doubt that Josef Mengele died in Brazil in 1979."[68]

It was over—or was it? The Israelis wanted one more inconsistency resolved—that of the osteomyelitis. Marwell was up to the task. When he researched German records, he learned that not all the conditions were "detectable on X-rays"; therefore, the failure of X-rays of the corpse to display evidence of osteomyelitis did not necessarily mean that the body was not Mengele's. Although a paleopathologist identified markings that could indicate the evidence needed, the Israelis were not satisfied. They wanted to run one more test—a DNA analysis. A judge issued an order releasing part of the skeletal remains. The OSI acquired a piece of the skull that was transported to the United States for DNA analysis. Because there was no DNA sample from Mengele, however, authorities believed that analysis of samples from Mengele's first wife, Irene, and their son, Rolf, would be sufficient for the determination. Unfortunately, both refused to cooperate by providing blood samples.

A German prosecutor involved in the case proposed a clever ruse, which, when implemented, worked. Steps were taken to convince the Mengele family that German officials intended to exhume the body of Karl Mengele Sr. As a result, Rolf Mengele and his mother provided the samples needed for the DNA analysis, which conclusively proved that the exhumed body indeed belonged to Josef Mengele.[69] The Angel of Death was dead, but was that the end of it?

Questions Answered?

Even with the OSI resolution of the Mengele case, questions—fueled by pop culture and rumor—remained. The 1978 movie *Boys from Brazil*—released in 1978, several years prior to the OSI investigation—added to the uncertainty. Although a fiction, the movie suggested a somewhat realistic scenario. In the film Dr. Josef Mengele—portrayed fantastically by Gregory Peck—cloned ninety-five Adolf Hitlers, whom he intended to raise in Brazil. His ultimate goal was the creation of a band of Nazi leaders who would form the Fourth Reich and pick up the pieces that resulted from the real Hitler's demise. It could happen, couldn't it? Surely, there was a grain of truth in the film.

The rumors of Mengele's influence did not end when the remains buried in Brazil were definitively identified as those of the Angel of Death. According to a *Telegraph* article written by Nick Evans and published in 2009, Mengele had continued his experiments with twins in Brazil. Evans based his article on an interview with Argentine historian, Jorge Camarasa, author of *Mengele: The Angel of Death in South America*. Although "for years scientists have failed to discover why as many as one in five pregnancies in a small Brazilian town have resulted in twins—most of them blond haired and blue eyed"—Camarasa claimed to have the answer: Mengele and his "notorious experiments." While the historian admitted that no one knows when Mengele first began visiting the Brazilian town of Cândido Godói, twins births commenced there in 1963. According to Evans, Camarasa was confident "in his claim that Mengele was successfully pursuing his dreams of creating a master race, a real-life *Boys from Brazil*"—in Cândido Godói.[70] Camarasa's bizarre contentions, as reported by Evans, add to the fog that still exists around Mengele and his legacy.

Legacy?

Mengele's tenure at Auschwitz had a lasting impact on the inmates who suffered at his hands and survived and those who lost family there. For these survivors, although one nightmare ended with liberation from the concentration camp, another has remained with them ever since. The horrible memories—from arrival at the camp, to the lack of food, to the torture or labor, to all that they experienced or witnessed—have not diminished over time. Decades after the war Alice Lok Cahana described her bipolar life at Auschwitz: "The train station always had a wonderful memory for me, because Father had a business office in Budapest and we would always accompany him to the station on Monday and then wait for him to come back on Thursday, and he would always bring us something. . . . We saw cattle trains! I told my sister, 'It's a mistake! They have cattle trains here—they can't mean we should go in cattle trains. Grandfather cannot sit on the floor in a cattle train!'" Unfortunately, the cattle train was there for Alice Lok Cahana, her family, and the others who had been rounded up by the Germans. For four days they endured the indignity of traveling to Auschwitz in a cattle car. The cramped conditions, the lack of food and water, and the stench from "sweat and excrement" only partially prepared them for what they would experience at Auschwitz.

Children, like Lok Cahana, could not begin to imagine what they faced.

> "When we arrived," says Alice, "I told Edith that nothing can be so bad as this cattle train—I'm sure that they will want us to work, and for the children there will be better food." Once out of the train and milling around on the ramp inside Birkenau, Alice was told by her sister to go and stand with the children, because they were both convinced that children would be better treated than adults. After all, they reasoned, the Germans came from a civilized country. So Alice, who was tall for her age, stood with the children and their mothers—the very group, of course, that in the warped logic of the camp the Nazis wished to murder most quickly.

Mengele happened to be on duty on the ramp that day. When he noticed Alice Lok Cahana, he asked if she was a young mother. Learning that she was only fifteen, Mengele redirected her to a different line—one containing adolescents and adults who were deemed useful for labor. Lok Cahana soon had the appearance of an inmate—shaven head and "ragged clothes three times too big for her."[71]

Alice Lok Cahana was not the only Holocaust survivor to be plagued by memories of Auschwitz. She, like the Ovitz family, the Slotkin and Kriegel twins, and others, were personally saved from the gas chambers by Mengele, but, unlike them, she was not the subject of his laboratory experiments. None of them, however, ever forgot their benefactor—"Uncle Mengele." The survivors are haunted by their nightmares, but not all the children survived. Approximately 1,500 sets of twins arrived at Auschwitz and participated in Mengele's experiments. When the Soviets arrived at Auschwitz, only 200 of the 3,000 children were still alive.[72] While Mengele never achieved the academic acclaim that he coveted, he did achieve notoriety of a different sort—a legacy. Encounters with the Angel of Death are forever etched in the memories of those who survived their encounter with Dr. Josef Mengele.

4

Otto von Bolschwing and the
Central Intelligence Agency

Otto von Bolschwing and Adolf Eichmann worked together to create programs designed to both persecute and terrorize the Jewish population in Germany. As a chief SS officer, von Bolschwing received postings to Romania and Greece. He had the distinction of being the highest-ranking German prosecuted by the Office of Special Investigations. A member of the Allgemeine SS, "the racial elite of the National Socialist Movement," von Bolschwing established a career with the SD, the intelligence-gathering arm of the Nazi Party. While working for the Jewish Affairs Office from 1937 to 1939, he presented a report titled "The Jewish Problem." In it, von Bolschwing advocated eliminating Jews from Germany "by forcing them to emigrate" and, on more than one occasion, offered suggestions for accomplishing his proposed plan.

In 1940 von Bolschwing received a posting to Romania, where he was instrumental in facilitating the escape of Romanian Iron Guard leaders to Germany. Before the war ended, however, he transferred to Austria and, in an effort to protect himself, actually cooperated with the Allies by helping them capture a number of high-ranking Nazi officials and SS officers. By 1949 he found employment with the CIA, which turned a blind eye to his past, his SS membership, and his work for the SD. In 1954 the CIA helped von Bolschwing move to the United States. In 1979, however, the newly created OSI began an investigation of the German. How did the CIA help this von Bolschwing? More important, how could the CIA help this Nazi? What did he bring to the table? Did he provide crucial information for the Cold War battlefront after World War II? Was his work for the CIA more important than holding him accountable for his past actions? Who was Otto von Bolschwing?

Early Years

Born on 15 October 1909 in the small village of Schönbruch, Prussia, Otto Albrecht Alfred von Bolschwing was the son of a Junker, a member of the aristocracy, and a possible descendant of the prestigious Bodelschwingh family. His parents were Richard Otto Wilhelm Ferdinand von Bolschwing and Ella Mathilde Karoline Julie von Bolschwing. Otto Albrecht Alfred was the youngest of five children and ten years younger than his next oldest sibling. His siblings were Ruth Ella Marie Gertrud Mathilde (born 3 July 1893), Gerda Marie Sophie Henrietta (born 4 June 1894), Elisabeth Paula Sophie (born 17 November 1895), and Karl Ludwig Richard (born 27 February 1899). Little is really known about his life between 1909 and 1919. One can imagine, however, his life of privilege. His family's place in society brought with it certain benefits, which young Otto would have enjoyed. The von Bolschwing's idyllic life was disrupted by the outbreak of World War I. Although fifty-one years old, Papa von Bolschwing did what was expected of him. He went off to war and died on the Eastern Front on 30 October 1914—when his youngest was only five years old.

Although he was no longer directly influenced by his father, that did not stop Otto von Bolschwing from being molded by, or embracing, the characteristics and mindset of his class. Educated at the public school Koenignsberg, he passed his exams in 1926. By the time he entered the University of Breslau, the young German had already displayed a gift for languages—and an aristocratic bearing that occasionally rubbed his peers the wrong way. Following his tenure at the University of Breslau, he pursued additional studies at the London School of Economics.[1] Once he graduated, von Bolschwing had to face reality. As the younger son, he probably did not stand to inherit much—if any—of the family assets. Although he was one of the elite, he did not necessarily have the financial resources that would permit him to live a life of leisure. It was time to get a job. The question was what that job would be. Even though it took him a while to settle on a career, events would propel him down a path to an unexpected profession. Initially, however, von Bolschwing tried his hand with "trading companies and other businesses in Germany, Great Britain, and elsewhere in Europe."[2] From 1928 to 1930 he worked for the East Asia Trading House, C. Illies Company, in Hamburg. For the next year or so he managed the Oberon Investment and Development Company in Berlin and Vienna. Beginning in 1931 he was a continental representative for several London investment houses. In 1932, however, he began an association with the German Foreign Office, for whom he traveled to Palestine. While in Palestine, he hoped to increase his future employment possibilities in addition to conducting services for the Foreign Office. Little did he know what the move to Palestine would ultimately mean for his future—both in the short and in the long term.

Although being a member of the Junker class did not automatically mean that he was antisemitic and although he had not demonstrated prejudice against, or hatred for, Jews in his early years, von Bolschwing would join a group that expected its members to embrace antisemitism, and he did—and then some. In 1929 von Bolschwing became a member of the Nazi Party.[3] By the early 1930s he was a member of the Nazis' intelligence-gathering branch, the Allgemeine SS, which recruited for the Gestapo and the SD. In addition, he became a liaison for the SD in Palestine.

Initially, however, it is possible that his antisemitic stance was one of "cynical opportunism," which his time in Palestine would demonstrate, but that would change within a relatively short period. Living and working in Palestine had another effect on von Bolschwing. He became more interested and engaged in politics and "political operations," particularly with regard to the British presence in Palestine.[4] He tried to work both sides of the aisle. At the same time that he was encouraging the Jews to rebel against British authority, he made efforts to meet with Arab leaders. He wanted to persuade them to support Jewish attempts to remove the British presence in the region. What better way to gain useful Middle Eastern allies for Germany?

Although his activities, particularly with Arab tribal leaders, were covert, von Bolschwing's meddling did not go unnoticed by the British, who booted him from Palestine in 1936. He returned to Berlin, where he reestablished a connection with Leopold von Mildenstein, the director and founder of the Jewish Affairs Department. They eventually had the responsibility of crafting "policies for the elimination of Jewish influence from German life." Wanting to take advantage of his expertise on Palestine and other matters, von Mildenstein offered von Bolschwing a job with the Jewish Affairs Department. In a move that would later prove to be a fortuitous one, von Bolschwing declined a regular position in Mildenstein's office. For him an official job brought with it two downsides: an entry-level ss rank and a "formal chain-of-command" that had to be respected.[5] His visions of his proper place made an entry-level rank unacceptable. Furthermore, because he wanted a certain amount of freedom in his job and because he did not want to be bound by the rules, he did not want his connection with Mildenstein's department to be an official one. Instead, he countered with an alternative suggestion. Von Bolschwing would come on board in the Jewish Affairs Office—but only as a consultant. Because this was a win-win solution for both men, Mildenstein acquiesced, and von Bolschwing consulted with him from 1937 until 1939. It was also during this period that von Bolschwing married for the first time—to Brigitte Klenzendorff. Seventeen months later the couple had a son, Gisbert Otto Richard Ernst.

Although classified as a consultant, von Bolschwing demonstrated a willingness to work hard for the Jewish Affairs Office and very quickly justified Mildenstein's faith in him. The stated purpose of the Jewish Affairs Office from the beginning was to gather information about the Jewish population—"statistical, economic, and cultural information"—containing any and all data that would be useful for the Nazi government when it developed an official Jewish policy.[6] In his new position von Bolschwing hit the ground running. Within a few weeks he had crafted a report about Palestine, based to some extent on his personal observations and activities. This report was passed up the chain of command and was read by some influential government officials. For example, after reading his report, ss chief Heinrich Himmler, who was impressed by what he read, decided to keep his eye on von Bolschwing. Himmler realized that von Bolschwing might be useful to the Reich in the future. It did not take von Bolschwing long to figure out, however, that although his report was interesting and informative, it did not marry up completely with the stated mission of the Jewish Affairs Department. If he really wanted to be noticed and to gain the career advancements that he deserved, he would have to keep that mission in mind in his subsequent analyses.

Quickly shifting his focus, von Bolschwing addressed the "Jewish problem" in his next report, which he submitted in January 1937. Through this report he attempted to shape policy by suggesting ways in which to eliminate the Jewish presence in Germany—primarily by forced emigration and the limitation of Jews' economic power. At the time he completed his Jewish Problem report, German policy, which was dedicated to the elimination of the Jewish presence in Germany, advocated exodus, not extermination. Although the Nazis were not yet ready to talk Final Solution, Von Bolschwing, who advocated extreme methods if necessary, recommended terror as a way to convince Jews to participate in a mass exodus.[7] He argued,

> A largely anti-Jewish atmosphere must be created among the people in order to form the basis for the continued attack and the effective exclusion of them. . . . The most effective means is the anger of the people leading to excesses in order to take away the sense of security from the Jews. Even though this is an illegal method, it has had a long-standing effect as was shown by the "Kurfurstendamm riot." . . . Psychologically, this is even the more comprehensible since the Jew has learned a lot through the pogroms of the past centuries and fears nothing as much as a hostile atmosphere which can go spontaneously against him at any time.[8]

Recognizing that using targeted terror against the Jews might not accomplish the ultimate goal of the mass exodus of Jews from Germany, von Bolschwing recommended steps—that is, requiring that Jewish businesses apply for a license to operate—that would be the precursor to the Nazi government appropriating Jewish-owned businesses. This suggestion tied in with von Bolschwing's second recommended approach to solving the Jewish Problem.[9] Taking on the Jewish Problem in Germany and placing it into a broader context, von Bolschwing focused on the economic parameters. He argued, "The Jews in the entire world represent a nation which is not bound by a country or by a people but by money. . . . The leading thought . . . is to purge Germany of the Jews. This can only be carried out when the basis of livelihood, i.e., the possibility of economic activity, is taken away from the Jews in Germany."[10]

Von Bolschwing recommended additional steps to encourage Jews to vacate Germany that would limit their travel. He suggested that Jewish passports in particular have immediate identifiers on them. That way officials reviewing a person's passport would instantly know whether or not the passport holder was a Jew. Admitting, however, that there was some risk involved in adopting this practice, particularly since the goal was to convince Jews to relocate, von Bolschwing wrote, "It is expressly emphasized that such an identification can only be effected [sic] internally in order to avoid that foreign consulates refuse the issuance of a visa to the holder of such a passport."[11] To prevent that from happening, he suggested that passport applications be approved only for Jews who were emigrating and that limitations be placed on the amount of assets that emigrating Jews could remove from the country.

As far as von Bolschwing was concerned, this was a perfect solution. Jews would no longer reside in Germany, *and* the Nazi government would confiscate the bulk of their financial resources at the time of their departure. Subsequent documents and memoranda created by von Bolschwing suggested ways in which to facilitate and control this policy, if adopted. Acknowledging that Jewish organizations would, in all likelihood, endeavor to expedite Jewish emigration, he proposed that these organizations be required to work directly with the SD. Furthermore, if the money to fund Jewish émigrés came from other countries, then the proposed protocol would stipulate that the foreign currency be transmitted directly to the SD rather than to the Jewish organization arranging the evacuation.[12] Allowing the SD unofficially to exact a fee for approving the departure of the applicant or applicants would be another financial benefit for the SD—and by extension for the Reich.

Von Bolschwing's work did not go unnoticed by his superiors, and soon he had added responsibilities. In 1938, following the Anschluss, or German annexation of Austria, the Nazis almost immediately put in place a plan to address the Jewish Problem there. Although

Adolf Eichmann was placed in charge of implementing a solution, von Bolschwing received orders to assist him. The two were tasked with constructing a program whose proposed outcomes mirrored the goals of the policies being implemented by the Jewish Affairs Office in Germany. More specifically, the Austrian program needed to accomplish two things: confiscation of Jewish property and forced expulsion of the Jewish population. The two men knew each other. Von Bolschwing had previously briefed Eichmann on both Zionism and Palestine. Of similar mindsets regarding the future of Jews in Austria, the two men worked well together on crafting the program to be implemented—one that would allow the achievement of their mission with regard to the presence of Jews in Austria.

But—times they were a changin'. Things really started to pick up steam in 1939—a year of important events, some of which had global consequences. First, Germany set its sights on Czechoslovakia. At the Munich Conference in September 1938, Neville Chamberlain of Britain and Édouard Daladier of France, in an effort to achieve a lasting peace for Europe and the world, accepted Adolf Hitler's promises and agreed to the German annexation of the Sudetenland, one of Czechoslovakia's key industrial regions. Six months later, in March 1939, Hitler demonstrated how good his word was when German troops crossed the border into Czechoslovakia and occupation began. In April the Spanish Civil War, which had been raging since the summer of 1936, ended. Despite the end of conflict in Spain, tensions in Europe, instead of decreasing, actually increased. All eyes were on Germany. What would Germany do next? Who was safe? Secret and not-so-secret negotiations occurred, as the world held its breath and hoped that war—again—could be avoided. Nations breathed an uneasy sigh of relief when they learned that on 23 August Joachim von Ribbentrop and Vyacheslav Molotov, representing their respective governments, signed the Treaty of Nonaggression between Germany and the Union of Soviet Socialist Republics. War had been avoided—or had it? The world quickly learned that peace in Europe would not last very long. On 1 September German forces invaded Poland. Recognizing that they could no longer delay action, Britain and France declared war on Germany. With the commencement of the conflict in Europe and with battles ongoing in the Pacific, World War II was on.

There was another event that occurred in 1939 that—at the time— did not seem to have global consequences. The RSHA (Reichssicher- heitshauptamt), or Reich Headquarters of the Security Service and Security Police, received control of the Jewish Affairs Office. The cre- ation of the RSHA resulted in the streamlining of government ser- vices when the SD, the Gestapo, and the Criminal Police became united under its jurisdiction. This also meant that Adolf Eichmann returned from Austria with orders to assume control of the Jewish Affairs Office. This change meant that von Bolschwing had a new boss—the RSHA. For his part, Otto Albrecht Alfred von Bolschwing was ready for bigger and better things, for more responsibility, for a chance to demonstrate the ways in which he could contribute to Hitler's plan for Germany's greatness in a world that did not include "undesirable" races.[13] It would not be long before he would be called on to do his part.

Wartime Activities

In early 1940 von Bolschwing received a new position—"a plum for- eign posting."[14] Heinrich Himmler sent him to Romania, where he was tasked with overseeing all SD activity, including the supervi- sion of SD agents. What exactly "overseeing all SD activity" actu- ally meant is not known. It is clear, however, that whether or not he received specific instructions to do so, von Bolschwing took steps to get close to the Romanian Iron Guard. The Iron Guard was an "ultra- Fascist" movement in Romania.[15]

Also known as the Legion of the Archangel Michael, the Iron Guard had the distinction of being "one of the largest and most enduring fas- cist movements in interwar Europe."[16] One of the top leaders in the Iron Guard was Valerian Trifa. A complex, educated man, Trifa was a theologian and a historian. He was also a graduate of the Gestapo school and editor of *Libertatea*, the Iron Guard's antisemitic newspa- per. A loyal Iron Guard commander, Trifa also led the National Union of Romanian Christian Students, a university fraternity known for its anticommunism and antisemitism. Like Adolf Hitler, Trifa was a charismatic speaker who could move a crowd, particularly by equating communism to a "worldwide Jewish conspiracy."[17] The Iron Guard's activities, particularly political ones, created potential problems for Hitler. Although antisemitic, which was a good thing as far as the Nazis were concerned, the Iron Guard did not acquiesce to Hitler's control. The Iron Guard's volatility jeopardized the one resource that the Nazis needed from Romania—its oil. Consequently, part of von Bolschwing's assignment was possibly to get close to the Iron Guard, especially its leadership, and to keep Germany informed about its political activities. By getting close to Trifa, he certainly acted as if it was. Furthermore, von Bolschwing seemed to buy into Trifa's message—as events would soon demonstrate.

If that was in fact part of his mission, then von Bolschwing's assignment was somewhat counterproductive, because the Iron Guard ultimately came into conflict with the influential, pro-German, Romanian marshal Ion Antonescu. Despite its efforts, Iron Guard leadership was unsuccessful in acquiring government positions. There was, however, a chance that situation could change. In October 1940, however, with Iron Guard support, Antonescu forced the Romanian ruler, King Carol II, to relinquish his crown. This paved the way for some Iron Guard members to gain positions in the new government. Almost immediately, possibly due to von Bolschwing's influence, the new administration adopted a series of anti-Jewish measures that mirrored those implemented in Germany and Austria. One of the new policies was the requirement that Jewish property be registered. Von Bolschwing was in a prime position to advise the Romanian government on a program to solve the country's Jewish Problem.

It did not take long, however, for the honeymoon between Antonescu and the Iron Guard to end. Early in 1941 the Iron Guard made the first move to sever ties with Antonescu and to pursue their agenda. While von Bolschwing's role in these events as they unfolded is unclear, Hitler and the Nazi Party would perceive the Iron Guard's actions as problematic. On 20 January, following the murder of a German officer in Bucharest, Valerian Trifa publicly issued his—and by extension the Iron Guard's—manifesto by reading it over the radio.[18] The manifesto reflected the Iron Guard's position, which was both antisemitic and antigovernment. Trifa used the manifesto as an opportunity to attack Antonescu. He criticized the Romanian leader on two counts. Trifa accused Antonescu of protecting the men who had assassinated the high-ranking German officer. He called the assassins "Satanic." Furthermore, he reproached Antonescu for continuing to allow Jews to hold government jobs, which was definitely contrary to the Nazi Party's position.[19]

Not one to let an opportunity for demagoguery to pass, Trifa concluding his manifesto by issuing a plea: "We beseech General Antonescu to do justice by [the] Romanians. We demand the replacement of all Masonic and Judized persons in the government. We demand a Legionnaire government."[20] With this manifesto Trifa and the Iron Guard directly challenged Antonescu. This was only the beginning. Momentum was building.

Trifa did not plan to let the grass grow under his feet. He was slated to give a speech the next night, 21 January, near the state university. A large group of Iron Guard students—between three thousand and ten thousand—gathered in the square where Trifa would speak. In Hitleresque fashion, Trifa, using a loudspeaker, delivered a rousing, thirty-minute-long emotional speech that struck a chord with his audience. Emotions raged as he expanded on the themes of his manifesto—and then some. Trifa advocated a regime change: the establishment of a new government, an Iron Guard government, a Legionnaire government in place of Antonescu's. In other words, he was suggesting a coup d'état—the overthrow of Antonescu. Trifa also praised the world's savior—Adolf Hitler. But that was not all. After highlighting Savior Hitler, Trifa hit his stride and identified the groups that should have targets on their backs—all Jews and Freemasons—and should be executed. According to Trifa, Freemasons were just as bad as Jews. Not only were they pro-Jewish, but they were also antifascist.

When the crowd was sufficiently riled, Trifa led them through the streets of Bucharest. They sang Legionnaire songs and shouted "Death to Freemasons and Kikes" as they marched through the streets. Although their route seemed random, there was a plan. Trifa led the crowd passed the German legation, where their chanting briefly changed. A resident at the German legation, von Bolschwing, undoubtedly heard the Iron Guard students yelling, "Sieg Heil!" and "Long Live Germany!" The crowd, which had doubled in size, surged toward its final destination—the headquarters of Ion Antonescu. Once there the students continued their angry shouting and chanting.[21]

Trifa's "call to action" achieved immediate results and, to some extent, spiraled out of control. It inspired a "military coup and a three-day, anti-Semitic pogrom in Bucharest that quickly spread to eleven other Romanian cities." Although he did not seek approval from his superiors in Berlin and probably would not have received it had he asked, von Bolschwing threw his support behind Trifa and the Iron Guard. His real usefulness would come later with the conclusion of the coup.[22]

Not content to attack the regular army, the Iron Guard "Green Shirts," whose name reflected the color of the shirts they wore, unleashed unspeakable violence against the groups that Trifa targeted, particularly those in the Jewish quarters. The Green Shirts burned synagogues. They destroyed sacred Torah scrolls. Bringing some of their captives to a meatpacking plant, the Green Shirts used hooks to hang Jews, whom they subsequently skinned alive. These skins later showed up as "trophy lampshades and shoes." In other instances, they mimicked kosher rituals by cutting the throats of Jewish captives and hanging "Kosher Meat signs" around their necks. They raped some Jews and stoned or decapitated others. Once unleashed, the violence spun out of control. Evidence indicates that three naked Jewish women were forced into a temple that a group of Green Shirts then set on fire. By the time the carnage ended, a river of tortured, dead Jews—numbering between five hundred and one thousand—flowed through the streets of Bucharest.[23]

Trifa and the Iron Guard's coup did not go unanswered. Antonescu authorized military force to extinguish the rebellion. The regular army easily quashed the coup d'état. Where the army failed was in rounding up Iron Guard leadership and the rank-and-file membership. Many of them fled Romania for other European cities. Once there they established intelligence networks and instituted plans for the eventual liberation of Romania from Antonescu. Not inclined to be lenient, Antonescu issued orders for the execution of all captured members of the Iron Guard. Topping the list of Iron Guard "Most Wanted" was Trifa. Unbeknownst to Antonescu, Trifa had found sanctuary in the German legation, thanks to von Bolschwing. In fact, several Iron Guard leaders—a total of thirteen—also found safe haven at the German legation, in the SD residence.

Von Bolschwing saw it as his duty to help these men as much as he could. Although they had been unsuccessful in overthrowing Antonescu, the Iron Guard had instituted a pogrom in Bucharest, and von Bolschwing had, since 1937, been advocating the use of pogroms as a way to control Jews and mold their behavior. But he did more than provide a hiding place for these men. He organized their relocation—to Germany. Time was short to achieve their escape because von Bolschwing and other SD colleagues were no longer welcome in Romania. The government had officially requested that Himmler's men, particularly von Bolschwing, leave the country. Before his departure von Bolschwing had escape plans underway for the "Iron Guard Thirteen," who left Romania for Germany a few weeks after their "savior's" departure. Although their attempted coup was not condoned by the Reich, the Nazis welcomed their pro-Nazi brothers to Germany and placed them in "protective custody."[24]

Helping Iron Guard leadership escape retribution aside, von Bolschwing's superiors, with the exception of Himmler, were generally not pleased with his support for Trifa and the rebels. His actions sparked complaints from the German Foreign Ministry, which objected to the SD inserting itself into external affairs of the Reich. His critics accused him of interfering in the internal affairs of another country— Romania. The irony here is that Hitler and the Nazi Party had earned a reputation for interference in other countries, but they saw events in Romania as not furthering the Reich's plan for the future. Political upheaval could jeopardize the Reich's access to Romania's oil fields. Certainly, in January 1941 it was more advantageous for the Third Reich to support the Antonescu government rather than the Iron Guard coup, which at the time did not fall in line with Germany's foreign policy. Although the Nazis were committed to the elimination of the Jewish presence in Germany and other countries under their control, the Iron Guard's attack on the Jewish population provided the Romanian people with an idea of what could happen should the Nazis seize control of the country. Hitler's concern was that the Iron Guard's treatment of the Romanian Jews could spark general resistance to a Nazi presence and cause unrest that would make the upcoming invasion of the Soviet Union more difficult.[25]

The result of his support of Trifa and the Iron Guard was that von Bolschwing was—in his mind, harshly—reprimanded. Perhaps reprimanded is not the right word to describe his reception when von Boschwing returned to Berlin. At the very least, he had been insubordinate; had not followed protocol; and had, on his own initiative, interfered in the internal politics of Romania in way that was counterproductive in Hitler's view. Von Bolschwing received more than a poor assessment rating by his superiors. In 1942 he was dispatched to a Gestapo prison, where he cooled his heels for less than a year. Whether he learned his lesson or not while in prison, von Bolschwing, now somewhat of a persona non grata, would not receive another plum foreign assignment. Instead, he returned to work similar to what he organized when he worked as a consultant for the Jewish Affairs Office.

Back in the day von Bolschwing had recommended policies that would not only result in the expulsion of Jews from Germany but would also allow the SD—and by extension the Third Reich—to appropriate Jewish businesses and financial resources. He quickly became reengaged in the latter activities. In other words, he was in the "Jewish extortion business."[26] One of the targets of his new position was Pharmacia, which was a Jewish-owned medical-supply company in Hamburg. Von Bolschwing accomplished his task and then some. Ever the opportunist, he lined his own pockets by illegally acquiring 20 percent of the company and then facilitated the use of the Pharmacia's Vienna office as a cover by German military intelligence.

By 1944, however, von Bolschwing, recognizing that the war was not going swimmingly for Germany and facing the reality that a German victory was becoming increasingly unlikely, began to think about his life after the war. Survival was key. He had to have a plan to guarantee his survival—a plan that would prevent him from being a recipient of the retribution that the victors were sure to hand out. By 1944 he had married for the second time. His new wife was Austrian. In

October 1943, after having divorced his first wife, Brigitte, a year earlier, he had married Ruth von Pfaundler, whose brother was a member of a resistance movement, called O-5. In 1943 the Allies had indicated that after the war Austria would not be considered a part of Germany, but a separate nation. In response to that announcement, a resistance movement—O-5—emerged in Austria. Learning of his brother-in-law's affiliation with O-5 gave von Bolschwing the seed of an idea, one that grew and bore fruit.

By late 1944 von Bolschwing had moved his family to Salzburg, Austria. The German situation was looking worse, and he saw the handwriting on the wall. It was time to put his plan into motion. He joined O-5, and his work with a unit situated in the Tyrolian Alps began. He was in the process of recrafting himself. He could no longer be a Junker aristocrat. He had to become a "Tyrolian underground operative." Like a chameleon, von Bolschwing reinvented himself and was convincing in his new skin. In fact, the leader of his local resistance unit bought his act and after the war signed "an affidavit attesting to Bolschwing's career in the Austrian resistance." Von Bolschwing was positioning himself to be on the right side at war's end. If all went well, he would be ready to embark on the next phase of his plan—hiding certain aspects about his past and making himself useful to the victorious Allies.[27] Who knew? Perhaps a move to the United States with his family was in his future.

Postwar Work

Unbeknownst to von Bolschwing, he was actually on Allied intelligence's radar—or at the very least they had heard of him. British intelligence had amassed a list of "known German intelligence officers." Von Bolschwing's name was on the list. Included in the limited information about him was reference to von Bolschwing's 1934 trip to Palestine, where he apparently, according to British sources, planned to search for a "treasure chest" hidden by the German army at the end of World War I. British intelligence had given the list to two U.S. intelligence organizations—the Office of Strategic Services (OSS) and the army's Counter Intelligence Corps (CIC), which was the forerunner of the Central Intelligence Agency. Although they had information about his involvement with the Iron Guard and with helping the group's leaders flee from Romania to Germany, Allied counterintelligence groups considered von Bolschwing a "minor" player, not worth additional investigation or concerted effort to capture. It was probably fortuitous, therefore, that when von Bolschwing initially crossed paths with Americans, they were not members of the OSS or the CIC but rather a military government unit eventually tasked with occupation.[28]

As the end of the war neared, von Bolschwing established a connection with an American unit—the 410th Infantry—in general and, more specifically, with Lt. Col. Ray F. Goggin and offered his services. He successfully drew attention to his "resistance work" in Austria and helped the Americans against his former compatriots in the final days of the conflict. Goggin emphasized von Bolschwing's contributions when he gave him credit for "materially assist[ing] the armed forces of the United States during our advance through Fern Pass and Western Austria prior to the surrender of the German Army." Furthermore, the officer claimed, "during our occupation, he personally captured over twenty high ranking Nazi officials and SS officers and led patrols that resulted in the capture of many more."[29] There is also no suggestion that he was able to provide useful information about the German V-2 rocket, including its location. Von Bolschwing wanted to be on the winning side at the end and took steps to ensure that he was.

Von Bolschwing's plan was working. By making himself valuable to the Americans, they bought into his "resistance fighter" persona and did not carefully question his previous wartime work. In addition, he cultivated a relationship with the Americans for another reason. If the Americans considered him a valuable asset, they might help him avoid prosecution for his "role in the persecution of the Jews." He probably thought that he needed all the help he could get to avoid prosecution, trial, and punishment for his affiliation with the Jewish Affairs Office and SD in Romania. His work with the U.S. military personnel who occupied southern Germany continued into 1946, but there were signs that his position was not a permanent one. Believing that he could prolong his beneficial relationship by taking advantage of his experience in intelligence work, von Bolschwing took steps to "seal the deal." He reached out to the Gehlen Organization, which was receptive and hired him.[30]

Created by Reinhard Gehlen, "Hitler's senior most military intelligence officer on the eastern front," the Gehlen Organization consisted of a "group of former Nazi intelligence operatives" and was funded and supervised by the U.S. Army. How did this relationship occur? How could the U.S. Army get into bed with Nazi intelligence operatives? Following the end of World War II, the United States and its Western Allies soon found themselves at loggerheads with their Eastern Ally—the Soviet Union. The two sides had different visions of what postwar Europe should look like and where and how their spheres of influence would be clearly delineated. Security was the order of the day, but what security meant for the Soviets and what it meant for western Europeans was not necessarily the same. In fact, five months after V-J day (2 September 1945, when the Japanese formally surrendered), Winston Churchill made his now famous Iron Curtain speech at Westminster College in Fulton, Missouri. His speech publicly acknowledged the tension or, more accurately, the split between Britain, the United States, and the West on the one hand and the Soviet Union and its allies—willing and unwilling—on the other. Recognizing that the United States, among other Western nations, would want to gather as much intelligence about its former ally as possible, Reinhard Gehlen and the Gehlen Organization willingly offered to provide that information. After all, the Nazis had been compiling information about the Soviets for years, and, with financial support from U.S. officials as well as protection from prosecution, the Gehlen Organization would not only turn over intelligence already acquired but also continue to accumulate information—not for the Third Reich this time, but for its new bosses, the Americans. As a new member of the organization, von Bolschwing received a relatively easy, but important, assignment. Gehlen tasked him with identifying ethnic German and former Romanian Iron Guard contacts who would be potentially useful sources of information.[31] Although the backgrounds of von Bolschwing, Gehlen, and other members of the Gehlen Organization were dubious, their American bosses were willing to look the other way because the possibility of acquiring information useful in the Cold War battle against the Soviets was more important than turning any of these men over for war crimes prosecution. The members of the Gehlen Organization got something from the deal with the Americans—legitimacy and a certain amount of protection from war crimes prosecution—at least for a time.

Always the opportunist, von Bolschwing was not satisfied working for the Americans through the Gehlen Organization. He wanted a position directly with the Americans—preferably with their Central Intelligence Group (CIG), "the immediate predecessor of the CIA," and sought employment with the organization. Von Bolschwing had another incentive. Rumor had it that, because he had not provided the quality contacts desired by Gehlen, his future with the organization was an uncertain one, although the security agency was not ready to sever ties yet. A position working directly for the Americans was not, however, a sure thing. The CIG's initial assessment of von Bolschwing was not a favorable one. For one thing the CIG was not sure that he could be trusted. Used to making good first impressions and to being considered "exceedingly bright," von Bolschwing would not give up. Although his role in the Gehlen Organization had not ended, he continued his efforts at recruitment by the CIG and then by the CIA, which was established when President Harry S. Truman signed the National Security Act of 1947 into law. Over the next couple of years, the CIA assessments of von Bolschwing remained consistent with the CIG's initial evaluation. According to the CIA, "Most evaluations of B (based almost without exception on study of biography rather than personal association) run as follows: self-seeking, egotistical, and a man of shifting loyalties. His protests of democracy and, more particularly, feelings of Austrian nationalism seem to contradict his history."[32]

While the CIA was aware of some of his wartime story, the agency had not yet learned of his association with the Jewish Affairs Office or with Adolf Eichmann—factors that could potentially turn the tide against him. Although von Bolschwing referred to himself as a "Nazi gadfly," the CIA was not fooled. According to another CIA assessment, "He is an adventurer, a lover of intrigue, and a wire-puller who is fond of power. Bolschwing states that in his position in Rumania he was able to frustrate many of the evil designs of the Nazi regime, but it should be remembered as a black mark against him rather than a point in his favor that he arranged the escape of [Horia] Sima and others at a time when these men were at the height of their crimes." The author of the report suggested that there were other problems with von Bolschwing: "If one adds to these objections the difficulties inherent in Bolschwing's involvement with political reporting in Austria, it is hard to see how, among all our other commitments, much could be gained by having MOB [Munich operations base] take him over as the principal agent for three Rumanian projects."[33]

While first the CIG and then the CIA pondered whether or not to recruit him, von Bolschwing demonstrated his usefulness to the Gehlen Organization, which by 1947 was enlarging its operations. Of particular note for the spy organization was the Balkan region. Gehlen turned to von Bolschwing for his assistance. Surely, von Bolschwing could turn to his former SS colleagues to create a network consisting of ethnic Germans and former Iron Guardsmen in Romania. Although he was confident of his capabilities, von Bolschwing did not live up to Gehlen's expectations. His recruitment record was not what Gehlen had hoped it would be. When he contacted the Iron Guardsmen he had helped, they—although grateful to von Bolschwing—did not want to join the intelligence ranks. He talked a good game, but "the proof was in the pudding." After working with him for over a year, the Gehlen Organization decided "that the smooth-talking Bolschwing was an operational blowhard, not worth the black market gas, cigarettes, and U.S. dollars required to pay him." Gehlen seriously considered cutting ties with von Bolschwing.[34]

Oddly enough, despite his poor track record, the CIA had second thoughts about rejecting von Bolschwing's overtures. The German gained an unexpected CIA advocate: James Critchfield, CIA station chief in Bavaria. It was well known that von Bolschwing had been angling for a transfer from the Gehlen Organization to the CIA. In late 1949 to early 1950, the CIA decided to hire several members of the Gehlen Organization, including von Bolschwing. The CIA bought into von Bolschwing's assessment of his intelligence career that had spanned from 1934 until 1949, even though it was a less than stellar one. After all, he had been booted out of both Palestine and Romania and had been rewarded for his activities in Romania with jail time. In addition, the CIA was also aware that he had given sanctuary to Iron Guardsmen who had perpetrated the nights of terror in Bucharest. Although recognizing that he was not a skilled agent, the CIA— particularly James Critchfield—viewed him as a controllable, valuable asset who had connections in Austria and with the Iron Guardsmen who could possibly be useful.[35]

The problem was—or rather had the potential to be—the fact that von Bolschwing had not disclosed everything about his career. For instance, he did not volunteer information about his association with the Jewish Affairs Office or with Adolf Eichmann. Critchfield did, however, know that von Bolschwing had helped the Iron Guard leaders, who were responsible for the Bucharest pogrom, but beyond that CIA field representatives did not seem inclined to investigate the veracity of von Bolschwing's version of his past. Overworked and short-staffed, they were more focused on what they needed from the German in Austria than anything else, including his past record. Unfortunately for the CIA, things were about to get more complicated.

It had become apparent that von Bolschwing had been padding his résumé, which would eventually cause some problems. His claim to an expertise in Austrian politics led to questions from the Austrian government. In early 1950, when the Austrian Ministry of the Interior requested copies of von Bolschwing's Nazi Party records from the U.S. Army's Berlin Document Center, those files conveniently "disappeared." Critchfield's superiors supported this action. The CIA did not want von Bolschwing's past publicized because that could lead to problems. The fact remained, however, that the CIA's actions to whitewash his past gave von Bolschwing a certain amount of leverage. There was concern that CIA support of von Bolschwing opened the door to him becoming a "major political problem if not managed carefully."[36] Perhaps it was time for a change in the relationship.

Retirement in the United States

In all likelihood, the CIA was relieved when von Bolschwing agreed in September 1952 that it was time for him to leave Austria and move to the United States. It would, however, take some time to accomplish this move. Despite his underwhelming performance in his job for the CIA and the potential political problems that could arise from the association with him, CIA Austria agreed to help von Bolschwing obtain U.S. citizenship, which was his long-term goal, and recommended that Washington bestow it on him. The plan was that if he was a U.S. citizen, then von Bolschwing could be sent back to Austria as a CIA officer. The U.S. government agreed that citizenship was a possibility, but recommended that the CIA sever its ties to von Bolschwing.

In August 1953 CIA headquarters contacted its field office in Austria with permission for von Bolschwing's move to the United States but noted that the process might be delayed by his Nazi Party membership. Headquarters further announced its intention to part ways with the troublesome German once he had emigrated. With the CIA's help, von Bolschwing applied for admission to the United States as part of the "regular German quota." The CIA provided the Immigration and Naturalization Service (INS) with the background information that they had on him at the time. The INS granted his request. Von Bolschwing went to the U.S. consulate in Munich and received his immigration visa. He was on his way to the United States and almost home free.[37]

Prior to his emigration, however, the CIA expressed concerns about von Bolschwing's ability to obtain U.S. citizenship lawfully and made certain dubious recommendations:

> Grossbahn [von Bolschwing's code name] has asked a question which has us fairly well stumped. What should his answer be in the event the question of NSDAP [Nazi party] membership arises *after* his entry into the U.S., for example, on his citizenship application forms? We have told him he is to deny any party, SS, SD, Abwehr [German military intelligence], etc. affiliations. Our reason for doing so runs as follows: his entry into the U.S. is based on our covert clearance. In other words, in spite of the fact he has an objectionable background, [ ] is willing to waive their normal objections based on our assurance that Grossbahn's services . . . have been of such a caliber as to warrant extraordinary treatment. Should Grossbahn later, overtly and publicly, admit to an NSDAP record, it strikes

us that this might possibly leave [ ] with little recourse than to expel him from the U.S. as having entered under false pretenses. . . . At the same time, we feel such instructions might give Grossbahn a degree of control against us, should he decide he wants our help again at some future date—an altogether undesirable situation. What has Headquarters' experience been on this point? Have we instructed Grossbahn incorrectly? Cabled advice would be appreciated, as time to the planned departure date is running short.[38]

Although the response advised that von Bolschwing tell the truth to INS, it later became apparent that there were discrepancies. There is evidence of a letter from the CIA to the INS commissioner confirming the fact that the intelligence organization had employed von Bolschwing, who was not a security risk. The letter, which failed to note his "Nazi background," requested that INS expedite his file and his entry into the United States. At the time, the INS collected all immigration records in one "A-file"; however, a later investigation by the Office of Special Investigations revealed that INS had a "secret second file" on von Bolschwing—a file that the INS could not locate years later when the OSI requested it.[39]

By January 1954 Otto Albrecht Alfred von Bolschwing had immigrated to the United States with his wife and son. Although he was no longer employed by the CIA nor would he be able to work for any other U.S. intelligence agency, he was not worried. As his past demonstrated, he had always landed on his feet. He was an opportunist. He would find work again. He was confident that he would be successful— and he was. He found employment as a "high-ranking executive for various multi-national corporations." For instance, focusing on the language skills that he brought to the table, von Bolschwing eventually found a position with Warner Lambert Pharmaceutical Company, where he assisted the vice president for foreign exports. Employment was not the only thing that he wanted. Von Bolschwing desired permanent status in the United States—citizenship—but he bided his time.[40]

In 1959 von Bolschwing decided to try for the brass ring. He submitted an application for citizenship. On the form he neglected to provide certain information—that about his Allgemeine SS, Nazi

Party, SD, or RSHA memberships—information that he should have supplied had he truthfully answered the questions on his naturalization application. Oddly, however, he subsequently contacted the INS, admitted that he had omitted some information in his application, and offered to supply it verbally. His omission did not hurt his application. Von Bolschwing received U.S. citizenship in 1959. He could breathe a sigh of relief. Now he could focus on moving his career forward.[41] Unfortunately for von Bolschwing, various bits about his past began to surface that would eventually lead to a government investigation.

Things did not go as smoothly as von Bolschwing had hoped. He was used to being in a position of power—of having a certain status—and he wanted to achieve such a position again in his new country. What he really wanted was to work as a political analyst. In 1960, however, a wrinkle began to develop that could potentially derail his dream. On 2 May Israeli secret agents captured his former colleague Adolf Eichmann in Argentina. Although Eichmann's arrest did not have an immediate impact on von Bolschwing, later events would begin to shine the spotlight on him. Still, at the time he was concerned. Von Bolschwing contacted his former CIA handler and expressed his concern that he would be kidnapped in the United States by Israeli intelligence agents. Uncertain about the source of this fear, the handler sought information from the CIA's Counterintelligence Staff and was shocked to learn about von Bolschwing's Nazi past and connections to Eichmann and the Jewish Affairs Office. After reading this information in German documents that had been discovered in a torpedo factory, the handler claimed, "We would not have used him at that time had we known about it."[42] The question of who knew what and when about von Bolschwing is up for debate. Despite his fears to the contrary, von Bolschwing was not abducted by Israeli intelligence agents, but things were about to heat up.

In 1961 von Bolschwing took steps to obtain a political position. Some New Jersey politicians, with whom he had established connections, nominated him for a Department of State overseas assignment to India. It looked like he was about to embark on the political career that he desired. One could almost hear him rubbing his hands together with glee. He was on his way! About the time von Bolschwing was seeking a foreign posting, the CIA—his old employers—were attempting to establish a closer relationship with Israeli intelligence organizations by searching their files (captured German documents, documents in the Berlin Document Center, and so on) for the names of German officers who were connected to Eichmann. In 1961 Eichmann went on trial for war crimes in Israel. Locating information that the Israelis could use against Eichmann at his trial was the goal. Some of what was uncovered, however, the CIA would have preferred had remained hidden.

On the list of known Eichmann associates was one Otto Albrecht Alfred von Bolschwing. The evidence was even more damning. The former CIA agent had, among other things, helped Eichmann persecute Austrian Jews. Von Bolschwing's past—if it became public knowledge—could potentially be a major headache for the CIA. It could not get any worse—or could it? It could. Further CIA investigation into the "architect of the Final Solution" revealed that von Bolschwing's SS role was greater than previously thought. CIA officials questioned those who had worked closely with von Bolschwing at the Austrian station. One of those interrogated in 1961 claimed that after von Bolschwing had left Austria, it became clear that at least one of the German's agents was "fraudulent." The question then became what the CIA should do with this information and what action should they potentially take against von Bolschwing.[43]

CIA officials met with von Bolschwing. During the meeting they informed their former employee that falsification of his records was grounds for legal action against him. In fact, because von Bolschwing was not honest—had actually lied—about his "role in the persecution of the Jews," the CIA should contact either the U.S. Department of Justice or the West German government. If the agency did this, things did not bode well for von Bolschwing. The CIA struck a deal with him instead. The agency did not turn him over to the Department of Justice or to the West German government; in exchange, von Bolschwing withdrew "his application for a U.S. Government-sponsored position in India." At this point, the agency, which hoped to avoid political embarrassment, did not want to acknowledge—publicly or privately—the role it played in bringing von Bolschwing to the United States. Furthermore, if von Bolschwing faded away into the sunset, the agency would be relieved, but it feared that would not happen. Consequently, CIA officials made it clear to von Bolschwing that if asked, they "would not lie on his behalf." The CIA went a step further and put the word out in 1963 to "its German station and bases" that although von Bolschwing was traveling to Europe, he was doing so as a private citizen, not as an agency representative.[44]

Things had been a bit dicey for a while, but once the agreement with the CIA was in place, von Bolschwing breathed a sigh of relief. Although he had to abandon his dream of the State Department job in India, he was safe from prosecution for war crimes by the Department of Justice or the West German or Austrian governments. He settled down to live a quiet life—for a time. By 1969 he and his family had relocated to Sacramento, California, where von Bolschwing found employment with Trans-International Computer Investment Corporation, a computer-leasing company with lucrative Department of Defense contracts. Von Bolschwing worked his way up in the company to vice president. Unfortunately, that did not last long. First the company found itself in the middle of a financial scandal, which ultimately contributed to its demise. In 1971 the Trans-International Computer Investment Corporation filed for bankruptcy. By this time von Bolschwing was sixty-two years old and not exactly employable. While he was eligible to retire with reduced social security benefits at sixty-two, von Bolschwing could not receive full social security benefits—depending on eligibility—until he was sixty-five. Nothing is really known about his employment history for the next decade. He basically lived under the radar, with one exception. In 1978 his wife, Ruth, committed suicide. That same year von Bolschwing came to the attention of the Special Litigation Unit of the INS because of its investigation into U.S. bishop Valerian Trifa's wartime record. This time the scrutiny would not just fade away. In the midst of the growing brouhaha, von Bolschwing married for the third time.[45]

OSI Investigation

A snowball started rolling downhill in 1977 when two members of the House Subcommittee on Immigration, Citizenship, and International Law, which was responsible for INS oversight, requested that the chair of the subcommittee, Rep. Joshua Eilberg, hold hearings about Nazi criminals living in the United States. Seeing the handwriting on the wall, the INS announced a plan to revise the established policies for investigating suspected Nazi criminals. The INS general counsel David Crosland created a task force called the Special Litigation Unit—or the SLU—that year. Headed by Martin Mendelsohn, who was assisted by four trial attorneys, the SLU was tasked with "review[ing] all INS files and material connected with alleged Nazi war criminals." If sufficient evidence existed, then the next step would be denaturalization and deportation. Although created in 1977, the new task force was not fully operational until the summer of 1978. In addition to the four trial attorneys, Mendelsohn added "two INS agents, four graduate students who were fluent in German, and one archivist" to make the task force complete. The SLU mandate from Crosland was a weighty one: "Crosland ordered all closed cases involving alleged Nazi war criminals still alive and in the United States reopened for investigation."[46]

This was a big task. In pursuing its mandate, the SLU began an investigation of Bishop Valerian Trifa, who had been an Iron Guard leader in Romania—which led the task force to von Bolschwing. One of the SLU attorneys, Eugene M. Thirolf, tasked with amassing information about German officials based in Romania in 1941, approached the CIA for material about von Bolschwing. Afraid that a can of worms was about to be opened, the CIA was not pleased about the request. When Mendelsohn reviewed the documents, CIA officials had to agree that von Bolschwing was less than honest on his naturalization application in 1959, when he failed to admit his Nazi Party membership. The worms were starting to crawl out into the open. The SLU was concerned by what it learned, particularly in light of what war crimes von Bolschwing might have committed. By 1979—the year that the Office of Special Investigations was established—the SLU launched a full scale investigation into Otto von Bolschwing, including "his immigration and his wartime activities," which made Mendelsohn's original plan to have von Bolschwing testify against Trifa problematic, if not impossible.[47]

In March 1979 the CIA informed Mendelsohn that an investigation of von Bolschwing could compromise the agency. Undeterred, the SLU scheduled an interview of von Bolschwing in June. The results of the meeting were quite interesting. When questioned by Eugene Thirolf, von Bolschwing categorically denied being a member of the SS. Von Bolschwing did admit to helping members of the Romanian Iron Guard leadership escape, but he claimed purely altruistic motives—an attempt to "create a peaceful settlement between two warring parties."[48] In the summer of 1979 there was a change in the lead investigator, when Thirolf was replaced by Jeffrey Mausner. In November Mendelsohn, who by this time was deputy director of OSI, sent a list of specific questions to the CIA. Mendelsohn asked if the potential for blackmail existed, if the CIA would vouch for von Bolschwing, if the CIA would have helped him gain entry to the United States if it had known the truth about his past, and if the CIA had told von Bolschwing to be honest about his Nazi past. Mendelsohn also inquired about what information the CIA had provided to the INS about von Bolschwing and whether or not von Bolschwing had worked for the agency after his move to the United States.

Initially, the CIA dragged its feet in responding to Mendelsohn. In fact, Allan A. Ryan Jr., the new OSI director, had to prod the agency to respond, which it finally did in the summer of 1980. The responses to these questions indicated the level of cooperation that the OSI could expect from the CIA. Despite its earlier reticence, the CIA did not oppose the OSI investigation and indicated that there was no possibility of blackmail. The CIA acknowledged von Bolschwing's value but agreed to testify about, among other things, what facts von Bolschwing did or did not supply. The agency was on the fence, however, about whether or not it would have supported von Bolschwing had all the facts about his past been known at the time. While the CIA claimed that it had told von Bolschwing to answer the naturalization questions truthfully, it could not guarantee that he had received that message. Finally, the agency denied helping von Bolschwing obtain naturalization or employing him after his move to the United States.[49]

It was very clear to the OSI investigators that von Bolschwing had not been honest on both his visa and his citizenship applications;

therefore, he had entered the country illegally. In addition, he had fraudulently received naturalization. Although the case seemed to be straightforward, it was far from that. There were a number of cases that made the situation less than ideal, as far as the OSI was concerned. First was the missing secret file. Von Bolschwing could claim that the missing file contained the omitted information, and the OSI would not be able to disprove it—even if that scenario was not likely. Without the file the CIA could not definitively confirm or deny that von Bolschwing had provided the information either in a written statement or in an interview.

The second problem was related to von Bolschwing's citizenship application. In 1959 the INS had received a letter from him, in which he referred to "additional information which might be in a file" and offered to expand on that information verbally. In an effort for clarity, OSI investigators questioned the INS agent who had reviewed von Bolschwing's forms and had interrogated him. After consulting his case file notes, the agent confirmed that von Bolschwing had failed to supply information about his various troublesome affiliations. The OSI was also concerned that von Bolschwing might assert that the CIA had told him to omit certain information. Those concerns were justified because von Bolschwing did just that. This was particularly problematic for the OSI because von Bolschwing's CIA contact—who may or may not have told him to be truthful—was deceased by this time.[50]

The OSI sought additional information from the CIA. Jeffrey Mausner contacted the agency in writing. In his letter Mausner stated that "most of our cases are based on a claim that the defendant misrepresented his Nazi background at the time of his entry into the United States or at the time of his naturalization. It is therefore important to know exactly what INS, State Department and CIA knew about von Bolschwing at the time of his entry and naturalization."[51] Unfortunately, the CIA was unable to satisfy this request completely.

In early 1981 the OSI had a formal "sit-down"—official and on the record—meeting with von Bolschwing at his California home. His son Golman (Gus) V. von Bolschwing represented him. During the interview Gus, who did more talking than his father, defended him vociferously. Arguing that American authorities had all of the facts about his father before he moved to the United States, Gus von Bolschwing asserted that the OSI investigation was hypocritical at best. He claimed, "It is just as difficult for my father at this point to prove his case, to disprove pieces of paper that are now 40 years old, as it was for certain individuals who did try to do justice to find and to prosecute Germans when there were no living witnesses or it was very hard to obtain living witnesses."[52] According to the son, further complicating the situation was von Bolschwing's declining health, which made it difficult for him to remember the past accurately.

In spite of these issues, Director Ryan was confident that the OSI had a case against von Bolschwing that could be won and wanted to move forward, but Deputy Assistant Attorney General Mark M. Richard did not completely agree. Arguing that the visa application case was too weak, Richard recommended that Ryan file charges based only on the naturalization case. In May 1981 the OSI made its move against von Bolschwing by filing a "three-count complaint" in the U.S. District Court for the Eastern District of California. The complaint alleged "(1) that von Bolschwing had procured his naturalization by concealment or misrepresentation since he failed to reveal his wartime activities and associations as part of his naturalization applications; (2) that these memberships and activities were evidence of a lack of good moral character requisite for citizenship; and (3) that his swearing to the truth of his naturalization application, when in fact the application was not truthful, was further evidence of lack of good moral character."[53] Listed in the complaint were the memberships that von Bolschwing had held—in the Nazi Party, the SS, the SD, and the RSHA. The International Military Tribunal in Nuremberg had ruled that all of these groups constituted criminal organizations.

Adding a new twist to the story, von Bolschwing responded to the charges in the press. He claimed that he had actually worked for the OSS during the war. In the article he was quoted: "It's not true. I never served in the SS or Gestapo or SD (the intelligence branch of the SS). I did serve in the OSS for the Americans, and I did parachute into Austria. It was dangerous work in Germany (for the Americans)." In another interview von Bolschwing added to the fantasy by claiming to have met William J. Donovan, the director of the OSS, in New York before the war. Ryan issued his own statement to refute von Bolschwing's claims. According to Ryan, "What he said is not true. Our case relates from the middle 1930s through the war, and, during that period, he was not a double agent for the United States or anything like that. He was not affiliated in any way with the U.S. Government."[54]

This case was not a slam-dunk for the OSI, but not because the organization did not have the evidence to make its case in court. The problem was von Bolschwing. Even though he made statements to the press, he had serious health issues that raised questions about his ability to understand the court proceedings. In addition, participation in his own defense was not certain. At the time the OSI filed the complaints against him, von Bolschwing had been admitted to a nursing home. The doctors diagnosed him with a "progressive neurological disorder which impaired his memory and intellectual functioning." Von Bolschwing's attorneys had apprised Ryan of the situation before he filed the complaint in an effort to resolve things without going to trial. Ryan recognized the problems that could result from going to trial under the circumstances. He believed that, at the very least, the press would have a field day "if the government tried to deport someone unable to understand or assist in his defense." Richard concurred.[55]

An agreement was reached with von Bolschwing and his attorneys. He would surrender his citizenship certificate but be allowed to remain in the United States. The district court had to sign off on the plea agreement, and it did. As part of the agreement, von Bolschwing publicly admitted that he had failed to disclose his memberships in criminal organizations—the Nazi Party, the SS, and the SD—on his citizenship application, but he did not, again, mention his work for the Jewish Affairs Office. Von Bolschwing stated that he would not contest his loss of citizenship, and the United States announced that it did not intend to deport von Bolschwing unless his health improved. Per the agreement, von Bolschwing's situation would be evaluated annually. The judge made the agreement official on 22 December 1981. Ten weeks later, at the age of seventy-two, Otto Albrecht Alfred von Bolschwing died.[56]

At the end of the day, because von Bolschwing relinquished his naturalization certificate, Richard considered the outcome a victory. Questions remain about the CIA: how much it knew about von Bolschwing's past, how much it chose to forget. The second secret file remains missing; therefore, the CIA can maintain "plausible deniability"—always a good thing in the intelligence game. In addition, von Bolschwing's actual usefulness to the CIA is equally questionable. His track record was not very good. His intelligence work for the Gehlen Organization, which was about to fire him before he got hired by the CIA, was less than stellar. It is worth asking the CIA if teaming up with von Bolschwing was worth it. Did the information and connections that he provided outweigh the negatives? In an honest assessment, the scale is probably more weighted by the negatives than the positives.

Von Bolschwing's record does demonstrate, however, that he was good at some things. The Jewish Affairs Office was pleased with his consulting work for them. It adopted a number of his recommendations regarding the Jewish Problem. He found favor with Himmler and Hitler for a time—at least until his screwup in Romania. He was very good at landing on his feet, as his activities with the resistance movement in Austria at the end of the war demonstrates. He successfully teamed up with U.S. military forces before eventually signing on with the CIA. He was able to hide his Adolf Eichmann association for quite some time. These connections allowed him to escape prosecution and punishment for his criminal activities of the 1930s and 1940s—for decades. It was not until the late 1970s that his luck really began to run out. In the end, although he lost his citizenship, von Bolschwing did not have to suffer the added humiliation of deportation. He did not, however, get to enjoy his reprieve for very long.

5

Kurt Waldheim—Patriot or Villain?

Former president of Austria Kurt Waldheim has the notorious distinction of being the only head of state ever placed on the U.S. Immigration and Nationalization Service's Watch List. People placed on the Watch List are those who are undesirable, suspected of having assisted the Axis powers in persecution based on race, religion, national origin, or political persuasion; of committing human rights crimes or terrorism; or of posing a security threat to the United States. Ideally, people who are on the Watch List are stopped at the border and denied entry into the United States. Waldheim gained prominence in the 1970s because of his two terms as secretary-general of the United Nations. In the mid-1980s he was a candidate in the Austrian presidential election. He had unsuccessfully run for the highest office in Austria in 1971. Although there had been rumors for years, Waldheim had deflected all questions about his wartime activities by presenting a brief standard narrative that investigators and pertinent political officials had accepted.

A more in-depth investigation of Waldheim began in late January 1986, after the World Jewish Congress (WJC) received a tip about his military service as a senior intelligence officer with the German army in the Balkans. According to Waldheim's autobiography and official statements, after he had been wounded in 1941 on the Russian front, he became a law student in Vienna and did not return to his unit on the front lines. Acting on the tip, the WJC sought and found documents that presented a vastly different story. These documents indicated "that Waldheim had served in a unit that had taken civilian hostages, burned homes, and shot male prisoners."[1] The WJC released this information to the media, and Waldheim admitted that he had served in the Balkans but denied knowledge of any atrocities. The investigation by the WJC put the organization at odds with one of Waldheim's staunchest supporters—Nazi-hunter Simon Wiesenthal. At the end of the day, Wiesenthal's adamant defense of Waldheim led him to launch public, personal attacks against the WJC investigators. Wiesenthal's behavior ultimately tarnished his prominent, global reputation.

By April 1986 the Office of Special Investigations had commenced its investigation of the Austrian president and would release a detailed report a year later. Throughout this period the WJC shared information with OSI. The two organizations pursued documents and witness testimonies to answer the following questions: What was the complete story of Kurt Waldheim's wartime service? How had he managed to perpetrate a cover-up for forty years? What did countries like the United States, Yugoslavia, the Soviet Union, and Israel know about Waldheim's history from 1942 until 1945? When did they know it? If they had unearthed evidence about Waldheim and war crimes, why did they keep silent?

It was one thing for the WJC to investigate Kurt Waldheim to determine whether or not he had committed war crimes. It was another altogether for the OSI to get involved. Waldheim was not a U.S. citizen, and he was no longer secretary-general of the United Nations. He had not immigrated—legally or illegally—to the United States after the war nor had he applied for entry in 1986. At the time the OSI commenced its investigation into Waldheim, he was running for president of his home country: Austria. Before OSI submitted its report a year later, Waldheim had won a runoff election and was Austria's president. What gave the OSI the authority to investigate a head of state? Who was the real Kurt Waldheim? Was he a patriot who had just done his duty during the war, as he had suggested, or was he a villain, a perpetrator of crimes against humanity?

Early Years

On 21 December 1918 Kurt Josef Waldheim was born in Austria, in the village of Sankt Andrä-Wördern, which is approximately fifteen and a half miles from Vienna. His parents were Josefine Petrasch and Walter Waldheim, although Waldheim was not his father's original surname. Born in 1889, Walter Watzlawik, a Roman Catholic, was of Czech descent. His father was a blacksmith in Tulln. Not wanting a physically hard life like his father, Watzlawik qualified as a teacher and obtained a job nearly ten miles away, in Sankt Andrä-Wördern. Shortly after the outbreak of war in 1914, Watzlawik met his future wife, whose father was a "well-to-do farmer."[2] The couple married and moved to Tulln because Watzlawik was headed off to war.

Watzlawik came back from war to a fractured empire and to a country with fewer opportunities for citizens with Czech surnames. Even though he had the skills to get a provincial teaching post and contacts from his wife and father-in-law to help on the job front, he did not find it easy to gain employment—until he took advice from a colleague. Because his Czech surname cast him as an outsider in his homeland and because he needed to be more of a "German Austrian," Walter Watzlawik became Walter Waldheim. Changing his name proved to be fortuitous because shortly thereafter doors opened up for the elder Waldheim.

During the interwar period, when Kurt Waldheim was growing up, his father achieved success. After being chosen as "head of the Wieselburg Boys School," he became "superintendent of schools for the entire Tulln district." His work as superintendent and his involvement in adult education earned him the title of Regierungsrat— "government counselor." His father's career successes and improvement in Austria's economy made life for Kurt; his brother, Walther; and his sister Gerlinde easier than it had been for their father, who had grown up impoverished.[3] Kurt, like his siblings, had access to an excellent education, thanks to his father. He was a graduate of the Vienna Consular Academy and the University of Vienna, where he earned a doctor of jurisprudence in 1944. Both achievements would eventually facilitate his career.

As a young man, Waldheim was tall and thin. Amiable, he exuded a quiet confidence. Growing up in the interwar period, he was intrigued by global politics. Setting his sights on becoming a diplomat, Waldheim focused on learning the law and multiple languages, which he knew would stand him in good stead. Driven by his father's hopes for him and a determination to succeed, he worked hard. Waldheim was focused on his career and was not to be deterred. Prior to the university, his father enrolled him in the gymnasium in Klosterneuburg. Every morning Waldheim commuted an hour by train to the town, which was north of Vienna. While attending the gymnasium, he "joined the Catholic Comagena fraternity," excelled in all subjects except mathematics, and played the violin in the school orchestra. He also participated in extracurricular activities—swimming, boating, and tennis.[4]

Despite appearances, life was not all a bed of roses. Waldheim pursued his studies against the backdrop of political turmoil, as three political groups vied for "political dominance": the Christian Social Party, the Social Democrats, and the "Greater German or pan-German groups. All three movements had roots in the defunct empire, and all three held views and prejudices that made it difficult for them to adjust to the changed environment" of post–World War I Austria and the world. Following the violence of riots by socialist workers in 1927, the Austrian chancellor imposed a more authoritarian system and "introduced a new constitution" that granted the chancellor more power and made the position an appointed, rather than elected, one.[5] By the time the chancellor retired in 1929, on the eve of a worldwide economic crisis, the new constitution was in place. The political situation that existed in Austria became more tenuous during the Depression—a time when desperation and violence plagued the nation.

In 1932 Christian Socialist Engelbert Dollfuss became chancellor at a time when political and social unrest was pervasive throughout the world. To the north of Austria, Adolf Hitler and the Nazis came to power in Germany. Although there was talk of Anschluss, unification with Germany, Dollfuss and his party "officially rejected the idea" in favor of a closer relationship with Benito Mussolini and Italy. Dollfuss took things to the next level and indicated his rejection of the Nazis by June 1933. He made the Nazi movement illegal in Austria. "From then on—until the Nazis were allowed aboveground again in March 1938—all members of the National Socialist German Workers Party, NSDAP, were known as 'Illegals.'"[6]

When the chancellor created a "Patriotic Front, a mass organization intended to encompass the entire nation," Waldheim's father .

joined. Dollfuss's plan with the Patriotic Front was to abolish political parties, even the Christian Social Party. Citizens felt pressure to become members: "State employees were required to join." Waldheim's father, who saw the "Front" as the solution to Austria's problems, did not have to be pressured to embrace membership. Dollfuss's goal was the recrafting of Austria into a "*Ständestaat*, a Christian corporate state." The chancellor established a Central Police Directorate and continued efforts to limit the presence of Nazis, communists, and socialists by suggesting that these groups introduced "poisonous '*fremde Ideen*' (foreign ideas) into Austria."[7]

Not only were these political machinations the order of the day during Waldheim's impressionable years, but they were also on Hitler's radar. Hitler was unwilling to tolerate Dollfuss's political agenda and took steps to foment regime change in neighboring Austria. The first attack was an economic one. Germans planning to vacation in Austria would have to pay a hefty fee to the German government for that privilege. Then on 25 July 1934 the Nazis staged an "uprising" in Austria. During the violence that resulted, seizure of government facilities in Vienna and elsewhere and the assassination of Dollfuss occurred. Because he sent troops to the Brenner Pass, Benito Mussolini, who condemned the uprising, possibly saved Austria from occupation—at least temporarily.

While he, like the rest of his family, was appalled by the uprising and the murder of Dollfuss, Waldheim realized that not all of his classmates at the Klosterneuburg gymnasium felt the same way. Some vocalized their solidarity with the Nazis. The irony here is that, while Waldheim seemed to reject the violence perpetrated by the Nazis in 1934, he later came to embrace their policies, despite his protests to the contrary. Dollfuss's successor, Kurt von Schuschnigg, who faced an uphill battle from the very beginning, moved to increase the size of the Federal Army, which would have the dual role of providing internal and external protection. In the spring of 1936, as he completed his studies at the gymnasium and prepared to enter an uncertain world, Waldheim—age seventeen—made a decision that would have an enormous impact on his future. Upon his graduation on 22 June 1936, he enlisted in the "Austrian army as a 'one-year volunteer,'" which would fulfill the mandatory military service requirement for new government employees. His twelve-month enlistment would commence on his eighteenth birthday—21 December.[8]

While Waldheim waited for his eighteenth birthday and his first posting, the political chaos within Austria continued, as von Schuschnigg awkwardly tried to shift the country's orientation from Italy to Germany. The chancellor hoped to accomplish two goals with this reorientation: an easing of the economic situation and help in curtailing the violence committed by Austrian Nazis. On 11 July 1936 von Schuschnigg and Hitler formalized a "gentlemen's agreement" between the two countries. As a result, Austria became a "German state." Anti-German—or anti-Nazi—press was consequently forbidden.[9] Unfortunately for Austria, the situation did not improve. Its economic situation worsened instead. Only Austrians with government jobs, like Waldheim's father, had job security. Thus was the situation in Austria as Waldheim prepared to perform his military service.

When his orders arrived in late 1936, Waldheim was pleased. He had hoped to receive posting to a cavalry unit, which is exactly what happened. He was sent to "Stockerau, the headquarters of the elite Dragoon Regiment 1." For Waldheim, this was an ideal assignment. Not only was Stockerau about ten miles from Tulln, but, as a member of an elite unit, he would also have the opportunity to "meet the right sort of people," who could potentially facilitate his future career. As far as he was concerned, it was a win-win assignment. A model recruit, Waldheim "worked hard, was a good comrade, and coped well with the inevitable stress and tedium of military service." In addition to standard military training, he participated in "dress parades." Waldheim "cut a splendid figure in his cavalry uniform, tall, slim, and self-assured, and he took real pride in the symbols of imperial greatness—the banners and standards—that surrounded him."[10]

When his year was up, Waldheim mustered out and applied for admission to the Vienna Consular Academy, which was the next logical step in pursuit of his chosen career. Not only was he accepted to the academy, but he also received a scholarship. His chosen fields of study were diplomacy and law. Waldheim commenced classes in the fall of 1937. During his first academic year, he completed courses in "languages, diplomacy, international studies, and law" while also dabbling in political science and finance. Waldheim also received training in other aspects of diplomatic service: "etiquette and protocol," hand shaking and bowing, speaking, and rank and status.[11] After a somewhat idyllic first year, Waldheim had little inkling that his life would soon change dramatically.

While Waldheim was taking classes at the Vienna Consular Academy, Hitler indicated his determination to alter the recently established Germany-Austria relationship. If all went according to plan, Austria would have the short end of the stick. Receiving a summons from Hitler on 12 February 1938, von Schuschnigg traveled to Bavaria to meet with the führer, who gave the Austrian leader an ultimatum: either a "National Socialist 'coalition government'" in Austria or a German invasion of Austria. According to Hitler, if von Schuschnigg accepted the latter option, he would be responsible for the "spilling of innocent blood." The Austrian leader found himself between a rock and a hard place. Accepting the reality that neither England nor Italy could help Austria avoid a German invasion, he conceded and "agreed" to a wide range of "Hitler dictated" concessions, including "the appointment of Nazi lawyer Artur Seyss-Inquart as minister of security." Von Schuschnigg did stand firm on one issue. The Austrian Nazi Party was still banned, but that became a moot point, because he also agreed to the release of Nazis from Austrian prisons and to allowing Nazis to protest publicly.[12]

As might be expected, news of the new German-Austrian agreement emboldened Austrian Nazis. The release of imprisoned Nazis from the Linz prison on 18 February 1938 exacerbated the situation. The Nazis offered the poor an alternative to socialism—National Socialism—and the economically and socially disadvantaged flocked to the call. Targeting Jews and Jewish businesses also garnered support for the "cause." As the situation deteriorated, von Schuschnigg demonstrated that he was not giving up without a fight. He called for a referendum to be held on 13 March. The Austrian people would have an opportunity to vote for—or against—independence. Choosing not to remain detached from the situation, Waldheim campaigned with his family for an independent Austria, despite the risk. The family suffered reprisals for their political activity. In addition to graffiti being painted on their house, Kurt Waldheim was physically attacked.

Hitler demanded the cancelation of the referendum vote and the establishment of a "decent" government in Austria. Not confident that von Schuschnigg would comply, the führer upped the ante.[13] "At 1 a.m. on March 11, less than forty-eight hours before the voting was to begin, Hitler signed the final orders for a German invasion of Austria. The only thing that could forestall bloodshed now, he said, would be the immediate ouster of the 'traitor' Schuschnigg and the installation of a Nazi-dominated government."[14] Von Schuschnigg caved. With his resignation, the minister of security—Artur Seyss-Inquart—became the new chancellor. The Anschluss would happen. Moving forward, Waldheim would think more carefully before publicly taking a political stand.

Violence, particularly against Jews, increased, but while in class Waldheim was removed from it. On 10 April a plebiscite to "ratify the *Anschluss*" occurred, and "over 99 percent of the voters" supported unification with Germany. While some truly supported unification, others accepted reality and acknowledged the consequences of not voting yes; however, not all Austrians escaped unscathed. The Gestapo paid a visit to the Waldheim house and arrested Walter Waldheim. Although he was only detained for a couple of days, when he was released, he no longer had a job, and his pension had been drastically reduced. Furthermore, according to Kurt Waldheim, he lost his Vienna Consular Academy scholarship. The harassment continued. SA (Sturmabeilung) men periodically searched the family home for "subversive literature." They arrested Walter Waldheim and briefly detained him a second time. Harassment spawned ostracism by the neighbors.[15] According to Waldheim, "Our family was under constant surveillance. We lived in daily apprehension."[16]

Waldheim remained focused on his studies, but his future at the Vienna Consular Academy was not a certainty. Without a scholarship, he was responsible for tuition. Although relatives loaned him money, Waldheim supplemented those funds by tutoring students in Latin and Greek. The tentacles of the Nazi octopus, which reached into all aspects of Austrian society, touched the Vienna Consular Academy

1. Klaus Barbie, Butcher of Lyon, as a young officer before he gained notoriety in Lyon. Unknown source.

2. Josef Mengele, Angel of Death. Police photograph, Mengele's Argentine identification document, circa 1956. Wikimedia Commons.

3. (*opposite top*) Secretary-General Kurt Waldheim (*second from left*), pictured with Secretary of State Henry Kissinger, Senator Jacob Javits, and Senator Abraham Ribicoff at a UN conference in Nairobi, Kenya. National Archives and Records Administration.

4. (*opposite bottom*) Andrija Artuković, Butcher of the Balkans (*center*). Artuković hearing, 10 March 1958. USC Libraries, Los Angeles Examiner Photographic Collection, 1920–1961.

5. (*above*) Karl Linnas, executioner in Estonia. Courtroom sketch drawn during Linnas's trial for war crimes, circa 1980–81. Courtroom Sketches of Ida Libby Dengrove, University of Virginia Law Library.

6. Project Paperclip team at Fort Bliss, 1946. Row 1: Bernhard Tessmann (*second from left*), Arthur Rudolph (*fourth from left*), Wernher von Braun (*seventh from right*). Row 2: Karl L. Heimburg (*sixth from left*). Wikimedia Commons.

7. Arthur Rudolph, father of the Saturn V rocket, holding part of a Saturn V model. NASA Marshall Space Flight Center, Huntsville, Alabama. Wikimedia Commons.

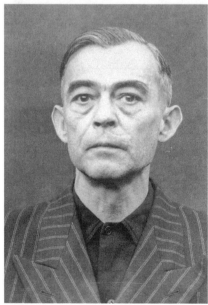

8. Kurt Blome, Dachau doctor. Photograph taken when Blome was a defendant in the Nuremberg Medical Case Trial, circa 1946–47. United States Holocaust Memorial Museum, courtesy of Hedwig Wachenheimer Epstein.

as well. The result was *Gleichschaltung*, or Nazi coordination. Despite the disgrace his family faced, Waldheim was able to continue at the academy—even while other students, especially Jewish ones, were expelled—because Director Hlavec von Rechtwall supported him. Waldheim, however, recognized the precarious nature of his position, and, although he later denied it, he joined the National Socialist German Students' League on 1 April 1938. His later army records acknowledged his position as a "full member."[17]

The end of the academic year brought obligation before pleasure—military service before vacation—and military service in the German, not the Austrian, army. On 17 August Waldheim reported to a "cavalry instructional unit," where he remained until 9 September, when he left for additional "combat training" at Stockerau. His assignment was to the Fourth Squadron of the Eleventh Cavalry Regiment—formerly Dragoon Regiment One—with "the rank of *Wachtmeister*, or sergeant." While Waldheim performed his military obligations, the situation in Europe continued to deteriorate. Conflict between Germany and Czechoslovakia was avoided only by negotiations, which resulted in the Munich Pact, signed on 30 September 1938 by British prime minister Neville Chamberlain, French prime minister Édouard Daladier, and Adolf Hitler. While the world collectively sighed in relief and Chamberlain announced to the British people that they had achieved "peace for our time," the German annexation of the Sudetenland would change Waldheim's life yet again.[18]

The German annexation of the Sudetenland dictated occupation, and the Fourth Squadron of the Eleventh Cavalry Regiment—Waldheim's unit—received this assignment. Waldheim's tour, however, concluded by the end of October. He received the designation "reserve officer candidate" and returned to his studies at the Vienna Consular Academy. In mid-November, after the infamous Reichskristallnacht—Reich Crystal Night—during which the Nazis launched violent attacks against Jewish citizens, businesses, and homes, Waldheim became a member of the SA. His initial assignment in a SA cavalry unit, the Reitstandarte, was to Storm Detachment Five, Unit Ninety, in Vienna. Years later, when he was under scrutiny, he denied being a member of the "N.S. Student League or the SA." According to Waldheim, "his

SA 'Unit' was merely a riding group at the Consular Academy that was 'coordinated' by the regime." He suggested that he had participated in just "two or three harmless horseback outings" with the group.[19]

In the spring of 1939 Waldheim completed his studies at the Vienna Consular Academy and graduated. Although he would have preferred a trip to Italy, he was required for military service and proceeded to the Eleventh Cavalry Reserve Section in Stockerau by August. By the end of that month his unit was incorporated into the Forty-Fifth Reconnaissance Unit. Waldheim received posting to the unit's First Mounted Squadron. Because he was accepted as an "officer candidate," his next assignment was to the "Krampnitz Cavalry Academy near Berlin," where he would receive several months of reserve officer training. Although his plan was to visit Italy after completing his training, but before resuming his law studies in Vienna, events in Poland would intervene.[20]

Wartime: Waldheim's Narrative

On 1 September 1939 German forces invaded Poland. The move was the culmination of a crisis situation between the two countries. The declaration of war on Germany by France and Britain made Waldheim's planned trip to Italy impossible. Instead, he reported—as ordered on 19 November—to the Forty-Fifth Reconnaissance Unit's First Cavalry Squadron. Although many hoped that, as a result of the "German victory in Poland," the war would be short lived, that would soon prove to be wishful thinking. The resolution of the situation in Poland, however, enabled Waldheim to apply for leave successfully. While hoping that Germany would sign a peace agreement with Britain and France, he returned to his law studies in Vienna. When no peace agreement had been announced by the time his leave was over, Waldheim's return to duty was unavoidable. By March 1940 he was with the First Cavalry Squadron in Hesse, Germany. Impatient to resume his law studies and begin his desired career in foreign service, Waldheim hoped that the "phony war" would be the end of things because he knew that a campaign in the west would signal a lengthy conflict.[21]

The war provided an unwanted complication in Waldheim's life.

It derailed his career plans. He was not exactly pleased, but he was stuck. In all likelihood, he would be in the Wehrmacht until the end of the war. He could only hope that the conflict would be over sooner rather than later. Waldheim did, however, understand that his wartime military service could only help him when he pursued his postwar career. He knew "that a respectable military record would look good on his résumé, cleansing him of the taint of having a suspected anti-Nazi for a father."[22]

Waldheim also understood how lucky he was not to be ordered to a combat situation, even during the "phony war." Being based in Hesse allowed him to continue his preparations for the "basic" law exam, which he took on 15 March 1940 in Vienna. Ten days later, because he had "passed with a satisfactory grade," he earned the probationary title "junior barrister." A month later Waldheim's unit—the Forty-Fifth Reconnaissance—was put on alert, which was not a good sign. On 10 May 1940 the German invasion of France, Belgium, and the Netherlands began. When the dust cleared five weeks later, the Germans had achieved victory in the west.[23]

Waldheim and his unit did not experience much action as they traveled to Boulogne-sur-Mer, France. By the time he received his next leave home in August, Waldheim had received promotion to "senior noncommissioned officer." He joined his family in their new home in Baden. While in Baden, Waldheim petitioned the "chief of the Nazi Party Personnel Office for the Lower Danube region" for permission to "pursue a legal career" and received approval. Luckily for him, his dubious political past did not sink him. In his assessment, the chief wrote, "The above-mentioned was, like his father, a supporter of the Schuschnigg regime, and . . . boasted ample evidence of his hateful attitude towards our movement. The above-mentioned has now been conscripted and is said to have proven his worth as a soldier of the German Army, so that I do not oppose his admission to judicial service."[24] Breathing a sigh of relief, Waldheim returned to his unit a few weeks later. By 1 December he received a commission as a reserve lieutenant.

Although France capitulated, the unwillingness of Britain to follow suit meant that the war continued. Because the front was quiet, however, Waldheim obtained "study leave" and started the next step toward his diplomatic career goal.[25] He enrolled in an international law doctorate program. He obtained leave to take classes but was back in France with his unit by mid-February 1941. Waldheim's easy life in France came to an end in the summer of 1941. He and his comrades would participate in Operation Barbarossa—the 22 June invasion of the Soviet Union. Tasked with attacking Soviet defenses around Brest-Litovsk, they learned what combat really entailed. It was dirty, noisy, and bloody. After Brest-Litovsk fell to the Germans, Waldheim received his first battlefield award: Iron Cross, Second Class.

Following the battle, Waldheim's unit became part of Vorausabteilung (Vanguard Unit), or VA, Forty-Five and received new responsibilities. SS forces joined them with the express purpose of "cleansing" the region of partisan forces. Unlike the situation in the west, Soviet forces did not crumble. There were attacks and counterattacks. It seemed never ending to Waldheim and his fellow soldiers. Waldheim did his part and then some. This did not go unnoticed by his superiors. On 18 August Lieutenant Waldheim received the Cavalry Assault Badge. On 8 October, in the absence of his squadron leader, he stepped in as temporary First Squadron, VA Forty-Five, leader. That same month Waldheim and his men found themselves near Moscow, in the Orel sector, and tasked with mopping up enemy resistance in the area.[26]

While conditions—on the battlefield and in terms of weather—were not great, Waldheim survived unscathed as winter neared. In early December the Soviets launched a counteroffensive in Army Group Center's sector, and Waldheim and the men in his unit found themselves hard pressed. On 14 December his luck ran out, and Waldheim was injured. He would turn twenty-three exactly one week later. Although not life threatening, the shrapnel wound to his leg was serious. It took several days to transport Waldheim to the field hospital in Minsk, where he received treatment from an Austrian doctor. In one sense, however, his luck held out. Waldheim did not lose his leg. Evacuated to Austria, Waldheim received treatment in Reserve Field Hospital Twenty-Three in Vienna. He recovered enough to spend Christmas with his family before beginning physical therapy. On 23 January 1942 Waldheim received another medal: the Wounded Badge in Black.

According to Waldheim, his injury ended the war for him. In numerous postwar accounts he claimed that—after a year-long recuperation—he was "discharged from military duties." Consequently, he returned to Vienna and continued his doctoral studies in law, which he completed in 1944.[27] For forty years this was Waldheim's version of his wartime activities. It was rarely questioned. In fact, Waldheim's short biography on the United Nations website does not even mention what he did during the war except earn his law degree in 1944. Later Waldheim, who denied his membership in a Nazi youth organization, confirmed this narrative in a 19 December 1980 letter to U.S. congressman Stephen J. Solarz. Not completely satisfied, the congressman contacted the Central Intelligence Agency to determine what information, if any, that agency had with regard to Waldheim's membership in Nazi organizations and his military service during the war.[28] The CIA's legislative counsel, Frederick P. Hitz, responded to Solarz's query:

> We believe that Waldheim was not a member of the Nazi Youth Movement, nor was he involved in anti-Jewish activities.
>
> We have no intelligence reporting in detail on Waldheim's military service. However, we have gleaned the following from German open source materials. Upon the outbreak of war in 1939, Waldheim was drafted at age 20 into the German Army. He served as a staff intelligence officer with the rank of lieutenant, assigned to the 45th Infantry Division. This Division saw action in the Polish Campaign (September 1939) and the assault on France (May 1940). It was sent to the eastern front in June 1941 to take part in the invasion of the USSR. Waldheim's service with this Division ended in 1941 when he received a leg wound. There is nothing in the files to suggest that while in this unit Waldheim participated directly or indirectly in anti-Jewish activities.
>
> His recuperation from the leg wound required almost a year; he was discharged from military duties following his recovery and returned to study law in Vienna. He received his doctorate in law in 1944 and in 1945 began his diplomatic career in the Austrian Ministry of Foreign Affairs.[29]

Several years would pass before Waldheim's wartime narrative would be more thoroughly investigated, challenged, and proven false.

Illustrious Postwar Career

As the war neared an end, Waldheim was ready to move on to bigger and better things—especially a diplomatic career. The year 1944 was a good one for Waldheim. Not only did he complete his law degree, but he also married Elizabeth "Cissy" Lieselotte Ritschel. Shortly after the war in Europe ended, Waldheim was reunited with his wife in Ramsau and met his daughter, Lieselotte, who had been born on the day that Adm. Karl Dönitz had given Germany's unconditional surrender to Gen. Dwight Eisenhower and senior officers from the United States, Britain, France, and the Soviet Union.[30] It was time to put the past behind him and move toward the future. Waldheim was ready. The past was just that—the past. There was no need to discuss it, to dwell on it, to provide a long narrative when asked what he did during the war. Waldheim apparently concluded that an abridged version of his wartime military service was the way to go. He embraced his version of events, repeated it when asked, and was reluctant—years later when challenged—to abandon it.

With the war over, Waldheim needed to be officially separated from the army if he hoped to pursue his chosen career. Consequently, he presented himself at the Wehrmacht "demobilization" center in Ramsau, surrendered his weapon, "and had his paybook stamped." Unfortunately, that was not the end of it. While he was no longer in the Wehrmacht, he had to be cleared by the U.S. Army; therefore, he reported to the "American processing center" in Schladming in mid-May. Waldheim was not overly worried because his military rank at the beginning—and the end—of the war was lieutenant. Although he thought that he would not be held for long, he did not know that the Americans had received information from British military intelligence that suggested Waldheim had been Gen. Alexander Löhr's intelligence officer in the Balkans. Consequently, he learned that his tenure with the Americans would be longer than he had expected—or hoped it would be—and he found himself "an inmate at the POW [prisoner of war] camp near Bad Tölz" in Bavaria. During his subsequent interrogations, Waldheim did not raise any red flags for the Americans. Because he was appropriately anticommunist, Waldheim was back with his family in Ramsau within a month.[31]

After temporarily relocating to Obermettenback, Austria, Waldheim and his family returned to Baden in early August 1945, and he began to look for a job. With help from Herr Schwanzer and Heinrich Wild, both well-known anti-Nazis who wrote letters of support, he returned to his prior position ("junior magistrate at the district court in Baden"), but he had his sights on bigger things—on a foreign-service job. The letters from Schwanzer and Wild, which he had "formally notarized," would help. Waldheim composed a résumé that glossed over what he did during the war. Because of a shortage of Austrian diplomats, he believed that he had a good shot at success. His plan was to get his ducks in a row and then to make his case to Secretary of State Karl Gruber.[32]

On 25 November 1945 Austrians went to the poll and voted for a new government. The Austrian People's Party (ÖVP), Volkspartei, which was a recrafted Christian Social Party, achieved an overwhelming victory. The election results solidified Gruber's position. Gruber's aide was Fritz Peter Molden. Approximately six weeks earlier, on 8 October, Waldheim showed up at Gruber's office and asked Molden for directions to the personnel office, where he submitted his credentials. After consulting Molden, Gruber summoned Waldheim and announced that, if he passed the requisite security checks, he would be the minister's "new personal diplomatic secretary." Molden received the task of conducting Waldheim's background check. After a cursory investigation in which his party memberships did not surface, Molden reported that Waldheim was "clean."[33] In the 1980s, when questions arose, Molden claimed "that it was clear to him and Gruber at the time that they were dealing with 'a man who is not a hero, not the type of guy who goes into the underground.'" He also admitted that he failed at the time to solicit much information from Waldheim himself. Furthermore, he did not investigate Waldheim's military record.[34] Consequently, Waldheim's secret remained safe. He was able to craft a narrative of limited service until he was wounded and released from military duties.

As a result of his "vetting" by Molden, Waldheim had the job and a fancy title—"Provisional Attaché in the chancellor's office, Department of Foreign Affairs." With his new position secured, Waldheim, confident that he was on his way to a lucrative diplomatic career, stopped working at the Baden court, effective 30 November, five days after the People's Party swept into power. At a young age—not quite twenty-seven—Waldheim had gotten his foot in the door and was on the path to his dream job, or at least he hoped that he was. He had a three-month probationary period in which to prove himself. He would draw on the lessons that he had learned at the Vienna Consular Academy. Waldheim presented himself with "the same modesty, enthusiasm, and dedication that had so impressed his superiors in the Wehrmacht," and Gruber was suitably impressed.[35]

Waldheim—by demonstrating his competence and efficiency—worked his way up the diplomatic ladder. In 1948 he became "First Secretary of the Legation in Paris," a position that he held until 1951, when he returned to Vienna to assume a new position as "head of the personnel department of the Ministry for Foreign Affairs." After four years Waldheim received his next assignment, which seemed to suggest that he had "arrived." In 1955 he traveled to New York to assume the duties of "Permanent Observer for Austria to the United Nations." Later that year, when Austria became a member of the UN, the head of the new, official "Austrian mission" was Waldheim, who was now positioned to put his diplomatic skills into action.[36]

Waldheim did not let the grass grow under his feet. Like Gruber, who by this time was the Austrian ambassador to the United States, his superiors were pleased with the ways in which he represented Austria's interests. The reward was a new posting to Canada in 1956. Although initially he was "Minister Plenipotentiary," before he left Canada four years later he was the Austrian ambassador. Waldheim returned to Vienna and had responsibility for the "Political Department (West)" at the Ministry for Foreign Affairs until 1962, when he was transferred to a new position—"Director-General for Political Affairs"—before returning to the United Nations in June 1964 to assume the role as Austria's "Permanent Representative." For the next four years he chaired the Committee on the Peaceful Uses of

Outer Space. Waldheim, who served as committee chair with distinction, was rewarded in 1968, when the UN called the first United Nations Conference on the Exploration and Peaceful Uses of Outer Space and elected him as the conference president.[37]

Although he ran the UN conference, Waldheim returned to Austria, where he served as "Federal Minister for Foreign Affairs" from January 1968 to April 1970. After a unanimous vote elected him "Chairman of the Safeguards Committee of the International Atomic Energy Agency (IAEA)," Waldheim officially returned to the United Nations, where he resumed his previous position—"Austrian Permanent Representative to the United Nations"—in October 1970. In less than a year, however, he decided to go in a different direction, although he was able to do so without resigning his position at the UN. He ran for president of Austria but was defeated in the April 1971 election. Luckily, the defeated candidate was able to return to the UN, where an unexpected door opened.

On 21 December 1971—on his fifty-third birthday—the United Nations Security Council put Waldheim's name forward for consideration as the next secretary-general. On 22 December "the General Assembly approved it by acclamation."[38] On 1 January 1972 Waldheim officially became UN secretary-general, which was a five-year appointment. He was reelected in 1977 and served a second five-year term as secretary-general. Although there were suggestions in the 1980s that the Soviets had exerted undo influence over him when it came to important appointments, Waldheim had been an active secretary-general who was involved in numerous causes that were important to the UN membership.

Being engaged in these causes spurred Waldheim to travel to the various "hot spots" on the UN radar, particularly during his first term. In March 1972, after receiving a Security Council mandate to determine the best way to resolve problems that existed in Namibia, Waldheim proceeded to South Africa and visited the country, which was plagued by a migrant workers' strike and involved in an independence war that had already been waging for six years and would continue for another sixteen. The crisis over Cyprus resulted in three visits by Waldheim to the island. He purpose was two-fold: facilitate leadership talks and "inspect" the UN's "Peace-keeping Force" based on Cyprus. His final visit, in August 1974, occurred approximately a month after a coup and an invasion by Turkish forces. Waldheim successfully orchestrated the commencement of negotiations between Glafcos Clerides, a Greek Cypriot politician and "Acting President" of Cyprus; and Rauf Denktash, a Turkish Cypriot politician and first president of Northern Cyprus.[39]

Waldheim was very much involved with trying to bring peace to the Middle East. The result was multiple trips and meetings over a sixteen-month period beginning in August 1973, when he sat down with government officials in "Syria, Lebanon, Israel, Egypt, and Jordan." Ten months later he returned to those countries for additional discussions. His personal efforts to broker a peace in the Middle East culminated with a final round of talks in "Syria, Israel, and Egypt in connection with the extension of the mandate of United Nations Disengagement Observer Force (UNDOF)" in November 1974. In each case Waldheim combined diplomatic conversations with inspections of UN peace-keeping operations, including "the United Nations Truce Supervision Organization (UNTSO), the United Nations Emergency Force (UNEF), and UNDOF." Undeterred by the varying degrees of success—or failure—of these missions, he continued to travel the globe, meeting with governmental leaders, participating in international conferences, and attending Security Council meetings held abroad.[40]

Waldheim served two terms as UN secretary-general—from 1 January 1972 until 31 December 1981. He did not run for a third term. Although there are no limits on the number of terms a secretary-general serves, there has never been a case when one has received appointment for more than two consecutive terms.[41] Once his tenure was over, it was time for Waldheim to return to Austria. After the excitement of the life that he had led for a decade, it could not have been easy to adapt to a quiet life of retirement. By the mid-1980s Waldheim would make a decision that would result in controversy, a resurgence in antisemitism in Austria, a scrutiny of global proportions, and a very public, verbal "trial" that pitted friend against friend, organization against organization, professional against professional, nation against nation and that would have unexpected—and to some extent unacceptable—consequences for Waldheim and for the Austrian people. Waldheim decided to make a second run for president.

Floodgates Opened: A New Narrative Emerged

Although rumors about his military activities had circulated behind the scenes for years, particularly when he was secretary-general, Waldheim's decision for a presidential bid opened the floodgates. Various groups—including the World Jewish Congress, the OSI, and news organizations—initiated investigations into his wartime past. The man who basically got the ball rolling was Eli Rosenbaum, a former OSI attorney. While working as WJC's general counsel in January 1986, Rosenbaum received "a tip that Waldheim had served as a senior intelligence officer with the German army in the Balkans from 1942 to 1945."[42] Rosenbaum was curious because the "tip" contradicted Waldheim's narrative that had been part of the public discourse since his UN days. Waldheim reiterated his account in his autobiography, which had been released after he left the UN. According to the narrative, after he had been wounded in December 1941, he had been released from military duties, and he returned to the University of Vienna, where he completed his law degree. Rosenbaum wondered what Waldheim had to hide and decided to dig deeper.

During the course of his investigation, which lasted for over a year, Rosenbaum located German documents that contradicted Waldheim's version of events. The documentary evidence placed Waldheim "in a unit that had taken civilian hostages, burned homes, and shot male prisoners." In an effort to expose Waldheim's past, the WJC provided the *New York Times* with "its preliminary findings." The newspaper conducted its own research to corroborate the WJC story and published an article in which it claimed that "Waldheim had served with a German Army command that fought 'brutal campaigns against Yugoslav partisans and engaged in mass deportations of Greek Jews.'" Furthermore, according to the article, Waldheim's commanding officer—Löhr—"had been executed for war crimes."[43]

As a result of the article, Waldheim was forced to admit that he had served in the Balkans during the period in question, but he issued the first of many denials of culpability: "He denied knowing about, or being involved in, any atrocities or persecution."[44] He also suggested that his political opponents were trying to undermine his presidential bid, and he accused the WJC of interfering in an Austrian political election. As Rosenbaum described in his coauthored book, *Betrayal: The Untold Story of the Kurt Waldheim Investigation and Cover-Up*, the WJC's release of "its preliminary findings" and the documentary evidence that it continued to uncover provided a target for Waldheim and his supporters, including Simon Wiesenthal—the Nazi hunter. Not only did they accuse the WJC of fabricating lies about Waldheim and of trying to change the course of the presidential election, but they also blamed the organization for a resurgence of antisemitic rhetoric and violence. Before the election was over, however, the Waldheim campaign actually adopted both Nazi and antisemitic rhetoric to promote the candidate. Waldheim opponents frequently found themselves the brunt of physical and verbal harassment, particularly when they tried to protest the Austrian at his rallies.

The *New York Times* article, however, would also have ramifications outside of Austria. The U.S. attorney general, Edwin Meese, received requests to prevent Waldheim from traveling to the United States by placing him on the "Watchlist." The requests came from the WJC and Elizabeth Holtzman, who by this time was a "former Congresswoman." Meese tasked OSI with looking into the matter. Even before completing an investigation, however, OSI supported the requests from WJC and Holtzman. On 7 April 1986 OSI director Neal Sher justified his recommendation:

> As a counterintelligence officer in a unit which—according to orders of its commander—was engaged in activities which included reprisals against civilians, the taking of hostages, the burning of homes and destruction of villages, and the shooting of male prisoners, Waldheim must be considered implicated in activities which fit squarely with[in the Holtzman Amendment]. This conclusion is strengthened by the fact that among his responsibilities were prisoner interrogations (and we know from the military order that prisoners were treated very harshly) and "special tasks." . . . If such a person was a United States citizen (who had concealed his war-

time service in the Balkans, as Waldheim has done for decades) he would be an OSI subject and a prime candidate for denaturalization proceedings.[45]

Although he suggested that Meese delay a decision until initiating another request to the UN for its war crimes files, Deputy Assistant Attorney General Mark M. Richard supported Sher's recommendation.

Despite Sher's and Richard's positions, the Waldheim case was not necessarily a cut-and-dried one, and Meese took his time in making a decision. His decision was complicated by the opinion offered by Assistant Attorney General Stephen S. Trott after he met with Waldheim's son, Gerhard, who provided a written letter from his father, in which he refuted the allegations. The AAG stated,

> I am not persuaded that we ought to take any action at this juncture other than to continue privately to review with great care the evidence on the subject. I remain very skeptical based on the timing of these charges, the fact that Kurt Waldheim has been a world-renown person for years without any of this coming to the fore, Waldheim's assertions that he can refute or explain everything, and Waldheim's support by no lesser an authority than Simon Wiesenthal.
>
> So, let's get the United Nations (UN) file and continue to study the evidence, and let's do it *without any* public comment whatsoever. . . . We have a special obligation under these unusual circumstances not only to enforce our own laws but also to not allow ourselves to be used as a wedge in the Austrian electoral process. It also goes without saying that we do not want to slander any person before we get all the facts and determine what they mean.[46]

When the UN files arrived, investigators received a shock. "Waldheim's name was on a UN War Crimes Commission list of persons who 'should be delivered up for trial.'"[47] This was not what Department of Justice (DOJ) investigators expected, but it affirmed the need to carry on with the investigation into Waldheim's wartime military record, especially in light of another bombshell dropped by the WJC weeks earlier. According to a WJC statement released at a press conference in New York on 22 March, the Central Registry of War Criminals and Security Suspects of 1948 listed Kurt Waldheim "as being sought by Yugoslavia for 'murder' and other crimes allegedly committed during the service in the Balkans."[48] Because of the seriousness of the information from the UN files and from documents provided by the WJC, Sher renewed his recommendation to the attorney general, but a leak complicated matters and caused strained relations between the United States and Austria.

Less than two weeks before the presidential election in Austria, a former DOJ official leaked Sher's memos to the attorney general in which he had recommended adding Waldheim's name to the Watch List—to the press. Not surprisingly, the media published the leaked information about the DOJ's internal investigation and the Watch List recommendation. In an official communication the Austrian ambassador to the United States informed Meese that the placement of Waldheim on a Watch List would constitute "interference in the current presidential campaign." Meese immediately tried to reassure the Austrian ambassador that DOJ "would act 'with due regard for the sensitivities of the Presidential campaign to avoid as much as possible any appearance of interference.'"[49] He did not, however, promise to drop it. Despite the attorney general's assurances, demonstrations protesting U.S. interference in the Austrian election broke out, and the Waldheim campaign used the incident to its best advantage. Whether or not the leak affected the outcome of the election, on 4 May Waldheim received 49.64 percent of the vote, which propelled him into the runoff election approximately a month later.[50]

Continuing his investigation into Waldheim's wartime military record, Rosenbaum regularly passed information to Sher, who was a friend from his OSI days. Meanwhile, Sher reiterated his recommendation about Waldheim and the Watch List in another internal memo to Meese. He also ordered an OSI inquiry into the allegations resulting from the UN file and those that continued to emerge from the WJC investigation. In addition to the information provided by the WJC, OSI obtained information from the Yugoslavian archives with regard to Waldheim's unit's involvement in "processing prisoners for deportations and executions." Besides reviewing the documents as they arrived, OSI was also inundated with explanations from Waldheim every time new facts became public. The drip, drip,

drip of information about Waldheim's wartime service did not generally come from OSI, but Waldheim was aware of the DOJ investigation. Waldheim's repeated explanations did not necessarily help his case: "OSI found his responses riddled with inconsistencies, distortions, and misleading statements. One could argue that Waldheim's statements were deliberately convoluted." Perhaps he was trying to deflect or discourage additional investigation of his military record. Unimpressed, "Trott thought Waldheim's submissions were starting 'to sound like the "I-just-worked-there-and-followed-orders" explanation.'"[51] Waldheim's statements had an unintended consequence. They raised questions that he did not want pursued—not just about his record but also about what he had been hiding for forty years.

Waldheim's attorneys issued a covert threat to the U.S. government. If the DOJ placed Waldheim on the Watch List, "the U.S. Government would seriously undermine larger U.S. interests in which Austria is a factor." They also suggested that a "Watchlist" designation would negatively affect Waldheim's ability to lead Austria as president. His attorneys had a point, because in the midst of the controversy surrounding Waldheim, the runoff election took place. On 8 June, in a close election, Waldheim edged out his opponent with approximately three hundred thousand more votes (53.89 percent) and became the president of Austria.[52] Waldheim's election and his attorneys' implied threats did not derail the OSI investigation, which continued until the next spring.

On 9 April 1987 OSI submitted its report on Kurt Waldheim to Attorney General Meese. Four OSI names graced the cover of the report, "In the Matter of Kurt Waldheim": Director Neal M. Sher, Deputy Director Michael Wolf, Historian Patrick J. Treanor, and Supervisory Historian Peter R. Black. In the most important section of the two-hundred-plus-page report, OSI itemized the "Chronology of Mr. Waldheim's Military Service." This chronology refuted Waldheim's claims that he had been discharged from military service after he was wounded during the fighting around Moscow in December 1941 and that he "did not know about, nor was he involved in, any atrocities or persecution." Although the chronology commenced with the summer of 1936, when "Waldheim entered the Austrian Army as a volunteer and served as a reserve officer cadet in a cavalry unit until August 31, 1937," for the purposes of refuting Waldheim's narrative of his military service, this story begins in December 1941.[53]

According to OSI, Waldheim was engaged in fighting near Orel, Russia, in December 1941, when he received a leg wound, which earned him the "Wounded Badge in Black." After recuperating in Austria—generally in Baden—for four months, Waldheim "was declared fit for service on March 6, 1942. His convalescent leave ended on April 7, 1942."[54] While he was still recuperating, he received notification of his next assignment: the Twelfth Army, which was based in the Balkans. By this time, at the age of twenty-three, he was a Wehrmacht officer in the German army, and after four years in the military he had participated in two major campaigns and "had been promoted, decorated, and wounded." He was an "experienced junior officer." According to the OSI report, while in the Balkans, "Lieutenant Waldheim was assigned to various staffs, usually as a special missions staff officer (*Ordonnanzoffizer*) and sometimes as an interpreter (*Dolmetscher*). In the German Army, special missions staff officers were essentially aides-de-camp or adjutants. That is, they were usually junior officers who were attached to the senior staff officers."[55] Furthermore, "special missions staff officers had permanently assigned duties within the appropriate staff departments. . . . Special missions staff officers thus occupied responsible and very sensitive positions on the staff, one step below general staff officers."[56]

Waldheim also performed the duties of an interpreter. According to the OSI report, an interpreter did more than translate and liaise: "One of the primary functions of interpreters in the German Army was the interrogation of prisoners and the evaluation of captured documents." The designation "interpreter," therefore, was a misnomer. Interpreters functioned as intelligence officers and were "assigned to the Intelligence Branch of the staff, where they might have performed other duties as well."[57]

Beginning on 22 March 1942 "Waldheim was assigned to Battle Group Bader, a unit of the Twelfth Army, and attached to the Italian Fifth Mountain (Pusteria) Division as an interpreter in a liaison detachment."[58] His new unit's mission was the elimination of "guerrilla activity in eastern Bosnia." To that end, the commander issued the following order: "The more unequivocal and harsh the reprisal measures are from the beginning, the less necessary they will be later. No sentimentalism! It is better if 50 suspected persons are liquidated than if one German soldier goes to ruin."[59] Consequently, the elimination of guerrilla activity involved "the routine shooting or hanging of captured insurgents and any persons who were either found in their company or had supported them in any manner whatsoever." Interrogation to obtain intelligence only delayed execution.[60] The Twelfth Army commander also authorized reprisals against civilians when "insurgents" could not be located, and he specified the numbers who should be punished. He encouraged "the shooting of male inhabitants of villages located in areas of guerrilla activity at the ratio of 100 civilians for every German soldier killed and 50 civilians for every German soldier wounded."[61] In July 1942 Gen. Alexander Löhr replaced the acting Twelfth Army commander, Lt. Gen. Walter Kuntze. After the war Löhr was tried for war crimes in Yugoslavia, convicted, and executed on 26 February 1947. Although Löhr was held accountable for committing war crimes, Waldheim could not be deemed equally guilty just because he served under the general; however, Waldheim did, on occasion, report directly to Löhr. By November 1943 Waldheim "enjoyed an increasingly personal relationship" with Löhr. "Löhr enjoyed discussing intellectual matters with the young Austrian doctoral candidate on his intelligence staff, and he occasionally took Waldheim along on plane trips to the Greek islands"[62]

When Waldheim joined Battle Group Bader in March 1942, it included several different ethnic units: German, Italian, and Croatian. Waldheim's assignment was to the German Liaison Detachment Five of the Italian Fifth Mountain (Pusteria) Division, and he reported in early April 1942 after his convalescence had ended. When Waldheim arrived, Battle Group Bader was engaged in fulfilling its mission—targeting and eliminating partisan activity in the region—although with limited success due to unenthusiastic support from the Italians. Although the Germans—and later Waldheim—suggested that only armed partisans fell victim to the area "cleansing" operations, the documents reputed that contention. By 15 May 1942 a total of "154 people had been killed (including 10 shot for possession of weapons) and 1,610 had been captured (of whom 10 were shot and 5 hanged)"; however, very few weapons were recovered. The Italian Pusteria Division had captured 488 (presumably) civilians and transferred them to the SS and the Belgrade police chief. The majority were deported to Norway for slave labor. The rest were "used as forced laborers on road construction." Although he denied knowledge of the deportations, Waldheim later admitted that he was "the" liaison officer in German Liaison Detachment Five. As the OSI report indicated, Waldheim's claim was unsustainable: "Waldheim, as the liaison officer, would have played a role in this transfer of approximately 500 persons to the SS for slave labor. Such an operation would have required communication and coordination between the Pusteria Division and German authorities, precisely the functions which liaison officers are assigned to perform."[63] The deportations indicated that eastern Bosnia was secured, which ended the battle group's usefulness.

By 28 May, however, with the disbanding of Battle Group Bader, Lieutenant Waldheim received a new assignment—in the operations staff of Battle Group Western Bosnia, which was also tasked with eliminating guerrilla activity. His base of operations was Banja Luka. His position as the quartermaster's deputy put Waldheim in the thick of things, particularly since this officer was responsible for more than supplies. As the "Second General Staff Officer," the quartermaster was tasked with "various matters including, inter alia, the processing of prisoners, rear area security and questions of executive authority and administration in operational areas." To carry out his numerous tasks, quartermaster utilized "supply troops and security forces such as the Field Gendarmerie." As "chief assistant," it would have been Waldheim's responsibility to see that the quartermaster's orders were executed.[64]

Two months later the operations staff, including Waldheim, relocated forty miles northwest to Kostajnica on the Una River. Two weeks later they were on the move again—this time northeast to Novska, twenty miles away. By the end of August Battle Group Western Bosnia no longer existed. Before it was disbanded, however, the battle group committed "acts of persecution against civilians during a most brutal campaign in the Kozara mountain region." Although he again contended that he was not involved in the committing of atrocities, one factor suggests otherwise: On 22 July 1942 "Waldheim was awarded a high Croatian military decoration, the Silver Medal of the Crown of King Zvonimir with Oak Leaves."[65]

After digging deeper into the events that had occurred in the Kozara Mountains and into Waldheim's award, the OSI succeeded in unearthing evidence that provided a clearer picture than had been previously available. On 5 July 1942 Battle Group Western Bosnia commenced an operation to destroy partisan forces based in the Kozara Mountains "north of Banja Luka." According to Kurt Neher, "an official German war correspondent on the scene," the Kozara operation was "a struggle against Partisans who were 'rotten sub-humans subjected to "final liquidation" without pity or mercy.'" By 18 July it was all over except the "mopping-up." A couple of weeks later an official report documented the outcome. The "battle group put enemy losses at 4,310 dead and 10,704 captured. The dead included an unknown number of persons previously apprehended (i.e., prisoners) as well as several hundred people shot in reprisal, while the prisoners included approximately 3,000 women and children." Additional "refugees" were transported to "Croatian concentration camps."[66]

The massacre in the Kozara Mountains is only part of the story. While Waldheim was assigned to Yugoslavia, the deportation of Jews also occurred. In fact, there was a Jewish community based in Banja Luka, where Waldheim was sent when he was first posted to Battle Group Western Bosnia. In early April 1942 Banja Luka police requested the deportation of the Jewish population to a camp "in the interest of public order and security." Following multiple requests "arrests and deportations" commenced in mid-June—after Waldheim's arrival. First, Jewish refugees were deported, but soon the local Jewish population was targeted as well. Bowing to pressure from the Germans, the Croatian II Home Defense Corps embraced the Nazi attitude toward Jews and other "undesirable" groups. According to the corps, "the Jews, like the Gypsies, 'should be 100% eliminated from public life,'" as subsequent action demonstrated. Beginning on 3 July Banja Luka's Jews had to wear "visible markings" identifying their ethnicity. Officials in Zagreb sent a thousand copies of the documents needed for the deportations on 23 July. The "roundup" of Banja Luka Jews occurred "on the night of July 27–28." Within a couple of days, 160 Jews—the entire Jewish population of Banja Luka—were on their way to Stara Gradiska concentration camp. While it was possible that German forces did not participate in the deportation of Banja Luka Jews, they did capture and transfer thirteen Jews to Croatian police a week later.

Although he denied knowledge of the deportations, Waldheim was physically present in Banja Luka at the time, and it would have been established protocol for the quartermaster to have facilitated the deportations. Although the OSI could not find specific evidence linking Waldheim to the Kozara campaign, the fact that he received one of the highest decorations awarded by the "Nazi Puppet State of Croatia"—"the Silver Medal of the Crown of King Zvonimir with Oak Leaves"—was significant.[67] The King Zvonimir medal was reserved for soldiers who demonstrated "valorous conduct in fights against rebels in Western Bosnia in spring and summer 1942." While German soldiers could receive this decoration, it was rare for them to receive one with "Oak Leaves." That honor was reserved for "distinguished service under enemy fire." Of the twenty thousand soldiers—both German and Croatian—involved in the massacre, only thirty-four received "special mention." Waldheim was number twenty-five on the list of those honored after this operation. Waldheim received the decoration shortly after the conclusion of the Kozara campaign, but before he participated in any other action.[68] His posting to Bosnia was not the end of Waldheim's wartime military career, nor was it the only part of his service that fueled the controversy in the 1980s.

As the campaign in Bosnia ended, Waldheim received orders to proceed to Arsakli, Greece, which was less than ten miles from Salonika. Between 19 November and 31 March 1943, he was on study leave back in Austria. On 1 December 1942 Waldheim received a promotion to first lieutenant. When his study leave ended, he did not return to Greece. His new orders sent Waldheim to Tirana, Albania, where he "was assigned to the German liaison staff attached to the Italian Ninth

Army," a position he held from April to July 1943, before returning to Greece. From 19 July to 4 October Waldheim "served as the First Special Missions Staff Officer ('o 1') in the Operations Branch of a new German staff in Athens" and "Third Special Missions Staff Officer ('o 3') in the Intelligence and Counterintelligence (IC/AO) Branch of the High Command Army Group E" from October to April 1945. He was granted study leave three times—23 November to 25 December 1943, 25 February to 16 April 1944, and 15 August to 4 September 1944. His leaves paid off: on 14 April 1944 he earned his law doctorate from the University of Vienna after submitting his dissertation.[69]

Although the earning of his law degree in the midst of a war was laudable because it illustrated Waldheim's focus on his postwar career plan, one final episode warrants mention—the Komeno Massacre, 16 August 1943. In some respects, the discovery of this event in relation to Waldheim was the final nail in the coffin of his postwar account that remained the accepted narrative for forty years. After his four month stint in Albania, Waldheim returned to Greece, where he was attached to the "planning office of the German general staff in Athens." Waldheim's duties included collecting troop reports, analyzing "their implications for the overall strategic situation," and including a summary of these reports in his daily brief to Army Group E Headquarters in Salonika. Waldheim generally sanitized the language for his briefs. For example, he substituted the word "victims" for "civilians" when referring to casualties within the local civilian population. He also used the term "bandits" when referencing "civilians shot by Wehrmacht troops."[70]

In August 1943 a Wehrmacht raid on the Greek village—Komeno—resulted in the execution of 317 villagers. The youngest victim was one-year-old Alexandra Kritsima; the oldest was Anastasia Kosta, aged seventy-five. Among the victims seventy-four were children under the age of ten. At least twenty families were completely wiped out. According to historian Mark Mazower, the raid was conducted by "highly trained regular soldiers from one of the elite divisions of the Wehrmacht."[71]

Why did the Wehrmacht carry out this raid, and where did Waldheim fit in? The villagers had managed to live peacefully next to their

Italian occupiers for two years, but that changed when members of the Greek resistance—*andartes*—moved into the area to gain access to locally produced food. The Italian commandant in Arta initially ignored the situation, and the villagers could not prevent the andartes from entering the village. On 12 August 1943, when a group of armed andartes entered Komeno to "collect" food, however, they were spotted by a "two-man Wehrmacht reconnaissance team," who did not have the same lackadaisical response that the Italians had. When the Germans quickly retreated from the village, the inhabitants suspected that was not the end of things. They were particularly concerned because Germans had never entered their village before. A village delegation traveled to Arta and met with the Italian commandant. The villagers were worried because they normally put on a celebration for the Feast of the Assumption—15 August. The Italian commander's assurances allowed the villagers to continue their preparations and to celebrate the feast day as they usually did.[72]

Meanwhile, the German reconnaissance unit returned to its home base—First Mountain Division Headquarters, Jannina—and notified their superiors of the presence of andartes in Komeno. The German commander, who needed a successful operation against the andartes, tasked the Ninety-Eighth Regiment with carrying out a raid against Komeno. The regiment was in position on the night of 15 August. D-day was 16 August. Around dawn on the sixteenth, German vehicles and "about one hundred men from 12 Company," entered the village.[73] Lieutenant Röser, the company commander, gave his men clear orders: "They were to go into the village 'and leave nothing standing.'"[74] Röser's order suggested that all villagers either were andartes or they supported the resistance—both crimes punishable by death, according to the Germans. The attack on the village lasted for six hours, during which time German soldiers shot as many villagers as they could—including the priest who was shot by Röser—and set fire to the village. The inhabitants, even if they had weapons and were able to use them, did not fire on their attackers. By 1:00 p.m. the Germans left the burning village behind and returned to base. They took the village livestock with them.

The Ninety-Eighth Regiment submitted two accounts of the

operation—one a couple hours after vacating the village, the other in the evening. The first description is revealing:

> This morning during the encirclement of Komeno, which was carried out on three sides, 12 Co. came under heavy gunfire from all the houses. Thereupon fire was opened by the Co. with all weapons, the place was stormed and burned down. It appears that during this battle some of the bandits managed to escape to the south-east. 150 civilians are estimated to have died in this battle. The houses were stormed with hand-grenades and for the most part were set on fire as a result. All the cattle as well as wool were taken away as booty. Booty-report follows separately. In the burning of the houses large amounts of ammunition went up in smoke and hidden weapons are also likely to have burned with them.[75]

As was the case with similar reports, they were written in such a way to mask the actual events that had occurred. Even the later Ninety-Eighth Regiment report, however, acknowledged that the villagers were unable to put up any resistance. In addition to being caught off-guard when the dawn attack began, the villagers had only a total of six weapons on hand—"5 Italian carbines, 1 Italian machine pistol"—six weapons against a hundred armed soldiers. The report concluded, "Result of this action confirms once again the opinion and report of this Division that a strong guerrilla centre is located on the east bank of the Gulf of Arta, including strong, active bandit groups."[76] Although he did not physically participate in the raid, Waldheim reported its occurrence the next day "in his unit's War Diary: '17 August: Increasing enemy air raid activity against the Western Greek coast and Ionian islands. In the area of 1st Mountain Division, the town of Komeno (north of the Gulf of Arta) is taken against heavy enemy resistance. Enemy losses.'" He also included an account in his daily brief to Army Group E Headquarters: "'heavy enemy resistance against the *Säuberungsunternehmen*' and . . . 'enemy losses' . . . totalled 150." Like the troops in the field, Waldheim used language to disguise what had actually occurred.[77] He conveniently "forgot" about this event when describing his wartime experiences.

The rest of Waldheim's service during the war did not raise any flags for the OSI investigators. According to the German wartime record, Waldheim served with distinction. His medals provide a testament to that fact: on 1 January 1944 he received "the War Merit Cross Second Class with Swords" and on 20 April 1945, "the War Merit Cross First Class with Swords." In late April 1945 Waldheim received orders transferring him from the Army Group E staff in Zagreb to an "infantry division" near Trieste. According to Waldheim, "conditions prevented him from reaching this unit," and when Admiral Dönitz tendered Germany's surrender, he was in southern Austria around Villach. As noted earlier, on 9 May Waldheim received his formal discharge from the German Wehrmacht.[78] To Waldheim's dismay—and Wiesenthal's—the OSI chronology of his wartime military record was vastly different from the one that Waldheim had presented to the world for forty years and damning to the reputation that he had so carefully built during that time.

Results of WJC and OSI Investigations

During the period in which Waldheim was under investigation by the WJC and the OSI, January 1986 through April 1987, Simon Wiesenthal remained a steadfast supporter of his fellow Austrian. On numerous occasions he issued public statements in which he criticized WJC officials, including Israel Singer, WJC secretary-general; Elan Steinberg, the executive director; and Eli Rosenbaum, the general counsel. In addition to accusing them of attempting to interfere in the Austrian presidential election, Wiesenthal questioned their integrity. He, in effect, accused them of conducting an unsubstantiated witch hunt. Furthermore, Wiesenthal failed to acknowledge the validity of the documentary evidence unearthed by both the WJC and the OSI. In fact, although he declined an invitation to review the WJC's evidence, he publicly accused the organization of not letting him review the documents that they had acquired. According to Rosenbaum, Wiesenthal's support of Waldheim had begun at least as early as 1971—when Waldheim ran for president the first time.[79] Despite the evidence unearthed by the WJC and the OSI that painted an entirely different picture of Waldheim, he remained steadfast in his support. Wiesenthal also found fault with the OSI investigation, which he claimed was evidence of the U.S. government's efforts, like those of the wjc's, to influence the outcome of the 1986 Austrian presidential election. The more evidence that emerged about Waldheim's military record, however, the less credibility Wiesenthal had, although few of his critics wanted to take him on publicly. It is highly possible that the Waldheim case destroyed Wiesenthal's reputation, which had been built on a shaky foundation. Apparently, not all of his Nazi-hunting activities had been above reproach. Some of his unsubstantiated claims had been proven to be false. Wiesenthal's attacks on the wjc did not, however, deter Rosenbaum or his bosses. They continued to search for the truth—even after Waldheim was officially persona non grata outside of Austria.[80]

Like the wjc, the osi did not abandon the investigation into Waldheim's wartime service. The evidence compiled by both the wjc and the osi proved that Waldheim had been responsible for "identifying areas of suspected resistance activity."[81] Within days of his identification, cleaning operations occurred. It was just a matter of connecting the dots. When it was released, the April 1987 osi report destroyed Waldheim's version of events. It provided a detailed description of his service record from 1942 until 1945. In analyzing the evidence, osi

concluded that Waldheim—who was awarded a prestigious medal by the Nazi puppet regime in Croatia—had been involved in the transfer of civilian prisoners to the ss for exploitation as slave labor, the mass deportation of civilians to concentration and death camps, the use of anti-Semitic propaganda, the turning over of Allied prisoners to the ss, and reprisal executions of hostages and other civilians. Moreover, as the officer responsible for assessing prisoner of war interrogation reports at the headquarters of his Army Group, Waldheim played a key role in determining the fate of individual prisoners. His wartime record thus established that he had "assisted or otherwise participated in persecution because of race, religion, national origin or political opinion."[82]

When submitting the report "In the Matter of Kurt Waldheim"—to Attorney General Meese, the osi reiterated its earlier recommendation "that he be placed on the Watchlist."[83] After reviewing the osi report, Meese rendered a decision, which was announced by the doj and the Department of State on 27 April 1987. Kurt Waldheim's name was added to the Watch List. Consequently, Waldheim became the first sitting president to be denied entry to the United States—even on official state business. Furthermore, Waldheim found himself unwelcome in many other nations. Even though the British government did not put him on a similar watch list, Waldheim never received an invitation to visit Britain while he was president, which would have been a normal courtesy extended to a newly elected head of state.

The pressure that he faced convinced Waldheim not to run for reelection in 1992. His decision did not result in removal from the Watch List, even though numerous appeals were made by Waldheim and his supporters. In 1998 Waldheim failed to receive the visa that would have allowed him "to attend a UN celebration of its fiftieth anniversary of peacekeeping operations."[84] The Department of Justice stood behind its decision not to let the good work that Waldheim had done while he was secretary-general of the United Nations whitewash the acts that he had committed as a Wehrmacht lieutenant in the Balkans between 1942 and 1945.

6

Andrija Artuković—"Butcher of the Balkans"

Andrija Artuković, the "Butcher of the Balkans," was the highest-ranking Nazi collaborator ever found in the United States. A Croatian by birth, he worked in several different positions within the Ustasha government, including minister of the interior, as well as minister of justice and religion. In his capacity as a government official, Artuković instituted policies for the persecution of Serbs, Jews, Gypsies, Orthodox Christians, and communists. These policies permitted broad powers, including mandating internment of these "undesirables," empowering summary courts to impose death sentences, calling for the execution of communist hostages, confiscating Jewish businesses, and limiting state and academic employment to Aryans. Between 1941 and 1945 more than 250,000 people (primarily Serbs, with Jews as the second largest group) died in Croatia as a result of these policies. In 1948 Artuković obtained a ninety-day visitor's visa under a false name, traveled to the United States, and got a job in California. After he received two visa extensions, his real identity was discovered, and the government instituted deportation and extradition proceedings. Although efforts to extradite him began in 1951 and predated the establishment of the Office of Special Investigations (OSI), which eventually became involved in the case, they finally culminated in his expulsion in 1986. How did Artuković escape detection for three years? Why did it take three decades for the U.S. government to succeed in kicking him out of the country? How did he earn the title of Butcher of the Balkans? Who was Andrija Artuković? Did his crimes warrant deportation?

Andrija Artuković was born to Marijan and Ruža Artuković on 29 November 1899, in Croatia.[1] At that time Croatia was part of the Austro-Hungarian Empire. Devoted Catholics, the Artukovićs sent their son to the Franciscan monastery school in Široki Brijeg. At the end of World War I, with the dissolution of the Austro-Hungarian Empire, the victors cobbled together several Balkan states into one country—Yugoslavia. Over twenty ethnic groups found themselves part of a nation that had no real identity. Included in this were two traditional enemies: Serbians and Croatians. For the next decade, as the fledgling nation struggled to unify the different groups into a Yugoslav citizenry, not every Balkan state embraced its new home. Andrija Artuković came to maturity during this contentious period.

After graduation, Artuković earned a law degree at the University of Zagreb. From 1924 to 1926 he worked as a court clerk in Zagreb before opening his own law office in Gospić, a city about 130 miles from Zagreb. Located in the northwestern part of Croatia, Zagreb was the second largest city in Yugoslavia during this time.[2] As Yugoslavians tried to craft a Yugoslav identity, not all ethnic groups embraced unification, and some began to explore the possibility of separation from the larger state. As he lived and worked in Zagreb, Artuković crossed paths with a man who would have a big impact on his future— Ante Pavelić.

Pavelić was a lawyer and politician, a member of the Croatian Party of Rights, and a supporter of an independent Croatia. By the late 1920s he publicly advocated that Croats rebel against the Yugoslav state. He formed an alliance with an Italian protectorate that supported a separate Croatia. In January 1929, after King Alexander I banned political parties, Pavelić left his homeland and formed another alliance—this time with the Internal Macedonian Revolutionary Organization—in an effort to undermine the Yugoslav state. Although he was tried in absentia and sentenced to death, Pavelić continued his effort by moving to Italy and founding the Ustaše—the Croatian Revolutionary Organization—which was dedicated to the creation of an independent Croatian state. Fierce nationalists and primarily Catholics, the Ustaše also embraced Bosnian Muslims as their blood brothers. Artuković would soon abandon his law career and embrace a life of political activism. Like Pavelić, he would advocate for an independent Croatia.

In 1929 Andrija Artuković also traveled to Italy and joined the

Ustaše. As Pavelić's trusted adjutant and commander of the Italian Ustaše, Artuković prepared to hit the ground running. In September 1932 he briefly returned to Croatia, where he led a small uprising in Lika, called the Velebit uprising, after the mountains in which the small town is located. The small armed attack on a police station was a test to see if it would spark a general Croatian revolt against the Yugoslav state. After a thirty-minute firefight in which no police officers were killed and nine of the ten Ustaše participants escaped, Artuković successfully returned to Italy. Although the attack did not result in an uprising, the government's harsh treatment of Croatians in the region provided a propaganda weapon that the Ustaše wielded to their advantage when they advocated an independent Croatian state.

Heralded as a hero on his return to Italy, Artuković, the Ustaše intellectual, was ready for his next assignment.[3] Leaving Italy, he traveled to Budapest and then Vienna, where he was arrested, imprisoned, and expelled in 1934. In September 1934, after a meeting with Pavelić in Milan, he traveled to London, where he was arrested a month later. The catalyst for his arrest was King Alexander I's assassination on 4 October 1934. Because of his political activities, the authorities suspected that Artuković played a part in the assassination plot. After being transferred to a Paris prison, he was extradited in 1935 to Yugoslavia, where he spent sixteen months in prison before being acquitted of having a role in the king's death and released in April 1936. Following his release, Artuković returned briefly to Gospić before setting out once again to advocate for the Ustaše cause—first in Austria, then in Germany. Being an advocate for a nationalist group that did not hesitate to implement terrorist tactics brought him to the Gestapo's attention in 1937. Although he fled Berlin just prior to his arrest, Artuković did not let the Gestapo threat deter him. Following a circuitous route—France to Hungary and back to Germany again—he returned to his work in Berlin, where he apparently remained for the next few years.

Two events, however, occurred in April 1941 that propelled Artuković's return to his homeland and a career trajectory that ultimately resulted in his condemnation by the global community. On 6 April German troops invaded Yugoslavia. Four days later, with the German dismemberment of Yugoslavia, Slavko Kvaterkik, the most senior home-based Ustaše, proclaimed the establishment of the Independent State of Croatia. Artuković returned to Zagreb and quickly became a member of the Croatian State Leadership, the temporary government established by Kvaterkik. Prepared to assume the reins of power, Ante Pavelić also returned to Zagreb. At that point things moved quickly. On 16 April 1941 the Ustaše founder appointed Artuković the minister of interior in the new government, thus making him a member of Pavelić's inner circle and the enforcer of his orders. A short, stocky, accomplished orator, Artuković fulfilled multiple roles in the new Croatian government. He helped negotiate the Ciano-Pavelić agreement, which was the result of boundary negotiations between Italy and Croatia. In June 1941 he accompanied Pavelić to a meeting with Adolf Hitler.[4] It was not, however, Artuković's negotiating or oratory skills that shaped the public's later opinion of him. It was, rather, the Nazi policies that he helped to implement in Croatia.

Evidence suggests that from the beginning the Independent State of Croatia government was more than just sympathetic to the Nazi cause; it was pro-Nazi: "It was dedicated to a clerical-fascist ideology influenced both by Nazism and extreme Roman Catholic fanaticism. On coming to power, the Ustaše Party dictatorship in Croatia quickly commenced on a systematic policy of racial extermination of all Serbs, Jews and Gypsies living within its borders."[5] Artuković embraced the racist views as espoused by the Croatian government, the Ustaše Party, and the Nazi regime, as evidenced by a speech that he made to the Croatian State Assembly. During the speech, "he described Jews as having: 'prepared the world revolution, so that through it the Jews could have complete mastery over all the goods of the world and all the power in the world, the Jews whom the other people had to serve as a means of their filthy profits and of its greedy, materialistic and rapacious control of the world.'"[6]

After his meeting with Hitler, one of Pavelić's ministers, Mile Budak, announced the state's racial policy, but it wasn't the first such policy. The precedent had been set months earlier. On 17 April 1941 "the first Legal order for the defense of the people and the states" dictated the death penalty as punishment for "infringement on the honor and vital interests of the Croatian people and the survival of the Independent State of Croatia." On 30 April the government issued the "legal order of races" and the "legal order of the protection of Aryan blood and the honor of the Croatian people." On 4 June the government ordered the "creation and definition of the racial-political committee."[7] Apparently, Artuković signed these orders. It was part of his job to implement Pavelić's directive to "save Croatia for the Croatians."[8] This ultimately meant eliminating the Serbian and Jewish presence in Croatia. In addition, enforcement of these orders was legal both through the preexisting courts and through the "new out-of-order courts as well as mobile court-martials with extended jurisdictions."[9] Those who harbored Jews were subject to the death penalty as well.

Jews were not the only targets of these policies. The Serbian Orthodox Church was also affected by these racial laws, which became more and more violent in their implementation. By late 1941, for example, three Orthodox bishops and almost all of the Orthodox priests had lost their lives, although not as a result of the legal implementation of these laws. They were violently murdered. By the end of the war the Ustaše had destroyed 450 Orthodox churches and forced the conversion of many Serbs to Catholicism.[10]

Artuković did not oppose these policies. In fact, he embraced them and supported their implementation and, as a result, was rewarded. By October 1941 Artuković could put another title after his name— minister of justice and religion. Two years later he was named secretary of state, a position he held from October 1943 until the war's end in May 1945.[11]

Expediency dictated the adoption of another Nazi policy—the establishment of concentration camps. Approximately twenty camps were situated in Croatia. Estimates of the number of deaths that occurred at these camps varies depending on the source. According to the OSI, "approximately 25,000 Jews, 250,000 Serbs, and numerous Gypsies, Orthodox Christians and Communists perished in the Independent State of Croatia between April 1941 and May 1945."[12] Other sources suggest that 30,000 Jews and 750,000 Orthodox Christians perished, while another 240,000 Orthodox Christians were forcibly converted to Catholicism.[13]

After the war the government accused Artuković, who was responsible for overseeing the concentration camps in Croatia, of being personally responsible for at least 700,000 deaths, which is almost the number who perished in one camp alone—Jasenovac. This is perhaps what earned him the name Butcher of the Balkans.[14] The Independent State of Croatia (Nezavisna Država Hrvatska) established a total of twenty-two concentration camps. Jasenovac was in existence from August 1941 until April 1945. Established and maintained by Department III of the Croatian Security Police (Ustashka Nadzorna Sluzba), Jasenovac, which fell under the command of head of the security police, Vjekoslav Maks Luburic, "became the largest and most important concentration camp and extermination camp complex" and was "crucial in the systematic and planned genocide of the Orthodox Serbs of the Srpska Vojna Krajina and of Bosnia-Hercegovinia by the Croats and Bosnian Muslims. . . . Jasenovac was in fact a system or complex of concentration and extermination camps occupying a surface of 130 square miles, set up under decree-law, No. 1528-2101-Z-1941, on September 25, 1941, legally authorizing the creation of 'assembly or work camps for undesirable and dangerous persons.'" The "undesirable and dangerous persons" arrested and sent to Jasenovac included "Jews, Bosniaks, Gypsies, and opponents of the Ustaša regime." Prior to August 1942 the majority of Jews who lost their lives were exterminated at Jasenovac. That changed after the Wannsee Conference on 20 January 1942, with the formulation of the "Final Solution to the Jewish Problem" and a German proposal. For a fee of thirty reichsmarks per person, the Germans would transport Jews, arrested by the Independent State of Croatia, to concentration camps in the east, particularly to Auschwitz. Any confiscated Jewish property would be retained by Croatia. This agreement indicated the level of cooperation that existed between the Nazis and the Independent State of Croatia.[15]

As a top government official, how could Artuković have been held personally responsible for a government policy that resulted in thousands of deaths? In 1984 his Ustaše motorcycle escort—Bajro Avdic—testified against him in a sworn affidavit. According to his statement, Avdic "had heard Artukovic order thousands of deaths, including:

(1) the machine-gun firing of approximately 450 men, women, and children for whom there was no room in a concentration camp; (2) the killing of all the inhabitants of a town and its surrounding villages; (3) the murder of approximately 5,000 persons near a monastery; and (4) the machine gun execution of several hundred prisoners who were then crushed by moving tanks."[16]

It is hard to imagine that Artuković's role in these atrocities, particularly since he was a high government official, escaped unnoticed. This begs the question: how was he able to enter the United States and live in obscurity for several years? Two days before the war in Europe ended, Artuković, seeing the handwriting on the wall, left Zagreb and traveled to Austria, where he was briefly detained by the Allies at Spittal an der Drau camp in the British zone. Although the British extradited some Croatian government officials, including the prime minister, Artuković slipped under the radar and obtained release with several other ministers. He quickly left the British zone and traveled to meet his family in the American zone. Around the time when his career as a public official in Croatia was cemented, Artuković had married Ana Maria Heidler. By the end of the war, the couple had two children.

Reunited, the family proceeded to Switzerland. With the help of some dubious church officials, he obtained a Swiss passport under a different name—Alois Anich—and traveled to Ireland. According to Artuković, "I stayed in Switzerland until July 1947. Then with the knowledge of the Swiss Ministry of Justice I obtained personal documents for myself and my family, which enabled us to travel to Ireland. Using the name of Anitch [*sic*], we stayed there until 15 July 1948. When our Swiss documents expired, the Irish issued new papers and under Irish papers we obtained a visa for entry into New York."[17] Artuković and his family traveled to Ireland at a time when Franciscan religious leaders were negotiating with the Irish government in an effort to get the country to accept a small number of Croatian refugees. Furthermore, the road to the United States was not necessarily as easy as Artuković suggested, or was it?

Artuković was not the only one with a dubious wartime record who sought help from Catholic Church officials to escape prosecution. Furthermore, since the end of the war, allegations asserting the participation of some religious orders—in particular the Franciscan order—in wartime atrocities had surfaced. Evidence seems to suggest, however, that Ireland knew little about possible connections between the Catholic Church and collaboration with the Nazis. In early 1946 some religious began to explore the possibility of Ireland as a safe haven for those fleeing persecution or prosecution. Father Charles Balić put out feelers on behalf of the College of St. Jerome—the Franciscan House in Rome—to ascertain if Ireland would be willing to accept some Croatian students. According to Balić, these students, who were at that time based in Italy and Austria, had fled communist Yugoslavia. Joseph Walshe, Ireland's Department of External Affairs secretary, suggested that his country might be open to receiving these students if they obtained the appropriate travel documents. For various reasons, however, including opposition from some Irish officials, the possibility of Ireland admitting Croat student refugees seemed to be a nonstarter; therefore, for a time Ireland did not seem to be an option for Artuković, who certainly was not a student.

As one door closed, another appeared to open. In 1946, after publicly condemning the Yugoslav government, Aloysius Stepinac—cardinal archbishop of Zagreb—faced trial for wartime collaboration with the Independent State of Croatia. To the Irish, his conviction signaled Catholic persecution by communist Yugoslavia. In response to Stepinac's conviction, Irish officials intimated a vague desire to help persecuted Catholic Croats. The door to freedom opened a little wider for Artuković, although he used circuitous means to go through it.

In March 1947 Frank Cremins, Irish minister to Berne, received visa applications from a Franciscan priest and his professor uncle—Rev. Father Louis Ivandić OFM and Alois Anich (Andrija Artuković). The two men indicated a desire to spend a year in Ireland to pursue "philological and historical studies and to learn English." The delegate general of the Franciscans of Switzerland, who facilitated the visa requests, also indicated Anich's desire for his family to follow him to Ireland to escape "Yugoslav persecution." To sweeten the request, the delegate general noted that his order in Dublin would look after the Anich family, who had sufficient personal financial resources for the trip. Both Ivandić and Anich (Artuković) received Swiss identity documents and the requested visas.[18]

On 15 July 1947 Artuković, traveling under the name Alois Anich, arrived in Dublin with his family—his wife, Ana Maria, and their daughters, Katherina and Anna—and Father Ivandić. Upon their arrival, when questioned by immigration officials, Artuković made two statements that eased the family's entry into Ireland. First, Anich's brother, who lived in Los Angeles, would provide financial support for the family while they were in Ireland. Second, after a year in Ireland the family would relocate permanently to South America. By the time the year in Ireland was up, however, the family's ultimate destination would change, although it was, perhaps, their real plan from the beginning. One thing was certain, however—the Artuković family would not return to Switzerland, where Swiss authorities instituted an entry ban on Artuković two days after the family's departure.

For the next year the Artukovićs lived quietly in Dublin. In addition to teaching history periodically, Artuković attended daily Mass at the Church of the Three Patrons. The family welcomed a new addition when Radoslav was born. In June 1948 the Irish Department of Justice issued Alois Anich and his wife identity documents, at which time the couple relinquished their Swiss identity papers. The new documents allowed them to return to Ireland without a visa for a year. With the new documents in hand, Artuković submitted an application for a "non-immigrant" U.S. visa and swore under oath before the American vice-consul that his name was Alois Anich. On his application he listed his occupation as professor and the purpose of the trip as a "six-month holiday." Ironically, when he applied for the identity documents from Irish authorities, Artuković indicated that he was moving to the United States permanently. This was not the first time that Artuković was less than honest—and it would not be the last time either. Visas in hand, the Artukovićs left Dublin and arrived in New York on 16 July 1948—a year and a day after their plane had touched down in the Irish capital. Instead of passports, they carried temporary visas and Irish identity papers.[19]

The family did not stay in New York. Artuković's brother John, who lived in California, owned a construction company. The family joined him, and Artuković, or Anich, went to work for John as his bookkeeper. According to the OSI, Artuković was in the United States on a "90-day visitor's visa." He applied for and received a visa extension twice but was unlikely to receive a third extension. The expiration date on the second visa extension was April 1949. Desperate to remain in the United States, Artuković had John approach his local representative for help. Unfortunately, this created multiple problems for him. Following established protocols, "his Congressman introduced a private bill to retroactively bestow lawful admission on Artuković and his family." The bill went nowhere because of opposition from the chair of the House Subcommittee on Immigration, who killed it. Although the bill died, Congress followed the routine procedure of sending it to the Immigration and Naturalization Service for review. Consequently, the bill initiated an INS investigation of Artuković, because it identified him by his real name—not as Alois Anich. The INS very quickly discovered two troubling facts. First, because he had been admitted under a false name, Artuković had entered the United States unlawfully. Second, he was wanted in Yugoslavia, where the government wanted to try him for war crimes. Because of his efforts to remain in the United States, the Butcher of the Balkans had inadvertently outed himself.[20] In the meantime, as INS debated what to do about Artuković, he remained in the United States.

The government had two options to eject Artuković—deportation or extradition—and pursued them both. Thus began the decades' long effort of the Department of Justice to return Andrija Artuković to his homeland to face the music and answer for his role in the extermination of Serbs, Jews, and other groups. The government took the case to court and filed both proceedings in 1951. While he did not challenge deportation on the grounds that he had entered the country under a false name and that he had stayed under an expired visa, Artuković petitioned to be granted refuge under a provision that would suspend deportation under specific circumstances—that he was of "good moral character" and that deportation would have severe economic consequences.[21] The wrinkle was that his fourth child, born in the United States, was a U.S. citizen. Artuković's argument was that his deportation would create undue economic hardship for his infant daughter.

Ignoring the economic issue, the INS argued that Artuković's lack of "good moral character" made him ineligible for an exemption to the rules. Providing evidence of his record as a cabinet minister who had been responsible for the execution of Serbs and Jews, among others, the INS convinced an immigration judge, who ruled against Artuković. The judge's ruling stood up under appeal. In crafting his opinion, the judge wrote,

> There appears to be little doubt (1) that the new Croatian state, at least on paper, pursued a genocidal policy in Croatia with regard to Jews and Serbs; (2) that Artukovic helped execute this policy in that, as Minister of Interior, he had authority and control over the entire system of Public Security and Internal Administration; and (3) that during this time there were massacres of Serbs and, perhaps to a lesser extent, of other minority groups within Croatia. . . . It is difficult for us to think of one man, other than [the Croatian president] who could have been more responsible for the events occurring in Croatia during this period than was [Artukovic].[22]

Deportation now seemed a real possibility. Scrambling, Artuković tried a new tactic. Acknowledging that as cabinet minister, he authorized the persecution of communists, he argued that he would, consequently, be subject to similar persecution if he were deported to Yugoslavia; therefore, Artuković requested a deportation stay. Because the extradition case against the Croat had not yet been resolved, the judge postponed a ruling on the deportation stay request until the other case had been resolved. By postponing a decision, the judge had given Artuković a reprieve, albeit a brief one.

Filed on 29 August 1951, the Extradition Complaint was based on the allegation that Artuković had "murdered, or caused to be murdered, 22 persons, including the Archbishop of Sarajevo." A warrant was issued, and Artuković was arrested. He was denied bail at a 10 September hearing. His extradition hearing was placed on the docket for 22 October. Throughout the month of September, various petitions were filed in the court. Although bond had initially been denied, which was normal, it was set at $50,000 on the nineteenth for two reasons. The judge believed that, because of his ties to the community, Artuković would not flee. In addition, he was dubious about the case's merits. The judge said,

> I am impressed by the date of the offenses, 1941; and the fact that Yugoslavia was invaded by Germany on April 6, 1941, and thereafter occupied by Germany until 1945 and that the whole world and especially that portion of the world, was in a terrible turmoil. . . . I cannot help but think that it might be possible, if extradition treaties with various countries were carried out to the letter in connection with charges that might be made, they might demand the extradition of every person who was a member of any armed forces against them and charge them with having committed murder, because surely people who are members of armed forces do kill other people, and they kill them just as dead as they would if they privately did it and with as much intention.

Artuković posted bail and was released the next day, 20 September. A week before the extradition hearing, the complaint was amended.[23]

Over the course of these proceedings, Artuković acquired numerous influential advocates who championed his cause. The day of his extradition hearing finally arrived, and Artuković was able to argue his case against being extradited. His case rested on two contentions. His first argument revolved around the nature of the 1902 U.S. extradition treaty with Serbia. It was his argument that the treaty was no longer valid. Serbia no longer existed as an independent country. How could the United States have a legitimate treaty with a state within a country? In 1951 the United States did not have an extradition treaty with Yugoslavia, which wanted Artuković returned to face trial for war crimes. The troubled relations between Serbia and Croatia was also an issue. Artuković's second contention was that the charges against him, which were political in nature, were not extraditable offenses.

The case dragged on . . . and on. Both sides filed motions, and the judge granted continuances. The judge finally issued a ruling on 14 July 1952. In the judge's opinion, "the Treaty between the United States and the Kingdom of Serbia of 1902 is not now in force and effect between the United States and the country now known as Yugosla-via." By making a decision on the first contention, the judge decided that he did not have to address the second one related to political offenses.[24] The judge's decision, since it voided an existing treaty, was of particular concern to the U.S. government. Concerned that the ruling might set a problematic precedent, the government teamed up with the government of Yugoslavia in filing an appeal.

The U.S. Court of Appeals for the Ninth Circuit heard the appeal—*Ivancevic v. Artukovic*—and on 19 February 1954 issued a ruling over-turning the district court decision. The higher court in effect decided that the "treaty between the United States and Serbia in 1902 was a present, valid and effective treaty between the United States and the Federal People's Republic of Yugoslavia." The Ninth Circuit Court of Appeals sent the case back to the district court with instructions to consider whether or not Yugoslavia's charges against Artuković were political in nature. On 3 April 1956 the district court judge issued his decision. He concluded that the charges were political and rooted in deep-seated ethnic problems. Siding with the defendant, the judge ruled that the charges lodged by Yugoslavia indicated the "animus which has existed between the Croatians and the Serbs for many hundreds of years, as well as the deep religious cleavage known to exist among the peoples in the Balkans." The government filed an appeal and refused to give up when the Ninth Circuit Court of Appeals upheld the district court decision. The case went all the way to the U.S. Supreme Court. On 10 March 1958 the Supreme Court ruled in the government's favor by "vacating the judgment of the United States Court of Appeals affirming the judgment of the District Court." The Supreme Court went a step further and returned the case to the dis-trict court with instructions to decide if Artuković had committed offenses that were extraditable under the 1902 treaty.[25]

The wheels of justice turned slowly. The case dragged on . . . and on, as additional motions were filed by both sides. From the time of the initial court filings in 1951, eight years passed by the time Theo-dore Hocke, U.S. commissioner for the district court, issued a deci-sion as charged by the Supreme Court. On 15 January 1959 Hocke ruled that there was insufficient evidence to support the government's contention that Artuković had committed extraditable offenses under the 1902 treaty with Serbia. According to the judge, "Absolutely no evidence was presented that the defendant himself committed murder. The complainant [Yugoslavia] relies entirely upon their evidence that members of the 'ustasa' committed murders upon orders from the defendant." The judge criticized two aspects of the governments' case. It was based primarily on hearsay evidence, and the submitted affidavits from witnesses used language—"children of tender years, new-born babes, aged persons, cruel and inhuman treatment, etc."—designed "to incite passion and prejudice." Furthermore, unlike the complainant, the defense presented witnesses who could be cross-examined. Although acknowledging that his orders resulted in "internment, deportation, and in some cases killing, of civilians," Hocke "rejected the Nuremberg concept that leaders are accountable for decrees signed by them but carried out by others."[26] In rendering his decision, Hocke also made clear his opinion about cases such as the one against Artuković:

> Upon consideration of all of the evidence presented and the authorities cited [*392] by both parties I can reach but one conclusion. The complainant has not shown by sufficient competent evidence that there is a reasonable or probable cause to believe the defendant guilty of any of the crimes charged. I hope I do not live to see the day when a person will be held to answer for a crime in either the California or United States courts upon such evidence as was presented in this case on behalf of the complainant. It would be mere speculation or surmise to find the acts charged were done upon orders from the defendant.[27]

The judge's ruling on the extradition case could not be appealed; therefore, this legal action was over.

Artuković could breathe a sigh of relief. He would not be extradited. But his request for a deportation stay remained unresolved. Four months later the INS rendered its decision. Agreeing that, in all likelihood, Artuković would be persecuted if he were returned to Yugoslavia because as cabinet minister he had opposed the communists, the INS supported a stay of deportation but did stress the support could be withdrawn. Although he could celebrate another victory, Artuković could not rest easy. One day the INS could change its mind and rescind the stay.

The Artuković case, which dragged on for years, ebbed and flowed with the winds. After receiving the stay, he stayed out of the limelight until he was thrust into it again with Israel's prosecution of Adolf Eichmann in 1961. Witnesses in the Eichmann case claimed that Yugoslav Jews were deported and executed at Artuković's request. In 1963 Artuković came onto the radar of the Los Angeles Federal Bureau of Investigation. Plans were underway for a visit to the United States by the president of Yugoslavia—Josip Broz Tito. Fearing assassination of the communist leader while on American soil, the Department of State requested from the Yugoslav government a list of all those who might pose a threat. Andrija Artuković's name was on the list and prompted an FBI assessment. Although they did not seem to deem him a threat, the FBI interviewed Artuković in 1967 in the wake of bombings at the Yugoslav consulates in Canada and the United States. During the interview Artuković, who was sixty-seven and semiretired and living in Surfside, California, acknowledged that he was both anti-Tito and anticommunist but noted that his activities in Yugoslav circles had ended years earlier. Furthermore, he was appreciative of his life in the United States and of the fact that he had not been extradited to Yugoslavia. The FBI report was straightforward, but lacked recommendations or conclusions.

Although living peacefully in Surfside, Artuković continually faced scrutiny; therefore, uncertainty was frequently the order of the day. Periodically, the INS would review the Artuković case to ascertain whether or not to lift the deportation stay. As late as 1974, however, the INS, based on an assessment by the Department of State, acknowledged the likelihood that Artuković would be persecuted if sent to Yugoslavia. But things were about to heat up again for the Croat.

Enter Elizabeth Holtzman, a graduate of Harvard University Law School, who, after practicing law for a few years, decided to enter politics. In 1972 she ran for Congress and, when she beat the incumbent Emanuel Celler, became the youngest woman elected to the House of Representatives. Passionate about the record of the INS and the Department of Justice in identifying and prosecuting Nazi criminals who were living in the United States, Holtzman sought and received a coveted position on the House Subcommittee on Immigration, Refugees, and International Law. By 1978 she authored and persuaded Congress to pass the Holtzman Amendment. What does this have to do with Artuković? The Holtzman Amendment filled a loophole for the INS. It authorized the deportation of war criminals. Included in the list of war criminals were persons who engaged in "Nazi persecution, genocide, or the commission of any act of torture or extrajudicial killing."[28]

Even before Congress passed the Holtzman Amendment, Elizabeth Holtzman became interested in several INS cases, including the one related to Andrija Artuković. She was troubled by what she read in Artuković's file. While Holtzman considered how to move forward with regard to Artuković, the House Judiciary Committee launched its own investigation and traveled to Eastern Europe in 1977 on a fact-finding mission. Upon their return, the committee reported on the Yugoslav government's position with regard to Artuković. Unhappy that he had not already been extradited or deported, the Yugoslavs asserted that they wanted to try Artuković for war crimes and promised to have an open trial that copied the due-process standards practiced by the United States. After hearing the House Judiciary Committee's report, the INS notified Artuković that the stay would not be renewed and gave him thirty days to provide just cause for an extension. Instead of complying, Artuković filed a lawsuit against the government to prevent it from moving forward. Ruling "that the government could not summarily lift the stay," the judge gave Artuković some breathing room. The case would go to the immigration courts for a decision.[29]

At this point, things really began to heat up and move more quickly to a climax. The passage of the Holtzman Amendment gave the government a way around the judge's ruling. The case landed on the OSI's desk shortly after its establishment, and in October 1979 the office immediately filed paperwork in court to have the stay lifted. In June 1981 the Board of Immigration Appeals (BIA) ruled on the OSI petition.[30] The BIA "is the highest administrative body for interpreting and applying immigration laws."[31] According to the BIA, Artuković "had offered no new evidence sufficient to call into question the soundness of the BIA's 1953 determination that Artuković had been a leader in the Nazi puppet government in Croatia and that he had, in that capacity, participated in the persecution of Serbs, Jews, and others."[32] Arguing that the Holtzman Amendment should be applied to the case, the BIA agreed with the OSI argument. Granting the OSI request to lift the stay, the BIA issued orders for Artuković's deportation to Yugoslavia.

It appeared that the path to the deportation of Andrija Artuković was open—or was it? As was to be expected, on the same day that the BIA handed down its decision, Artuković and his lawyers filed an appeal in the Ninth Circuit Court. Pending a decision there, the stay would remain in place. Rendering a ruling that was perhaps a bit unusual, the Ninth Circuit Court argued that the BIA could not use "the 1953 finding to justify deportation in 1981." The underlying issue for consideration had changed. In the 1950s it was whether or not Artuković's deportation would provide undue economic hardship on his infant daughter. In 1981 the underlying issue was whether or not Artuković met the criteria of the "newly-enacted Holtzman Amendment." In other words, the government would have to collect more evidence and request a new hearing by an immigration judge, which it did in February 1984. In January 1985 Artuković would be back in front of an immigration judge.[33]

As might be expected, the Yugoslav government followed these proceedings carefully and contemplated filing a new extradition request, an option that it had begun exploring as early as 1981. In July 1983 three members of the Department of Justice—the deputy assistant attorney general, Mark M. Richard; the acting OSI director, Neal Sher; and the associate director of the Office of International Affairs, Murray Stein—traveled to Yugoslavia to discuss the possibility.[34] While these explorations were underway, the OSI was gathering information for a new deportation hearing. In November 1983 the OSI sent a historian to search Yugoslav archives for information. He located and forwarded pertinent documents to his supervisors at OSI. Things began to snowball.

In August 1984 Yugoslavia reentered the fray by formally requesting Artuković's extradition. Justification for the request was the contention that thousands of murders fell at the former cabinet minister's door. In November 1984 Artuković found himself arrested again and behind bars. His request for bail was also denied—again. Here we go again, he must have thought. Although his deportation hearing was scheduled for January 1985, it was put on hold pending the outcome of the new extradition case.

Artuković fought both deportation and extradition with every weapon available—even, legitimately, his failing health. Artuković and his lawyers filed a motion to block the extradition hearing by requesting a contempt ruling against the government. Although he argued—correctly—that the government was attempting to do an end run around the deportation hearing, the judge threw out the motion and paved the way for the extradition case against Artuković to move forward.

Before allowing the case to begin, however, the extradition court had to determine whether or not Artuković was "mentally competent to understand the proceedings and to assist his counsel."[35] At eighty-four he was plagued by numerous ailments and was in poor health. The court-appointed doctor testified that Artuković was not competent to stand trial. He recommended a delay for appropriate treatment. Relying on his own observations of Artuković in the courtroom and declaring that the defendant had both good and bad days, the judge rejected the doctor's recommendation and ordered the trial to proceed, but he did establish parameters that took Artuković's health into account. Not only would the doctor make daily reports about Artuković's condition, but the proceedings would occur in half-day increments every other day, depending on the defendant's health.

Not to be deterred, the defense tried again to have the case derailed by filing a motion arguing that "federal officials had impermissibly encouraged Yugoslavia to request extradition." For Artuković, the encouragement was not the issue. It was the lapse in time between when the first extradition request had been denied and the current proceedings—twenty-five years. The defense argued that the gap created a disadvantage for the defendant and that his client had, as a result, been denied due process. This argument got the judge's attention. He challenged OSI director Sher: "If it develops that some politician was trying to run for higher office by railroading Mr. Artukovic back to Yugoslavia, that would be impermissible." Unfortunately for Artuković, Sher's response satisfied his concerns. The judge determined that the Department of Justice had not committed misconduct and that the extradition proceedings had been initiated by the Yugoslav government. Things were not going Artuković's way this time.[36]

The next issue at hand before the court was the merits of the government's case for extradition. The government presented fifty-two sworn affidavits to the court, which focused on only two of them. These two statements were from eyewitnesses who testified to Artuković's role in the "murder of civilians."[37] These witnesses were Franjo Trujar and Bajro Avdic.

An Ustaše police official, Franjo Trujar was deposed in 1984, at which time he swore an affidavit that he had been interviewed in July 1952. The transcript of the first interview factored heavily in the one conducted in 1984 because by that time the elderly Trujar's memory was faulty. According to the 1952 statement, Trujar was present when Artuković ordered the elimination of a former Yugoslav parliamentarian who had been an outspoken critic of the government. The case against Artuković was mounting, and the next witness statement would put another nail in his coffin.

As noted earlier in this chapter, Bajro Avdic was an Ustaše motorcycle escort. In his sworn affidavit Avdic accused Artuković of being responsible for the deaths of thousands of people. He claimed that he had overheard the cabinet minister issuing orders for the elimination of concentration camp overflow when there was no possibility of interning more people in the camp. According to Avdic, Artuković authorized the extermination of an entire town's population, along with that of the surrounding villages, and several thousand people who were near a monastery. Perhaps the most egregious charge was that Artuković ordered "the machine gun execution of several hundred prisoners who were then crushed by moving tanks."[38]

The Avdic affidavit was even more damning than Trujar's. Citing the sworn affidavits from Trujar and Avdic, the judge ordered that Artuković be extradited to Yugoslavia to face the music—in other words, where he would be tried for war crimes. Fighting to the bitter end, Artuković and his defense team filed a motion for an emergency stay. Artuković had his answer five days later, when the appeals court denied his request. Artuković appealed to the Supreme Court. On 12 February 1986 Associate Justice William Rehnquist issued his decision. He denied Artuković's request that the Supreme Court delay his extradition. Within minutes of the 1:00 p.m. announcement of the Rehnquist ruling, Andrija Artuković, who had been imprisoned since November 1984, found himself on a plane to Yugoslavia. After decades he had lost the battle that he had been fighting since 1951, when the government first filed deportation and extradition proceedings against him. Artuković was finally going home—not to Surfside, California, but to Yugoslavia. The Yugoslav government, which had been advocating for this moment for just as long as Artuković had been fighting it, would finally achieve justice.

One month later, in March 1986, Artuković stood trial for war crimes and was convicted and sentenced to death by firing squad, although his poor health brought an indefinite postponement in carrying out the sentence. He would instead be sent to prison. On 18 January 1988 a Yugoslav press release announced that Andrija Artuković had died in a prison hospital in Zagreb. For Andrija Artuković the nightmare that had lasted for over three decades was finally over.[39]

Although it did not end well for Artuković, the OSI had picked up the gauntlet from the first INS case against the Croat, stayed the course despite setbacks, and achieved a victory that affirmed its existence. "The Artukovic case stands out in many respects. It was OSI's first filing. Artukovic was the only Cabinet official and the only Croat ever prosecuted by the office. And he was the first OSI defendant to be extradited, though he was followed just two weeks thereafter by John Demjanjuk. Artukovic matters have spanned decades. If one begins with the original INS deportation filings in 1951, the case and its progeny have been around for over half a century."[40]

Artuković, as a government official, was in a position to craft policies that resulted in mass execution. Serbs, Jews, Orthodox Christians, and others paid the ultimate cost as a result of these policies. Artuković did more than rubber stamp them. He embraced them.

Therefore, his crimes were as, if not more, egregious than those committed by Karl Linnas—the subject of the next chapter—because they had broader implications. His policies potentially affected a much larger group of people than those in the one concentration camp where Linnas was based. At the end of the day, Andrija Artuković's work with the Ustaše—perhaps aptly—earned him the title Butcher of the Balkans.

7

Karl Linnas—Executioner in Estonia

Karl Linnas ran a Nazi concentration camp in Estonia. He was one of the highest-ranking Nazi collaborators ever found in the United States. His orders to execute Jews at the Estonian camp provided the basis of the denaturalization and deportation case against Linnas: "As the head Estonian in the camp, he ordered guards to fire on prisoners kneeling along the edge of an anti-tank ditch; the dead fell directly into their graves."[1] The Office of Special Investigations became involved in 1979 and filed its first legal documents in November of that year. Although he did not contest the accusations, Linnas did not cooperate with the investigation. He considered depositions of Soviet witnesses to be unreliable because they were taken with Soviet officials present. In addition, he refused to answer certain questions when he was deposed and failed to submit evidence that would contradict the government's case. In 1982 Linnas's citizenship was revoked, and he was deported five years later. How was Linnas able to enter the United States in the first place? How and when was he able to obtain U.S. citizenship? What led to the discovery of his real past? Who was Karl Linnas?

Early Years

In many respects Karl Linnas was an enigma. Not much is known about his early life. What is known is that Karl Linnas was Estonian. He was born on 6 August 1919, in Estonia, possibly in Tartu. Located on the Baltic Sea, Estonia has had a checkered past. Prior to the eighteenth century Estonia found itself under the control of Denmark, the German Knights of the Livonian Order, and Sweden.[2] The Russians incorporated the small Baltic state into their empire in the eighteenth century. Although they desired control over their own land,

Estonians did not gain independence until the cracks in the Russian Empire, which commenced with revolution in 1917, resulted in collapse in 1918 after World War I had ended. The Treaty of Versailles guaranteed the independence of the Baltic states—Latvia, Lithuania, and Estonia. For the next two decades, Estonia struggled to define itself politically as it vacillated between democratic and autocratic governance. Born in 1919, Linnas grew up during this contentious political period of Estonian history. Government upheaval and uncertainty influenced his outlook and perhaps shaped the decisions that he made during World War II.

As Estonia struggled to define itself politically, Europe encountered different difficulties in the 1930s. There were multiple flashpoints and unrest that threatened Estonia's independence from outside. To the east Russia had undergone a communist revolution and now had a new name: the Union of Soviet Socialist Republics, or the USSR. First Lenin and then Stalin had instituted rapid change—in industry, in agriculture, and in the military—and this resulted in purges of the intelligentsia and the officer corps. To the west Adolf Hitler's ascension to power unleashed a series of challenges to political autonomy and nationhood, as well as to certain ethnicities.

Within Germany Hitler and the Nazis targeted Jews by limiting types of employment available to them, boycotting their businesses, and passing the 1935 Nuremberg Laws, which restricted them in other ways, including marriage. Nazi persecution of Jews during this period culminated in a campaign of mob violence known as Reichskristallnacht (Reich Crystal Night). In addition, Jews were forced to wear a yellow Star of David. Furthermore, the Nazis took steps to control Christian churches within Germany and negotiated an agreement with the Vatican in which they pledged to maintain the traditional rights of the Catholic Church—although they would not hesitate to violate that pledge if it suited their purposes. They also targeted the physically and mentally handicapped and non-Aryan groups. Hitler and the Nazi Party did not, however, limit their aggressive persecutions to religious or political groups within Germany. It didn't take long for them to turn their gaze beyond their own borders.

In 1936 German troops entered the Rhineland, in violation of the

Versailles Treaty. Emboldened by the lack of response from his country's European neighbors, particularly France, Hitler embarked on a plan of expansion while everybody nervously watched. In 1938 he orchestrated the Anschluss, and Austria became united with Germany. Next he set his sights on the Sudetenland, the industrial region of Czechoslovakia that bordered Germany. In September 1938 at the Munich Conference, the prime ministers of Great Britain, France, and Italy acquiesced to Hitler's request and, without permission from Czechoslovakia, handed control of the Sudetenland over to Germany. Europe breathed a sigh of relief. They had avoided war. As Prime Minister Neville Chamberlain had so famously announced, they had achieved peace for all time. After all, they had Hitler's assurances that Germany would not engage in further aggressive action. Six months later, however, the agreement would be broken, when German troops crossed the border and proceeded to occupy the rest of Czechoslovakia. Abandoned and betrayed by its European allies, Czechoslovakia could not go it alone against Germany and did not put up much resistance. This period of uncertainty shaped Linnas's world view. As Linnas reached maturity, tensions in Europe came to a head.

"Could things get any worse?" the Estonians must have wondered. As they watched, things did indeed get worse. Rhetoric from Berlin suggested that the Polish government was oppressing that nation's German minority and made much of Europe nervous about what would happen next.[3] Like Estonians, they would soon find out, when a startling announcement was made on 23 August 1939. Germany and the Soviet Union had reached an agreement—the Molotov-Ribbentrop, or the Soviet-Nazi, Non-Aggression, Pact—which, among other provisions, allowed the two nations to acquire spheres of influence in central and eastern Europe. Unbeknownst to Estonians, the Germans agreed not to oppose the Soviets' reacquisition of Latvia, Lithuania, and Estonia. Tensions in Europe intensified. Soon Europe would be ablaze, and Estonians would ask themselves several questions. Could Estonia stay out of it? How would Estonians respond? Which side would they support? Furthermore, Karl Linnas would have to decide what he would do. Where did his loyalties lie? As events unfolded and he had to take a side, whose cause—Nazi Germany's, the Soviet communists', or Estonia's—would he embrace?

Wartime Service

On 1 September 1939 German troops invaded Poland. Thus World War II began in Europe. Although other European nations would quickly, but reluctantly, enter the fray, Estonia chose another path—complete neutrality—or at least that was the plan. The Soviet Union would force a change in Estonia's stated neutrality, and it wouldn't take long. Less than three weeks after German troops invaded Poland from the west, the Soviet Union honored its part of the Molotov-Ribbentrop Pact. Soviet troops entered Poland from the east; moreover, a large number of additional Soviet troops were concentrated on the Soviet border with Finland, Latvia, Lithuania, and Estonia. Estonians, including Karl Linnas, held their breaths, not sure what their government would do. Would Estonia be able to stick to its stated complete neutrality, or would the nation bow to pressure from the east?

It did not take the Soviet Union long to impose its will on Estonia. Using the presence of their troops on the border and threats of military force, the Soviets pressured the Baltic nation to sign a "so-called mutual military assistance pact" on 28 September 1939. Under one of the provisions of the pact, the Soviets established military bases in Estonia. Furthermore, the Soviets coerced Latvia and Lithuania to sign similar agreements. Although the Baltic nations were perhaps tempted to resist, the Soviet invasion of Finland persuaded them that resistance was futile. Despite hope to the contrary, things actually got worse. Citing authority granted under the terms of the Molotov-Ribbentrop Pact, the Soviet Union, after occupying them, "forcibly annexed" the three Baltic countries the following summer.[4] Soviet occupation brought Estonia's status as a free nation to an end, and the nation would not reclaim it for over fifty years. It was not until 1992 that Estonia regained its independence.

Uncertainty was the order of the day in Estonia beginning on 1 September 1939, when the first German troops entered Poland, and continuing with Soviet occupation. The situation in Estonia took another turn after 22 June 1941, when Operation Barbarossa—the German invasion of the Soviet Union—commenced. Soon pressure on the Baltic nations would come from multiple sides. Occupying Soviet troops would no longer pose the only threat to Estonians. Less than a month after the commencement of Barbarossa, the first German troops assaulted Estonia. The German onslaught forced Soviet forces to retreat. Shortly thereafter occupation by German troops, which would last until 1944, began. During the period of German occupation, the Nazis executed approximately eight thousand citizens or residents of Estonia. In addition, they housed over twenty thousand Jews, Soviet prisoners of war, and other "undesirables" in prison camps in Estonia. Many of these prison internees did not survive German occupation.[5]

Advancing along with German combat forces were mobile killing units—Einsatzkommandos—that had specific tasks. Einsatzkommandos were divided into battalions called Einsatzgruppen, which received orders to implement policy, particularly policy with regard to the Jewish population and other "undesirables," such as communists, in Estonia and other occupied territories. The Einsatzgruppen elicited and received help in carrying out their duties from the Estonian Home Guard—the Selbstschutz—with some success. According to captured German records,

> Einsatzgruppe A, aided by the Selbstschutz, successfully achieved one of its major objectives. By mid-January 1942, the Chief of the Security Police and the Security Service was able to report that Estonia was "judenfrei" (free of Jews) and that the execution of Jews had been handled in such a manner so as to minimize public attention to the fact of the German extermination process (Record at 58, GX-6). While Jews were shot solely based upon the determination of their religious ancestry, Communists were shot only if they were active in the party, with the balance either being set free or detained in concentration camps (Record at 56).[6]

Where does Karl Linnas fit into this story? As the Germans occupied Estonia and persecuted Jews, communists, and others, what was Karl Linnas doing? Between 1940 and 1943 Linnas lived in Tartu, Estonia, during which time he was supposedly a student at the university, or at least that is what he indicated on his application to the Immigration and Naturalization Service (INS) in 1959. While it is true that Linnas attended the University of Tartu, by 1 July 1941 he was no longer enrolled there or at any other university. Evidence exists, however, that shortly after the German occupation in July 1941, Linnas became a member of the Selbstschutz. There is also evidence that he joined, for almost two years, another organization during this time—the Omakaitse (Estonian Self-Defense), a paramilitary group working with the Nazis to arrest, imprison, abuse, and execute civilians.

On 10 July 1941 the first German troops arrived in Tartu. By the twelfth Maj. Friedrich Kurg, "leader of the forest brothers in Southern Estonia," issued orders for the arrest of all Jews in the area.[7] Recognizing that provisions had to be in place to house the arrested Jews, even if only temporarily, Field Cmdt. Maj. Hans Gosebruch requisitioned the Kuperjanov Barracks as the temporary holding center. Within a month, however, a more permanent facility—a concentration camp—was established. Even before the camp was finished, Linnas had joined the staff at Kuperjanov Barracks.

Although subordinated to Maj. Walter Scheichenbauer, the commander of the military police (Feldgendarmerie), Capt. Juhan Jüriste, as camp commandant, was in charge of hiring camp guards at the barracks. After interviewing prospective guards, he made his recommendations to Roland Lepik, who had the ultimate hiring authority. On 1 August Jüriste was replaced as camp commandant by Lepik; he had another task. Lepik's new title was "chief of the Special Department of the Tartu Concentration Camp's Commandantur." Jüriste and Linnas were tasked with supervising the construction of the Tartu concentration camp. Upon completion of the construction, they subsequently supervised the transfer of Jews and others from Kuperjanov Barracks to the new concentration camp. Once the camp was up and running, Linnas was based there until at least May 1942. He wore a second lieutenant uniform, and his position at the Tartu concentration camp allowed him to wear a sidearm. Things gradually settled down into a routine—one that involved the execution of Jews.[8]

According to Jüriste,

In late afternoon, the officer with special tasks Koolmeister arrived at the concentration camp and instructed about 8–10 guards on the square. After some time, a closed truck drove up to the death barrack. The guards led by Koolmeister, as well as Lepik, Chief of the special department, also arrived. The door of the death barrack was open. Lepik stood at the door with a list, as did one of the guards who was at the disposal of the special department. Lepik read the name of a detenus, and the guard standing beside him stepped behind the detenus. This way, all the 8–10 detenus were brought out of the barrack, their hands were tied with a rope and they were placed in the truck. Before they were brought out, the people to be executed had been undressed in the barrack, they were brought to the truck in their underclothes and without shoes. After an attempted escape, the executees were also tied together with a rope.[9]

Until February 1942 the executions occurred at an antitank ditch called the "Jalak (or Jalaka) line," which was adjacent to the Tartu-Riga Road.[10]

In October Linnas recruited Olav Karikosk to be a concentration camp guard. In the Tartu area, there were two concentration sites—first the exhibition grounds and then the Kuperjanov Barracks. According to Hans Laats, who supervised the guards at Kuperjanov Barracks, Linnas was a guard at the exhibition grounds before becoming "chief of the relocated concentration camp at the Kuperjanov Barracks." Camp guards were also members of the Selbstschutz (Estonian Home Guard).[11] According to Karikosk and Laats, detainees marked for execution were housed in special barracks: "Laats confessed to his own presence at one execution conducted at an anti-tank ditch (known as the 'Jalaka Line') outside Tartu. This excavation had been converted by the Einsatzkommandos into a mass grave site for the victims of their extermination process. In recounting a portion of Jalaka Line execution, he stated that Linnas was the individual who had announced the death sentence and had commanded the guards to fire on the prisoners who were kneeling at the ditch's edge."[12] Although he did not witness the execution described by Laats, Karikosk, who also identified Linnas as the concentration camp chief, claimed that his boss ordered his presence at an execution.

Additional eyewitness testimony places Linnas at the Kuperjanov concentration camp barracks. Oskar Art transported prisoners—Jews and non-Jews—via bus to the Jalaka Line for execution on three occasions. According to Art, Linnas supervised the loading of the prisoners onto the bus. Another witness, Elmer Puusepp, crossed Linnas's path in a different context—that of prisoner. A Soviet political officer, Puusepp was arrested by Selbstschutz in the summer of 1941 and imprisoned at Kuperjanov Barracks along with forty other prisoners, half of whom received assignment to the special barracks. Puusepp testified to Linnas's participation in an incident at Kuperjanov Barracks. "This incident occurred in the City of Tartu when Linnas helped direct Jews being ordered from a Jewish school onto a red bus which had been used on occasions to remove prisoners from the death barracks at the concentration camp. Linnas was seen helping a little girl '5 or 6 years old' with a doll as large as she was onto the bus. Puusepp noticed a guard carrying the little girl's doll to storage that very same evening together with clothing and other personal effects taken from those persons who had just been executed."[13]

In addition to eyewitness accounts, documentary evidence places Linnas at the Tartu concentration camp. After the war the Soviets discovered four documents, dated between November and December 1941. Each of these documents was signed by Karl Linnas over the title "Chief of Concentration Camps" or "Chief of Tartu Concentration Camp." "The documents concerned the routine operation of the camp" and consisted "of orders and correspondence pertaining to prisoners" and other camp matters.[14] In addition, they support the notion that Linnas had a supervisory role at the Tartu concentration camp and suggest that he was a member of the Selbstschutz.

Later charges against Linnas stemmed from the mass executions that occurred during his time as camp commander. Primary responsibility for organizing mass executions fell under the auspices of the Department of Special Affairs, which established a specific protocol.

Under the direction of the DSA, the executions proceeded as follows. A small red bus came to a "death barracks" for the condemned. These turned in their clothing and possessions before boarding. Their hands were tied behind their backs, and in many cases the group was tied together with a long rope. Witnesses indicated that the condemned were treated with unusual cruelty, including beatings and in some cases rape. Guards rode with the victims, usually were very drunk, and abused the condemned along the way. As prisoners were loaded onto the bus, remaining inmates of the death barracks were ordered to lie on the floor and not look out the windows. But the guards, preoccupied with the condemned, were unable to enforce this prohibition. Other prisoners and guards observed the activities and testified about them later.[15]

The execution site was the antitank trench, approximately three miles from the camp proper. A guard escorted each prisoner from the bus to the trench, where a sentence was read, though for Jews this might simply be "worthless race." The guards then shot their victims. When Linnas supervised killings, he inspected the bodies to be certain there were no signs of life, following up with a final shot when necessary. Despite this, witnesses testified that at least some victims were buried still alive. According to the witnesses most of the shooters were volunteers.[16]

By May 1942 Linnas had moved on to military service and served with several groups that were part of the German army. First, he joined the Estonian Schutzmannschaft, or Auxiliary Police, and served in the capacity of a junior lieutenant. Between 1942 and 1944, after his service in the Estonian Schutzmannschaft, Linnas joined the Thirty-Eighth Estonian Police Battalion by July. On 3 August 1944 he suffered a shrapnel wound to his right shoulder and arm.[17] With the Soviet advance westward into Germany, German forces retreated back into their homeland, and Linnas and his wife, Linda Saks, whom he had married a month earlier, and other collaborators went with them.

Postwar Years

Although he initially moved around, Linnas ultimately established residence "in or near Neuberg" in West Germany, where he established contact with U.S. military authorities. On 22 August 1945 he received an American Expeditionary Force Registration Record, or DP-2 (Displaced Persons) card. Approximately a year later Linnas filed a sworn questionnaire with the "Third United States Army at Geretsried Displaced Persons Camp in Germany." When he submitted the questionnaire, which was completed in Estonian, he was questioned by authorities about his information. In response, Linnas claimed "that during the years 1941 and 1942, his occupation was as a temporary draftsman and student." When questioned about his military and political activity from 1936 to 1946, Linnas, downplaying his wartime work, stated, "that his only service was in the Army of the Democratic Estonian Republic, 1938 to 1940, as a sergeant, and in an Estonian security battalion in Tartu, Estonia, 1943 to 1944, as a sergeant." On 5 July 1947 Linnas received an American Expeditionary Force Registration Record, or DP-3 card, from U.S. military authorities.[18]

Linnas and his family remained in Neuberg until the United States opened a door to another option on 25 June 1948, when Congress passed the Displaced Persons Act (DPA), which established a limited window during which certain displaced Europeans could obtain permanent residence status in the United States. In particular, Congress envisioned the DPA helping "those individuals who were victims of persecution by the Nazi government or who were fleeing persecution" or those "who could not go back to their country because of fear of persecution based on race, religion or political opinions."[19]

For Linnas, the key protected group included individuals who could not return to their native countries because they faced persecution. With his homeland reoccupied by Soviet troops, it was too hot to go home. After all, among the groups targeted during his tenure at the Tartu concentration camp were communists. In Linnas's case, however, the grounds for persecution or prosecution were war crimes, not race, religion, or political opinions; therefore, he decided to take advantage of the new U.S. legislation. Doing so, however, would mean being less than completely honest when he made his case for relocation and hoping that U.S. officials would not look too deeply into his wartime past. Linnas was banking on the fact that, because so many people would apply for displaced-persons status, staffs handling these cases would be so overworked that they would not scrutinize applications too closely. He might—just might—escape detection.

Those requesting admittance to the United States under the Displaced Persons Act had to follow a three-part process. "First, a refugee filed an application for International Refugee Organization, or IRO, assistance." An IRO eligibility officer interviewed the applicant about his personal and family history, particularly during the war, to determine his qualifications under the established guidelines. "The primary source of background information inevitably came from the applicant himself." If the applicant met the criteria, he was granted IRO assistance. The next step was "to qualify as an eligible displaced person under the DPA." The basis for the Displaced Persons Commission determination was the IRO report. After conducting a security check on the applicant's background and determining eligibility, the case analyst would issue "a report certifying that the applicant was a person eligible for admission into the United States under the DPA." At that point the case analyst would forward the applicant's file, which included the "preliminary IRO certification and the Displaced Persons Commission report to the appropriate American Consulate."[20]

The possibility of obtaining permanent residence status in the United States under the DPA was an appealing one for Linnas, who by this time had a family to support. He had married Linda Saks on 7 July 1944 in Estonia. After escaping to Germany, the couple had two daughters—Anu (in 1945) and Tiina (in 1947). Remaining in Germany was not the safest option for Linnas. Because he now had a family, Linnas realized that escaping detection by Soviet investigators was becoming increasingly difficult. Although he lived in West Germany, only a porous border between West and East Germany protected him from his enemies to the east. Consequently, if he could move to the United States, he would then be farther from the reach of the Soviets, who were aggressively pursuing perpetrators of war crimes. Linnas chose, however, to pursue the displaced-persons avenue through a circuitous route. In February 1948, August Linnas, Karl Linnas's father, filed a signed and sworn application for assistance with the Preliminary Commission for the IRO. His request was for himself and his family, including his son, whom he characterized as a university student and technical artist from 1940 to 1943. The elder Linnas's application did not, however, include his daughter-in-law, Linda, or his granddaughters. Linda Linnas submitted an "IRO Resettlement Registration Form" for herself and her children in December 1949.[21]

During that same month Linnas overcame the first hurdle, when the IRO, based on false information, certified his eligibility for a displaced-persons and refugee designation. The IRO then forwarded Linnas's file to the U.S. Displaced Persons Commission for review, and James McDonald became his case analyst. As part of the background check, Linnas was interrogated by members of the U.S. Army's Counter Intelligence Corps (CIC). By this time he really had his "story" down pat. During the interrogation Linnas confirmed the information that his father had provided. He could not do anything but confirm it. From 1940 to 1943 he was a university student in Tartu, Estonia. He "had never served in the German army." He had not held membership in any political group or organization. He did admit, however, that after being drafted, he had served in the Estonian army from 1 July 1938 until June 1940. Drafted a second time by the Estonian army, he served with the "Estonian Home Guard, Kreis Tartu" from 22 May 1943 until August 1944, when he was wounded. Linnas could not do anything but confirm these facts. To tell the truth at this stage would derail his efforts to move to the United States with his family, at the very least. He had no way of knowing if criminal charges could be filed against him if he spilled the beans under CIC questioning. He could not go down that road; therefore, maintaining the lie was crucial to his plan for his future—and, by extension, for his family's future.[22]

The CIC did not seem to recognize the apparent contradiction between Linnas's statement and the narrative provided by his father and confirmed by Linnas. Whether or not the CIC took steps to verify Linnas's testimony is not known. What is known, however, is that the CIC passed Linnas with flying colors. Consequently, on 27 April 1951 McDonald confirmed his eligibility for consideration for admission to the United States. Hurdle two passed. A few weeks later, with evidence of his official displaced-persons status in hand, Linnas went to the U.S. consulate in Munich, where he "filed a signed and sworn Application for Immigration Visa and Alien Registration" form and immediately received an immigrant visa. Four days later, on 21 May,

Walter Ziemak, an INS officer, questioned Linnas to assess the validity of his application. Linnas also signed two copies of INS Form I-144, the contents of which Ziemak thoroughly explained. By signing the form Linnas confirmed that he had "never advocated or assisted in the persecution of any person because of race, religion or national origin." He was almost home free. Linnas and his family arrived in the United States three months later, and on 17 August 1951 he swore that the INS Form I-114 with his signature was accurate.[23]

Linnas initially found employment first as a draftsman and then as a surveyor in New York State, when he got a job with Norton Brothers in Sayville, where he worked for approximately six years. In 1957 he got a job with Lockwood, Kessler & Bartlett in Syosset. A year later he bought a home in Greenlawn, New York, which was closer to his new job and where he and his family lived quietly until 1961.[24] Linnas was living the good life. He had put his past behind him, or so he thought. Little did he know that his past was about to catch up with him. His life would begin to unravel, and he would be unable to stop the collapse of the fictitious narrative that had provided the backdrop for his new life in the United States. Before the unraveling began, however, Linnas started the process to make his life in the United States permanent.

After moving to Greenlawn Linnas took steps to legitimize his residence in the United States by filing a naturalization petition with the INS on 4 July 1959. As part of the review process, an INS officer met with Linnas on 14 December 1959 to discuss his responses to questions on the application. As was customary, the interview of Linnas was "conducted under oath. Linnas attested the accuracy of the information included in his application at that time." It does not appear that, beyond the interview, the INS investigated the validity of Linnas's application. If the INS had investigated further, however, the officers did not unearth any information that contradicted Linnas's statements on his application. Relying on the INS assessment and with no access to contradictory information regarding the Estonian's wartime activities, the supreme court of Suffolk County, New York, conferred citizenship on Linnas on 5 February 1960.[25] Linnas was home free—or—was he?

Controversy

While Linnas might have assumed that the Soviets would eventually give up trying to find him, he would soon discover that the contrary was true. Unsuccessful in locating him through his parents because they were also in the United States, they pursued another angle— Linda Linnas's parents, who still resided in Estonia. Under questioning, Jaan Saks, Linda Linnas's father, provided his Soviet interrogators the information they sought—Karl Linnas's address: 21 Goldsmith Avenue, Greenlawn, New York. It is possible that Saks did not communicate this information to his son-in-law, who would be blindsided a short time later.

Little did Linnas know, when he left for work on 23 May 1961, that his world was about to fall apart. That morning, a *New York Times* article indicated that the Soviet Union had charged six Estonians for crimes related to their associations with the Tartu concentration camp. None of the six lived in the Eastern Bloc, and the Soviets planned to take steps to bring them there for trial. One of those identified in the article was Karl Linnas, who was listed as warden of the camp. Either he had not read the *New York Times* that morning or had not done so carefully. The morning of 23 May 1961 seemed like any other when he joined his usual carpool companion and coworker, Richard Siebach.

Siebach, who had always lived on Long Island, regularly read a local daily, *Newsday*, which had picked up the *New York Times* article. That morning *Newsday* had published a sensational article—"Reds Accuse LIer [Long Islander] of Nazi War Crimes."[26] When he read the paper before leaving for work that morning, Siebach was startled to see that one of the accused was Linnas. As they rode to work, Siebach brought up the article and pressed his coworker. When questioned by a colleague, Linnas admitted to being a guard, but not a supervisor, at the camp, a fact that he had omitted from both his displaced persons and his citizenship applications.

In October the USSR filed a formal petition with the U.S. government, requesting Linnas's extradition. There was immediate opposition to granting the request, primarily on the grounds that the Soviet occupation of Estonia was illegal. Despite the U.S. refusal to comply with the request, the Soviets "charged Linnas with having taken an active part in the killing of 12,000 persons during the war" and tried him in absentia for war crimes committed at the Tartu concentration camp. The three-day trial commenced in Tartu on 16 January 1962—after the verdict had been rendered and announced a month earlier. Linnas was convicted and sentenced to death. Linnas was not the only Estonian defendant on trial in Tartu that day. Capt. Juhan Jüriste and Ervin Richard Adolph Viks were also accused of the killing of twelve thousand civilians interned in the Tartu concentration camp. Like Linnas, both Jüriste and Viks were convicted and sentenced to death in absentia. Although in all likelihood he would not be shown mercy, Jüriste pled guilty. Fortunately for Viks, he was living in a country—Australia—that declined to extradite him to the Soviet Union for a trial.[27]

As indicated earlier, although the Soviets first requested extradition in October 1961, the U.S. government refused the request and did not initially pursue the issue further for a couple of reasons. Now part of the Soviet Union, as it had once been part of the Russian Empire, Estonia was not an ideal location for the deportation of Linnas. The announcement of the conviction and sentencing of Linnas guaranteed that deportation could very well result in Linnas's death. Deporting Linnas to the Soviet Union during the Cold War could have multiple ramifications for the United States, particularly in terms of foreign relations. A fellow Estonian American contacted Secretary of State Dean Rusk to voice his support for Linnas and to campaign against his compatriot's extradition. For this Estonian American, as was the case with other members of the Baltic American community, his opposition was grounded in one particular issue—"the illegality of the Soviet Union's continued occupation of Estonia" and the other Baltic states.[28] He argued that if the United States allowed the extradition to move forward, then the government was in effect recognizing the incorporation of the Baltic states into the Soviet Union. Consequently, it was better to let the matter fade away and die, but it eventually resurfaced. It is important to note, however, that well into the 1980s the issue of deportation to Estonia was a recurring "political conundrum."[29]

The Department of Justice did not initiate an investigation of Linnas until 1979, after the creation of the Office of Special Investigations (osi). There were three reasons for the delay. Because of strained Cold War relations, the Kennedy administration was reluctant "to deport naturalized citizens to the USSR regardless of any wartime offenses." In addition, the Department of Justice had no mechanism in place to prosecute war criminals. That became possible only with the establishment of the osi. Finally, prior to 1978 U.S. law made it easier to fight deportation.[30]

osi Investigates

The Linnas case was one of the first taken up by the Office of Special Investigations shortly after its establishment. In November 1979, after reviewing the case, the osi filed denaturalization proceedings against Linnas, who then learned that he was on the Department of Justice's radar. Because the Department of Justice was taking steps to strip him of his citizenship, Linnas knew that his life was about to change—dramatically. He had to decide what to do. Could he successfully fight the Department of Justice? What did denaturalization mean? If he lost his citizenship, was the next step extradition to the Soviet Union? With his life turned upside down, Linnas had to devise a strategy that would thwart the legal case against him. Unfortunately for Linnas, the Department of Justice—particularly the newly created osi—had a new weapon in its arsenal to use against alleged criminals like Linnas: the Holtzman Amendment to the Immigration and Nationality Act, which closed a loophole. The government could now deny "discretionary relief" to anyone who allegedly lied about criminal wartime activities to enter the United States. Reasons for discretionary relief included marriage to a U.S. citizen, exhibition of good moral character while in the United States, or the inability to get a fair trial in the Soviet Union. Because he had already been convicted and sentenced to death, Linnas could definitely argue the latter. Because of the Holtzman Amendment, however, that argument no longer mattered in the Linnas case.[31]

The osi scheduled its first deposition of Linnas on 15 December 1980, but he skipped the meeting and sent his attorney to claim his

"Fifth Amendment right against self-incrimination."[32] He chose not to participate in the deposition of the witnesses who testified against him. Like Andrija Artuković, he argued that the presence of Soviet officials during the questioning tainted the witnesses' testimony. Linnas repeatedly pled the Fifth and refused to answer any questions. In addition, he produced no evidence to refute the government's case. A month later Judge Jacob Mishler ordered Linnas to answer questions within ten days. For the judge refusal to answer the questions was tantamount to acknowledging that the government's claim was valid. At the end of the day, refusal to answer questions did not prevent a trial.

Beginning on 16 June 1981, Mishler sat in judgment over a trial that lasted for three days. Rodney G. Smith and Martha Talley presented the government's case, while Ivars Berzins represented Linnas. A Latvian American, Berzins established his career by "defending alleged Nazi offenders." After highlighting the defendant's failure to cooperate with the OSI investigation and to obey the judge's order, Talley presented the government's position in a nutshell. According to Talley, "to become a U.S. citizen, the law required one to be of 'good moral character' and to have entered the U.S. legally; by lying about his wartime record, Linnas had made himself ineligible for immigration into and citizenship of the U.S." Consequently, the court must, Talley argued, revoke Linnas's citizenship.[33] In presenting the defense's case, Berzins failed to live up to his later reputation. Not all the witnesses that he called provided information that was germane to the case. In many respects Berzins did not seem to have his head in the game, nor did his strategy necessarily appear sound. Rather than trying to exonerate his client, Berzins attempted to discredit the witnesses and evidence presented by the government's attorneys. After the defense attorney had complained on multiple occasions that he had not had time to read all of the government-provided documentation, Mishler reminded Berzins that he had had five months in which to examine the documentary evidence. The crux of the defense's strategy was to refuse to "accept any Soviet evidence against Linnas, arguing that it was all prima facie unreliable." At the end of the day, Judge Mishler did not buy it.[34]

Two weeks later, on 30 June 1981, Mishler "denaturalized Linnas, citing two major reasons in his rulings." Because he had lied to the CIC and to INS, Linnas had been admitted to the United States unlawfully. In addition, Mishler asserted that, because of his actions at the Tartu concentration camp, Linnas "lacked the requisite moral character" to enter the United States.[35] Although Linnas appealed the decision, the Second Circuit Court of Appeals upheld Mishler's ruling six months later, when on 25 January 1982 Judge Wilfred Feinberg denied the defense request to have the Soviet documents thrown out. Linnas's lawyer continued to file appeals on his client's behalf. On 5 April the Second Circuit Court of Appeals threw out Linnas's request for another hearing. As a result the INS began the deportation process on 25 June, but Linnas and Berzins were unwilling to throw in the towel. They were dealt another blow when the Supreme Court on 4 October decided against hearing the case.

To give him credit, Berzins, although he seemed to display some incompetence in the first trial, continued to fight for Linnas. He filed another appeal in immigration court. Judge Howard I. Cohen reviewed the entire case—including documentation and transcripts from the denaturalization trial and the Second Circuit Court of Appeals decision—and issued a ruling on 19 May 1983. The judge stated that "deportability [was] established by clear, convincing and unequivocal evidence." Furthermore, in issuing his decision, he referenced a previous decision in *Fedorenko v. Inus* (1981). In that case, Cohen ruled that "service as a concentration camp guard, whether voluntary or not, disqualified a person for a U.S. visa." Based on the evidence presented at the denaturalization trial, Cohen reaffirmed Mishler's ruling that Linnas, because of his wartime record, was not eligible for DP status. Since DP status was a prerequisite for immigration and citizenship, Linnas was not entitled to those privileges either. Linnas received deportation notification two years after Mishler's ruling was upheld. Then began the fight over where to deport him. Not only did this play out diplomatically, but it also resulted in additional litigation.[36] Things were not yet over.

Interestingly, when the deportation order was issued, Linnas received an order to identify where he wanted to be deported. Not one to give up easily, Linnas provided an answer that was sure to delay his deportation. He chose the "free and independent Republic of Estonia." To prevent any confusion, Linnas emphasized that he did not mean the country "with the puppet government formed by the Soviet occupiers of Estonia." The way in which Linnas referenced Estonia also reflected two realities. First, as late as 1984 the United States recognized not the Soviet-controlled Estonia but the "free and independent Republic of Estonia," which in effect meant the émigré-led government-in-exile that operated in New York City. Second, Linnas recognized what it would mean to be placed into Soviet hands. Sending him to Estonia in 1984 would do just that, and the end result would be the loss of his life.[37] In the court's opinion it had two options—Estonia or the Soviet Union. Cohen chose the Soviet Union because in 1983 Estonia was part of the Soviet Union. Emphasizing Cold War tensions and problems, Linnas and his supporters turned to the court and the general public to challenge the ruling. In addition, on 14 June 1983 his daughters sent a letter to the Estonian community, in which they suggested that Soviet-backed activists had infiltrated the U.S. government. They connected the creation of the OSI, which had a pro-Soviet agenda, to discrimination against anticommunists. "The persecution of so called 'war criminals,' 40 years after it supposedly happened, is just an attempt to silence anticommunist groups by leading Soviet style court cases in the U.S. and to promote communism in the free world. The denaturalization of our father . . . by [a judge] who accepted Soviet supplied 'witnesses and documents' in U.S. courts is only the continuation of the 1962 Soviet 'show trial.' . . . As a final measure, the immigration judge . . . also accepted the Soviet 'information.'"[38]

In this heated atmosphere, the Board of Immigration Appeals weighed in. While Linnas raised numerous issues in the appeal heard by the BIA, at the end of the day only one mattered—that of where Linnas was to be deported. On 31 July 1984 the BIA rendered its decision. While it upheld the majority of Cohen's ruling, the BIA called into question the judge's decision to deport Linnas to the Soviet Union, particularly since the U.S. government had yet to recognize the Soviet annexation of Estonia. Ordering a new hearing, the BIA ordered Cohen to "consider the implications of the United States' refusal to recognize the Soviet annexation of Estonia, [to] designate a country of deportation pursuant to the appropriate [statutory] provisions . . . and [to] articulate the statutory basis for selection, whichever country is designated." The BIA had an underlying concern that had to be addressed. If the ultimate decision was to deport Linnas to the Soviet Union, would that undermine the current nonrecognition policy of the United States?[39]

What was clear to Linnas was that he was to be deported. What was not clear was where he would be sent. Linnas could only hope that the process of finding him a host country would be a long and drawn-out one. The longer it took, the longer he could stay in the United States with his family and—perhaps—the less likely it was that he would be sent to the Soviet Union. Going to the Soviet Union was not a life-prolonging option, and Linnas still hoped to avoid paying the piper.

The OSI now had to find a new home for Linnas. What better place to look than his previous place of residence. Because he had lived in West Germany from 1945 to 1951, the U.S. government attempted to send Linnas there, but to no avail. The West German government "remained steadfast in the position it had adopted" in an earlier case. "It would only admit German citizens." Because he had never applied for German citizenship, Linnas did not qualify. Consequently, the United States could not send him to West Germany.[40] The OSI had to find another solution. While the OSI endeavored to find another possible host country for Linnas, the BIA gathered information to allay its concerns about sending Linnas to the Soviet Union. Unfortunately for Linnas, being deported to the Soviet Union was still a possibility.

Even the Department of State, which did not think that deporting Linnas to the Soviet Union was the best option for the United States, joined the fray. The State Department tasked its embassies to put out feelers in seventeen countries to determine if any would be a viable alternative to the Soviet Union. The list of countries included "Brazil, Columbia, Czechoslovakia, Germany, Greece, Israel, Italy, the Philippines, South Africa, Sri Lanka, Sweden, Switzerland, Thailand, Turkey, Venezuela, the United Kingdom, and the USSR." The OSI also contacted Canada, Germany, Israel, and the Soviet Union.

To Linnas's dismay, the only country that was willing to accept him was the very country that he hoped to avoid—the Soviet Union. The Department of State contacted the White House and then prepared a statement for the deportation judge that addressed the BIA's concern about jeopardizing existing U.S. policy. Noting the futility in finding a country other than the Soviet Union to accept Linnas, the Department of State asserted that deporting Linnas to the Soviet Union "would not as a matter of law contravene the longstanding and firmly held United States policy of nonrecognition of the forcible incorporation of Estonia into the USSR."[41]

Linnas's heart must have dropped when he heard the news. Now it was up to Judge Cohen to follow the BIA directive and officially designate the deportation country. The statement from the State Department eliminated his and the BIA's concerns about shipping Linnas to the Soviet Union. Linnas vehemently argued against being sent to the Soviet Union. He reminded the court that he had been sentenced to death in absentia by the Soviets in 1962—before the trial had even occurred—and asked the court to reconsider sending him to the Soviet Union, where he would most certainly be executed. Confident that the earlier conviction and sentence would not be enforced, the OSI argued that, as early as 1984, the Soviet Union had promised the U.S. government that they would give Linnas a new trial. Hearing this did not bring comfort to Linnas, who was equally certain that a new trial would not be a fair one and would have the same outcome.

On 9 April 1985 Cohen was ready to give his decision. According to Cohen, "Linnas could be deported under either of two provisions out of the seven that the INS designated as warranting deportation."[42] He reiterated that under the law the best option was to deport Linnas to the country where he was born—Estonia. If, however, that was not possible, then he could be deported to any country that would take him. Only one country fit that bill—the Soviet Union. The OSI had won their case. In an effort to cut further appeal off at the pass, the BIA held a second hearing on 16 October 1985 but ruled against Linnas's request for a review of Cohen's decision. Persuaded by the OSI contention that the Soviet Union was the only country willing to accept Linnas, the BIA, in effect, upheld Cohen's 9 April ruling.

One would have thought that at this point Linnas had exhausted all of his appeals. As might be expected, he was not ready to give up, nor was Berzins. After all, Linnas was fighting—quite literally—for his life. During this time his daughters continued to write letters "to the U.S. Baltic community and to public officials" on his behalf. They contacted anyone who could possibly help. They even wrote to President Ronald Reagan. In addition for requesting support to stay their father's deportation, the daughters solicited financial contributions to defray court costs, which amounted to over $300,000 by July 1986. Berzins filed an appeal of the most recent decision in the Second Circuit Court of Appeals.[43]

Judge Frank Altimari of the Second Circuit Court of Appeals heard the case in March 1986. Rudolph Giuliani presented the government's case. While the case was being heard, the OSI became concerned that Linnas was a flight risk—that he was laying plans to flee to Canada using an "underground support network."[44] The OSI took steps to prevent Linnas from leaving the country, if that was indeed his plan. Cooperating with the OSI, the U.S. Attorney's Office contacted Berzins and requested a meeting with him and his client. The purpose of the meeting was a discussion of custody in the event the court ruled against Linnas. When Berzins and his client arrived for the meeting, Linnas was placed under arrest.

This unexpected turn of events was a harbinger of things to come. Judge Altimari was ready to render his decision. Linnas and his family, Berzins, OSI representatives, Giuliani, and concerned citizens arrived in court and waited for Altimari to issue his ruling. First addressing the request to be deported to the "free and independent Republic of Estonia"—in New York—Altimari suggested that Linnas had wasted a chance of finding a legitimate deportation site. The judge was not amused, nor did he take the request seriously. Although he noted that under certain conditions the court could intervene, Altimari denied that such a case was before him. He stated, "The foundation of Linnas' due process argument is an appeal to the court's sense of decency and compassion. Noble words such as 'decency' and 'compassion' ring hollow when spoken by a man who ordered the extermination of innocent men, women and children kneeling at the edge of a mass grave. Karl Linnas' appeal to humanity, a humanity which he has grossly, callously and monstrously offended, truly offends this court's sense of decency."[45] Linnas and his family could see where this was going even before the judge gave his final ruling. Altimari upheld Cohen's order of deportation to the Soviet Union.

Linnas and his lawyer—his new lawyer, Ramsey Clark—continued to fight his deportation, and the case went all the way to the Supreme Court. In requesting that the high court hear the case, Clark, who had been President Lyndon B. Johnson's U.S. attorney general, argued "that the pending death sentence in the Soviet Union made it an improper destination for deportation." The Department of Justice countered with assurances from the Soviet Union that there was a "strong likelihood" that Linnas would receive a new trial.[46]

While the Supreme Court considered whether or not to hear the Linnas case, the OSI, confident that the ruling would be the desired one, commenced planning for deportation. The lack of direct flights to the Soviet Union was a complication. The concern was that Linnas would request asylum during a layover. Believing that Eastern European countries would not accept such a request, the OSI started contacting the Soviet-satellite countries. With an agreement to allow a layover in Czechoslovakia, the OSI's plans began to jell. Things were coming together, but the OSI could not relax until Linnas was on the plane to the Soviet Union, and that would not happen until there was a decision from the Supreme Court.

In the meantime pressure was mounting. Attorney General Edwin Meese received a memo on White House letterhead from Patrick Buchanan, President Reagan's communications director. While not mentioning the Linnas case directly, Buchanan noted that almost fifteen thousand cards, letters, and phone calls regarding "the denaturalization, deportation and prosecution of suspected war criminals" had landed on his desk.[47] In general, these communications were supportive of the policy, but many did express some concerns. Buchanan's memo sparked a meeting between Meese and members of the émigré community and resulted in a promise from the U.S. attorney general to investigate alleged OSI improprieties. This appeared to be a roundabout way to circumvent the order for Linnas's deportation. There was even discussion within the OSI about whether or not deporting Linnas to the Soviet Union was the right thing to do. There was also a flurry of activity during this time, as all sides continued to pursue possible alternative countries for the Linnas deportation destination. At the end of the day all avenues failed. Linnas's fate remained in the hands of the Supreme Court.

Although the Supreme Court "rejected a petition to hear the Linnas case" in January 1987, the Manhattan Federal Appeals Court agreed to a deportation delay on 2 April to allow Linnas's lawyers to appeal to the highest court one more time. A few days later "Supreme Court Justice Thurgood Marshall blocked the deportation of alleged Nazi war criminal Karl Linnas to consider, one final time, whether the United States should deport Linnas to the Soviet Union, where a Soviet court had sentenced him to death in absentia."[48]

On 20 April, however, Chief Justice William Rehnquist presented the majority opinion, in the six-to-three decision. The "Supreme Court vacated the Marshall stay," which opened the way to Linnas's deportation to the Soviet Union the next day. Because of his declining health, the Soviet government did not implement the execution punishment decreed in January 1962, but he was incarcerated in Tallin prison. In June prison officials transferred Linnas to a Leningrad (Saint Petersburg) hospital, where he had two operations. The operations failed to prolong the sixty-eight-year-old's life for long. Linnas died on 2 July 1987. His long battle to escape his past was over.[49]

For the Soviets, bringing Karl Linnas back to the Soviet Union to face justice was a high priority. While the U.S. government was not on good terms with the Soviet Union and was conflicted about deporting an alleged war criminal to a country where his fate was predetermined, the Department of Justice was under pressure to do the right thing. There was irrefutable evidence that Karl Linnas had entered the United States and obtained citizenship through illegal means. That alone warranted denaturalization and expulsion. Evidence of the crimes perpetrated by Linnas also stacked the deck against him. For multiple reasons, however, it took the U.S. Department of Justice, in conjunction with the Office of Special Investigations (after its founding in 1979), over twenty years to deport Karl Linnas to the

Soviet Union for justice to be served. Although he died approximately two months after he arrived in the Soviet Union, Karl Linnas was not executed. Consequently, the families of those who died in the Tartu concentration camp between 1941 and 1942 might legitimately question whether or not justice was served. After all, Linnas died from poor health, not execution. At the end of the day, did he pay the price for his role in the execution of twelve thousand innocent people?

8

Operation Paperclip—Antecedents and Dubious Draftees

A plan that began during World War II and continued during the postwar period, Operation Paperclip targeted top German scientists and technicians.[1] The goal was to identify scientists and technicians who were working on specific projects and to bring them to the United States. Of special interest were scientists and technicians working on rocket projects, particularly the V-1 and V-2, and aerodynamics, as well as those conducting experiments with chemical weapons, chemical reaction technology, and medicine.

U.S. intelligence and military services designed and implemented Operation Paperclip without the knowledge or approval of the Department of State. They successfully brought hundreds of scientists and technicians, along with their families, to the United States. Because they did not have State Department's approval, these people had to hide information about their service to the Third Reich and, in some cases, their membership in the SS, the SD, or the Nazi Party. These scientists and technicians worked on guided missile and ballistic missile technology and other sensitive projects before and during the war.

The goal of this chapter is to provide background on Operation Paperclip and discuss its mission and its implementation, particularly with regard to Department of State policy. Knowledge of Operation Paperclip is vital to understanding why so many Nazis were able to enter the United States—legally and illegally—and to evade punishment for so long. In some cases, even if punishment seemed to be warranted, they eluded it permanently. It must be noted first, however, that the United States was not the only nation interested in the knowledge that German scientists and technicians could provide on a variety of subject matters. Both Great Britain and the Soviet Union threw their hats into the ring and tried to put their hands on the people deemed important to their nations' futures as well. To a certain extent the United States and Great Britain conspired together to keep numerous scientists and technicians out of the hands of the Soviet Union. Although it may seem strange that two allies conspired against the third ally, as the hot conflict faded into a cold one, the position of the United States and Great Britain toward their erstwhile ally seemed justified. All three nations wanted to expand and improve production of certain goods—such as ordnance or rockets—to facilitate an advantage in potential future conflicts, particularly as the Cold War took shape in the wake of World War II.

To achieve this objective the acquisition of certain technologies and technological know-how was crucial. Capturing the technology and the documents was only part of it. Having access to the scientists and technicians who had worked on these programs for the Nazis and who could provide possible shortcuts, particularly on the technology front, was the other part of the equation. Therefore, in the final days of the war, American, British, and Soviet forces raced against one another to capture documents, intact rockets, rocket parts, other technologies, and personnel to further their agendas. In fact, as the war in Europe ended and the participants celebrated V-E day (Victory in Europe), the British implemented a plan—Operation Backfire—during the summer and fall of 1945, in an effort to obtain as much information as possible about the German V-2 rocket program and to construct and test fire V-2 rockets with the assistance of captured German scientists and technicians. Before the ink was dry on the V-E documents, the British, like their American and Soviet counterparts, were already focused on the next phases—ending the Pacific war and preparing for the postwar world.

With the war winding down in Europe, American forces accepted the surrender of hundreds of rocket scientists and technicians and found important documents about the program from Peenemünde that had been moved for safety to the isolated village of Dörnten, which was slated as part of the British occupation area. Desiring their fair share, the British used diplomatic means to gain access to the information and people who would allow them to evaluate the German program completely.[2]

Recognizing the importance of the German V-2 program and wanting to utilize German technological advancements to further their own program, the British organized Operation Backfire. The goal of Operation Backfire was to conduct a thorough investigation into the German rocket program with the endgame of determining what would potentially be most directly useful to the British. The Special Projectile Operations Group, which was the British section of the Allied Air Defense Division, went on the hunt for information. The group wanted more than information, however; it wanted to be able to translate the information into usable products. For the British that usable product was a reliable rocket that would allow them to project power in the Pacific Theater, where the war was still being fought, or in a future conflict. Whether or not an eventual space program was on the table was beside the point. More immediately, the British hoped to apply successful German technology to their ordnance and to utilize additional resources to the war in the Pacific. In that sense the British were like the Americans. Ironically, V-J day, or the end of the Pacific Theater conflict, arrived before Backfire had reached its culmination.

Ultimately, Operation Backfire had three phases: (1) evaluation of the V-2 assembly, (2) interrogation of V-2 scientists and technicians, and (3) test firing of rockets across the North Sea. Unlike the Americans, who captured intact V-2 rockets, however, the British found only parts of V-2 rockets. This would make phase three more challenging to accomplish and made phases one and two that much more crucial. Phases one and two required a high degree of success if the British hoped for even modest results in phase three. Pressure for success was intense, and the window of opportunity was limited. The British would have a relatively short period in which to achieve the outcomes dictated by the three phases of Backfire. Failure was not an option.

To achieve Backfire's goals, the British employed scientists and technicians who had worked on the Nazi's V-2 project. When the Operation Backfire mandate had been completed, the War Office detailed the process in a report that filled five volumes. Furthermore, after the completion of Backfire, many members of the V-2 Division returned

213

to Germany or went to the United States as part of Project Paperclip. Consequently, an examination of Operation Backfire, particularly the British employment and possible exploitation of German scientists and technicians, is the first part of the Project Paperclip story.

On 7 November 1945 Maj. Gen. A. M. Cameron, commander of the Special Projectile Operations Group, issued his report on Operation Backfire. In it, Cameron noted the mandate that he had received from the Supreme Commander, Allied Expeditionary Force, on 22 June 1945. The stated objective was "to ascertain the German technique of launching long range rockets and to prove it by actual launch. As complete, undamaged and fully tested rockets are not available, it is necessary first to assemble rockets from the available components. In addition to the primary object, the operation will therefore provide opportunity to study certain subsidiary matters such as the preparation of the rocket and ancillary equipment, the handling of fuels, and control in flight."[3]

Cameron got to work, but as the war wound down, things changed a bit. On 11 August the War Office assumed responsibility for Backfire and gave Cameron further instructions. The overall primary objective would remain the same, and Cameron would still have access to the German technical staff that had already been assembled. The expectation was that Cameron and his staff would compile a complete slate of information related to the launching of long-range rockets. In addition, "The intention is that you will collect this information by carrying out the operation of assembly and filling in Germany, using German disarmed personnel supervised by British technical experts, and that the successful completion of the operation will be proved by the firing of a number of A-4 rockets. Observation of the trajectory and photographic records will be taken as far as possible and the drill employed for firing the rockets will be recorded in detail."[4]

Although British and German teams would not attempt to launch a rocket until October, British interaction with captured Germans began much earlier. At the end of April, with the surrender of the German A-4 Division, personnel who built and fired A-4 rockets, the Allies chose over one hundred officers and men for interrogation. The criteria for interrogation included longevity of experience, particularly related to improvements in and launching of rockets. A month later these Germans became part of Operation Backfire. Included in the group temporarily released to the British by the Americans were Wernher von Braun, Arthur Rudolph, and Walter Dornberger. The British segregated them in a camp near Brussels and instituted even more intensive interrogations. By the beginning of July the number of Germans detained as part of Backfire had increased to 137, and the group was relocated to Altenwalde near Cuxhaven, on the North Sea near the mouth of the Elbe River.[5]

The complexity of building rockets soon became apparent, as did the need for more experienced personnel. Consequently, the British secured permission to obtain an additional seventy-nine technicians from the group in American custody at Garmisch-Partenkirchen. At the end of July these additional technicians joined the Backfire contingent at Cuxhaven. Because the intended program outcome exceeded the parameters of normal interrogations and because trust was an issue, the British divided the Germans into two groups. Lieutenant Colonel Weber, the senior German officer, received command of a military unit, which was created by grouping together soldiers and civilians who would work on the construction and launching of the rockets. The unit was designated the Altenwalde Versucha-Kommando. The second group, which was isolated near Brockeswalde, consisted entirely of civilian experts. The hope was that additional interrogation of these civilian experts would provide the information that would not only corroborate that provided by the other group but would also be crucial to the successful construction and launch of rockets.[6] Although Lt. Gen. Walter Dornberger was held separately from the other two groups, he was transported to England a short time later. Dornberger, an army artillery officer, led the v-2 rocket program and other projects at the Peenemünde Army Research Center, which made him valuable to the British and their Allied partners.[7]

Negotiation between the British and the Americans over the German scientists and technicians continued during the summer and into the fall of 1945—and, to some extent, had the feel of a National Football League (NFL) draft, albeit a draft that deemed the Soviets ineligible to participate. Because they considered them valuable, the British and the Americans believed that they had the right to control the destinies of the personnel in question, particularly once Germany lost the war. Unlike a normal wartime draft in which the majority were considered eligible, the British and the Americans wanted to draft only the best—"the cream of the crop." They did not consider this a game. It was a competition carried out by men who were more interested in acquiring assets than uncovering the dubious pasts of the Germans. They were also looking down the road to an unpromising postwar relationship with the Soviets. Furthermore, although they were not given a choice about being drafted, most German scientists and technicians, in all likelihood, would have chosen exploitation by the British or the Americans over the Soviets. Some, like Wernher von Braun, just wanted to continue their research. All of the players had an agenda. For the British and the Americans, it was fast-tracking their knowledge base to end the war on their terms. For the Germans it was a different future with the possibility of long-term employment instead of scrambling for their livelihood in Germany or facing a dubious lifetime under the control of the Soviets.

Events, however, diminished the Americans' early willingness to cooperate with the British regarding the temporary assignment of personnel prior to the conclusion of negotiations. Because the fight against the Japanese had not ended, the Americans requested the return of twenty-six civilians who were viewed as essential to the development of weapons for use in that conflict. The British, however, believed the transfer of these civilians back to the Americans would be detrimental to the successful completion of Backfire. While the two sides negotiated the fate of the contested civilians, the war in the Pacific ended. Under the terms of the agreement reached, however, the British returned fourteen civilians to the Americans and agreed to transfer the remaining twelve at the conclusion of Backfire.

Throughout this period the status, pay, and housing of the German soldiers and civilians were repeatedly evaluated. The British promised pay incentives to ensure cooperation. Included among the 600 Germans who participated in Backfire were 70 A-4 technicians and 128 A-4 Division troops.[8] Discussion between the British and the Americans over the "ownership" of German scientists and technicians also continued throughout this period, and the two sides negotiated and renegotiated that ownership. This dance foreshadowed postseason player exchanges, although there was no free agency involved. In many respects this part of the story is the most interesting. As the British and the Americans played "pass the rocketeers," two factors remained uppermost in their discussions. Each wanted to have access to the scientists and technicians who would best further their own weapon and rocket programs. Furthermore, both wanted to keep the German scientists and technicians out of the Soviets' hands, even though they had to acknowledge that the Soviets were crucial allies in the war that had just concluded. Not verbalizing that acknowledgment, however, also meant that the British and Americans could ignore the fact that they were figuratively stabbing their former ally in the back with their efforts to maintain control over the captured scientists and technicians.

Not only was the exchange of German scientists and technicians between Great Britain and the United States a contentious topic between the two countries, but it also sparked debate within the British government. As the British learned, reaching agreement over the German experts was not easy, whether it was the result of an internal debate or negotiations with their American Allies. For example, in a deputy chiefs of staff document dated 12 September 1945 and drafted in response to FMW 168, the author identified the previously agreed-on policy and noted that the committee was revisiting the issue, which was an indication of the fluidity of the situation. According to the memo, "Allocation of German scientists and technicians to be settled in Washington or London on the basis of requirements tabled by the Americans and ourselves. Each party to have the right to include in their lists personnel at present situated in either the British or American zones. Where both parties want the same individual and an acceptable substitute cannot be agreed approximate equality of allocation between the United States and the British Empire should be presumed."[9] The bottom line for the British, however, was the continuation of good relations with their American Allies, as is evidenced by the minutes from the 13 September meeting of the deputy chiefs of staff. The minutes clearly articulated their position: "There was general agreement that Anglo-American co-operation was more important than any question of using Germans in one country or the other."[10]

Which country—Britain or America—would have control over particular officers, scientists, and technicians was not easily resolved. Even as the British were conducting Backfire, discussions about "ownership" continued and were particularly contentious when both sides tried to draft someone or "claimed the same person." The personnel at Cuxhaven generally remained unaware of the negotiations going on in the background as they focused on their work. As indicated earlier, there were two separate groups working on the project. The technical group focused on the rockets and was tasked with both building and repairing them. The availability of materials proved frustrating at times, but the group worked well with their British counterparts in an effort to construct rockets that could be successfully tested.[11]

The second group provided information about field procedures to the British Field Staff, which assumed responsibility for the actual firing of the rockets once construction and repairs were completed. Col. W. S. J. Carter had command of the British Field Staff. The firing troop, although understaffed, consisted of 107 German operational personnel. The limitation of personnel meant that some of the operational personnel worked with the technical group to rebuild rockets and ground equipment. As a result, "elaborate rehearsals of the field operations" was not possible during the reconstruction stage. With the target date for the first launch set for 1 October, teams conducted launch rehearsals during the last week of September.[12]

On 1 October the first rocket was put into launch position. The gray skies perhaps foretold the outcome of the first attempt to launch a rocket. Two unsuccessful efforts were made to launch. Ignition failed to occur because the steam unit valves would not open. When attempts to resolve the problems and achieve a successful launch on 1 October did not come to fruition, the British Field Staff made the decision to postpone the launch for a day and to attempt it with a different rocket. Crews reconvened on 2 October. The day could not have been better for a launch. The sky was clear, and wind was minimal. At 2:43 p.m. the rocket left the launch pad. As Cameron noted in his report, "This was the first A-4 launching to be observed by Allied personnel at close quarters." Although the rocket was only in the air for just under five minutes, it reached a maximum height of 43.1 miles and a range of 155.0 miles.[13]

Two days later teams returned to the launch pad with another rocket for the next test fire. With clear skies and no wind, conditions were again perfect. Having been repaired, the rocket, which had not launched on 1 October, returned to the pad for another attempt. At 2:15 p.m. liftoff occurred. This time, because of engine failure, the rocket remained aloft for only slightly more than two minutes. Its maximum height was 10.8 miles, and its range was 14.9 miles. Although the launch was successful, the rocket's performance was disappointing. The mitigating factor this time was engine failure; the result was minimal success.[14]

Crews would have one more chance to get it right. The final launch date was 15 October. A number of representatives, including some from the United States and the Soviet Union, were on hand. Because the proximity of Cuxhaven to the Soviet zone made a secret launch unlikely, the British invited Soviet observers to be present, which allowed the British to control the amount and type of information that they shared. Weather conditions were less than ideal. Low clouds obscured the view, and surface winds of thirty miles per hour were potentially problematic. Since this test was meant to be a demonstration more than anything else, the Backfire team made the decision to proceed. The third rocket left the launch pad without a hitch at 3:06 p.m. and remained in flight for four minutes and thirty-seven seconds. Although its behavior was normal, the rocket fell short and slightly off target. Its maximum height reached 39.8 miles, and its flight range was 144.8 miles. Although less than perfect, the launch achieved its purpose and received a "success" rating.[15]

With the October rocket launches completed, it was time to dismantle the program and write an after-action report, which Cameron completed a short time later. Dismantlement did not, however, resolve one issue—what to do with the Germans officers, scientists, and technicians who had participated in Backfire. Discussion on various topics related to the Germans continued for some time after the operation's completion. At no point, however, did Soviet access to the personnel in question receive serious consideration—this despite the fact that Soviet representatives witnessed the final Backfire test on 15 October. Two weeks later, on 29 October, Group Captain Wilson received a memorandum titled "Exploitation of German Scientists." It referenced earlier "British proposals for the co-ordinated exploitation of German Scientists and Technicians in the United States and the United Kingdom" that had been put on the table for discussion a month earlier. Although no official reply had been received, the memorandum articulated the British understanding of the next step. Both countries would construct lists of the German personnel whom they wanted to acquire. The lists would provide a starting point for negotiations. British and American archives include numerous versions of those lists along with accounts of efforts to resolve ownership of jointly claimed scientists and technicians. It was a continuation of the draft discussions that had begun months earlier. Although the war was over, the desire to acquire experts, particularly in rocketry, remained. Understanding the technology would translate to better weaponry for future conflicts or in the short term as potential deterrents to their former ally, soon to be a Cold War adversary. The memorandum also identified the machinery to be employed during the negotiation process and proposed the exchange of completed work products.[16]

The exchange of German scientists and technicians with the Americans was not the British government's only concern. It also had to make decisions about factors related to those Germans who would reside in Britain for an unspecified period of time, including the length of their employment, pay, housing, and families. For example, the Cabinet Office had to address parliamentary questions about the future use of both personnel and information that were raised by the Board of Trade in December 1945. In crafting a response, the Cabinet Office stated,

> It is the Government's policy to secure from Germany a knowledge of scientific and technical developments that will be of benefit to this country and to make such knowledge available to those who can use it. This step seems desirable since although we were generally ahead, there were cer-

tain fields in which the Germans held a temporary lead. As part of this policy it is proposed to recruit, on the recommendation of the responsible department, a strictly limited number of German scientists and technicians of the highest grade for service in this country. Any Germans brought in under this scheme must be politically unobjectionable and they will be subject to strict supervision while they are here. They will be allowed to land in the first instance for a period of 6 months and any prolongation of this period will be made in consultation with my Rt. Hon. Friend the Secretary of State for Home Affairs.[17]

The Cabinet Office then delineated the kind of acceptable government work that these "aliens" could perform. While acknowledging that some Germans could be hired by "individual firms," their employment would be predicated on the fact that there were no British citizens available. Furthermore, even if they worked for private companies, these Germans would still be considered "Servants of the State." The Cabinet Office, to some extent, justified its position by noting that the Americans and the Soviets had adopted similar policies.[18]

What the records do not indicate is the extent to which the Germans scientists and technicians were willing participants in this process. Additional examination may reveal more of this side of the story. What is apparent, however, is that some Germans learned that there were perhaps unexpected consequences of cooperation with the British. For example, the British War Crimes Investigation Unit questioned Dornberger about the use of slave labor for V-2 rocket construction. As director of the V-2 program, he did have legitimate questions to answer. The British eventually allowed Dornberger, who spent two years in detention, to transfer to the United States under Operation Paperclip. Despite British warnings about Dornberger, whom they called a "menace of the first order," the Americans, not to be deterred, gave him a contract shortly after his release from British custody and chose to ignore his alleged connection to the use of slave labor. After signing his Paperclip contract on 12 July 1947, Dornberger spent the next three years developing guided missiles for the U.S. Air Force before gaining employment in the private sector at Bell Aircraft. Living a charmed life, Dornberger's past did not come back to haunt him. Not only did he achieve career success as a senior vice president for Bell Aerosystems Division, but his previous work with the U.S. Air Force also opened doors for him and afforded him the security clearances that allowed him to liaise with military agencies.[19] Although Dornberger—despite his past—was a success story, not all of the American associations with German scientists and technicians were as smooth sailing as Dornberger's.

As noted, the Americans faced some of the same issues as the British when they considered importing captured scientists and technicians for critical wartime and postwar work. In fact, the Americans and the British conducted discussions during the summer of 1945 in an effort to craft policies and procedures for the appropriate importation of these captured assets. On 6 July the War Department, General Staff (WDGS), constructed a document enumerating the "principles and procedures," which were to govern the "exploitation of German specialists in science and technology in the United States," and sent it to the Joint Chiefs of Staff (JCS), the British Chiefs of Staff, and the Navy Department for review. All three weighed in on the WDGS's proposed policies. The JCS accepted the policies as articulated. Not wishing to be committed completely, the British Chiefs of Staff hedged its bets by signing on to participation "in principle." The Navy Department agreed to cooperate with the stated policies, but with a caveat. It would do so if the War Department maintained "administrative control."[20]

The new directive acknowledged that the WDGS envisioned procedures that would permit the "exploitation of chosen, rare minds whose continuing intellectual productivity we wish to use."[21] The directive clearly articulated the WDGS plan for exploitation:

> The specialists brought to the United States will be those whose exploitation to the fullest cannot be accomplished in Europe and whose presence here will enable them to fit in as a part of a definite program of activity of a continuing character. Careful selection will be made by the Assistant Chief of Staff, G-2, WDGS for those German specialists whose actual presence is indispensable.
>
> No known or alleged war criminals should be brought to the United

States. If any specialists who are brought to this country are subsequently found to be listed as alleged war criminals, they should be returned to Europe for trial.

To improve the chances of cooperation on the part of the specialists, protection should be afforded dependent members of their immediate families while the specialists are in the country. The specialists are to be paid a modest per diem from funds under the control of the Secretary of War.

The purpose of this plan should be understood to be temporary military exploitation of the minimum number of German specialists necessary. In these instances where exploitation is completed, the specialists will be returned to Europe.[22]

Ironically, the program did employ alleged war criminals, whose pasts were somewhat obscured, and was, at the end of the day, anything but temporary. In addition, President Harry S. Truman was unaware of the WDGS exploitation plan. Although the WDGS's intentions were quite mercenary, one must remember that at the time the directive was crafted, the United States was still at war. The Germans might have waved the white flag, but the Japanese had yet to do so. Furthermore, Truman had not yet approved the use of an atomic bomb against the Japanese city of Hiroshima.

Although the American program was ultimately known by its code name Paperclip, Operation Overcast was the initial U.S. importation policy created by the JCS, but plans for tapping into a wellspring of knowledge—albeit generated by the enemy—actually predated Operation Overcast. As early as 1943, U.S. officials, including the chief of staff, George Marshall, turned their attention to an issue of primary importance—the state of the German atomic bomb program. Although they asked a number of elementary questions, at the end of the day, it all boiled down to one question. How close were the Germans to producing a weapon of this caliber? Crucial to answering that question were all related materials, including documents, equipment, and the scientists and technicians who were involved in atomic bomb research for the Reich. To that end, an Alsos Mission had the task of locating those who played an integral role in the German atomic bomb program.

The Alsos Mission was the code name for the intelligence-gathering operation that fell under the auspices of the Manhattan Engineer District. Falling under the umbrella of the U.S. Manhattan Project and commanded by Gen. Leslie Groves, the Alsos Mission received orders to proceed to occupied Europe, where their members were to gather intelligence about the German atomic bomb program.[23] Thinking ahead to future needs, the U.S. chief of staff, George Marshall, who was the driving force behind the establishment of the Manhattan Engineer District, mandated the parameters of the mission:

> While the major portion of the enemy's secret scientific developments is being conducted in Germany, it is very likely that much valuable information can be obtained thereon by interviewing prominent Italian scientists in Italy. . . . The scope of inquiry should cover all principal scientific military developments and the investigations should be conducted in a manner to gain knowledge of enemy progress without disclosing our interest in any particular field. The personnel who undertake this work must be scientifically qualified in every respect. . . . It is proposed to send at the proper time to allied occupied Italy a small group of civilian scientists assisted by the necessary military personnel to conduct these investigations. Scientific personnel will be selected by Brig. Gen. Leslie R. Groves with the approval of Dr. [Vannevar] Bush and military personnel will be assigned by the Asst. Chief of Staff, G-2, from personnel available to him. . . . This group would form the nucleus for similar activity in other enemy and enemy-occupied countries when circumstances permit.[24]

Although Italy was the initial target for gathering information about the German atomic bomb program, the evolving nature of the war allowed the Alsos Mission to expand into other countries on their fact-finding mandate. In fact, the Alsos Mission operated in three phases, the first of which—Alsos I—was in Italy. In the summer of 1944 Alsos II began operating in France. By February 1945 the mission entered its final phase, when Alsos III set up shop in Germany.

During the final months of the war, while several Allied technical teams gathered intelligence about the German v-1 and v-2 programs, others pursued information about the atomic bomb angle. In April and early May 1945, the Alsos Mission hit the mother lode.

The team succeeded in detaining ten atomic scientists. Included in the group that fell into the Alsos Mission net were three Nobel Prize winners—Otto Hahn, Werner Heisenberg, and Max von Laue. Following their capture, the ten atomic scientists found themselves cooling their heels in an internment camp in England for almost a year.[25]

As noted earlier, the British and American intelligence agencies shared information. This exchange occurred under the umbrella of the Field Information Agency, Technical, which was established by a directive issued by Gen. Dwight D. Eisenhower on the advice of his assistant chief of staff for intelligence (G-2), Maj. Gen. Kenneth W. D. Strong. The purpose of the Field Information Agency, Technical, was "to fill the need for one clearing house to 'plan, establish policies, control, direct and coordinate on an integrated basis' all activities of the various technical units and projects operating in territory controlled by Eisenhower's forces." In addition to the Allied intelligence agencies, Alsos, Backfire, and Overcast fell under the umbrella of the Field Information Agency, Technical.[26]

The cooperation that resulted from information sharing by the Allied intelligence agencies first facilitated the British Project Backfire and then the American Project Overcast, but all did not run smoothly. Recognizing that the scientists and technicians who worked on the German atomic, v-1, and v-2 programs could not be exploited to their fullest potential while they remained in war-torn Europe and faced possible appropriation by the Soviets, the JCS commenced Overcast in June 1945 to solve this problem by relocating carefully chosen assets to the United States.[27] Although begun in June, Overcast was not officially codified until 20 July. The JCS's motivation was clear from the beginning—"to assist in shortening the Japanese war and to aid our postwar military research." Overcast was never meant to be anything other than a military program. Furthermore, the military had jurisdiction over the wartime disposition of prisoners. It is clear, however, that President Harry S. Truman was not initially brought into the loop and informed about Overcast.[28]

Overcast immediately ran into problems because it overlapped with the British initiative Backfire. As indicated earlier, many of the captured scientists and technicians became part of a tug-of-war, as both the British and the Americans vied for the cream of the crop—to draft the best scientists and technicians for their team. Despite the military and technological need for these assets, the Americans, who feared domestic fallout if average citizens learned of the plan to bring a large number of Germans into the country, worked hard with their British counterparts in devising a plan for "sharing the scientific spoils of war." The goal was to put Overcast into play quietly to avoid broadcasting information about the number of Germans relocating to the United States or about their wartime work. The sense of urgency that existed in June dissipated with the Japanese surrender, which made the rush to implement Overcast less imperative.[29]

Within weeks after Truman's announcement on 1 September 1945 that Japan had acquiesced to the unconditional surrender terms, the first German scientists, engineers, and technicians landed in Boston. Armed with six-month contracts, Dr. Wernher von Braun and six other V-2 rocket engineers—four Hermann Göring Institute scientists and a Messerschitt Me-262 test pilot and his mechanic—were ready to work for a new employer: the U.S. Army. Housed at Fort Strong, which earned the name "Operation Overcast hotel," the Germans were tasked with "undertak[ing] research, design, development, and other tasks associated with jet propulsion and guided missiles as may be assigned by competent U.S. authorities."[30] The question became where they would carry out their mandate.

By 29 September 1945 transportation of the Germans to their final destinations began. The first group traveled to Aberdeen Proving Ground, where they translated, cataloged, and evaluated captured German documents. On 6 October Wernher von Braun began his trip to Fort Bliss, Texas. Once there his work for army ordnance commenced immediately. Operation Overcast was moving forward—albeit slowly.

All did not, however, go smoothly. The German participants had signed six-month contracts. What would happen when the six months was up? Would enough replacements have arrived in the meantime to give the research bench depth and allow the return of the first draftees to Germany? Even before these first contracts expired, the planners had to admit that Overcast in its initial iteration was not enough. The demand for personnel—for specialists—by the military services far exceeded the numbers shipped in the first month of Overcast. In a 25 July communication the War Department instructed the Commanding General, United States Forces, European Theater, to "locate, screen, contract, and ship a maximum quota of 350 volunteer specialists; to afford protection for their families; and to obtain British concurrence to evaluate related equipment, documents, and records."[31] The War Department orders proved problematic because plans were already in place to supply that number of "volunteer specialists" to the U.S. Army Ordnance.

The need for ever-increasing volunteer specialists created unforeseen difficulties, only some of which could be resolved by extending the six-month contracts for another six-month or year period. The end of the war against Japan did not eliminate the need for these important experts. It did not take long for the Cold War to heat up and reinforce the importance of maintaining control of the draftees—who were needed to enhance American technological advancements. Keeping them out of the Soviets' hands was crucial to achieving that goal. Furthermore, expansion of Overcast to meet the ever-increasing demands eventually required Truman's approval.

The War Department received an unexpected ally in former vice president Henry Wallace, who was the secretary of commerce. Tasked with overseeing the acquisition of reparations from Germany in the form of scientific and technical information, Wallace was in a unique position to help the War Department initiative. Also involved was the Joint Intelligence Objectives Agency, or JIOA, which the JCS created in September 1945. The JIOA assumed control of the Nazi scientist program. If the Overcast specialists were to receive contract extensions and remain in the United States for a longer period, the Department of State would have to factor into the mix. Consequently, the State Department added a new member to the JIOA—Samuel Klaus—who was responsible for approving visas for the German scientists.

Klaus immediately clashed with his colleagues at the JIOA. He was not on board with Overcast or its expansion to admit an ever-increasing number of volunteer specialists into the United States. In fact, Klaus demonstrated early on that he would pose an impediment to the program when he suggested that the Germans in question were not "brilliant scientists" who had been caught up in an inescapable situation. Staunchly anti-Nazi, Klaus had a different perspective when it came to all Germans, especially the German scientists. He accused them of being "amoral opportunists of mediocre talent" and promised that he would do all is his power to limit the number of visas issued to German scientists to "less than a dozen." Klaus would make it difficult to ignore the scientists' pasts, their memberships in the Nazi Party and the ss, which were visa disqualifiers.[32] The JIOA faced a conundrum. Despite their dubious wartime backgrounds, the JIOA viewed the identified draftees as crucial to the future Cold War fight.

Wallace would help the JIOA do an end run around Klaus and the State Department. Wallace became involved because his office—the Department of Commerce—also had a representative on the JIOA: John C. Green. A supporter of the German scientist program, Green—in the face of Klaus's opposition—appealed to Wallace for help. Wallace, at first glance, was an unusual choice. During the war he had frequently vocalized his opinion of Hitler as the devil incarnate. Although, like Klaus, he was a staunch anti-Nazi, Wallace was a firm believer in the importance of science to the economic growth and prosperity of the United States. Unlike Klaus, he put the U.S. future before his hatred of all things Nazi. Wallace agreed to write a letter of support for Overcast, which he sent to Truman on 4 December 1945. In his letter Wallace directly linked the German scientist program to U.S. economic prosperity. Because of his past public position regarding Hitler and the Germans, Wallace's letter carried much weight and persuaded Truman to get on board as well.[33]

Even before the president agreed to support the initiative, the JIOA moved forward with expansion. By 1946 the number of required "former enemy specialists" greatly exceeded initial expectations and reached a thousand. By March 1946 Overcast had a new name—Paperclip—and a new supporter. Wallace's letter had the desired effect, and Truman acknowledged the benefits of the program. The idea of employing Germans in the American Cold War fight was an appealing one. Truman had one reservation, however. He was concerned about potential backlash if the American public got wind of Project Paperclip; therefore, his support came with caveats. Paperclip had to be a covert program. The public had to be blissfully unaware of the program in general *and*, more specifically, of the numbers of Germans involved. Furthermore, Truman put restrictions on the types of Germans who could participate in the program, when he officially authorized the JIOA plan in September 1946. Hard-core Nazis were not eligible to participate. Only "nominal" or "opportunistic" Nazis could take part in Paperclip.[34] Truman's restriction could potentially disqualify a number of key German personnel on the JIOA's A-list—those already in the country or those designated for transfer to the United States in the near future.

The first test would come six months after Truman approved Paperclip, when the director of JIOA, Bosquet Wev, submitted the first batch of scientists' dossiers to the Department of State and the Department of Justice for approval. These dossiers included carefully selected information and omitted potentially damaging data that could result in rejection of the applications. Missing from the dossiers was "raw intelligence reports on the German specialists' activities." Included instead were security reports issued by the Office of the Military Government of the United States (OMGUS), which was the occupation government's administration in postwar Germany. The OMGUS based the reports about the scientists on information provided by the U.S. Army's Counter Intelligence Corps. Because it knew that the phrase "ardent Nazi" was a disqualifier, the OMGUS generally inserted less inflammatory phrases instead when describing the scientists.[35]

Using less inflammatory terminology did not, necessarily, ensure approval of the dossiers by either State or Justice. For Wev and the JIOA, roadblocks would be put in place by State through Samuel Klaus, a known opponent of Project Paperclip. Klaus found all former Nazis suspect. Degree of commitment to the party did not factor into his world view when he assessed the dossiers. An additional problem in the mix was the nature of the OMGUS reports included in the first batch. Having not yet been informed of the desirability of utilizing the Germans to further an American agenda, the OMGUS was more honest in the initial reports than they were in later ones. That honesty caused problems for the JIOA. In assessing those brought to the United States as part of Project Overcast, the OMGUS categorized them as "ardent Nazis." Nor was the OMGUS assessment of the "specialists on the Paperclip recruiting list" any better.[36]

The climate was ripe for a confrontation between Wev and Klaus. The reality was that—no matter what the OMGUS reports said—over 50 percent of those recruited by Wev had been members of the Nazi Party or veterans of the SS. Not willing to play ball, Klaus rejected the recruits—drafted members of Paperclip. He ruled them ineligible under the criteria established by Truman. Furious at being thwarted, Wev had to rethink the process. Obtaining visas for members of the Paperclip team was crucial. Anxious to move forward, Wev suggested that the OMGUS dossiers be altered to make them more acceptable to Klaus—and by extension to the Department of State.

By late 1946 the military held approximately 230 Paperclip scientists in custody. The JIOA informed the State Department to expect visa applications for the scientists and their families and indicated that the OMGUS intelligence reports would include the "best information available." Ever suspicious, Samuel Klaus concluded that military intelligence officers would not include damaging information in these reports and that "the pipeline to bring ardent Nazis and their families into the United States was wide open." There was justification for Klaus's concerns. The proof was in the pudding, so to speak. Over 750 German volunteer specialists—scientists, technicians, and engineers—entered the United States during the decade after the war under a protected umbrella provided by Overcast, Paperclip, and other similar programs. Approximately 80 percent were former members of the Nazi Party—and in many cases of the SS as well. The Cold War continued to provide the driving force behind programs such as Paperclip. By the time Paperclip had served out its usefulness, approximately 1,600 German scientists had entered the United States, along with their families.[37] Most successfully applied for U.S. citizenship. For a time they were able to work and live quiet lives in the United States. At the end of the day, however, that changed for many of them.

When news got out about the background of members of the Overcast and Paperclip teams, Americans became more aware of—perhaps dubious—policies implemented by the U.S. government in the wake of World War II. Justified as necessary because of the Cold War, which began on the heels of World War II, Overcast and Paperclip gave the United States the edge it needed against the Soviet Union, but it did so with the help of Germans with checkered pasts, some of whom would later be investigated by the Office of Special Investigations. In some cases they faced trial, denaturalization, and deportation. Scientists and technicians such as Arthur Rudolph, Wernher von Braun, Bernhard Tessmann, and Kurt Blome, who were members of the Overcast or Paperclip teams, warrant further investigation. The next couple of chapters endeavor to answer some of the questions raised by this discussion of Backfire, Overcast, and Paperclip.

Before delving into the cases of Paperclip individuals, however, the following question deserves attention. Why did the scientists and technicians cooperate with Backfire, Overcast, and Paperclip? For some these projects provided them with the opportunity to continue the work that excited them. Von Braun and Rudolph, for example, were driven to build rockets. Initially, they built rockets for German ordnance, but they wanted to build and test even bigger and more powerful rockets. After working for U.S. Army Ordnance, both men found employment with NASA, and Rudolph saw his dream of putting a rocket on the moon come to fruition. For others participating in Paperclip allowed them to escape their past. By signing up and being drafted into service, many could and did avoid prosecution for alleged war crimes—at least for decades. Some Germans sought a better life for themselves and their families than they believed they would experience under Allied or Soviet occupation. Working for the U.S. military and other government divisions frequently led to naturalization and opened doors to job opportunities in the private sector. Furthermore, employment by the Americans or the British was possibly more attractive than employment in the Soviet system. At the end of the day, the German scientists, engineers, and technicians who participated in Backfire, Overcast, and Paperclip were perhaps motivated by a combination of factors—not the least of which was the chance for a new life.

At the end of the war in Europe, both the British and the Americans wanted to take advantage of German advances in weapons development—especially in cutting-edge, high-tech areas like rocketry, missiles, and jet engines. They also wanted to deny their Soviet Allies access to the same information. The result was a quick, and often haphazard, scramble as the Western Allies moved to transfer key enemy personnel out of Soviet reach. Thus began a period of talent scouting and ownership-rights negotiation—similar to the draft process in professional athletics. While the scientists and technicians did not profit as spectacularly as a top-flight quarterback or point guard as a rule, Paperclip participants secured something no less valuable to them: a more secure future for themselves and their families than they were likely to have if they had not "volunteered" to serve their conquerors and new masters.

The officers and civilians captured in April 1945 had at best limited control over their own futures. The lucky ones participated in Operation Backfire or Operations Overcast and Paperclip and avoided fates that awaited some of their peers, including the possibility of being tried for war crimes. The really lucky ones found gainful employment in Britain or the United States in the postwar era because they had something important, indeed unique, to offer—new knowledge and fresh skills. As a result, Britain's Operation Backfire, for example, had two important outcomes. Like a good sports' trade, both parties profited. The British successfully gained an important theoretical and technical understanding of the German v-2 rocket program. German personnel who participated in Operation Backfire also received long-term benefits, especially if they succeeded in gaining employment in key British and American industries after their direct usefulness to the Allied governments had ended. They escaped the material and emotional effects of living in a shattered society. Americans and Germans alike derived similar benefits from Backfire and U.S. operations, Overcast and Paperclip. And for some participants, the American package had a bonus—no particularly careful screening for possible war crimes. This oversight was sufficiently obvious that not a few beneficiaries of the American programs were eventually investigated by the Office of Special Investigations of the U.S. Department of Justice. That, however, occurred in the future—many years in the future.

9

Arthur Rudolph—Nazi Rocket Scientist, NASA Scientist, or Villain?

In August 1984, after receiving the Distinguished Service Medal from the National Aeronautics and Space Administration (NASA) and after thirty years as a naturalized American, seventy-eight-year-old Arthur Rudolph "forfeited his U.S. citizenship" and left the United States under a cloud of suspicion—never to return. According to the Office of Special Investigations, his actions while working as a rocket scientist for the Nazis reportedly involved persecution and mistreatment of Jews and other prisoners. Who was this mild-mannered man who had the distinction of being "the only Paperclip scientist prosecuted by OSI"? What set him apart from other scientists who came to the United States under Operation Paperclip? Were his crimes serious enough to warrant persecution by the OSI and the Department of Justice? After all, he was not convicted by the Department of Justice or stripped of his citizenship. He voluntarily relinquished it and agreed to leave the country. If he was innocent, as he claimed, why didn't Rudolph remain in the United States and provide evidence that would have forced the OSI to abandon its investigation into his background and his work for the Nazis?[1]

Early Life

On 9 November 1906 Arthur Louis Hugo Rudolph was born in Stepfershausen, Germany, to Gustav and Ida Rudolph, who were farmers. From a very early age Rudolph was fascinated with machinery. As a young boy, he had his share of chores on the farm, but he knew that he did not want to be a farmer because the work was so hard. Unfortunately, farm life would not remain peaceful and uneventful. World War I changed things for the Rudolph family, particularly after Gustav Rudolph died on the Eastern Front in 1915.

Rudolph began his education at the village elementary school. After completing eight years of school and receiving confirmation in the Lutheran Church, he attended a *Fachschule* in the town of Schmalkalden: three years of study similar to that offered at many American junior colleges. For the next three years Rudolph worked as a "practitioner in the silver-working industry" in Bremen before continuing his education at the College of Berlin in 1928.[2] In 1930 he graduated with an undergraduate degree in mechanical engineering.

After a brief stint as a draftsman, Rudolph began employment at Heylandt in Berlin on 1 May 1930. The company manufactured equipment used in the production, handling, and transportation of oxygen. On his second day at Heylandt, Rudolph witnessed the testing of a small rocket by two employees—Max Valier and Walter Riedel. In short order he asked to join Valier's team and was accepted. Little did he know that this was the beginning of a path that would lead to V-2 rockets, NASA, and Saturn V rockets and that would bring notoriety but would end in accusations and a tarnished reputation, in disgrace.

A couple of weeks later an accident cost the lead scientist, Valier, his life. Rudolph was hooked, his fascination with rockets, undiminished. The German redesigned the fuel injection system, which stabilized his former colleague's rocket design, and continued to research and design rockets, despite the company's ban on such activity after Valier's death. He even enlisted the help of his boss, Alfons Pietsch, who was works manager at Heylandt. In fact, Rudolph, Pietsch, and Riedel tested the new design at the plant when Dr. Heylandt was out of town. Rudolph had the rocket-space travel bug, and he was not going to let an accident and a company ban stop his work! Pietsch was equally enthusiastic. Unfortunately, he went too far, and Heylandt ultimately fired him.

Around this time the three Heylandt employees received an invitation to witness rocket tests performed by members of the German Rocket Society. Although the tests failed to result in an airborne rocket, the day had long-lasting ramifications for Rudolph. It was there that he met Wernher von Braun, the man who became one of the most famous of rocket scientists in both Germany and the United States.[3]

The lives and careers of these two men—Rudolph and von Braun—would become intertwined for the next several decades.

Nazi Years

With the start of the Great Depression in 1929, the ranks of the Nazi Party swelled. Many of Rudolph's friends joined. Although his interest was in rockets, not politics, Rudolph gave in to pressure from his friends and became a member of the party. He was also persuaded by his unfocused fear, widely shared in the "non-political" German middle and professional classes, that the Communist Party, which was also on the rise, would "become the government." As member No. 562007, he also enlisted in the SA. The Depression had serious ramifications both in Germany and abroad. While it increased the membership of the Nazi Party, it also cost Rudolph his job. He was laid off in May 1932. Joining the ranks of the unemployed, Rudolph was required to get his card stamped periodically at the Arbeitsamt, or Unemployment Office.[4] While there he encountered Pietsch, who was also unemployed. The two men agreed to continue their efforts to design and launch a rocket successfully. For Rudolph, who was responsible for the design end of things while Pietsch would seek funding, this marked an evolution from hobby to career.[5]

Within four weeks Rudolph had completed his rocket design. Although it took a while, Pietsch eventually got a contract from the German Ordnance Department, which had tasked Capt. Walter Dornberger with developing a "liquid-fuel rocket" that could be used as a weapon.[6] Unfortunately, things did not go as smoothly as expected. After Pietsch spent about half of the money on himself and then disappeared, Rudolph had to negotiate a new contract with Dornberger. Following a successful test of his design, which was assessed by Wernher von Braun, Rudolph accepted a job offer from Dornberger. He became a civilian employee with the army. Although his real interest was putting a rocket into space, for the time being, however, Rudolph had to put that aside and focus on the needs of the Ordnance Department—the development of artillery rockets.

Rudolph's initial posting was to Kummersdorf, where Dornberger, who would rise to the rank of major general and who was in charge of the German rocket program throughout the war, managed a small group of scientists, including Rudolph, Riedel, and von Braun. While at Kummersdorf Rudolph and the other scientists built and experimented with increasingly larger liquid-fuel rockets. In December 1934 a group from Kummersdorf, including Rudolph, tested two A-2 rockets on the island of Borkum in the North Sea. The rockets, which performed well, reached a height of one and a half miles. The scientists also conducted tests on a rocket engine that had been designed by Rudolph when he worked at Heylandt. During this time Rudolph and von Braun spent much time together—both at work and after hours. The two men shared an interest in space travel and a belief that it was possible to build a rocket capable of flying to the moon and beyond, and discussions of their ideas and designs kept them up all hours of the night.

As their work continued, the Kummersdorf scientists tested rockets that were twenty-five feet long, then ones approximately twice as long that could fly two hundred miles. The latter eventually received the designation "V-2." Despite successfully testing these rockets, both Rudolph and von Braun felt constrained by the space where they worked and sought a testing ground that would allow them to experiment with even bigger rockets—rockets capable of space travel. Consequently, taking advantage of Dornberger's temporary absence from Kummersdorf, the two approached the Luftwaffe because they considered the group more forward thinking and because they knew of Hitler's support of it. Their sales pitch worked, and in short order the Luftwaffe pledged five million marks and space for the creation of a rocket center. Learning of the Luftwaffe involvement, the army wanted in as well. Upon Dornberger's return, von Braun apprised his superior of events that had occurred in his absence. Recognizing the genius behind the actions taken by von Braun and Rudolph, Dornberger took charge, cut through red tape, and moved mountains to organize a facility at Peenemünde, on Usedom, a Baltic coastal island a hundred miles north of Berlin.

In May 1937 the new rocket center at Peenemünde became operational, and Rudolph and other Kummersdorf staff moved there. By mid-August his pregnant wife, Martha, whom Rudolph married in

October 1935, joined him. Three months later their daughter Marianne Erika was born. This was an exciting time for Rudolph, who, like his colleagues, worked long hours doing the work that both interested and intrigued them.

Testing on liquid-fuel rockets continued for the next several years, but it was not until 13 June 1942 that the first attempt to launch a v-2 rocket occurred. The first two tests ended in failure when the rockets exploded as they reached higher altitudes. The third time was the charm. On 3 October 1942 Rudolph and his colleagues successfully tested a v-2 rocket; following its designated trajectory, it traveled 125 miles from the launch site to its entry into the Baltic Sea. Success still did not bring the rocket program the full support of Hitler or the Nazi regime. That, however, would change within a relatively short period of time.

When Adolf Hitler first visited the rocket center at Peenemünde in March 1939, he barely reacted. Government support for the program subsequently declined. Four years later, however, after the successful testing of the v-2, that would change. In early July 1943 Dornberger and von Braun received a summons to show Hitler a film of the successful v-2 rocket launch from the previous October. Finally recognizing the "war-winning" potential of the weapon, the führer became enamored with the project and promised to authorize support for its expansion. When he learned about the v-2 program, Heinrich Himmler recognized the need for maintaining secrecy about the rocket program and its expansion and supposedly suggested that the best way to ensure security would be to utilize a workforce that consisted entirely of concentration camp internees. The plan received Hitler's approval. From this point on the rocket center at Peenemünde did not lack funds, equipment, or manpower, and Dornberger tasked Rudolph with designing the pilot production plant for the site.[7]

Working under Gen. Godomar Schubert, Rudolph began the design for the new facility and, as a result, temporarily relinquished his development work. By August Rudolph had the assembly line ready for the production of v-2 rockets, but production was disrupted by British bombing raids against the buildings at Peenemünde, including employee houses. Following the raid, the women and children were evacuated to safer locales in Germany. The production facility was moved as well. Its new location would be at Mittelwerk, and Rudolph received orders to move there as well to oversee operations.

Mittelwerk was not what Rudolph expected. It consisted of a series of factories located in tunnels constructed in the mountains. When he arrived at Mittelwerk, Rudolph learned that his workforce would consist of forced laborers, many of whom had originally been housed at Buchenwald. The SS would construct a new concentration camp—Dora-Nordhausen—to house the prisoners that they would supervise. The prisoners performed two functions: additional excavation of tunnels in the underground complex and work on the V-2 assembly line next to German civilians who were also employed in the latter.

While at Mittelwerk, Rudolph reported to Albin Sawatzki, who dictated that the first lot of V-2s (50 in number) would roll off the assembly lines in three months after their arrival, despite lack of equipment and design problems. Sawatzki drove the crews hard, but they were able to manufacture only 4 V-2 rockets by late December 1943. By the end of 1944, however, the kinks had been worked out, and production figures at the facility reached 800 V-2s a month. On 8 September 1944 the first V-2s struck London, and they caused much damage over the next several months. Though the Allied ground and air campaigns in 1945, however, caused a decline in production, Mittelwerk could boast the manufacture of 5,000 V-2 rockets by the time it was captured by Allied forces. The launching of these fearsome weapons caused 1,400 bombs to land in England between September 1944 and March 1945 and resulted in over 9,200 casualties, with corresponding effects on a war-weary population.[8]

Life at Mittelwerk was not easy for Rudolph or any of the other workers. Divided into two shifts, production lines ran twenty-four hours a day, seven days a week. Sawatzki was a difficult taskmaster, who frequently threatened to send Rudolph and others to the concentration camp for the least transgression. The SS and the Gestapo left subtle threats, which confirmed that they were keeping close watch on scientists and workers alike! The situation became increasingly tense in early 1945, when shortages of parts and shortages of food began to affect production adversely.

In mid-March 1945 all production at Mittelwerk ceased. Rudolph and others, like their counterparts at Peenemünde, received orders to relocate to Oberammergau in Bavaria. Wanting to avoid traveling with the ss, Rudolph joined Dornberger's group, and they headed south. Taking advantage of the confusion in and around Oberammergau, they parted company and moved around the area until they were captured by the Americans in late April. Rudolph found himself reunited with von Braun and Dornberger in Garmisch, where they and others underwent interrogation by the Americans, who were identifying scientists who could potentially be useful in furthering the development of missiles for the war effort.[9]

Postwar Moves

As soon as the war in Europe ended, the British instituted Operation Backfire to accomplish three goals. First, they undertook a thorough assessment of the v-2 assembly. Second, they interrogated German scientists who had expertise in all aspects of the program. Third, they conducted tests by firing missiles across the North Sea. Once the tests were completed, the British War Office released a five-volume report. Recognizing the importance of the project, the Americans approved the temporary transfer of Rudolph to the British. He participated in Backfire from July to October 1945, at which time Rudolph's transfer back to the Americans was affected.[10]

For the sake of facilitating the transfer of German scientists to the United States, Operation Paperclip (see chapter 8) targeted those who had experience with the development of guided missiles and aerodynamics, several of whom had participated in Backfire for the British. Arriving in the United States in December 1945, Rudolph was one of the first to travel under the auspices of Operation Paperclip, after he was vetted by the Immigration and Naturalization Service. Unfortunately, INS did not have the full story when it approved Rudolph. In addition, INS (at the time a division of the Department of Justice) was under pressure from the number two man at the Department of Justice to approve Rudolph's participation in Paperclip and transfer to the United States. Citing information provided by the Joint Chiefs of Staff and the Department of the Army, this official concluded that the country's national interests would be compromised if Rudolph's application was denied.[11] INS, accepting its superior's recommendation, chose not to delve more deeply into Rudolph's work on the V-2 project and provided the desired approval.

After undergoing interrogation in Boston, Rudolph and other members of the team traveled to the White Sands Proving Ground in New Mexico in January 1946 and continued their work on the V-2 project. A year later Rudolph received a new posting—the Ordnance Research and Development Division at Fort Bliss, Texas. A few months later his family finally arrived. For the next two years, while working at Fort Bliss, he also traveled back and forth to San Diego, California, where he served as a liaison to the Solar Aircraft Company.

Like other Paperclip scientists, Rudolph had come to the United States without a visa, a situation that eventually had to be rectified. Because he had to enter on a legitimate visa before applying for citizenship, Rudolph, like many of his colleagues, traveled to Ciudad Juárez, Mexico, Obtaining a visa, he officially immigrated to the United States on 14 April 1949, even though he could not enter the country under the Displaced Persons Act or the Refugee Relief Act.[12] Ironically, however, under the terms of the Department of State's visa regulations, the entry of an alien "who has been guilty of, or has advocated or acquiesced in, activities or conduct contrary to civilization and human decency on behalf of the Axis countries" was prohibited.[13] That regulation would eventually come back to haunt Rudolph.[14]

In early 1949, prior to his trip to Mexico, the FBI conducted an investigation of Rudolph, who completed a questionnaire in which he explained his reasons for joining the Nazi Party: "Until 1930 I sympathized with the social-democratic party, voted for it and was a member of a social democratic union (Bund Techn. Agst. U. Beamt.). After 1930 the economical situation became so serious that it appeared to me to be headed for catastrophe. (I really became unemployed in 1932.) The great amount of unemployment caused the expansion of nationalsoc. and communistic parties. Frightened that the latter one would become the government I joined the NSDAP ([Nazi Party] a legally reg. society) to help, I believed in the preservation of the western culture."[15] The FBI inquiry, including interrogations of Rudolph's

American associates, suggested that Rudolph had not been active in the Nazi Party. During its investigation, the FBI also consulted the Office of the Military Government of the United States. According to the FBI report, "The OMGUS report concluded that on the basis of available records RUDOLPH was not considered a war criminal, an ardent Nazi, nor in the opinion of the Military Governor likely to become a security threat to the United States."[16] The FBI concurred in that assessment.

Although Rudolph successfully immigrated to the United States in April 1949, the FBI periodically investigated him, particularly when he applied for citizenship. In mid-June 1950 the Fort Bliss group, including Rudolph, was transferred to a new facility—Redstone Arsenal in Huntsville, Alabama. In addition to a new location and new facilities, the group had a new name—the Ordnance Guided Missile Center. While at Redstone Arsenal for the next decade, Rudolph's life underwent some changes.

In 1951, according to an FBI report dated 22 September, Rudolph applied for U.S. citizenship. At the time he was married, had one child, and was in the process of purchasing a house. Three years later, on 11 November 1954, Rudolph traveled to Birmingham, Alabama, took the appropriate oath, and became a naturalized citizen of the United States of America. Life was good! Rudolph's life was full of positives—at home and at work.

A rising star, Rudolph received a new appointment in 1956. Not only did he become the technical director of the Redstone Project, but he also became the project manager for the Pershing missile project. Once fully developed, the Pershing missile was a "mobile, medium range, surface-to-surface missile." In 1961 control of the missile project shifted to Army Ordnance Missile Command. While he supervised the project, Rudolph was the recipient of other honors. In 1959 Rollins College in Winter Park, Florida, awarded him an honorary PhD in science, and he also received one of the highest civilian honors awarded by the army—the Exceptional Civilian Service Award. Although he was receiving accolades, Rudolph was hiding a secret—a secret that would tarnish his awards, his career, his life—but for the time being, his secret was safe. By the time the missile project became the Missile Command's baby, Rudolph was ready for something bigger and better—NASA![17]

NASA Scientist

In 1961 Rudolph joined the staff at NASA, where he was reunited with his old friend, Wernher von Braun, who became his boss. Building up his reputation and making a real name for himself in rocket development, Rudolph remained employed at NASA until his retirement in 1969. Within the first year he received an influential appointment as assistant director of Systems Engineering. As assistant director, he liaised between vehicle development at Redstone Arsenal's Marshall Space Flight Center and Houston's Manned Spacecraft Center.

At NASA Rudolph was finally at the point at which he could begin to fulfill his dream—a dream that began over thirty years earlier, when he witnessed Max Valier and Walter Riedel testing a small rocket on the grounds of Heylandt, where they all worked. Although his path had been long and he had been diverted at times, at NASA he was part of a program that considered space travel possible. It was no longer the stuff of movies and comic books. Rudolph was living the dream! He was where he belonged, *and* he was working on the development of spacecrafts, including manned spacecrafts. In fact, for five years—from August 1963 to May 1968—he was the Saturn V rocket program project director. Anything was possible!

Although the federal government provided funding for the space program, there were still questions about whether or not NASA could successfully launch a rocket. Dare they dream even bigger! Could they put a man on the moon? There was the added pressure of competition with the Soviets. The United States and the Soviet Union were in a race to put the first man in space, to have a rocket circle the moon, to land a man on the moon. The pressure was on. How would the Saturn V perform? As the testing date neared, tension increased. Rudolph and others on his team checked and rechecked the design and the prototype, but there was only so much that could be done in the lab. At some point they needed to take a leap of faith, reach for the stars, and launch a rocket.

The date for the first Saturn V launch was finally set. The launch site was the Kennedy Space Center in Florida. On 9 November 1967 Rudolph received the best birthday present ever imagined. The Saturn V rocket's flight was flawless! Less than two years later, in July 1969, a Saturn V rocket helped to put the first man on the moon! His work on the project earned Rudolph the title "Father of the Saturn V rocket." Even before astronaut Neil Armstrong stepped onto the moon, however, Rudolph received a promotion at NASA. In May 1968 he became the Marshall Space Flight Center director's special assistant, a position that he held until his retirement at the end of 1969. With the moon landing Rudolph had achieved his wildest dream, and at sixty-three he decided that he had reached the pinnacle of success, that he could not top his work on the Saturn V rocket, and that the time had come to retire while he was at the top of his game. He had already received the NASA Exceptional Service Medal, and with retirement came NASA's highest honor—the NASA Distinguished Service Medal.[18] It was time to rest on his laurels.

OSI Investigation

Life was good, or it was supposed to be. After he retired, Rudolph and his wife, wanting to be near their daughter, moved to San Jose, California. Unfortunately, shortly after they moved, Rudolph suffered a heart attack and had to have triple bypass surgery. Once he recovered, however, life got better, and for the next decade or so he had nothing to worry about, except to enjoy retirement, time with his daughter, and sunny California. That would all change in 1979, when Rudolph came onto the OSI radar. Rudolph's world was about to turn upside down!

The German had been investigated before, but, unlike the earlier investigations, the OSI inquiry would come to a different conclusion. What had been swept under the rug in 1945 would condemn him approximately four decades later. The powers that be turned a blind eye because, to them anyway, the bigger picture was much more important at the time. The long term goal—employing Nazi scientists to help beat the Soviets in the missile and rocket race—took precedence over questionable wartime activities. The decision to do so would be challenged by the OSI when it began to investigate alleged Nazi criminals, some of whom were peacefully residing in the United States, in 1979.

The OSI would soon set its sights on Arthur Rudolph, distinguished NASA retiree. But who was he really? After all, he had been investigated before—beyond the interrogations at Garmisch in 1945. In June 1947 the U.S. Army conducted an interrogation of Rudolph at the Office of Ordnance Research and Development Service Suboffice (Rocket) at Fort Bliss, Texas. Questioned extensively about his work during the years 1938 to 1945, Rudolph provided succinct, matter-of-fact responses. The focus of the questions was the Mittelwerk factory. When asked if any of the factory workers were foreigners or forced labor, Rudolph said that they were "Haeftlinge, that is, men in arrest" and that, while initially he thought they were all Germans, many were, in fact, "Russians, French, Polish, [and] Czech." He did admit that he supervised some of the Haeftlinge, although the number varied each day, but denied any of them worked in his office. He also answered specific questions about the Haeftlinge—where they slept (particularly those who slept in the tunnels); when, where, and what they ate; what their work hours were; what clothing they wore; what their working conditions were and if they were sanitary; how they were made to work harder; how they were punished—and about the differences between them and German civilian workers.[19]

Rudolph's interrogators also inquired about the changes in conditions and for the workers that had (or had not) occurred when Dr. Greg Rickkey became general director of the Mittelwerk factory. Based on the line of questioning, it appeared that in 1947 Rickkey was a "person of interest." They were more focused on Rickkey than on the foreign or "forced" workers. In addition, the interrogators were interested in how Rickkey handled workers who refused to work.[20] In addition to presenting himself in the best light possible, Rudolph claimed a fair amount of ignorance. His responses apparently did not have an impact on his transfer to the United States under Operation Paperclip or his work for NASA. Perhaps they should have. In any event, forced labor by Haeftlinge, whether prisoners of war or concentration camp internees, would be an important feature in the OSI investigation of Rudolph.

Shortly after he began working for NASA, the FBI looked into Rudolph's background and into his employment history, particularly his work in the United States. The FBI's conclusions about Rudolph were ultimately and inevitably based on incomplete information. Following a request by the Civil Service Commission, which was obeying provisions of the National Aeronautics and Space Act of 1958, the FBI ordered an investigation of the scientist in a memorandum dated 6 April 1962. The director's inquiry request was sent to several field offices, including those in Birmingham, El Paso, San Diego, Tampa, and Baltimore.

The initial response from El Paso basically provided no information, but a report from the Tampa Field Office dated 17 April 1962 did corroborate a few facts, in addition to verifying his date and place of birth. According to Tampa, Rudolph had received an honorary degree from Rollins College, and he had given a talk—"Looks of the Mars Ship"—for the college after von Braun had recommended him. The report also briefly confirmed some of Rudolph's employment history: "Kummersdorf Proofing Ground, 1934; Peenemuende South, 1937; Niedersachswerfen, 1943; Cuxhaven (with British), 1945; Fort Bliss, Texas, 1946; Redstone Arsenal, Alabama, 1950." This wasn't much because there were no real details, but it was a start.[21]

The FBI discovered, however, that it was difficult to confirm certain aspects of Rudolph's employment history in the United States—which did *not* necessarily mean that he was not being truthful or that it cast suspicion on him. The Albuquerque Field Office reported that it could not confirm Rudolph's employment at White Sands Missile Range (1946-47) because the facility's personnel office destroyed records after a decade, but further investigation revealed that Rudolph did not have an arrest record in Las Cruces, New Mexico, with the Provost Marshal's or the Sheriff's Office, nor was there a file on him with the Credit Bureau. The San Diego Field Office noted that there was no criminal or credit record on file for either Rudolph or his daughter. Although admitting that the Solar Aircraft Company had no records to confirm his employment with them, San Diego proceeded to recommend Rudolph, saying that he was "a man of excellent character, associates and reputation" and that an acquaintance "had no reason at all to question the loyalty of the applicant [Rudolph] and would highly recommend him for a position of trust."[22]

Acknowledging that Rudolph was "executing SF-86, entitled 'Security Investigation Data for Sensitive Position,'" the Birmingham Field Office provided a six-page assessment of the applicant, which was more extensive than what had been provided by the other field offices.[23] Noting that he had admitted membership in the Nazi Party, the report evaluated Rudolph's justification for associating with the group and accepted his explanation that the economic situation prompted what many considered to be questionable action. Unnamed witnesses were questioned and testified that Rudolph had not been actively involved with any fascist organizations. In fact, Rudolph received glowing accolades from all those questioned. There were no red flags. As far as Birmingham was concerned, there was much to recommend that Rudolph receive the requested security clearance for his job with NASA.

In a second communication the El Paso Field Office, after further investigation and assessments from the El Paso Police Department, Sheriff's Office, and Credit Bureau, concurred with Birmingham's conclusions. An IC report dated 5 May 1962, issued by the Baltimore FBI Office, affirmed that Rudolph's background had been thoroughly investigated in 1949 and 1953–54 and that they had three sworn statements from Rudolph dated 20 December 1947, 5 August 1952, and 29 October 1954. In addition to noting that it had also relied on pertinent information from the army, Baltimore found Rudolph's assertions about his Nazi membership credible.

In an effort to be thorough, the FBI also consulted CIA files but found no pertinent information about Rudolph or his family. In addition, the FBI ascertained that the House Committee on Un-American Activities did not have a file on the scientist.[24] The FBI concluded its investigation, which had been prompted by a request from the Civil Service Commission and Rudolph's efforts to work on sensitive NASA projects, and ultimately recommended that Rudolph be granted clearance. Rudolph appeared to be an upstanding citizen, whose membership in the Nazi Party and work in the Nazi rocket program could be logically explained by the Depression and the climate that existed in Germany at the time, particularly when the use of forced labor was more the norm than the exception. But was he? Was Rudolph any different from other nonpolitical middle-class and professional Germans who found themselves working for the Nazi regime during wartime?

Enter a new player—Eli Rosenbaum. In the summer of 1979, Rosenbaum was a summer intern at OSI. After the internship ended he happened to read two newly published books, which brought the name Arthur Rudolph to his attention. Although somewhat different, both of these books had one thing in common—rocket science. The first book was *Dora: The Nazi Concentration Camp Where Modern Space Technology Was Born and 30,000 Prisoners Died* by Jean Michel. As the dramatic title suggests, Michel examined the connection between the Dora concentration camp and the Nazi's rocket program.

The second book that Rosenbaum read, however, brought the rocket program home. It was Frederick I. Ordway's *The Rocket Team from the V-2 to the Saturn Moon Rocket: The Inside Story of How a Small Group of Engineers Changed World History*. What could be in these books, particularly the latter, that could pique Rosenbaum's interest in Rudolph? There were two things related to the same event that raised red flags for him. First, Rosenbaum read an account of a complaint by Rudolph who lamented the fact that he had to leave a New Year's Eve party because he had to supervise the movement of some rocket parts. The picture that accompanied the vignette revealed who was relegated to moving the rocket parts; Rudolph had to leave the party to supervise prisoners of war, who, in violation of the Geneva Convention, were handling rocket parts, which constituted munitions.

Based on Ordway's account of the event, Rosenbaum concluded that Rudolph was more concerned about missing a party than about prisoners of war being used for labor that was outlawed by the Geneva Convention. As a result, he became determined to investigate the German scientist at the first possible moment. What was his problem? What kind of person was he? Was there more to the story than that illuminated by Ordway? Was Rudolph connected to the Dora-Nordhausen camp in any way? Rosenbaum was so appalled by what he read in Ordway's book that, when he went to work for OSI a year later, he made every effort to persuade his boss to approve an investigation of Rudolph.[25]

Initial investigation revealed a couple of interesting facts. First, in 1947 a U.S. military court in Dachau, Germany, tried nineteen people who had worked at the Dora-Nordhausen complex. The National Archives and Records Administration housed not only the transcript from the trial but also related pretrial documents. Included in the material was a 1947 interview of Rudolph, who was listed as a potential witness. The interview revealed some interesting facts, many of which revolved around the execution of Dora internees. Of twelve inmates accused of sabotage, six were sentenced to hanging. Not only did Rudolph attend the hanging, but he also ordered laborers, whom he supervised, to witness the event as well. In addition to the interview, the file also contained a diagram of the underground rocket factory. The dotted line on the diagram represented the "Path of Overhead Crane Trolly [sic] On Which Men Were Hung." An examination of the diagram revealed the line's proximity to Rudolph's office. In addition, an examination of the trial transcript disclosed that Rudolph had more intimate knowledge of the prisoners than he revealed in his interview. According to trial transcripts, "Rudolph received daily prisoner strength reports which showed the number of prisoners available for work, the number of 'new arrivals,' and the number of people lost through sickness or death."[26]

The OSI now had the ammunition that it needed to confront Rudolph. OSI conducted two interviews of Rudolph. At the first, conducted in October 1982, the big guns were present: Allan A. Ryan Jr., director; Neal M. Sher, deputy director; and Eli M. Rosenbaum, trial lawyer. Sher and Rosenbaum conducted the second interrogation of Rudolph in February 1983. During these interviews Rudolph admitted a number of things that the OSI ultimately found problematic. He acknowledged that, while he was at Mittelwerk, he had been aware "disease, overwork, mistreatment, and malnutrition" had resulted in prisoners' deaths. These deaths caused a reduction in the available workforce for the production of V-2 rockets. Consequently, Rudolph "had requested labor replenishments from the SS, and knew that these replacements came 'probably from Buchenwald or somewhere else.'" Furthermore, Rudolph acknowledged that he had the authority to assign laborers to specific tasks within the Mittelwerk facility. Not only damning, these admissions also suggested that Rudolph had perhaps not been completely forthcoming when he was vetted for Paperclip and when he applied for citizenship.[27]

For the OSI the question then became what the next step should be. In determining that next step, the OSI had to answer the following questions: Did Rudolph's actions constitute persecution? Were they as bad as those perpetrated by the Nazis who ran the concentration camps or as bad as those committed by people such as Klaus Barbie or Josef Mengele? How much weight should be given to these revelations that Rudolph was more directly involved with prison labor than previous records had demonstrated? What, if any, consequences should result from the conferring of citizenship under what now seemed to be questionable circumstances?

After assessing the information contained in the file from the National Archives and Records Administration, including Rudolph's statement and his 1982 and 1983 interviews, the answer seemed simple for the OSI, which concluded that a mistake had been made in allowing Rudolph both to enter the United States formally and to obtain citizenship. Consequently, OSI advised that denaturalization action should be filed and cited the following as justification for its recommendation. Rudolph, as supervisor, "was directly responsible for exploiting slave laborers." On that premise the OSI concluded that Rudolph's actions "violated the State Department's regulation barring entry to persons who participated, advocated, or acquiesced in activities or conduct contrary to civilization and human decency." Furthermore, forcing inmates to witness the hangings of other laborers constituted a "form of 'terror'" that contributed to their persecution. As such, Rudolph's "persecutory" activities in themselves were heinous and indicated that he lacked the "good moral character" required for citizenship. Consequently, as far as the OSI was concerned, Rudolph should forfeit his right to be a citizen of the United States![28]

As further justification for its position, the OSI argued that, although the INS was aware that Rudolph had worked at Mittelwerk, it did not know the full extent of his activities there. Consequently, its decision to recommend his admission to the United States under Paperclip was based on incomplete information, and it was only the OSI investigation, including its two interviews with Rudolph, that brought the additional information to light. Furthermore, the OSI, unlike the INS, had uncovered a "clearer picture of his true accountability." Recognizing that its recommendation might meet with resistance because of Rudolph's contribution to the space program, the OSI provided a counterargument that "*failure* to bring charges would present more serious concerns." Part of the OSI's contention concerned the credibility of its office. The OSI feared that choosing not to pursue a case against Rudolph "would give credence to the criticism that the office discriminated against non-Germans (i.e., Lithuanian, Ukrainian and Latvian camp guards) who occupied low-level collaborationist positions during the war, never belonged to the Nazi party, and lived quiet lives in the U.S." Rudolph, on the other hand, belonged to the Nazi Party (even if he did not actively participate in party meetings), worked on the V-2 rocket program for the Nazis, and, by the OSI definition, persecuted prisoners of war and concentration camp laborers. If low-level non-German collaborationists were prosecuted, Rudolph, whose crimes could conceivably be considered more heinous, should be as well.[29]

Just because the OSI recommended that denaturalization papers be filed against Rudolph did not mean, however, that the Department of Justice would accept the proposal, even though the OSI felt that sufficient cause existed for such action. Apparently, the OSI was persuasive because the Department of Justice sanctioned the filing of the case, and the OSI received the task of notifying Rudolph. Informed that prosecution was imminent, Rudolph took an unexpected step. He instructed his attorney to negotiate a written agreement with the federal government. Under the terms of the agreement, the government would agree not to prosecute Rudolph in exchange for two concessions from the German, who would not only leave the United States but also renounce his U.S. citizenship. In exchange for the government's willingness to wait until he left before making any announcement about the situation, Rudolph consented not to dispute the government's contention that he had persecuted unarmed civilians during his time at Mittelwerk.

Three men signed the agreement in San Jose on 28 November 1983: OSI director Neal M. Sher, Arthur Louis Hugo Rudolph, and George H. Main, Esq., the attorney for Rudolph. In the signed agreement Rudolph admitted that during the time he served as "Operations Director" of the Mittelwerk "underground rocket fabrication plant" "forced laborers, including concentration camp inmates," worked there. As a result, he illegally obtained U.S. citizenship, was subject to denaturalization, and could be deported if he were not a citizen. In the signed statement Rudolph noted, "I agree permanently to depart the United States by March 29, 1984, at my own expense." He then stated that he would obtain the documents necessary for his departure and that "on or before June 1, 1984," he would renounce his citizenship at a U.S. embassy or consulate, at which time he would turn over his passport or have it stamped "canceled." He would take the steps designated by the Department of Justice to confirm that he had complied with both departure and the renunciation of citizenship, and he "agree[d] not to reapply for United States citizenship under any circumstances." All of this was predicated, however, on Rudolph's health, and the agreement spelled out the procedure that Rudolph would have to follow if health issues delayed his departure from the United States and the renunciation of his citizenship by the stipulated dates. In addition, Rudolph acknowledged what the penalty for noncompliance would be. Finally, he stated that he had entered into the agreement of his own free will, after consulting with his attorney, and that he had not been coerced or pressured into signing it.[30]

Just as Rudolph made concessions, the U.S. government articulated its part in the agreement, which was signed and executed by a representative of the Justice Department. As long as Rudolph upheld his end of the bargain, the federal government would not institute denaturalization or deportation proceedings against him, nor would it limit his access to his "federal retirement, health care and/or Social Security benefits." In addition to providing him with formal documentation verifying that he was no longer a U.S. citizen, the government agreed not to take steps to revoke the citizenship of Rudolph's relatives who obtained it because of his naturalization. In other words, Rudolph's wife and daughter could, if they chose, remain U.S. citizens. Furthermore, the government agreed not to announce the results of Rudolph's case until 1 June 1984, the day on which he formally relinquished his citizenship. Finally, both Rudolph and the federal government agreed that "this Agreement completely disposes of all the issues in this case."[31]

The OSI admitted, however, a hope that the resolution of the Rudolph case would send a message and that it would have an impact on other pending cases. As the office articulated, "when other OSI subjects and defendants see that the department is prepared to go after someone of Rudolph's stature and importance (and presumed official 'connections'), the depth of the Government's commitment to the Nazi prosecution program will become ever more apparent to them. The fact that a man of Rudolph's obvious sophistication and intelligence was willing to surrender without a fight cannot fail to make a powerful impression upon them and to increase significantly the likelihood of securing similar settlements in other cases."[32] Because of his stature, the Justice Department hoped that the resolution of the Rudolph case would lend credibility to its efforts to bring other Nazi criminals to justice.

Years in Exile

In October 1984 Rudolph traveled to Germany, where he formally gave up his citizenship. Because of his stature and his position at NASA, Rudolph's actions could not escape the media's notice. When pressed by the media, Rudolph asserted that he had done nothing wrong and claimed the opposite—that he had endeavored to "help the poor forced laborers to have their conditions improved."[33] The media's response, naturally, was to question why Rudolph had left the United States and given up his citizenship. Rudolph's justification was perhaps a bit unlikely, or perhaps it was just a compromise. According to Rudolph, in an effort to avoid both sensationalism and the cost of litigation, he had renounced his citizenship. His age and his health persuaded Rudolph to take that step. Many Americans were outraged by Rudolph's alleged activities, and they felt that losing his citizenship and the right to live in the United States was not enough. NASA received a request to revoke the Distinguished Service Medal that it had awarded Rudolph. Recognizing Rudolph's contribution to the space program and the development of the Saturn V rocket, NASA refused.

A bright spot! Rudolph could retain his NASA medal and find comfort in the fact that his work in the space program gave him some validation. Although NASA's position in some respects vindicated him, Rudolph would soon discover that his decision to move back to his homeland would bring a new set of trials and tribulations. The road would *not* be an easy one, and for the next decade Rudolph would struggle to clear his name and to suggest that he was not the Nazi criminal that the United States implied.

Although he returned home to Germany, Rudolph was not initially welcomed with open arms. What the West Germans objected to was the fact that the OSI did not notify them of the circumstances *before* Rudolph arrived in the country. Faced with a done deal, however, the West German government initiated an investigation of its own to ascertain whether sufficient evidence existed to prosecute Rudolph for murder, because they did not have a statute of limitations for that particular criminal offense. During the course of their investigation, the West Germans sought information from the OSI.

As the director of OSI, Sher drafted a letter to Elfriede G. Krueger at the Embassy of the Federal Republic of Germany on 26 April 1985 in response to a request for information about Rudolph that had been initiated by a Dr. Streim of the Zentrale Stelle der Landesjustizverwaltungen. Requesting that the documents being forwarded to aid the investigation remain confidential, Sher asked that his office be consulted before anything contained in them was released to the public. Sher also included a list of witnesses who agreed to communicate with the West German government. He then reminded the West Germans that the nature of the OSI investigation—denaturalization and deportation—was different from the criminal inquiry they would conduct. Included with Sher's letter were almost thirty documents and interview transcripts—the fruits of the OSI scrutiny into Rudolph's activities at Mittelwerk. Some of the materials were German in origin, and the period covered by the documents and transcripts spanned four decades, from 1943 to 1983.

After conducting a thorough investigation of their own, the West German government chose not to file murder charges against Rudolph and, after considering the matter carefully, chose to reinstate the German citizenship that Rudolph had given up in 1954 when he became a U.S. citizen. With the furor dying down, Rudolph's life had the potential of being quiet again—finally! Unfortunately, he did not leave well enough alone.

In 1989 Rudolph did what any German who wanted to travel to the United States did. He went to the U.S. consulate in Hamburg and submitted a visa application. Not surprisingly, the U.S. consulate rejected Rudolph's application. What Rudolph did, however, was unwittingly place himself on the Department of Justice's radar, and it set out to determine what the German had up his sleeve. When, a year later, the Justice Department gained information indicating that Rudolph planned to fly to Canada, the OSI contacted the Canadian government, briefed it regarding Rudolph's character and background, and notified it of Rudolph's plan to travel there. When Rudolph stepped off the plane, he was met by Canadian officials, who detained him until the decision was made to release him on bond until his deportation back to Germany.

Unfortunately for Rudolph, his problems in Canada did not remain a secret. In fact, not only was it reported in Canada, but American media got a hold of the story as well. It received extensive publicity in the United States, particularly because his supporters, including Ohio representative James Traficant, were vocal in their support of Rudolph. The media attention would have unintended consequences that adversely affected Rudolph and his case.

During his hearing in Canada, Rudolph presented a different account of events than he had given during his 1947, 1982, and 1983 interviews—an account that contradicted the agreement that he signed with the U.S. government in 1984. In the Canadian court Rudolph testified that "he had been shocked to learn that concentration inmates would be used as a source of labor at Mittelwerk." Ironically, the day after Rudolph's testimony, the OSI received evidence that challenged it. A Smithsonian Institution historian, who worked at the National Air and Space Museum, contacted the OSI in reference to two documents related to Rudolph that he had found in Germany. These documents indicated that Rudolph had indeed employed slave laborers from the Dora concentration camp, but they provided even more damning information. According to the documents, Rudolph "had in fact worked to institute that program." Was Rudolph even more culpable that the OSI had originally thought?[34]

What was this new evidence against the German scientist? Was it credible? What should the OSI do with it? The first document was a report dated April 1943 and signed by Rudolph. According to the report, Rudolph had just toured a factory that employed concentration camp "forced laborers" who were guarded by SS troops. He apparently saw merit in utilizing forced laborers. Ultimately, Rudolph concluded the rocket program would benefit from a similar labor system. The April 1943 report indicated that he was more intimately involved with the use of "forced laborers" at Mittelwerk than he had previously admitted. The second document—June 1943 meeting minutes—demonstrated that Rudolph's recommendation was about to bear fruit. At the meeting he received orders to coordinate with the commandant of the camp and to organize a forced laborer program at the underground facility. These documents painted a vastly different picture than the one of a scientist who had been given no choice but to work with the labor force that he was given.[35]

After acquiring copies of the documents, the OSI provided them to Canadian authorities, and they were entered into the record at Rudolph's hearing. As might be expected, this new evidence challenged Rudolph's testimony and affected the outcome of the hearing. In May 1992 the Canadian Federal Court of Appeals rendered a decision in *Rudolph v. Minister of Employment and Immigration*. According to the court, Rudolph "'called for, made use of and directed' slave laborers who suffered 'indescribably brutal' conditions."[36] The court ordered that he be deported back to Germany.

At this point, things got really interesting. Instead of returning to Germany quietly and letting the furor surrounding him die down, Rudolph added fuel to the fire by filing a lawsuit that named the

U.S. Department of Justice, the U.S. attorney general, the U.S. secretary of state, and four OSI attorneys, who had participated in the case against him, as defendants. In his lawsuit he hoped to accomplish two goals. First, he wanted the 1983 agreement between him and the U.S. government canceled. Second, he wanted to be allowed to return to the United States. Even though he knew that the OSI had recently acquired damning documents, a fact that he failed to address, Rudolph argued that he had been misled by the government. The government had suggested that they had enough evidence to get a denaturalization ruling in court, when in fact government officials had deposed a key witness who exonerated him. In 1993 he learned that *Rudolph v. U.S. Dep't of Justice, et al.*, no. C 92-20116 JW, would not move forward. The judge threw out the lawsuit because it was "barred by the doctrine of sovereign immunity."[37]

Acting the part of the wrongfully accused, Rudolph refused to let the matter rest. He filed a second lawsuit—*Rudolph v. U.S. Dep't of Justice, et al.*, no. C 94-20411 JW. Despite evidence to the contrary, he asserted that the denials in 1989 of a visa to enter the United States and in 1990 of his "right to enter Canada" were wrong and that those instances did not constitute the first time that his rights had been violated. It was his contention that his civil rights had been abused when he was interviewed by the OSI. According to the lawsuit, some of the questions posed by the OSI "had been 'incriminatory, impermissibly suggestive and argumentative.'" In addition, he maintained that prior to the second OSI interview he was unaware that he had a right to an attorney or that he actually needed one. Rudolph again met failure! The court dismissed his case—different parts of it for different reasons—in 1995. The court justified its decision because, in some instances, the law provided no basis for the lawsuit and, in others, as was the case in his first lawsuit, because of sovereign immunity.[38]

When the court rendered a decision in Rudolph's second lawsuit, he ultimately had no other recourse. He did not initiate further legal action against the U.S. government. In fact, Rudolph did not survive the setbacks. In 1996 he passed away. Rudolph will go down in history as the only scientist who came to the United States as part of Operation Paperclip who was investigated and prosecuted by the OSI. In many respects his case demonstrated that he was unable to escape his past. Interestingly, some Americans, including the former deputy director of the CIA Ray Cline, thought that his work for NASA allowed Rudolph to pay his "debt to society" and that, as a result, he should have been allowed to remain in the United States. The OSI disagreed and argued that it would have been far worse had they chosen a different path with regard to Rudolph.[39] According to the OSI, "Deciding to refrain from seeking Rudolph's denaturalization simply because of the work he performed for our government would, it can be argued, amount to a desecration of the memories of Albert Einstein, Enrico Fermi, Niels Bohr, and other leading scientists who made at least equally substantial contributions to our nation—but who did so either after being forced by the Nazis to leave Germany or after voluntarily risking their lives to flee the introduction of Hitler's racial policies in Europe."[40] The OSI contended that, his contributions to NASA aside, Rudolph did participate in a brutal system that victimized concentration camp inmates.

Questions about Rudolph remain but, in all likelihood, will never be answered to everyone's satisfaction. If he had not done anything wrong, why did Rudolph agree to renounce his citizenship and leave the United States for good? If, as he later claimed, the OSI had testimony from a key witness that exonerated him, why didn't he stay and fight? At the time he cited both his health and the cost as reasons for his decision, but a decade later, when he was in his late eighties, he filed lawsuits against the U.S. government in an effort to rescind the agreement that he had signed in 1983. Perhaps his apparently overwhelming desire to return to the United States caused him to throw caution to the wind. After all, how could he know that a Smithsonian Institution historian would find documents that suggested that he was more culpable than the OSI had thought a decade earlier? The evidence does support the fact that, even though he joined the Nazi Party and the SA, he did not actively participate in either group. Equally, recently revealed evidence does suggest that Rudolph recommended that concentration camp labor be utilized in the underground rocket factory at Mittelwerk.

Rudolph was either a complex individual with a complicated past or a simple, unreflective type in well over his head and going with the system. Should his past at Mittelwerk be ignored because he contributed greatly to NASA and to the development of the Saturn V rocket, or should he be held accountable for recommending and then overseeing a forced laborer program despite his contributions to the U.S. space program? In other words, was Arthur Louis Hugo Rudolph a NASA hero or a Nazi criminal, or was he both?

10

The Scientists Who Avoided OSI Investigation

Not all scientists and technicians who moved to the United States under the auspices of Operation Paperclip found themselves under investigation by the Department of Justice's Office of Special Investigations. How did they elude scrutiny by the OSI? The focus of this chapter is three prominent scientists who benefited personally and professionally from the Operation Paperclip program. If any of the three were investigated by the OSI, this was not indicated in the final OSI report submitted in 2006. Although others may have avoided detection, these three deserve particular notice because two of the three contributed to the U.S. missile program during the Cold War, while the third conducted experiments for the U.S. Army Chemical Corps. The scientists under scrutiny here are Wernher von Braun, the father of the U.S. space program; Bernhard Tessmann, a guided missile expert; and Kurt Blome, a high-ranking Nazi scientist who conducted cancer and bacteriological warfare research for the Germans. Who were these scientists? Why didn't the OSI investigate them? Should they have been investigated? Why weren't they tainted by the work of the OSI?

Numerous scientists and technicians who worked on the German V-2 project traveled to the United States after the war as part of Operation Paperclip. Two of the men who participated in both the German and the American programs were Wernher von Braun and Bernhard Tessmann. Of the two, von Braun gained the most notoriety in both countries. Von Braun and Tessmann worked together in Germany during the war and in the United States after the conflict. The two men entered the United States as government employees under Paperclip, and both eventually worked in Huntsville, Alabama, for the National Aeronautics and Space Administration. A third man who adds additional layers to this story is Karl Ludwig Heimburg, an engineer who, as a guided missiles expert, was part of von Braun's team, first in Germany and then later in the United States. The story of these three men, who were inextricably connected, is a complicated one that weaves together dreams, wartime obligations, and Cold War glory.

> The dream of planetary spaceflight that had driven [Hermann] Oberth and his disciples [in Germany] was finally shattered on 7 May 1945 by military and social collapse and total surrender. The Peenemünde project was a phenomenon of global importance not only because of its technological success but also because of the distorted purpose to which it was put and the horrific methods used in the process. The development, production, and deployment of AGGREGAT 4, renamed V2 (Retaliation Weapon 2), cannot be separated from the fact that over 30,000 prisoners died in the inhuman working and living conditions of the Dora concentration camp. Each of the 3,200 missiles launched against Belgium, England and France was steeped in their blood.[1]

The best place to start is with the man who emerged as the leader of the group, was the driving force behind their rocket experiments, and eventually earned the nickname of "Dr. Space," Wernher von Braun.

Wernher von Braun

Born on 23 March 1912 in Wyrzysk, Poland, Wernher Magnus Maximilian von Braun was the second of three sons born to Emmy von Quistorp and Magnus Alexander Maximilian Freiherr von Braun. Both of his parents were noteworthy in their own rights. A baron, Magnus von Braun, who was from an affluent family, was a conservative civil servant—eventually receiving appointment as the minister of agriculture in the Federal Cabinet. A descendant of medieval European royalty, Emmy von Quistorp was well educated. She was fluent in six languages and dabbled in ornithology and astronomy. She whetted the young von Braun's appetite for outer space by giving him a telescope after his Lutheran confirmation.

From an early age von Braun distinguished himself. He was able to read newspapers by the age of four, and in school his questions regularly stumped his teachers. Displaying a talent for music, the young von Braun played the piano and demonstrated an ability as a composer, completing three piano pieces by the time he was fifteen. In 1925 he began to study and play the cello. While it seemed he was headed for a musical career, von Braun had another—competing— interest. In 1920, when von Braun's father received a promotion, the family relocated to Berlin. Four years later he received another pro- motion—to Reichsminister of agriculture in the Weimar Republic by President Friedrich Ebert—a position that he held until 1932. It was after the family moved to Berlin that Magnus von Braun's son began to experiment with rockets.

Newspaper headlines announcing experiments with rocket- powered automobiles captured the young von Braun's attention in 1924. Thus began his first rocket experiment, which garnered him lots of attention, not the least of which was because he involved his brother in his adventure. Wernher von Braun and his older brother, Sigismund, purchased "six large skyrockets." The boys tied the rock- ets to Wernher's newly painted coaster wagon and brought it to Tier- garten Strasse, "Berlin's most upscale street." After the boys lit the skyrocket fuses, Wernher jumped into the wagon.[2] According to von Braun, "I was ecstatic. The wagon was wholly out of control and trail- ing a comet's tail of fire, but my rockets were performing beyond my wildest dreams. Finally they burned themselves out with a magnif- icent thunderclap and the vehicle rolled to a halt. The police took me into custody very quickly. Fortunately, no one had been injured, so I was released in charge of the Minister of Agriculture—who was my father."[3]

Sigismund's version of events was slightly different from his broth- er's: "The wild rocket ride had, in fact, caused a casualty or two. The runaway wagon 'crashed into the legs of a woman, ruining her stock- ings,' and then plowed into a fruit stand." Needless to say, there was some fallout from the boys' adventure. The police warned against fur- ther experiments. Baron von Braun, displeased with the boys' antics, which cost him "a fine to cover the damages," grounded his sons for two days. Von Braun's mother, on the other hand, advised caution and noted that "the world needs live scientists, not dead ones."[4]

Von Braun was hooked! He certainly did not learn the intended lessons from his grounding. Once released from "house arrest," he repeated the experiment, although he did not involve his brother this time. He did, however, utilize more rockets. Lighting the fuses, he boarded his wagon and flew down the street. The outcome was about the same. Not all of his energy, however, was devoted to these experiments. Around this time von Braun and a friend decided to build an automobile. It is possible that he hoped to make the automobile "rocket-powered." Between his "flying wagon" experiments and his automobile project, he began to neglect his schoolwork, and his grades suffered—dramatically. When he did not pass mathematics and physics, the von Braun parents made the decision to send their son to boarding school.[5]

In 1925 von Braun—age thirteen—began his tenure at a progressive Hermann Lietz boarding school located in the Ettersburg Castle (north of the town of Weimar and 124 miles southwest of Berlin). "Famous for their advanced teaching approach," the Lietz schools paired robust academics with hands-on craft courses in "woodworking, metalworking, carpentry, stonecutting, and masonry." Although he excelled in his new school, von Braun did not initially set the world on fire with his performances in mathematics and physics; however, that would soon change. A book on space travel—*Die Rakete zu den Planetenräumen*, or *The Rocket into Interplanetary Space*, by Hermann Oberth—peaked his interest and resulted in his drastic improvement in those academic fields. It also focused his attention on constructing objects that could propel people into space.[6]

Attending boarding school did not temper von Braun's fascination with space or his propensity to experiment. Within the first couple of years at Ettersburg Castle, he tried another experiment that did not go as expected—one that a former teacher recalled: "I still remember very well that very first rocket, which blew up in the faces of Edwin May, Jochen Westphal and Ernst August Saalfeld in the farmyard in Ettersburg, while the inventor, Wernher von Braun, was trying to get launch permission from me, and I was trying to tell him that the experiment couldn't go well, because without controlling the mixture ratio of acetylene and air, there was a constant danger of an explosion."[7] Undeterred, von Braun had caught the space bug that would never lose its hold on him. Although in his early teens he had contemplated a career in music and composition, the pull of space travel won out over his love for music.

In April 1928 a new Lietz school opened its doors on the North Sea island of Spiekeroog, and von Braun transferred there. During his two years at Spiekeroog, he demonstrated an increasing brilliance in science and math and developed a single-minded focus on rockets and space travel. When home on vacation in July 1928, he retried his initial experiment with his wooden wagon and rockets. Modifying his wagon, he again tied fireworks to it—six "of the largest fireworks rockets" he could find.

> In a sedate German thoroughfare called the Tiergarten Allee, I aimed the vehicle carefully down the pavement. The day was mild, and many strollers were taking the air. It never occurred to me that they were not prepared to share the sidewalk with my noble experiment.
>
> I got behind the wagon, lighted the fuses, and leaped aside as jets of flame thrust out from the rockets and my wagon began to roll. Unattended, it picked up speed. It swerved this way and that, zigzagging through groups. . . . I yelled a warning and men and women fled in all directions.
>
> I was ecstatic. The wagon was wholly out of control and trailing a comet's tail of fire.[8]

The outcome of this experiment was very much the same as it was the first time that von Braun tried it. The wagon stopped when the fireworks had "burned out," the police arrived on the scene, and von Braun was escorted to the police station. After questioning him about his antics that caused such havoc, the police released him into the custody of his father. Von Braun's father was less than pleased, to put it mildly. A lecture ensued, followed by "house arrest" for a day. Apparently, von Braun learned his lesson this time. He did not repeat the experiment—at least not on Tiergarten Allee—but from this point on, his career was settled. He was determined to design and launch a rocket that would allow space travel.[9]

After graduating with honors from high school at seventeen, von Braun received acceptance at the Charlottenburg Institute of Technology in Berlin for the 1930 spring term. In addition to declaring a major, "mechanical and aircraft engineering," he was accepted as an apprentice to Hermann Oberth—von Braun's idol and author of *The Rocket into Interplanetary Space*. Von Braun seemed positioned to pursue an avenue that would result in a choice career. Furthermore, to complete a requirement of his major, von Braun took a "practicum at the Borsig locomotive and heavy machinery factory." The practicum would last six months. Like the other employees at the factory, von Braun was required to join the union that represented the factory workers—the metalworkers' union. Despite his aristocratic upbringing, von Braun quickly learned that he was just another worker at the factory. He was treated no differently than the other workers. He was there to learn—and learn he did.[10]

Von Braun quickly learned that even the best-laid plans occasionally hit bumps in the road. Only a few months into his apprenticeship, Oberth returned to Romania. Unwilling to have his dream derailed, von Braun joined together with other rocketeers who had been working with Oberth to form their own company. The purpose of the company was to continue Oberth's experiments. Their base of operations was "an abandoned, three-hundred-acre ammunition storage depot and proving ground at Reinickendorf on the outskirts of Berlin," which they rented for a song.[11] To give legitimacy to their venture, the group gave the site a formal designation—Raketenflugplatz Berlin, or Rocket Flight Field Berlin.

Engaging in rocket research and testing was not an inexpensive venture, and money was not easy to acquire. A complicating factor was the overall economically poor conditions in Germany that had been caused by the Stock Market Crash in the United States. Unbeknownst to von Braun, he and the group of rocketeers had a benefactor—Lt. Col. Karl E. Becker—who was connected to army ordnance, specifically "ballistics and munitions." In fact, Becker had secretly supported Oberth prior to his departure. This had resulted in Oberth and his apprentices giving a public test of their rocket engine for the Chemisch-Technisches Reichsanstalt in July 1930. This would later open doors for von Braun. For the next two years, von Braun and his rocketeers received funding from the military.[12]

In 1932, at the age of twenty, von Braun graduated from the Charlottenburg Institute. He had a mechanical-engineering degree that acknowledged his focus on aeronautical engineering. Von Braun's circle continued to expand. In 1932 von Braun met Arthur Rudolph, a fellow rocketeer who had already successfully developed a rocket for the army. Within a couple of years, Rudolph would become an integral member of the von Braun team.[13] During the spring of 1932—a year that would bring a lot of change to von Braun's life—the rocketeers received a visit at Raketenflugplatz from army representatives, who endeavored to circumvent Versailles Treaty restrictions on military strength by investing in rockets. When the framers constructed the treaty in 1919, rockets had not been on their radar. The rocketeers were not in a place to be choosy about the sources of funding. According to von Braun, "the Army was desperate to get back on its feet. We didn't care about much about that, one way or the other, but we needed money, and the Army seemed willing to help us. In 1932, the idea of war seemed to us an absurdity. The Nazis weren't yet in power. We felt no moral scruples about the possible future abuse of our brainchild. We were interested solely in exploring outer space. It was simply a question with us of how the golden cow could be milked most successfully."[14] Among the visitors was a junior officer who would play an integral role in von Braun's future—both immediate and long term. Capt. Walter Dornberger held an advanced degree in mechanical engineering; therefore, their common interest forged a connection between the two men. In time, that connection would evolve into a work-related relationship.[15]

Although some of his fellow rocketeers were not thrilled with the prospect of working for the military, von Braun was willing to make a deal with the "devil" if it meant that he could conduct research that would result in putting man into space. Before the end of the year, his new connection with Dornberger and the military would bring von Braun great dividends such as "secret doctoral dissertation" work for the army, but it also meant that he had to join the army officially. Within a couple of years, based on his research for the army, he successfully launched rockets—the result of which was more funding, and not just from the army, for his own research. In December 1934 von Braun and his team successfully launched two "A-2 (A for *Aggregat* [Aggregate]) liquid-fueled rockets from the North Sea island of Borkum to altitudes of more than one and a half miles." The result was the opening of unexpected doors:

> Feats such as the A-2 flights soon caught the attention of the *Luftwaffe* (German air force). It offered the von Braun group a project budgeted at 5 million reichsmarks (about $1.2 million) to develop a rocket-powered fighter plane at a proposed facility larger than Kummersdorf. The German army would not allow the Luftwaffe to get the upper hand, so it came up with a 6-million reichsmark allocation in 1935 to support the group's rocket work along existing lines. It was not the last time competing forces maneuvered to gain the team's services. For von Braun, now twenty-three years old and responsible for 11 million reichsmarks in funding, rocketry was no longer small potatoes.[16]

The von Braun group had hit the big league. Their work was in demand by multiple government groups—particularly the army and air force, who were perhaps anticipating the war to come. Consequently, as he broadened his research, von Braun was able to expand his group. Working for both the army and the air force required an increase in personnel. Included among his new employees were Bernhard Tessmann and Karl Heimburg. Furthermore, the outbreak of war in 1939 made the work of von Braun's team on rockets even more important and opened doors that were slow to open earlier. It did not seem to matter that Hitler did not exactly embrace the team's experiments. What did matter was that army and air force leadership did.

Bernhard Tessmann

Bernhard Robert Tessmann, the son of Robert and Emilie Tessmann, was born on 15 August 1912 in Zingst, Germany. Zingst is located on the eastern end of the Fischland-Darß-Zingst Peninsula in Mecklenburg-Vorpommern, Germany, on the Baltic Sea. He received an education in Berlin because his father, who was a small contractor, obtained a job there. According to Tessmann, after attending "basic schools" and high school, he attended night school for five years and earned a degree in mechanical engineering in the summer of 1935. While pursuing his degree in night school, Tessmann gained employment at Orenstein & Koppel A-G, a large machine company. Initially, he was a detail designer. According to Tessmann, the company "built all kind of diggers for mine works and cranes and all kinds of heavy machinery. This had given me also a chance to make some business trips to Holland where we dried the Lake Zoider out to gain more land, you know. The company had contacts with copper mines in [the] south of France where I had to go occasionally as a trouble-shooter. And even to Russia near the Black Sea area."[17] While facts about much of Tessmann's life are somewhat hazy, he was not as much in the public realm as von Braun, which might explain why less is known about him and why he was able to fly under the OSI's radar.

In 1991 Tessmann gave an interview, and, as a result, more is known about his life before 1936. His father was an employee of UFA film studios, where Tessmann had seen the sets for the film *Frau im Mond*, or *Woman in the Moon*. He was married to Ilse, and in 1935 (or possibly 1936, according to some accounts) a colleague introduced him to Wernher von Braun. The two men met in mid-August in von Braun's Berlin office, which was, according to Tessmann, at the army headquarters, or WaPruf 11. Von Braun's office was located in Dr. Walter Dornberger's division. When Tessmann first met him, Dornberger held the rank of major with an honorary doctorate in engineering. By the summer of 1936 Dornberger had received a posting to the Army Weapons Department and was assigned specifically to oversee rocket development at the soon-to-be constructed Army Experiment Station at Peenemünde. When Tessmann first met them, however, von Braun and Dornberger answered to Gen. Prof. Karl Emil Becker at the German army's Ordnance Department.

During that first encounter von Braun offered Tessmann a job. According to von Braun, the research that he was doing was entirely new and exciting, but it did not pay very much, which was an understatement. Von Braun clarified that the salary was "practically nothing much." He admitted that his unit frequently had to make a convincing case for a better budget. Tessmann confirmed that von Braun's assessment about his income was spot on, but there was another complication. According to Tessmann, "for a couple of months I didn't even get any salary because he hired me, but he did not have a free and approved spot or the permission to add someone to his meager payroll. So through the Fliegerhurst Commandut, Rechlin, the German Air Force, I was hired later and got, finally after six months, my first check, and that was not much."[18] Salary issues aside, however, Tessmann admitted his new employer had not lied. Von Braun was correct. The work was exciting. Furthermore, that excitement would spread and grab the attention of other creative, young engineers.

Meeting von Braun would change Tessmann's life and the lives of many other engineers, such as Karl Heimburg. Although he was not initially interested in building rockets, much less sending one to the moon, Tessmann soon became part of a select group working with von Braun and participating in his efforts to design and construct a viable rocket. Von Braun, not *Woman in the Moon*, had piqued Tessmann's interest in sending a rocket into the outer atmosphere. Von Braun's vision, or perhaps obsession, drew his colleagues to him like moths to a flame. Tessmann, like the others, became intrigued and bought into von Braun's obsession. Who would not want to be part of making history? During the mid-1930s for young men such as Tessmann and Heimburg (the latter two years older than the former), getting involved with von Braun could possibly open up new career opportunities, job security, and eventually good salaries. As von Braun's flame burned brighter, so might theirs. After all, if von Braun was right, could any of them pass up the opportunity of being a part of a history-making venture and all that it might entail?

Von Braun used every opportunity to espouse his ideas—to advance his vision for the future. According to Tessmann, von Braun "invited a group of us to dinner at his house one night, but he never got around to cooking it. He kept drawing calculations on his blackboard for a rocket to the moon."[19] Von Braun's drive and vision were contagious, as Karl Heimburg noted. Born in Lindesfels, Germany, on 29 January 1910, Karl Ludwig Heimburg graduated from the Institute of Technology in Darmstadt, Germany, in 1935 with a master's degree in mechanical engineering. Between 1936 and 1941 he found employment as an engineer in the coal industry. In this capacity he worked for C. Illies Company in Germany, Japan, Korea, and Manchuria. In

1941, although Germany was at war, Heimburg decided to pursue graduate studies in coal gasification chemistry; therefore, he enrolled in the Institute of Technology in Karlsruhe. Within a year, however, Heimburg found himself in the Germany army and posted to Peenemünde. There he would work in "Germany's closely guarded rocket research and development facility" for the premier rocket scientist— Wernher von Braun.[20] According to Heimburg, "We always had space on our minds. If we talked about space, though, people thought we were crazy. It was too fantastic an idea."[21]

Although their ideological focus was on rockets and space, von Braun, Tessmann, Heimburg, and others had to face the reality of their jobs—their military jobs. Working under Lt. Col. (later Lt. Gen.) Walter Dornberger, they had the task of designing missiles for the Ordnance Department.[22] Their task was a crucial one, since the type of ordnance that Germany could develop was curtailed by the Versailles Treaty. Under the terms of the treaty, Germany could not experiment with or construct artillery that could project shells beyond a specific range—9.32 miles. Ever resourceful, the Germans found a loophole. Because the treaty did not specifically prohibit it, the Germans focused on the construction of missiles.

Von Braun and his team had to do more than design and build missiles. They had to determine whether or not the missiles worked as planned. Von Braun needed a testing site—one that allowed the team to fire the missiles out to sea—and he tasked Tessmann with designing one that would permit the group to test a variety of engines. Because von Braun liked his first designs, he gave Tessmann a new job—that of "facility planner and designer." The next step was to choose a location suitable for Test Stand 1, as the new facility would be called. According to Tessmann and Heimburg, von Braun's mother suggested a place where her brothers had hunted and fished—Peenemünde, which was situated in the province of Pomerania. Von Braun's mother hit the mother lode with her suggestion. As soon as he visited it, von Braun realized that Peenemünde was ideal. It was on a small island located on the Baltic Sea. By late 1936 Tessmann had the responsibility of making Peenemünde work.[23]

As in any major project, there were glitches. The first one resulted from funding. Although the von Braun team worked for the army, a lack of funds almost resulted in a shutdown before things got off the ground. Luckily for the team, the air force (Luftwaffe) stepped in, purchased the area, and received their own proving grounds approximately two miles away from the army's facility. According to Tessmann, it was Luftwaffe general Albert Kesselring who, because of his interest in the work von Braun was doing, pushed for and found the funds to buy the desired Peenemünde site. By the end of 1936 Tessmann had relocated to Peenemünde and begun overseeing the construction of the testing facility. By March 1937 the von Braun team transferred their operation to Peenemünde. Holding an "honorary doctorate in mechanical engineering from the Friedrich-Wilhelms University of Berlin," the newly promoted Col. Walter Dornberger was in charge.[24]

As soon as the facilities were ready, the team settled in and got to work designing and building missiles. The early missiles were the A series. On 7 May 1938 the rocket team conducted its first actual test of an engine for an A-4—a "long-range bombardment missile." It took years of research and testing before the A-4 was perfected and received a new designation—V-2 or "Hitler's Vengeance Weapon 2." Although not violating the letter of the Versailles Treaty, von Braun's work on the V-2 weapon was still in violation of the treaty. Germany was not at war. Why did it need missiles? War was on the horizon. Less than eighteen months later, Germany was at war—with Poland, France, and England.[25]

Once the English became aware of German efforts to construct a new type of weapon, the Royal Air Force received the task of bombing Peenemünde. Consequently, von Braun received orders to relocate the testing facility to a new location—a place where his staff could also oversee the construction of an underground factory that would produce the new V-2 rockets once they had been perfected. To complete construction and commence production as soon as possible, Hitler authorized the use of slave labor. He put the SS in charge of both the slave labor and the construction of the new facilities. The location chosen was near Kohnstein-Nordhausen. The complex—factory and testing facilities—eventually received the name Mittelwerk.

In late August 1943 the Germans were ready to commence construction at the new location. They transported 107 slave laborers fifty miles from Buchenwald to the construction site. With the SS supervising, the laborers—using their bare hands—enlarged two existing tunnels and dug "smaller cross-tunnels." In September the first shipment of machinery and personnel arrived from Peenemünde. The Germans were wasting no time in getting up and running. In fact, a sense of urgency drove them. The work was brutal, and the toll on the slave laborers was unbelievable. By the end of the war sixty thousand camp internees had been relocated to Nordhausen. Approximately half of them did not survive the work. By the spring of 1944, because of the constant need for replacement workers, the SS located a concentration camp—Dora—in proximity to the Mittelwerk complex, which eliminated the need to transport concentration camp internees from Buchenwald.[26] First construction, then production, proceeded at a frantic pace. Finally, success—on the rocket front anyway—was at hand. In September 1944 the Germans fired their first V-2 rocket. The target was Paris. Thus began a period in which the Germans launched four thousand V-2 rockets against numerous targets located in France, Belgium, and England.[27] While the Germans fired rocket at their enemies, the ground offense had begun to intensify.

During the time von Braun's team was ensconced at Mittelwerk and somewhat oblivious to the outside world, the Allied war against Germany had been heating up. By the summer of 1944, German forces found themselves being pressed on all sides. On the Eastern Front the Soviet steamroller had been gradually forcing German troops back toward their homeland. Slowly advancing up the Italian peninsula, British, American, and Canadian forces were duking it out with their enemy. The icing on the cake was D-day—when British, American, and Canadian troops stormed the beaches at Normandy, gained a foothold, and began advancing east toward Germany. While V-2 rockets were raining down on Germany's enemies, von Braun recognized that security conditions at Mittelwerk were becoming increasingly tenuous. By February 1945 Soviet forces were nearing Berlin from the east, and in the west the situation did not look any better for Germany. In addition to advances on the ground, Allied air forces launched virtually continuous attacks against German troops and infrastructure.

In late March, when he learned that American troops were getting close and would force the suspension of his team's work on the v-2, von Braun made a monumental decision that was based on a new directive. On 1 April Dornberger received orders for the evacuation of Mittelwerk from ss general Hans Kammler, and he informed von Braun and others on his staff about the edict. Acknowledging that the likelihood of Germany winning the war at that point was slim to none, von Braun decided to hide all of the documentation related to the v-2 rocket program. Fearing that the ss would destroy the written record of his team's work, von Braun took steps to prevent that from happening. After the war he did not want to be back at square one where his research and the progress that his team had made were concerned. Dieter Huzel, von Braun's personal aide, and Tessmann received the task of secreting fourteen tons of documents in the Harz Mountains. The Harz Mountains were approximately twenty-four miles from Mittelwerk.

With boxes of documents loaded into three trucks, Tessmann and Huzel, accompanied by seven German soldiers, drove to the Harz Mountains and began to search for a hiding place. They located an appropriate site for their task—an abandoned mine near Dörnten. Situated "at the northern edge of the Harz," Dörnten housed a small mining community. At the abandoned mine Tessmann and Huzel paid the caretaker for an antechamber that was large enough to fulfill their need. Once the money had changed hands, the engineers and their crew were ready to commence unloading of their precious cargo. While this was not an easy task, the infrastructure within the mine helped make the job less arduous.[28]

> The documents were contained in wooden boxes which were unloaded from the truck, and then from the two others which were driven to the mine during the night. Fourteen tons of numbered boxes were eventually loaded onto flatcars on the railroad track at the tunnel's mouth. Then the flatcars were pulled by an electric-battery-operated locomotive a thou-

sand feet into the tunnel, stopping at a gallery which branched off from the track. At the end of the gallery was a small, dry room that had once been a powder magazine.

Struggling and sweating in the damp chill of the mine, the nine Germans unloaded the boxes from the flatcars and hauled them to the small room. It was not until eleven o'clock the next morning—when American dive bombers were streaking over Dörnten—that the last box was in place. The room's iron door was locked. Then the gallery leading to it was hidden from view by rocks and timbers blasted into it by a charge of dynamite.[29]

Tessmann and Huzel had followed an agreed-on security strategy. Because of their instructions from von Braun to keep the depository secret from everybody else, including their bosses and the soldier crew who had helped conceal the files, Tessmann and Huzel had blindfolded the soldiers on the trip to and from the abandoned mine. Even if they were captured and pressured, the soldiers could not reveal the exact location of the stash. Although the caretaker knew that Tessmann, Huzel, and their crew had stored secret documents in the old mineshaft, he did not know that the boxes contained the technical record of the German V-2 project. Furthermore, neither von Braun nor the rest of his team knew the exact location either; therefore, they could not "spill the beans" during interrogation—even under "rigorous" interrogation.[30]

Tessmann and Huzel did not finish their task a minute too soon. As they departed from the Dörnten area on 7 April, the first American soldiers—from the U.S. Ninth Army—appeared on the scene. The Germans returned to Nordhausen-Bleicherode but within two days were on the road again, trying to avoid the advancing Americans. Having loaded his belongings into a truck, Tessmann drove down the Adolf Hitler Pass on the way to the Alps. His goal was to link up with von Braun. His hope was that he could travel the four hundred miles to the rendezvous point without being captured by the Americans or any other Allied troops. Weather conditions made his drive treacherous, as heavy snow shifted to driving rain.[31]

Tessmann and Huzel were not the only ones to hide documents. "On orders of Lt. Gen. DORNBERGER, a box was hidden by Capt.

KÜHNE, a member of his staff, at the end of April or the beginning of May 1945 at OBERJOCH, less than a mile from the Tyrolean frontier. The box contained (a) minutes of the discussions of the Arbeitsstab DORNBERGER at Bad SACHSA in March and April 1945, (b) various documents on guided missiles and some of the latest projects in this field, (c) possibly some of Prof. von BRAUN's private papers, and (d) other documents."[32] Like von Braun, Dornberger did not want precious documents to fall into the wrong hands—the SS or perhaps the Soviets. As both men would later demonstrate, they were willing to let the Western Allies—specifically the Americans—eventually get their hands on these materials, which would prove to be an excellent bargaining chip.

Von Braun was not concerned just about preserving the written record of his team's work. He also devised a plan to evacuate personnel. In addition to owing Tessmann a personal debt because he had saved his life following an automobile accident, von Braun wanted to get as many of his team members out of harm's way as he could. Consequently, he gave Tessmann and Huzel a rendezvous point in Bavaria. After hiding the boxes of crucial documentation, Tessmann was to proceed to that location. Although he did not want the SS to destroy the record of his life's work, von Braun did need the help of the SS to get the rest of the scientists and technicians to Bavaria. Once there the group would be safe from Soviet forces advancing into Germany from the east, and von Braun could figure out how to navigate a surrender to the right American troops.[33]

Although traveling separately, Huzel and Tessmann linked up with von Braun and the others in Oberammergau. Once his brother Magnus arrived with information about the status of the area, the location of American troops, and passes, von Braun was ready to put the next phase of his plan into operation. He and a select group would approach the Americans. Included in the select group were von Braun's brother Magnus, Dornberger, Lt. Col. Herbert Axster (Dornberger's chief of staff), Hans Lindenberg (a combustion-chamber engineer), Tessmann, and Huzel. Loading their personal possessions into three cars, the men sat back and were driven down the Adolf Hitler Pass. They were off to negotiate surrender to the Americans.[34]

During a 1991 interview Karl Heimburg continued the story:

So we were in southern Germany. Then von Braun and General Dornberger took up conversations with the United States. The idea of the United States at that time, the United States Army was, "We want to know what is that all about rockets?" They did not have the idea to build rockets themselves at that time. They only wanted to know, and the idea was if we would do that we should go in an area where we can launch the v-2 on land. Not as we had to do it in Germany, over water. You could not see anything about the impact. This was, of course, interesting for us, too, that we should see how that vehicle comes down. Therefore, the Army had the idea we go to White Sands, and they had headquarters available in Fort Bliss. So we, at that time one hundred and eighteen, were brought to the United States. Part of us in White Sands proving ground, part of us, the bigger part in Fort Bliss. We launched some vehicles in White Sands. After the Korean War broke out [June 1950] the Army changed its mind and said, "We better build rockets of our own too. Of course, we cannot do that in Fort Bliss and White Sands. We have to go somewhere else." And we—when I say we, the German group—was thinking, well, we should go somewhere close to an industrial center, either Los Angeles or San Francisco. The idea to go to the West, on our side, was the shipping on the western side is by far less than on the eastern side. If you go close to Los Angeles, we will launch the vehicles to the south, and if we go to San Francisco, we launch the vehicles to the north.[35]

Like Heimburg, Tessmann would also travel to the United States as part of Project Paperclip and work with von Braun and Arthur Rudolph on guided missiles at Fort Bliss, Texas, before eventually joining the team in Huntsville, Alabama.[36]

In the decade after the end of World War II, as the Cold War between the East and the West heated up, the Americans, British, and Soviets, among others, focused on increasing their military capabilities. They all recognized the importance of missile technology. In the summer and fall of 1945, the British—with the help of German scientists and technicians, including von Braun and Rudolph—constructed and successfully launched a v-2 rocket. Because both the British and the Americans wanted to take advantage of the knowledge and experience of the scientists, engineers, and technicians who worked on the v-2 program and because they wanted to keep this expertise out of the hand of the Soviets, representatives of the two nations entered into exhaustive negotiations to determine which scientists would be employed by which country. Although initially the British viewed the Germans' employment as temporary, the Americans were open to the idea of permanent residence status or even citizenship for those who would be most useful to the United States' Cold War agenda.[37]

Initially, von Braun, Tessmann, Rudolph, Heimburg, and others worked for army ordnance, but the game would change drastically in 1957. As Heimburg indicated, many of them worked on rocket technology at Fort Bliss, Texas, or White Sands Proving Ground in New Mexico before being transferred to the Redstone Arsenal in Huntsville, Alabama, in 1950. The United States was not alone in focusing on this technology or on pursuing the possibility of launching a craft of some sort into space—which was also von Braun's dream. On 4 October 1957 the Soviets' efforts bore fruit when they launched *Sputnik I*—the first artificial satellite—into space. Not pleased that the Soviets had beaten the United States to the punch and on his watch, President Dwight D. Eisenhower put the U.S. space program into high gear with the establishment of the National Aeronautics and Space Administration. On 1 October 1958—one year after *Sputnik I* wound its way into the outer atmosphere, NASA opened its doors for business.

Although von Braun, Tessmann, Rudolph, and Heimburg would all make important contributions to the NASA space program, von Braun did not immediately jump at the chance to be a part of this initiative, despite his desire to design a manned space craft that could be successfully launched into outer space. According to Heimburg,

> Von Braun did not join NASA right away. Somehow he did not want to step on the Army's feet. Or on the Army officer's feet. Once the top man of NASA was visiting Huntsville, and I was leading him around in the test facilities and he asked me, "What is the reason that von Braun refuses to enter NASA?" I said, "I have not the slightest idea. I cannot give you an answer on that." Then he asked me, "Would you please tell von Braun either he joins NASA or he will be pushed out of space completely." I said, "Okay, I

can do that." And I told von Braun and he said, "I'm fully aware and I will do that. The question was only I did not want to step on the Army's feet."[38]

Not willing to give up on his dream, von Braun joined the others at NASA. Almost from the beginning von Braun, Tessmann, Rudolph, and Heimburg were involved in important research that eventually resulted in the construction of the Saturn V rocket.

On 1 July 1960 the Marshall Space Flight Center (MSFC) was established at the Redstone Arsenal facility in Huntsville, Alabama. The MSFC—a government-owned civilian center dedicated to research on rocketry and spacecraft propulsion—had as its first mission the development of "Saturn launch vehicles for the Apollo moon program." Dr. Wernher von Braun became the first MSFC director on 1 July 1960 and served in that capacity until 27 January 1970. In that capacity von Braun was "the chief architect of the Saturn V launch vehicle, the superbooster that would propel Americans to the Moon."[39]

During his tenure at the MSFC, von Braun would work closely with Tessmann, Rudolph, and Heimburg. In fact, on 5 December 1968 he issued a memorandum in which he codified new duties and promotions of members of his team at the NASA facility.[40] "Effective December 16, Mr. Karl Heimburg will become the Director of the P&VE Laboratory. Also we are considering combining the P&VE and Test Laboratories. Pending the final decision on the proposed combination, Mr. Bernhard Tessmann will manage the Test Laboratory in his present capacity as Deputy Director."[41] Although the 5 December 1968 announcement did not specifically mention him, Arthur Rudolph was an integral member of the von Braun team at MSFC. Rudolph "was the project manager for the Saturn, a vital and complex component of Apollo."[42] In many respects, von Braun, a leading proponent of space exploration, was the face of NASA. Recognizing his importance to the program, NASA made von Braun the head of its "strategic planning effort" in 1970, which meant a move to Washington DC.[43] Two years later, however, he retired from NASA and began work with Fairchild Industries in Germantown, Maryland. Von Braun passed away on 16 June 1977.

When he first went to Huntsville, Heimburg participated in constructing first the Redstone Arsenal facility and then the Marshall Space Flight Center. He joined NASA in 1960 and directed test operations, including those associated with Projects Juno, Pershing, Jupiter, and Explorer I. His responsibilities also included testing Mercury, Gemini, and Apollo engines. In 1969, as director of the Astronautics Laboratory, Heimburg was operations director for Project Skylab, America's first space station. After a prolific career with NASA, Heimburg retired in 1974 and stayed in Huntsville, where he died on 26 January 1997.

As indicated earlier, Bernhard Tessmann traveled to the United States with von Braun and initially worked for the U.S. Army Ballistic Missile Agency—first at the Artillery Proving Ground in Aberdeen, Maryland, and then at White Sands, New Mexico. Relocated to Huntsville, Alabama, in 1955, he, like Heimburg, helped plan and design both the Redstone Arsenal missile-testing facilities and the Marshall Space Flight Center. He also joined NASA early on and worked on both the Saturn and Jupiter Projects. He briefly received assignment to the U.S. Atomic Energy Commission and was tasked with helping to design nuclear test facilities. In June 1973 Tessmann retired from MSFC. He also stayed in Huntsville until his death on 19 December 1998.[44]

Unlike Arthur Rudolph, von Braun, Heimburg, and Tessmann avoided investigation by the Department of Justice's Office of Special Investigations, despite the fact that they were all involved at Peenemünde and Mittelwerk. There is no indication in the OSI report that these men came under any scrutiny. Because he died in 1977, two years before the establishment of the OSI, it is perhaps easy to understand why von Braun avoided the OSI radar, particularly since Rudolph apparently made no effort to shift the blame for the treatment of the forced laborers to his friend and colleague. More than Rudolph, von Braun was the face of NASA, and it is possible that serious roadblocks would have impeded an investigation if one had been launched. The cases of Heimburg and Tessmann, on the other hand, are less obvious; however, before engaging in further speculation, there is one more Paperclip scientist—Dr. Kurt Blome—who must be investigated first, because he is also missing from the OSI report.

Kurt Blome

Not all Project Paperclip scientists, technicians, and engineers participated in the German v-2 program. The Germans also employed scientists in medical research of various types—including mass sterilization and gassing. Numerous books detail experiments on Jewish prisoners, the mentally ill and criminally insane, and the mentally and physically disabled—all in an effort to create a master Aryan race.[45] A virologist, Kurt Blome falls into the category of medical research. While not much is known about his early life, a few facts are available.

Born on 31 January 1894 in Bielefeld, Westphalia, Kurt Blome apparently attended medical school. In 1931, at a time when he was an "internationally renowned physician," Blome, a former lieutenant general in the SA, joined the Nazi Party. For the next decade information about Blome is remarkably absent. Although spotty, a record of his activities begins to emerge in 1942—the year in which he became involved with the Central Cancer Institute, University of Posen (Poznań University). That same year he published his autobiography—*Arzt im Kampf* (Physician in struggle)—"in which he exuberantly equated medical and military power in their battle for life and death." Blome's attitude is understandable within the context of the burgeoning "*militarized medical Führer*," which was the culmination of the "militarization of medicine." The Nazis initiated a revision of the German medical ethos as part of a program called Gleichschaltung, under which "all political, social and cultural institutions were to be virtually ideologized and controlled by trusted Nazis." All professional medical organizations were eliminated or incorporated into the Reichsärztekammer, or Reich Physicians' Chamber, which was led by "'old medical fighters' who had marched and fought in the streets in the early days." Professors and medical students took weapons training. Having a "prominent military background" became inextricably linked to the acquisition of "medical prestige." Categorized as medical "old fighters," physicians like Blome were viewed "as more *Nazi* than physician." Consequently, Blome, who, like his peers, had something to prove, embraced being a part of the newly created militarized medical Führer.[46]

By 1943, fully embedded into the Nazi Party and a full participant in the militarized medicine program, Blome had received promotions and new titles—Reichsgesundheitsführer, or deputy Reich physician führer, and "Plenipotentiary for Cancer Research in the Reich Research Council," a post created by Hermann Göring on 30 April 1943.[47] With these new positions he had new responsibilities and a new boss. As director of a unit at the Central Cancer Institute, Blome was involved in, and oversaw, biological weapons research. In addition, he received orders directly from Reichsführer-SS Heinrich Himmler to conduct specific research—including injecting concentration camp prisoners with the plague vaccine.

Not all the experiments ordered by Himmler were related to biological weapons. Following Himmler's directives, deputy Reich physician Führer Blome authorized various experiments on prisoners at the Dachau concentration camp. These experiments included prolonged exposure to cold. Prisoners were forced to strip and remain outside in harsh winter conditions for up to fourteen hours or to spend a minimum of three hours in a tank full of iced water. At one point, of the three hundred inmates forced to participate, eighty did not survive. What was most important to Himmler, however, was the development of biological weapons.

Between 1943 and 1945 Blome met multiple times with Himmler, who was the moving force behind the Reich's bioweapons program. Himmler was particularly interested in exploring the possibility of using the bubonic plague as an offensive weapon, and he tasked Blome with pursuing this line of research in July (or possibly August) 1943. To achieve the endgame as soon as possible, Himmler authorized Blome "to use human beings." In addition, the Reichsführer offered the doctor a testing facility that had an exploitable group of potential patients—the medical block at the Dachau concentration camp. When Blome noted that certain circles within the party strongly opposed conducting experiments on humans, Himmler's response demanded acceptance. The war effort demanded experimentation on humans. Refusal was treasonous. Agreeing to Himmler's demand, Blome suggested that, in order to conduct plague bacterium research, he would need his own facilities that were isolated from population centers.

Himmler agreed. The result was the establishment of the Bacteriological Institute at Nesselstedt, which was near what was once Poznań University. The Reich controlled the university by 1943.[48]

With construction on the Nesselstedt facility completed by February 1944, Blome and his staff were ready to hit the ground running. The facility included a number of buildings: a state-of-the-art laboratory, housing for staff, and an "animal farm." In the experimental block were "a climate room, a cold room, disinfectant facilities, and rooms for 'clean' and 'dirty' experiments." Furthermore, because they were experimenting with dangerous biological agents and might become contaminated, the staff also had an isolation hospital that could accommodate up to sixteen people at a time. Despite his best efforts, Himmler was displeased with the progress of Blome's team. Exacerbating the situation in the winter of 1944 were the constant rumors of an imminent Allied invasion.[49]

Blome's productivity was not enhanced by Himmler's harebrained ideas for a biological agent–delivery system. Beginning a month or two before the Allies invasion at Normandy, the two Germans met multiple times. Characterizing his superior as paranoid, Blome claimed that Himmler was convinced that the Allies planned to target the Reich with biological weapons. Promising to investigate Himmler's reports of multiple puzzling, as well as alarming, incidents, Blome turned the conversation to the serious threat to the institute and his research—the Soviet army. Acknowledging the threat, Himmler agreed to relocate Blome's research facility to "Geraberg, in the Thuringian forest, at the edge of the Harz Mountains." Construction on the new bioweapons research facility commenced in October 1944. Although not completely finished by the war's end, the Geraberg facility was clearly in use.[50]

Between 1943 and the end of the war, Blome and his research staff conducted experiments with a wide range of biological agents, including "plague, cholera, anthrax, and typhoid." The team also attempted to spread malaria and typhus by experimenting with mosquitoes at Dachau and with typhus-infected lice at Buchenwald. Blome's research extended to nerve agents—in particular tabun and sarin. According to the Centers for Disease Control and Prevention, tabun is "the most toxic of the known chemical warfare agents. It has a fruity odor reminiscent of bitter almonds. Exposure to tabun can cause death in minutes."[51] Sarin is a nerve agent. "Nerve agents are the most toxic and rapidly acting of the known chemical warfare agents" and are more potent than their relatives—pesticides.[52] Using aerosol dispersants and other methods to spray tabun and sarin from aircraft, Blome exposed Auschwitz prisoners to these nerve agents and evaluated their effects.

Despite Blome and his team's frantic work, they were not achieving results fast enough to satisfy Himmler or, ultimately, Hitler. Pressure assaulted them from all sides. As they conducted their research, the war played out all around them. The Soviet steamroller was bearing down on Germany from the east. After the failed offensive that earned the title of the Battle of the Bulge, the Western Allies were slowly pressing their advance into the German heartland. The war was not going well for the Germans. The situation became increasingly worse for the Reich in the spring of 1945. No one—especially scientists and physicians, like Blome, who had conducted experiments on concentration camp inmates—was safe.

Although he initially escaped capture, Dr. Kurt Blome's luck would not hold. He was on multiple watch lists, including that compiled by the Americans' Alsos Mission. Initially tasked with gathering information about the Germans' atomic bomb program, the Alsos Mission soon expanded to include intelligence gathering related to the enemy's biological weapons program. Consequently, Blome made the group's "most wanted list." Alsos had an additional mission—capture as many scientists as possible to keep them out of Soviet hands and determine which ones to exploit in order to advance American programs. The Alsos Mission was not the only agency trying to get their hands on Blome, who was not oblivious to the fact that he was probably a wanted man. But it was difficult, once the war ended, to travel in occupied territory without going through a manned checkpoint of one sort or another.

Amazingly, however, Blome avoided capture for almost two weeks after the war ended. Possibly because he wanted to elude the Soviets, Blome, like von Braun, Rudolph, Heimburg, and Tessmann, headed to Bavaria, where his luck ran out on 17 May 1945 at a U.S. checkpoint in Munich. Soldiers examined the papers of a man who matched the description of the man identified as the director of the bioweapons research facility at Geraberg. The man who approached the checkpoint was "well-dressed"—"134 pounds, five foot nine, with dark black hair, hazel eyes, and a pronounced dueling scar on the left side of his face between his nose and his upper lip." The man's German passport identified him as "Professor Doctor Friedrich Ludwig Kurt Blome."[53] Blome's name immediately raised a red flag, and the Americans detained him. Blome was formally arrested by Agent Arnold Vyth of the Counter Intelligence Corps, who dispatched him to the Twelfth Army Group Interrogation Center. Officials compiled documentation about the captured German. In addition to information provided by the War Crimes Office, they learned that the Office of Strategic Services also had Blome on their watch list.

Blome underwent extensive interrogation. Initially, he appeared cooperative, which raised the hoped of his interrogators, who thought that they were poised to hit the mother lode. During his first interrogation, Blome indicated that he did not agree with the use of medical science advancement in the commission of atrocities. When pressed, "Blome state[d] that in his capacity as deputy surgeon general of the Reich he had 'observe[d] new scientific studies and experiments which led to later atrocities e.g. mass sterilization, gassing of Jews.'"[54] His interrogators were practically salivating, but their excitement would not last. Maj. E. W. B. Gill, an Alsos Mission interrogator, conducted Blome's second interview. This time the German volunteered less and was more obstructionist. Claiming to be nothing more than a Reich administrator, Blome denied being personally involved in any research. Not only did Gill fail to learn anything new from Blome, but he was also convinced that the German was being less than truthful.[55]

A month later Blome was transferred to Castle Kransberg—codenamed Dustbin—for additional interrogation by Alsos agents Bill Cromartie and J. M. Barnes. The first session went no better than that conducted by Gill. A few days later, however, Blome "seemed anxious" to cooperate. Not certain that they could trust him, the agents also realized that it would be difficult to confirm Blome's version of events. For example, Blome suggested that the army, not his staff, conducted vaccine research and that the Reich surgeon general had jurisdiction over epidemic research and was responsible for protecting Germans from bioweapons. Furthermore, he provided information that would add to the tense postwar relationship between the United States and the Soviet Union. According to Blome, the Soviet biological weapons program was the best in the world, and a few months earlier the Soviets had seized the "Reich's most advanced biological weapons research and development facility" at Nesselstedt.[56]

Although there was concern about the extent of Blome's involvement in the development and testing of biological weapons for the Reich, the Joint Intelligence Objectives Agency identified him as one of the scientists who could provide crucial intelligence for the United States. Consequently, they placed Blome's name on the list of German and Austrian scientists whom they hoped to exploit. Recognizing that Blome's past as Reich deputy surgeon could not be spun in a positive light, the JOIA acknowledged, however, that the German's expertise would be crucial should the United States find itself at war with its soon-to-be former ally—the Soviet Union—but the agency was unclear about how many of the scientists on the list would actually be brought to the United States under Project Paperclip.

When the Dustbin came under the jurisdiction of U.S. Army Military Intelligence Service Center, the army moved the interrogation facility to its location at Darmstadt. Blome, who was also transferred to Darmstadt, found himself employed there as a doctor by the U.S. Army by the summer of 1946, while officials from the U.S. Chemical Corps took steps to transfer him to Camp Detrick, Maryland, where he could be interviewed at length by their bacteriologists. Unfortunately for Blome, this plan was derailed that same summer—by the Palace of Justice trials at Nuremberg. Soviet prosecutors announced their intention to put Maj. Gen. Walter P. Schreiber on the witness stand. Schreiber, the former Reich surgeon general, was expected to provide testimony against his former colleagues—including Blome.

The infamous Doctors' Trial began in 1946. U.S. officials held twelve trials of German doctors accused of war crimes. The first of these was the *United States of America v. Karl Brandt et al.* All but three of the twenty-three defendants were medical doctors. The prosecutors listed the charges against them: "The indictment consisted of four counts. Count one charged participation in a common design or conspiracy to commit war crimes or crimes against humanity. The ruling of the tribunal disregarded this count, hence no defendant was found guilty of the crime charged in count one. Count two was concerned with war crimes and count three, with crimes against humanity. Fifteen defendants were found guilty, and eight were acquitted on these two counts. Ten defendants were charged under count four with membership in a criminal organization and were found guilty."[57] Blome was one of the lucky ones. When the trial ended in 1947, he was a free man—acquitted of the charges primarily because the prosecution was unable to prove intent.

Blome's acquittal reopened the Project Paperclip door. The German received a visit from Dr. Harold W. Batchelor and three of his colleagues from Camp Detrick. All were "biological warfare experts." By this time, Blome realized that it was to his advantage to cooperate with the Americans. After all, he had just escaped conviction and possibly execution at Nuremberg. He could not take that chance again. If he made himself valuable to the Americans, then maybe they would protect him if he was targeted again. Finding Blome both helpful and a fountain of information, the Americans, willing to turn a blind eye to his past activities, offered him a contract to participate in Project 63, a job placement program. Many participants received jobs with American aviation companies. Although they believed that he had actually experimented on concentration camp inmates, the Americans believed that Blome's potential usefulness—particularly as the Cold War loomed—outweighed any atrocities that he probably committed.

In 1951 Blome received an offer of a real job. The U.S. Chemical Corps gave him a contract and a yearly salary of $6,800. There is evidence to suggest that the U.S. Army falsified Blome's Joint Intelligence Objectives Agency application by leaving out details of his employment history between 1945 and 1948. His agency file does not mention Blome's July 1945 admission "that Himmler had ordered him in 1943 to use concentration camp inmates for experiments on plague vaccine" and that he intended to "conduct human experiments," an admission that resulted in his war crimes trial. Not much is known about Blome's work for the United States after this. Apparently he was post doctor at Camp King in Oberursel, Germany, near the U.S. Military Intelligence Service Center, because he was unable to obtain a U.S. visa. There is also mention in his file that he worked on a top secret project: "Army, 1952, Project 1975." Information about this project remains classified.[58]

At the end of the day, however, Blome's past caught up with him. French authorities arrested him and tried him for war crimes. This time the charges stuck. Convicted, Blome received a twenty-year prison sentence, which perhaps confirmed allegations that the Americans had made a deal with Blome. In exchange for information about his experiments at Dachau and his expertise on biological warfare, they would ensure that he would escape conviction at Nuremberg. Dr. Kurt Blome died on 10 October 1969 in Germany, which means that he must have received early release.[59]

When considering the men discussed here—Wernher von Braun, Bernhard Tessmann, Karl Heimburg, and Kurt Blome—one question comes to mind. Why were they not investigated by the Department of Justice's Office of Special Investigations? All four men conducted research that affected the lives of concentration camp inmates and constituted war crimes, although not all of them directly interacted with the internees. What made one Nazi fair game for investigation when another got a pass? The first three men on this list—von Braun, Tessmann, and Heimburg—and Arthur Rudolph worked together on rocket research before and during World War II. The construction and operation of the rocket factory and testing facilities at Mittelwerk resulted in the establishment of the Dora concentration camp and cost many inmates their lives; however, only Rudolph found himself in the OSI headlights.

While some might argue that there was no reason for the OSI to investigate von Braun because he had died two years before the establishment of that branch of the Department of Justice, that does not explain why neither Tessmann nor Heimburg faced the same scrutiny that Rudolph did. After all, both lived until the late 1990s. Because the OSI report does not explain why some Nazis, particularly those who came to the United States as part of Project Paperclip, were not scrutinized by OSI, one must make an educated guess. Although they both worked on the Saturn rocket project, neither Tessmann nor Heimburg received the same notoriety that von Braun and, to a lesser extent, Rudolph did. As leader of the project that put a man on the moon, von Braun was "Dr. Space." He was the face of NASA. To question his background or his integrity would be same as impugning NASA's reputation. This suggests, perhaps, that it was not in the OSI's best interests to investigate von Braun. But there was a precedent for investigating a deceased Nazi. Unlike Rudolph, Tessmann and Heimburg had no direct control over concentration camp inmates; therefore, it seems likely that the OSI left them alone because they had done nothing to draw attention to themselves—which Rudolph did. Furthermore, Rudolph was integrally involved in the decision to use inmates at Mittelwerk, which made charges of war crimes against him more sustainable.

Where does this leave Blome? Although he was acquitted at Nuremberg, it is difficult—if not impossible—to deny that he and his staff conducted experiments on human subjects—on the unwilling inmates of Dachau and Buchenwald. He had to face the music a second time, and he was unable to escape unscathed when the French convicted him of war crimes. Although he died almost a decade before the establishment of the OSI, why did the deceased Blome escape scrutiny? The OSI helped to identify the remains of Josef Mengele, who died the same year that the agency was established. While it is possible that Mengele's war crimes were more egregious than Blome's, both men experimented on concentration camp prisoners and caused the deaths of many of them. There are three factors that might explain why the OSI did not shine their light on Blome. First, he worked for the United States, albeit briefly in the grand scheme of things. Second, he died almost a decade before the OSI was created, unlike Mengele, who died the same year. Finally, Blome never received the notoriety that Mengele—the Angel of Death—did. Consequently, Blome succeeded in flying below the OSI radar.

Although Blome, Tessmann, Heimburg, and von Braun escaped OSI scrutiny, many others did not. One could argue that without Rep. Elizabeth Holtzman and, to a lesser extent, Simon Wiesenthal, the Department of Justice would not have been pressured to create the OSI and attach it to the Criminal Division. One could argue that it took the Holtzman Amendment to give the OSI the tools that it needed to pursue its mandate. But the OSI took its responsibilities seriously. Tasked with investigating suspected Nazi criminals and pursuing denaturalization and, in some instances, deportation cases against them, the OSI was thorough and persistent. The evidence did not always substantiate the initial charges, which resulted in exoneration. Central to the U.S. justice system is the "innocent until proven guilty" mantra, which made the OSI's task all the more difficult. It was no easy task to collect evidence decades after the war. Documents had been destroyed or were sealed in archives behind the Iron Curtain. Witness testimony was frequently problematic. Some victims who survived the camps were too traumatized to provide coherent testimony. Statements provided by witnesses were contradictory. Some survivors were interviewed by Soviet officials in less than ideal circumstances, which sometimes raised questions about the veracity of their testimony. Furthermore, analysis of the evidence could be shaped by the issue of whether or not the "innocence meme" should, or in fact could, be applied to Nazis. The same conundrum exists in the current atmosphere created by terrorism and the nonconventional battlefield of the "war on terror."

Sometimes, however, the evidence told a different story, and the OSI went to court. Did the OSI win every case that it pursued? No, it did not, but the cases in the win column spanned a group of people who established concentration camp and extermination policy, who ordered or personally carried out executions, and who performed obscenely irrelevant experiments on camp inmates. Nor did a successful case necessarily end with denaturalization or deportation. In one case it was enough to place a sitting president on a Watch List, which prevented him from entering the United States, even in an official capacity. This was no mere "slap on the wrist." In the final analysis, as its 2006 report, "The Office of Special Investigations: Striving for Accountability in the Aftermath of the Holocaust," suggests, the OSI, working with limited financial and personnel resources, followed its mandate to achieve justice for those tortured and murdered under the auspices of the Nazi Final Solution.[60]

NOTES

Foreword

1. Bernanos, *France contre les robots*.
2. Cavanaugh, "Aquinas's Account."

Introduction

1. Eric Lichtblau, "Nazis Were Given 'Safe Haven' in U.S., Report Says," *New York Times*, 13 November 2010.
2. Feigin, "Office of Special Investigations," 74.
3. Feigin, "Office of Special Investigations," 77.
4. Feigin, "Office of Special Investigations," 78.
5. Feigin, "Office of Special Investigations," 79.
6. Feigin, "Office of Special Investigations," 85–86.
7. Feigin, "Office of Special Investigations," 150–74; "John Demjanjuk, Convicted Nazi Death Camp Guard, Dies Aged 91," *Guardian*, 17 March 2012; Robert D. McFadden, "John Demjanjuk, 91, Dogged by Charges of Atrocities as Nazi Camp Guard, Dies," *New York Times*, 17 March 2012.
8. Feigin, "Office of Special Investigations," 151.
9. Feigin, "Office of Special Investigations," 154.
10. Feigin, "Office of Special Investigations," 155.
11. Feigin, "Office of Special Investigations," 151–74, 575–76; "John Demjanjuk, Convicted Nazi."
12. Feigin, "Office of Special Investigations," 601. Several Internet sources, including articles for which historian Richard Breitman was interviewed, claim that he was born in 1924. That would have made him seventeen in 1941, which makes it difficult to accept that he was an SS or SD officer in August 1942. Therefore, the birth year of 1918 seems more likely. See Breitmen, "Tscherim Soobzokov"; "An American Nazi Living in New Jersey," *Atlantic*, July 12, 1974; Albert J. Parisi, "Pipe-Bomb Death Puzzles Authorities," *New York Times*, September 15, 1985; Robert Weiner, "CIA Sheltered NJ Man with Nazi Past: Justice Dept. Inquiry Saw War Criminals Were Given Safe Haven," *New Jersey Jewish News*, November 17, 2010.
13. Feigin, "Office of Special Investigations," 342–43.
14. Feigin, "Office of Special Investigations," 343.
15. Feigin, "Office of Special Investigations," 343–44; Brewda, "KGB and Mossad."

16. Feigin, "Office of Special Investigations," 345.

17. Brewda, "KGB and Mossad," 56.

18. Feigin, "Office of Special Investigations," 346.

19. Feigin, "Office of Special Investigations," 601.

20. Feigin, "Office of Special Investigations," 348.

21. Feigin, "Office of Special Investigations," 350.

1. Office of Special Investigations

1. Johnson, "Summary."

2. Feigin, "Office of Special Investigations," 1.

3. For an in-depth examination of Andrija Artuković, see chapter 6.

4. For a more detailed account of the Karl Linnas case, see chapter 7.

5. For a more detailed analysis of the Otto von Bolschwing case, see chapter 4.

6. Feigin, "Office of Special Investigations," 2. See also Rosenbaum, "Introduction to the Work."

7. "Simon Wiesenthal Biography: Activist (1908-2005)," Biography.com, 2 April 2014, www.biography.com/people/simon-wiesenthal-9530740.

8. "Simon Wiesenthal Biography"; United States Holocaust Memorial Museum (USHMM), "Janowska," Holocaust Encyclopedia, accessed 17 June 2016, www.ushmm.org/wlc/en/article.php?ModuleId=10005279.

9. "Simon Wiesenthal Biography."

10. "Simon Wiesenthal Biography."

11. "Holtzman, Elizabeth," United States House of Representatives, History, Art & Archives, accessed 17 June 2016, http://history.house.gov/People/Detail/15213.

12. "Holtzman, Elizabeth."

13. Feigin, "Office of Special Investigations," 2-3.

14. Feigin, "Office of Special Investigations," 3-4.

15. Ruffner, "CIA's Support." See also U.S. General Accounting Office, *Widespread Conspiracy*, 33-34.

16. Ruffner, "CIA's Support." See also U.S. General Accounting Office, *Widespread Conspiracy*.

17. Ruffner, "CIA's Support." See also U.S. General Accounting Office, *Widespread Conspiracy*; and *Hearings before the Subcommittee*, vols. 1-2.

18. Feigin, "Office of Special Investigations," 3-4.

19. Feigin, "Office of Special Investigations," 4-6.

20. Rosenbaum, "Introduction to the Work," 2.

21. Feigin, "Office of Special Investigations," 6.

22. Act to Amend the Immigration and Nationality Act.

23. Feigin, "Office of Special Investigations," 7-9.

24. Feigin, "Office of Special Investigations," 10-11.

25. Feigin, "Office of Special Investigations," 11.

26. Rosenbaum, "Introduction to the Work," 3-4.

27. Feigin, "Office of Special Investigations," 11.

28. Feigin, "Office of Special Investigations," 11–12.
29. Feigin, "Office of Special Investigations," 12–13.
30. Rosenbaum, "Introduction to the Work," 3–4.
31. Feis, "OSI's Prosecution," 8.
32. Feis, "OSI's Prosecution," 8.
33. See the chapters on Klaus Barbie (2) and Josef Mengele (3).
34. Feis, "OSI's Prosecution," 9.
35. Feis, "OSI's Prosecution," 10–12.
36. Feis, "OSI's Prosecution."
37. Rosenbaum, "Introduction to the Work," 5; Feigin, "Office of Special Investigations," v. See also White, "Barring Axis Persecutors." For more detail on Waldheim, see chapter 5.
38. Rosenbaum, "Introduction to the Work," 5; "Verfahren wegen Verbrechen."
39. "Former Secretary-General Kurt Waldheim," United Nations, 22 June 2016, www.un.org/sg/en/content/formersg/kurt-waldheim; Rosenbaum, "Introduction to the Work," 5; Jonathan Kandell, "Kurt Waldheim Dies at 88; Ex-UN Chief Hid Nazi Past," *New York Times*, 14 June 2007.
40. Rosenbaum, "Introduction to the Work," 5–6.
41. Rosenbaum, "Introduction to the Work," 6–7. See also Nazi War Crimes Disclosure Act.
42. USA PATRIOT Act.
43. Gordon, "OSI's Expanded Jurisdiction," 25.
44. Gordon, "OSI's Expanded Jurisdiction," 25.
45. Feigin, "Office of Special Investigations," 599; Ralph Blumenthal, "The Last Nazi Hunter," *Parade*, 4 April 2010.
46. Blumenthal, "Last Nazi Hunter"; Matt Pearce, "Holocaust Suspect Dies in Michigan after Avoiding Deportation," *Los Angeles Times*, 9 July 2014.
47. "Posts Tagged 'Office of Special Investigations,'" *Main Justice: Politics, Policy and the Law, Sunday*, 16 May 2010, www.mainjustice.com/tag/office-of-special-investigations/ (site discontinued).

2. Klaus Barbie

1. Morgan, *Uncertain Hour*, 204.
2. Holocaust Education & Archive Research Team (HEART), "Klaus Barbie: The Butcher of Lyon," Holocaust Research Project, accessed 20 January 2016, www.holocaustresearchproject.org/nazioccupation/barbie.html; American-Israeli Cooperative Enterprise (AICE), "Klaus Barbie (1913–1991)," Jewish Virtual Library, accessed 23 June 2016, www.jewishvirtuallibrary.org/jsource/Holocaust/Barbie.html; Morgan, *Uncertain Hour*, 204.
3. "Klaus Barbie: Department of Justice; FBI; Department of State; CIA; Counter Intelligence Corps Files," Paperless Archives, accessed 3 February 2016, www.paperlessarchives.com/barbie.html; Morgan, *Uncertain Hour*, 204–5; Paris, *Unhealed Wounds*, 41.

4. Morgan, *Uncertain Hour*, 205–6.

5. Paris, *Unhealed Wounds*, 43; Morgan, *Uncertain Hour*, 206; HEART, "Klaus Barbie." The facts about Barbie's life in 1937 and 1938 are a bit muddled. The record is muddied, which makes determining an exact timeline of events difficult. According to Paris, the school in Bernau was an SD, not an SS, school. She also claims that Barbie attended both the Bernau school and the leadership course in Berlin in 1937. Morgan concurs that Barbie attended a training course in Bernau in 1937, but at an SS school. Morgan also claims that Barbie's first postcourse deployment was to Düsseldorf. The Holocaust Education & Archive Research Team muddies the waters even more. According to the Holocaust Research Project, "After service in the Berlin vice squad he was transferred to Dusseldorf and in 1937 after joining the Nazi Party, and graduated from the SD school at Bernau and was sent to an exclusive leadership course in Berlin Charlottenburg. For three months from September 1938 he served with the 39th Infantry Regiment before returning to Charlottenburg for his final training and exams."

6. Paris, *Unhealed Wounds*, 43.

7. Paris, *Unhealed Wounds*, 43–44; Morgan, *Uncertain Hour*, 206.

8. Paris, *Unhealed Wounds*, 43–44; Morgan, *Uncertain Hour*, 206; HEART, "Klaus Barbie."

9. Paris, *Unhealed Wounds*, 44–45.

10. HEART, "Klaus Barbie."

11. "Murderous Barbie Has No Regrets about Crimes," *Digibron*, 10 March 1983.

12. HEART, "Klaus Barbie"; Paris, *Unhealed Wounds*, 44–46; "Ernst Cahn and Alfred Kohn Bridge Amsterdam," STIWOT, accessed 15 December 2016, http://en .tracesofwar.com/article/27733/Ernst-Cahn-and-Alfred-Kohn-bridge-Amsterdam.htm.

13. Paris, *Unhealed Wounds*, 45–46.

14. Paris, *Unhealed Wounds*, 76.

15. AICE, "Klaus Barbie (1913–1991)."

16. AICE, "Klaus Barbie (1913–1991)"; Paris, *Unhealed Wounds*, 27.

17. AICE, "Klaus Barbie (1913–1991)."

18. Paris, *Unhealed Wounds*, 93–94.

19. "Children's Ghosts Confront the 'Butcher of Lyons' in French Courthouse," *Guardian*, 28 May 2015; "May 11, 1987: Butcher of Lyon on Trial," History.com, accessed 15 December 2016, www.history.com/this-day-in-history/butcher-of-lyon-on-trial/print.

20. "Jean Moulin (1899–1943)," British Broadcasting Corporation, accessed 15 March 2016, www.bbc.co.uk/history/historic_figures/moulin_jean.shtml.

21. "Jean Moulin (1899–1943)."

22. AICE, "Klaus Barbie (1913–1991)."

23. Paris, *Unhealed Wounds*, 106; HEART, "Klaus Barbie."

24. AICE, "Klaus Barbie (1913–1991)"; HEART, "Klaus Barbie"; Paris, *Unhealed Wounds*, 101–9.

25. HEART, "Klaus Barbie."

26. "Earl Browning Obituary," *Telegraph*, 6 November 2013.

27. Feigin, "Office of Special Investigations," 372.

28. "Earl Browning Obituary."

29. Ralph Blumenthal, "U.S. Agents Tell of Shielding Barbie," *New York Times*, 17 July 1983.

30. "Earl Browning Obituary"; AICE, "Klaus Barbie (1913-1991)"; HEART, "Klaus Barbie"; Steinacher, *Nazis on the Run*, 203; Feigin, "Office of Special Investigations," 372, 374; Wolfgang Saxon, "Klaus Barbie, 77, Lyons Gestapo Chief," *New York Times*, 26 September 1991.

31. "Earl Browning Obituary."

32. "Earl Browning Obituary"; AICE, "Klaus Barbie (1913-1991)"; HEART, "Klaus Barbie"; Steinacher, *Nazis on the Run*, 203; Feigin, "Office of Special Investigations," 372, 374; Saxon, "Klaus Barbie, 77."

33. Steinacher, *Nazis on the Run*, 90.

34. Steinacher, *Nazis on the Run*, 90, 203.

35. Paris, *Unhealed Wounds*, 121.

36. Steinacher, *Nazis on the Run*, 203; "May 11, 1987."

37. "May 11, 1987."

38. "Earl Browning Obituary"; Saxon, "Klaus Barbie, 77"; Paris, *Unhealed Wounds*, 121-22.

39. Steinacher, *Nazis on the Run*, 204.

40. Steinacher, *Nazis on the Run*, 204.

41. Gustavo Sanchez, "In Pursuit of Bolivia's Secret Nazi," *Guardian*, 10 September 2008. See also Steinacher, *Nazis on the Run*, 203-4.

42. Georg Bönish and Klaus Wiegrefe, "From Nazi Criminal to Postwar Spy: German Intelligence Hired Klaus Barbie as Agent," *Spiegel Online*, 20 January 2011, www.spiegel.de/international/germany/from-nazi-criminal-to-postwar-spy-german -intelligence-hired-klaus-barbie-as-agent-a-740393-druck.html.

43. Steinacher, *Nazis on the Run*, 204-5.

44. "Solinger" was the handler's code name.

45. Bönish and Wiegrefe, "Nazi Criminal to Postwar Spy."

46. Bönish and Wiegrefe, "Nazi Criminal to Postwar Spy."

47. Bönish and Wiegrefe, "Nazi Criminal to Postwar Spy."

48. While some sources contend that Barbie's identity was discovered in 1971, others list the date as 1972. While it is possible that the discovery occurred in late 1971, Beate Klarsfeld publicly identified Altmann as Barbie on 28 January 1972.

49. Paris, *Unhealed Wounds*, 121-23; Goda, "Manhunts," in Breitman et al., *Intelligence and the Nazis*, 426-27.

50. Paris, *Unhealed Wounds*, 121-23; Goda, "Manhunts," in Breitman et al., *Intelligence and the Nazis*, 426-27; Feigin, "Office of Special Investigations," 371.

51. William Rogers, qtd. in Goda, "Manhunts," in Breitman et al., *Intelligence and the Nazis*, 427.

52. "Hugo Banzer, 75, Ex-Dictator; Guided Bolivia to Democracy," *New York Times*, 6 May 2002; Feigin, "Office of Special Investigations," 371-72.

53. "May 11, 1987."

54. Feigin, "Office of Special Investigations," 372.

55. Feigin, "Office of Special Investigations," 373.

56. Feigin, "Office of Special Investigations," 373-74.

57. Feigin, "Office of Special Investigations," 374.

58. Feigin, "Office of Special Investigations," 375.

59. Feigin, "Office of Special Investigations," 375.

60. Feigin, "Office of Special Investigations," 375.

61. Feigin, "Office of Special Investigations," 376-78.

62. "Klaus Barbie: Women Testify of Torture at His Hands," *Philadelphia Inquirer*, 23 March 1987; Paris, *Unhealed Wounds*, 27, 106-7; Steve Holland, "On Trial with Klaus Barbie: The French Resistance," *Philly.com*, 3 February 2016, http://articles.philly.com /1987-05-10/news/26161943_1_jews-and-resistance-fighters-jean-moulin-french -resistance (site discontinued); HEART, "Klaus Barbie"; AICE, "Klaus Barbie (1913- 1991)"; "May 11, 1987"; Rone Tempest, "Klaus Barbie, Wartime 'Butcher of Lyon,' Dies: Gestapo; Cancer Claims Ex-Nazi Convicted of Deporting French Jews to Death Camps in World War II," *Los Angeles Times*, 26 September 1991.

63. Tempest, "Klaus Barbie, Wartime."

3. Josef Mengele

1. Posner and Ware, *Mengele*, 4.

2. USHMM, "Josef Mengele," Holocaust Encyclopedia, accessed 20 January 2016, www.ushmm.org/wlc/en/article.php?ModuleId=10007060; "Angel of Death: Josef Mengele," The Holocaust: Crimes, Heroes and Villains, 20 January 2016, http:// auschwitz.dk/Mengele.htm; Posner and Ware, *Mengele*, 4-5.

3. Posner and Ware, *Mengele*, 4.

4. Posner and Ware, *Mengele*, 5.

5. "February 07, 1979: The 'Angel of Death' Dies," History.com, accessed 16 December 2016, www.history.com/this-day-in-history/the-angel-of-death-dies/print.

6. "February 07, 1979"; USHMM, "Josef Mengele"; "Josef Mengele, Nazi War Criminal," About Education, accessed 22 April 2016, http://latinamericanhistory .about.com/od/thehistoryofargentina/p/Josef-Mengele-Nazi-War-Criminal.htm; AICE, "Josef Mengele (1911-1979)," Jewish Virtual Library, accessed 25 July 2014, www.jewishvirtuallibrary.org/jsource/Holocaust/Mengele.html; "Angel of Death"; Posner and Ware, *Mengele*, 7-15.

7. Posner and Ware, *Mengele*, 14-16.

8. Posner and Ware, *Mengele*, 10-15. For more on the work of von Verschuer and others during this period, see Weingert, "German Eugenics."

9. Posner and Ware, *Mengele*, 17; "February 07, 1979."

10. "February 07, 1979."

11. HEART, "Josef Mengele: 'The Angel of Death,'" Holocaust Research Project, accessed 25 July 2014, www.holocaustresearchproject.org/othercamps/mengele.html.

12. Yehuda Koren and Eilat Negev, "How the Seven Dwarfs of Auschwitz Fell under

the Spell of Dr. Death: The Hideous Experiments Carried Out by Nazi Josef Mengele on Seven Trusting Brothers and Sisters," *Daily Mail*, 15 February 2013.

13. Rees, *Ultimate Infamy*, 180.

14. Posner and Ware, *Mengele*, 29–30.

15. Posner and Ware, *Mengele*, 29.

16. Andy Walker, "The Twins of Auschwitz," BBC *News Magazine*, 28 January 2015, www.bbc.com/news/magazine-30933718.

17. Walker, "Twins of Auschwitz"; Posner and Ware, *Mengele*, 34.

18. "Eva and Miriam," The Holocaust: Crimes, Heroes and Villains, 20 May 2016, www.auschwitz.dk/eva.htm.

19. Rees, *Ultimate Infamy*, 180–81. See also "Eva and Miriam."

20. "Eva and Miriam."

21. Yehuda Koren and Eilat Negev, "The Dwarves of Auschwitz," *Guardian*, 23 March 2013.

22. Koren and Negev, "Dwarves of Auschwitz."

23. Koren and Negev, "Seven Dwarfs of Auschwitz."

24. Koren and Negev, "Seven Dwarfs of Auschwitz."

25. Koren and Negev, "Seven Dwarfs of Auschwitz."

26. Koren and Negev, "Seven Dwarfs of Auschwitz."

27. Koren and Negev, "Seven Dwarfs of Auschwitz."

28. Koren and Negev, "Seven Dwarfs of Auschwitz."

29. Walker, "Twins of Auschwitz."

30. USHMM, "Josef Mengele."

31. Gerald L. Posner and John Ware, "Fugitive: How Nazi War Criminal Josef Mengele Cheated Justice for 34 Years," *Chicago Tribune*, 18 May 1986; Posner and Ware, *Mengele*, 59–60.

32. Posner and Ware, "Fugitive"; Posner and Ware, *Mengele*, 60–61.

33. Posner and Ware, "Fugitive"; Posner and Ware, *Mengele*, 61–62.

34. Posner and Ware, "Fugitive." See also Posner and Ware, *Mengele*, 61–62.

35. Posner and Ware, "Fugitive"; Posner and Ware, *Mengele*, 62–64.

36. Steinacher, *Nazis on the Run*, 24. See also Posner and Ware, "Fugitive."

37. Posner and Ware, "Fugitive"; Posner and Ware, *Mengele*, 63–65.

38. Posner and Ware, "Fugitive"; Steinacher, *Nazis on the Run*, 24; USHMM, "Josef Mengele."

39. Steinacher, *Nazis on the Run*, 25; Posner and Ware, "Fugitive"; USHMM, "Josef Mengele"; Posner and Ware, *Mengele*, 68–85.

40. Posner and Ware, "Fugitive"; Steinacher, *Nazis on the Run*, 25; Posner and Ware, *Mengele*, 86–87.

41. Posner and Ware, "Fugitive"; Steinacher, *Nazis on the Run*, 25; Posner and Ware, *Mengele*, 88–89.

42. Posner and Ware, "Fugitive"; Steinacher, *Nazis on the Run*, 25, 49–52, 97; Posner and Ware, *Mengele*, 89–93.

43. "Josef Mengele, Nazi War Criminal"; "Josef Mengele in South America,"

About Education, 22 April 2016, http://latinamericanhistory.about.com/od/Nazis
/fl/Josef-Mengele-in-South-America.htm; Posner and Ware, "Fugitive"; Posner
and Ware, *Mengele*, 94-106.

44. Posner and Ware, "Fugitive"; Posner and Ware, *Mengele*, 109-12.

45. HEART, "Josef Mengele"; Posner and Ware, "Fugitive"; Posner and Ware,
Mengele, 117-24.

46. Posner and Ware, "Fugitive"; Goda, "Manhunts," in Breitman et al., *Intelligence and the Nazis*, 431; Posner and Ware, *Mengele*, 124-32.

47. Posner and Ware, "Fugitive"; Goda, "Manhunts," in Breitman et al., *Intelligence and the Nazis*, 431-33; Posner and Ware, *Mengele*, 14-54.

48. Posner and Ware, "Fugitive."

49. Posner and Ware, "Fugitive." See also Posner and Ware, *Mengele*, 161-64.

50. Posner and Ware, "Fugitive"; Posner and Ware, *Mengele*, 165-73.

51. Posner and Ware, "Fugitive"; Posner and Ware, *Mengele*, 173-81.

52. Posner and Ware, "Fugitive."

53. Posner and Ware, "Fugitive."

54. Posner and Ware, "Fugitive"; Posner and Ware, *Mengele*, 220-29, 241-43.

55. Posner and Ware, "Fugitive"; "Josef Mengele, Nazi War Criminal." See also
Posner and Ware, *Mengele*, 271-83.

56. Posner and Ware, "Fugitive."

57. Posner and Ware, "Fugitive"; Posner and Ware, *Mengele*, 284-89.

58. See the Simon Wiesenthal Center website, accessed 16 December 2016, www
.wiesenthal.com/site/pp.asp?c=lsKWLbPJLnF&b=4441471#.V0w6s_krLIV.

59. Feigin, "Office of Special Investigations," 390-91.

60. Feigin, "Office of Special Investigations," 391-92. See also Goda, "Manhunts,"
in Breitman et al., *Intelligence and the Nazis*, 432-36.

61. Feigin, "Office of Special Investigations," 392-93.

62. Feigin, "Office of Special Investigations," 393.

63. Feigin, "Office of Special Investigations," 393-94.

64. Feigin, "Office of Special Investigations," 394-95.

65. Feigin, "Office of Special Investigations," 395.

66. Feigin, "Office of Special Investigations," 395-96.

67. Feigin, "Office of Special Investigations," 396.

68. Feigin, "Office of Special Investigations," 396-97.

69. Feigin, "Office of Special Investigations," 398-99.

70. Nick Evans, "Nazi Angel of Death Josef Mengele 'Created Twin Town in Brazil,'" *Telegraph*, 21 January 2009.

71. Rees, *Ultimate Infamy*, 226.

72. AICE, "Josef Mengele (1911-1979)."

4. Otto von Bolschwing

1. It is possible, however, that von Bolschwing actually attended London University, where he studied law. See "Romanian Projects: Available Info on Alfred Otto

von Bolschwing," CIA, accessed 16 December 2016, www.foia.cia.gov/sites/default /files/document_conversions/1705143/BOLSCHWING,%20OTTO%20(VON)%20 %20%20VOL.%201_0009.pdf.

2. Ruffner, "Case of Otto Albrecht," 62.

3. Feigin, "Office of Special Investigations," 259; Naftali, "CIA and Eichmann's Associates," in Breitman et al., *Intelligence and the Nazis*, 343; Ruffner, "Case of Otto Albrecht," 62-63; "Romanian Projects." There is some discrepancy about the year in which von Bolschwing joined the Nazi Party. According to Feigin, he joined the Nazi Party in 1932, while Naftali dates his membership in the party from 1929.

4. Naftali, "CIA and Eichmann's Associates," in Breitman et al., *Intelligence and the Nazis*, 343-44.

5. Naftali, "CIA and Eichmann's Associates," in Breitman et al., *Intelligence and the Nazis*, 339, 343-44; Feigin, "Office of Special Investigations," 259.

6. Feigin, "Office of Special Investigations," 259.

7. Naftali, "CIA and Eichmann's Associates," in Breitman et al., *Intelligence and the Nazis*, 344; Feigin, "Office of Special Investigations," 259; "Romanian Projects."

8. Naftali, "CIA and Eichmann's Associates," in Breitman et al., *Intelligence and the Nazis*, 344. See also Feigin, "Office of Special Investigations," 259. Von Bolschwing was referring to the anti-Jewish riots that occurred in the summer of 1935 along the Kurfurstendamm, which was the main shopping avenue in Berlin.

9. Naftali, "CIA and Eichmann's Associates," in Breitman et al., *Intelligence and the Nazis*, 344.

10. Feigin, "Office of Special Investigations," 259.

11. Feigin, "Office of Special Investigations," 259-60.

12. Feigin, "Office of Special Investigations," 259-60.

13. Naftali, "CIA and Eichmann's Associates," in Breitman et al., *Intelligence and the Nazis*, 340, 344-45; Feigin, "Office of Special Investigations," 259-60.

14. There is some discrepancy about when von Bolschwing received this new assignment. According to Feigin, he was sent in January 1940, but Naftali puts the date as March 1940. Feigin, "Office of Special Investigations," 260; Naftali, "CIA and Eichmann's Associates," in Breitman et al., *Intelligence and the Nazis*, 345.

15. Naftali, "CIA and Eichmann's Associates," in Breitman et al., *Intelligence and the Nazis*, 345.

16. Clark, "European Fascists."

17. Rashke, *Useful Enemies*, 59.

18. An alternate spelling of Valerian Trifa is Viorel Trifa.

19. Rashke, *Useful Enemies*, 59-60; Naftali, "CIA and Eichmann's Associates," in Breitman et al., *Intelligence and the Nazis*, 345-46; Feigin, "Office of Special Investigations," 260; Ruffner, "Case of Otto Albrecht," 63.

20. Rashke, *Useful Enemies*, 59.

21. Rashke, *Useful Enemies*, 59-60.

22. Rashke, *Useful Enemies*, 60.

23. Cummings, *Cold War Radio*, 151; Rashke, *Useful Enemies*, 59-60; Ruffner, "Case

of Otto Albrecht," 63; Naftali, "CIA and Eichmann's Associates," in Breitman et al., *Intelligence and the Nazis*, 345.

24. Feigin, "Office of Special Investigations," 260; Rashke, *Useful Enemies*, 60–61; Naftali, "CIA and Eichmann's Associates," in Breitman et al., *Intelligence and the Nazis*, 345–46.

25. Naftali, "CIA and Eichmann's Associates," in Breitman et al., *Intelligence and the Nazis*, 345–46; Ruffner, "Case of Otto Albrecht," 63.

26. Naftali, "CIA and Eichmann's Associates," in Breitman et al., *Intelligence and the Nazis*, 346.

27. Naftali, "CIA and Eichmann's Associates," in Breitman et al., *Intelligence and the Nazis*, 345–46; Feigin, "Office of Special Investigations," 260; "Romanian Projects."

28. Naftali, "CIA and Eichmann's Associates," in Breitman et al., *Intelligence and the Nazis*, 346.

29. Feigin, "Office of Special Investigations," 260–61; Ruffner, "Case of Otto Albrecht," 63; Naftali, "CIA and Eichmann's Associates," in Breitman et al., *Intelligence and the Nazis*, 346–47.

30. Naftali, "CIA and Eichmann's Associates," in Breitman et al., *Intelligence and the Nazis*, 354.

31. Simpson, *Blowback*, 40; Naftali, "CIA and Eichmann's Associates," in Breitman et al., *Intelligence and the Nazis*, 347; Feigin, "Office of Special Investigations," 261; Rashke, *Useful Enemies*, 68. For more information about the Gehlen Organization, see Rashke, *Useful Enemies*.

32. Ruffner, "Case of Otto Albrecht," 63; Naftali, "CIA and Eichmann's Associates," in Breitman et al., *Intelligence and the Nazis*, 346–47; Goda, "Tracking the Red Orchestra," in Breitman et al., *Intelligence and the Nazis*, 296; Feigin, "Office of Special Investigations," 261.

33. Feigin, "Office of Special Investigations," 261; Ruffner, "Case of Otto Albrecht," 63.

34. Naftali, "CIA and Eichmann's Associates," in Breitman et al., *Intelligence and the Nazis*, 347–48.

35. Ruffner, "Case of Otto Albrecht," 63; Feigin, "Office of Special Investigations," 261; Naftali, "CIA and Eichmann's Associates," in Breitman et al., *Intelligence and the Nazis*, 348–49.

36. Naftali, "CIA and Eichmann's Associates," in Breitman et al., *Intelligence and the Nazis*, 350; Ruffner, "Case of Otto Albrecht," 63–64.

37. Ruffner, "Case of Otto Albrecht," 67; Feigin, "Office of Special Investigations," 261; Naftali, "CIA and Eichmann's Associates," in Breitman et al., *Intelligence and the Nazis*, 352–53.

38. Feigin, "Office of Special Investigations," 261–62.

39. Feigin, "Office of Special Investigations," 262.

40. Ruffner, "Case of Otto Albrecht," 63–68; Feigin, "Office of Special Investigations," 262–63; Naftali, "CIA and Eichmann's Associates," in Breitman et al., *Intelligence and the Nazis*, 353.

41. Ruffner, "Case of Otto Albrecht," 69; Feigin, "Office of Special Investigations," 263; Naftali, "CIA and Eichmann's Associates," in Breitman et al., *Intelligence and the Nazis*, 353.

42. Naftali, "CIA and Eichmann's Associates," in Breitman et al., *Intelligence and the Nazis*, 343; Tamara Feinstein, ed., "Uncovering the Architect of the Holocaust: The CIA Names File on Adolf Eichmann," National Security Archive, http://nsarchive.gwu.edu/NSAEBB/NSAEBB150/.

43. Ruffner, "Case of Otto Albrecht," 69.

44. Ruffner, "Case of Otto Albrecht," 69; Naftali, "CIA and Eichmann's Associates," in Breitman et al., *Intelligence and the Nazis*, 345; Feinstein, "Uncovering the Architect."

45. Ruffner, "Case of Otto Albrecht," 69; Naftali, "CIA and Eichmann's Associates," in Breitman et al., *Intelligence and the Nazis*, 354; Operation Gladio, "Otto von Bolschwing," 12 December 2012, http://operation-gladio.net/otto-von-bolschwing (site discontinued).

46. Feigin, "Office of Special Investigations," 2-4.

47. Ruffner, "Case of Otto Albrecht," 69.

48. Feigin, "Office of Special Investigations," 263.

49. Ruffner, "Case of Otto Albrecht," 69-70; Feigin, "Office of Special Investigations," 263-65.

50. Ruffner, "Case of Otto Albrecht," 70; Feigin, "Office of Special Investigations," 264-65.

51. Ruffner, "Case of Otto Albrecht," 70.

52. Ruffner, "Case of Otto Albrecht," 70-71.

53. Feigin, "Office of Special Investigations," 265-66; Ruffner, "Case of Otto Albrecht," 71.

54. Ruffner, "Case of Otto Albrecht," 71; "Man, 71, Is Ordered to Reply to Charge of Serving the Nazis," *New York Times*, 29 July 1981.

55. Feigin, "Office of Special Investigations," 266.

56. Feigin, "Office of Special Investigations," 266-67; Ruffner, "Case of Otto Albrecht," 71-72; "Man, 71, Is Ordered"; "Otto von Bolschwing: Ex-Captain in Nazi SS," obituary, *New York Times*, 10 March 1982; Operation Gladio, "Otto von Bolschwing."

5. Kurt Waldheim

1. Feigin, "Office of Special Investigations," 310.

2. Herzstein, *Waldheim*, 27.

3. Herzstein, *Waldheim*, 27, 34-35; Jonathan Kandell, "Kurt Waldheim, Former UN Chief, Is Dead at 88," *New York Times*, 15 June 2007; "Kurt Waldheim," obituary, *Telegraph*, 15 June 2007.

4. Herzstein, *Waldheim*, 35-37; "Former Secretary-General: Kurt Waldheim," United Nations, 4 July 2016, www.un.org/sg/en/content/formersg/kurt-waldheim.

5. Herzstein, *Waldheim*, 37, 38.

6. Herzstein, *Waldheim*, 37-40.

7. Herzstein, *Waldheim*, 40-41.

8. Herzstein, *Waldheim*, 40-45.

9. For more on the "gentlemen's agreement," see Herzstein, *Waldheim*, 48.

10. Herzstein, *Waldheim*, 47-49, 50.

11. Herzstein, *Waldheim*, 50; Sher et al., "Matter of Kurt Waldheim," 21.

12. Herzstein, *Waldheim*, 51.

13. Herzstein, *Waldheim*, 50-53.

14. Herzstein, *Waldheim*, 53.

15. Herzstein, *Waldheim*, 53-55.

16. Waldheim, qtd. in Kandell, "Kurt Waldheim Dies."

17. Herzstein, *Waldheim*, 55-56.

18. Herzstein, *Waldheim*, 55-56; Kandell, "Kurt Waldheim Dies"; John M. Goshko, "Kurt Waldheim; Led U.N. Austria; Suspected of Nazi Ties," *Washington Post*, 15 June 2007; Kandell, "Waldheim, Former UN Chief"; Rosenbaum and Hoffer, *Betrayal*, 22, 23, 84, 430; Sher et al., "Matter of Kurt Waldheim," 21.

19. Herzstein, *Waldheim*, 58.

20. Herzstein, *Waldheim*, 48.

21. Herzstein, *Waldheim*, 57-59; Kandell, "Kurt Waldheim Dies"; Kandell, "Waldheim, Former UN Chief"; "Kurt Waldheim," obituary, *Telegraph*; Rosenbaum and Hoffer, *Betrayal*, 22-23, 77, 84, 88; Sher et al., "Matter of Kurt Waldheim," 22.

22. Herzstein, *Waldheim*, 61.

23. Herzstein, *Waldheim*, 61-62.

24. Qtd. in Herzstein, *Waldheim*, 62-63.

25. Herzstein, *Waldheim*, 63.

26. Herzstein, *Waldheim*, 63-65; Sher et al., "Matter of Kurt Waldheim," 22-23.

27. Herzstein, *Waldheim*, 65-66; Rosenbaum and Hoffer, *Betrayal*, 7.

28. Rosenbaum and Hoffer, *Betrayal*, 15. For a more complete discussion of the CIA assessment, see "Waldheim, Kurt," vol. 1, and "Waldheim, Kurt," vol. 2, Second Release of Name Files under the Nazi War Crimes and Japanese Imperial Government Disclosure Acts, RG 263, Records of the Central Intelligence Agency, 1894-2002, NARA.

29. Qtd. in Rosenbaum and Hoffer, *Betrayal*, 15-16. See also Ruffner, "Kurt Waldheim," 54; and Goshko, "Kurt Waldheim."

30. Herzstein, *Waldheim*, 155.

31. Herzstein, *Waldheim*, 156, 159; Rosenbaum and Hoffer, *Betrayal*, 83.

32. Herzstein, *Waldheim*, 159, 163-64.

33. Herzstein, *Waldheim*, 166-69; Rosenbaum and Hoffer, *Betrayal*, 174-75.

34. Herzstein, *Waldheim*, 169. See also Rosenbaum and Hoffer, *Betrayal*, 175.

35. Herzstein, *Waldheim*, 170.

36. "Former Secretary-General."

37. "Former Secretary-General."

38. "Former Secretary-General."

39. "Former Secretary-General."

40. "Former Secretary-General."

41. "Former Secretary-General"; "Appointment Process," United Nations, accessed 8 July 2016, www.un.org/sg/appointment.shtml.

42. Feigin, "Office of Special Investigations," 310. For a detailed account of his investigation and release of information about Waldheim's World War II military record, see also Rosenbaum and Hoffer, *Betrayal*.

43. Feigin, "Office of Special Investigations," 310.

44. Feigin, "Office of Special Investigations," 310-11; Sher et al., "Matter of Kurt Waldheim," 31-34.

45. Feigin, "Office of Special Investigations," 311.

46. Feigin, "Office of Special Investigations," 311-12.

47. Feigin, "Office of Special Investigations," 312.

48. Wistrich, *Austrians and Jews*, 257. See also Rosenbaum and Hoffer, *Betrayal*, 129-36.

49. Feigin, "Office of Special Investigations," 312.

50. Rosenbaum and Hoffer, *Betrayal*, 257-58; Feigin, "Office of Special Investigations," 312.

51. Feigin, "Office of Special Investigations," 312-13.

52. Rosenbaum and Hoffer, *Betrayal*, 291.

53. Sher et al., "Matter of Kurt Waldheim," 21.

54. Sher et al., "Matter of Kurt Waldheim," 23.

55. Sher et al., "Matter of Kurt Waldheim," 28-29.

56. Sher et al., "Matter of Kurt Waldheim," 30.

57. Sher et al., "Matter of Kurt Waldheim," 30.

58. Sher et al., "Matter of Kurt Waldheim," 23.

59. Qtd. in Sher et al., "Matter of Kurt Waldheim," 36.

60. Sher et al., "Matter of Kurt Waldheim," 36.

61. Sher et al., "Matter of Kurt Waldheim," 37.

62. Sher et al., "Matter of Kurt Waldheim," 39; Herzstein, *Waldheim*, 108, 113-14.

63. Sher et al., "Matter of Kurt Waldheim," 41-43. For more information on Waldheim's role in the deportations, see Rosenbaum and Hoffer, *Betrayal*, 418-20.

64. Sher et al., "Matter of Kurt Waldheim," 45-48.

65. Sher et al., "Matter of Kurt Waldheim," 24-25, 50.

66. Sher et al., "Matter of Kurt Waldheim," 51-52. For a more detailed account of the aftermath of the operation, see Sher et al., "Matter of Kurt Waldheim," 52-74; and Rosenbaum and Hoffer, *Betrayal*, 122-25.

67. Sher et al., "Matter of Kurt Waldheim," 70-73.

68. Sher et al., "Matter of Kurt Waldheim," 70-75; Rosenbaum and Hoffer, *Betrayal*, 123.

69. Sher et al., "Matter of Kurt Waldheim," 25-26.

70. Mazower, *Inside Hitler's Greece*, 190.

71. Mazower, *Inside Hitler's Greece*, 191-92.

72. Mazower, *Inside Hitler's Greece*, 192.

73. Mazower, *Inside Hitler's Greece*, 192-94.

74. Mazower, *Inside Hitler's Greece*, 194.

75. Qtd. in Mazower, *Inside Hitler's Greece*, 196-97.

76. Mazower, *Inside Hitler's Greece*, 197.

77. Mazower, *Inside Hitler's Greece*, 197-98. For more on Waldheim's activities in Greece, including the deportation of Jews from Corfu, see Rosenbaum and Hoffer, *Betrayal*, 192-98, 220-24.

78. Sher et al., "Matter of Kurt Waldheim," 26-27.

79. Rosenbaum and Hoffer, *Betrayal*, 453-54.

80. For additional information about the World Jewish Congress–Wiesenthal feud, see Rosenbaum and Hoffer, *Betrayal*.

81. Rosenbaum and Hoffer, *Betrayal*, 217-18, 221-23.

82. Feigin, "Office of Special Investigations," 314; Sher et al., "Matter of Kurt Waldheim," 204.

83. Feigin, "Office of Special Investigations," 313.

84. Feigin, "Office of Special Investigations," 314-15, 321-23; Rosenbaum and Hoffer, *Betrayal*, xvii.

6. Andrija Artuković

1. Feigin, "Office of Special Investigations," 239. Some sources suggest that Andrija Artuković was born in Klobuk, Herzogovina. See Ryan, "Attitudes toward the Prosecution," in Braham, *Contemporary Views*, 213-14.

2. Feigin, "Office of Special Investigations," 239.

3. Tomasevich, *War and Revolution*, 35.

4. Feigin, "Office of Special Investigations," 239-40; Ryan, *Quiet Neighbors*, 3; HEART, "The Jasenovac Extermination Camp: 'Terror in Croatia,'" Holocaust Research Project, accessed 16 December 2016, www.holocaustresearchproject.org /othercamps/jasenovac.html.

5. HEART, "Jasenovac Extermination Camp."

6. Feigin, "Office of Special Investigations," 239.

7. HEART, "Jasenovac Extermination Camp."

8. Ryan, *Quiet Neighbors*, 3.

9. HEART, "Jasenovac Extermination Camp."

10. HEART, "Jasenovac Extermination Camp"; Ryan, *Quiet Neighbors*, 3; Goda, "Nazi Collaborators," in Breitman et al., *Intelligence and the Nazis*, 230-31.

11. HEART, "Jasenovac Extermination Camp"; Ryan, *Quiet Neighbors*, 3; Goda, "Nazi Collaborators," 230-31; Feigin, "Office of Special Investigations," 239; Butler, "Artukovitch File."

12. Feigin, "Office of Special Investigations," 240.

13. Butler, "Artukovitch File."

14. Butler, "Artukovitch File"; Nesho Djuric, "Yugoslav War Crimes Trial to Begin: Artukovic Was Croatian Officer," *Sun-Sentinel*, 13 April 1986; "Andrija Artukovic, 88, 'Butcher of the Balkans,'" *Chicago Tribune*, 19 January 1988; Ryan, *Quiet Neighbors*, 3.

15. HEART, "Jasenovac Extermination Camp."

16. Feigin, "Office of Special Investigations," 248.

17. Butler, "Artukovitch File"; Kennedy, "Deed Agreeable to God," 194.

18. Kennedy, "Deed Agreeable to God," 193-94.

19. Kennedy, "Deed Agreeable to God," 191, 193-99.

20. Feigin, "Office of Special Investigations," 251; Rashke, *Useful Enemies*, 58.

21. Feigin, "Office of Special Investigations," 240-41.

22. Feigin, "Office of Special Investigations," 240-41.

23. Feigin, "Office of Special Investigations," 241-42; United States of America ex rel. Branko Karadzole, Consul General, Federal People's Republic of Yugoslavia, Complainant, v. Andrija Artukovic, Defendant, 170 F. Supp. 383 (S.D. Calif. 1959).

24. Artukovic v. Boyle, 107 F. Supp. 11 (S.D. Calif. 1952); Feigin, "Office of Special Investigations," 242.

25. Feigin, "Office of Special Investigations," 242-43.

26. Feigin, "Office of Special Investigations," 242-43; *Karadzole*, 170 F. Supp. 383.

27. *Karadzole*, 170 F. Supp. 383.

28. Ryan, "Attitudes toward the Prosecution," in Braham, *Contemporary Views*, 213.

29. Feigin, "Office of Special Investigations," 244.

30. Feigin, "Office of Special Investigations," 240-45; Ryan, "Attitudes toward the Prosecution," in Braham, *Contemporary Views*, 213. There is a slight discrepancy regarding the date of the Board of Immigration Appeals' ruling. Feigin says June 1981, while Ryan claims the ruling was issued on 1 July 1981.

31. "Board of Immigration Appeals," U.S. Department of Justice, 24 March 2016, www.justice.gov/coir/board of immigration appeals.

32. Ryan, "Attitudes toward the Prosecution," in Braham, *Contemporary Views*, 213.

33. Feigin, "Office of Special Investigations," 244-45.

34. Feigin, "Office of Special Investigations," 245-46. The Office of International Affairs, which was housed in the Department of Justice, was in charge of extraditions.

35. Feigin, "Office of Special Investigations," 246-47.

36. Feigin, "Office of Special Investigations," 247.

37. Feigin, "Office of Special Investigations," 248.

38. Feigin, "Office of Special Investigations," 248.

39. Ralph Blumenthal, "Andrija Artukovic, 88, Nazi Ally Deported to Yugoslavia, Is Dead," *New York Times*, 19 January 1988; "War Criminal Andrija Artukovic Dies in Yugoslav Prison Hospital," *Jewish Telegraphic Agency*, 19 January 1988; Feigin, "Office of Special Investigations," 246-48, 569.

40. Feigin, "Office of Special Investigations," 253.

7. Karl Linnas

1. Feigin, "Office of Special Investigations," 271.

2. In 1202 Bishop Albert of Livonia founded the Livonian Brothers of the Sword. The Livonian Knights were a German military and religious order. Wearing a white robe with a red cross and sword, the Livonian Knights pursued their purpose of conquering and Christianizing the Baltic region.

3. Under the terms of the Versailles Treaty, Poland gained complete independence. In addition, Poland acquired the German provinces of Posen and Western Prussia and half of Silesia.

4. Toomas Hiio, "German Occupation in Estonia, 1941–1944," Estonica: Encyclopedia about Estonia, 12 August 2009, www.estonica.org/en/History/1939-1945_Estonia_and_World_War_II/German_occupation_in_Estonia_1941-1944/.

5. Hiio, "German Occupation in Estonia."

6. United States of America, Plaintiff, v. Karl Linnas, Defendant, 527 F. Supp. 426 (E.D. N.Y. 1981).

7. Maripuu, "Execution of Estonian Jews," in Hiio, Maripuu, and Paavlo, *Estonia, 1940–1945*, 652.

8. *Linnas*, 527 F. Supp. 426; Maripuu, "Execution of Estonian Jews," in Hiio, Maripuu, and Paavlo, *Estonia, 1940–1945*, 652; Weiss-Wendt, *Murder without Hatred*, 198, 200.

9. Maripuu, "Execution of Estonian Jews," in Hiio, Maripuu, and Paavlo, *Estonia, 1940–1945*, 653.

10. Maripuu, "Execution of Estonian Jews," in Hiio, Maripuu, and Paavlo, *Estonia, 1940–1945*, 653.

11. Maripuu, "Execution of Estonian Jews," in Hiio, Maripuu, and Paavlo, *Estonia, 1940–1945*, 653; Weiss-Wendt, *Murder without Hatred*, 198, 200; *Linnas*, 527 F. Supp. 426.

12. *Linnas*, 527 F. Supp. 426.

13. *Linnas*, 527 F. Supp. 426.

14. *Linnas*, 527 F. Supp. 426.

15. Legge, "Karl Linnas Deportation Case," 32.

16. *Linnas*, 527 F. Supp. 426; Legge, "Karl Linnas Deportation Case," 32–33.

17. *Linnas*, 527 F. Supp. 426; Legge, "Karl Linnas Deportation Case," 29.

18. *Linnas*, 527 F. Supp. 426, app. B.

19. Hinojosa, "Summary."

20. *Linnas*, 527 F. Supp. 426.

21. *Linnas*, 527 F. Supp. 426.

22. *Linnas*, 527 F. Supp. 426.

23. *Linnas*, 527 F. Supp. 426; Legge, "Karl Linnas Deportation Case," 29–30; Rashke, *Useful Enemies*, 253.

24. Allen, "Nazi War Criminals," 6; Legge, "Karl Linnas Deportation Case," 26, 29–30.

25. *Linnas*, 527 F. Supp. 426.

26. Legge, "Karl Linnas Deportation Case," 30.

27. Legge, "Karl Linnas Deportation Case," 30–32; Feigin, "Office of Special Investigations," 271; Rashke, *Useful Enemies*, 253.

28. Legge, "Karl Linnas Deportation Case," 30.

29. Feigin, "Office of Special Investigations," 271.

30. Legge, "Karl Linnas Deportation Case," 34.

31. See chapters 1 and 6 for a detailed discussion of the Holtzman Amendment.

32. Legge, "Karl Linnas Deportation Case," 34.

33. Legge, "Karl Linnas Deportation Case," 34-35; Feigin, "Office of Special Investigations," 271-72.

34. Legge, "Karl Linnas Deportation Case," 34-38; Feigin, "Office of Special Investigations," 271.

35. Legge, "Karl Linnas Deportation Case," 38-39.

36. Legge, "Karl Linnas Deportation Case," 34, 38-40; Feigin, "Office of Special Investigations," 271-72.

37. Feigin, "Office of Special Investigations," 271-72; Legge, "Karl Linnas Deportation Case," 38-40.

38. Feigin, "Office of Special Investigations," 272.

39. Feigin, "Office of Special Investigations," 273.

40. Legge, "Karl Linnas Deportation Case," 40; Feigin, "Office of Special Investigations," 273.

41. Feigin, "Office of Special Investigations," 273-74.

42. Legge, "Karl Linnas Deportation Case," 40.

43. Feigin, "Office of Special Investigations," 274-75; Legge, "Karl Linnas Deportation Case," 39-40.

44. Feigin, "Office of Special Investigations," 276.

45. Feigin, "Office of Special Investigations," 276-77.

46. Feigin, "Office of Special Investigations," 278.

47. Feigin, "Office of Special Investigations," 279.

48. Beiner, "Due Process for All," 293; Feigin, "Office of Special Investigations," 277-85.

49. Legge, "Karl Linnas Deportation Case," 44-45; Beiner, "Due Process for All," 293-94; "Karl Linnas Deported," *Jewish Telegraphic Agency*, 22 April 1987; William J. Eaton, "Deported War Criminal Dies in Soviet Hospital," *Los Angeles Times*, 3 July 1987; Feigin, "Office of Special Investigations," 287.

8. Operation Paperclip

1. For a more extensive examination of Operation Paperclip, see Intelligence and Investigative Dossiers: Impersonal File, 1939-80, Containers 79-85, Army Staff: Office of the Assistant Chief of Staff for Intelligence, G-2, Entry A1 134-A, RG 391, Records of the Investigative Records Repository, NARA; Jacobsen, *Operation Paperclip*; Lasby, *Project Paperclip*; Beyerchen, "German Scientists"; Simpson, *Blowback*; and Hunt, *Secret Agenda*.

2. The hiding of these files and their subsequent recovery by American forces is discussed in greater detail in chapter 10.

3. Report on Operation "BACKFIRE," vol. 1, *Scope and Organization of the Operation*, WO file 33/2554, TNA, 1.

4. Report on Operation "BACKFIRE," 1:1. Film footage of the rocket-firing tests

still exists. See the following website to view some of the film: "Operation Backfire Tests at Altenwalde/Cuxhaven,"-v2rocket.com, accessed 16 December 2016, www .v2rocket.com/start/chapters/backfire.html.

5. Report on Operation "BACKFIRE," 1:12; Jacobsen, *Operation Paperclip*, 176; Neufeld, *Von Braun*, 211-12. Both von Braun and Rudolph are discussed in greater detail in chapters 9 and 10.

6. Report on Operation "BACKFIRE," 1:12.

7. Jacobsen, *Operation Paperclip*, 8.

8. Jacobsen, *Operation Paperclip*, 12.

9. Deputy Chiefs of Staff Committee, DCOS (45) 66, Draft Reply to FMW 168, 12 September 1945, CAB file 121/427, TNA.

10. Deputy Chiefs of Staff Committee, Extract from DCOS (45), Twelfth Meeting, 13 September 1945, CAB file 121/427, TNA.

11. Report on Operation "BACKFIRE," 1:21.

12. Report on Operation "BACKFIRE," 1:21, 23.

13. Report on Operation "BACKFIRE," 1:26; "Operation Backfire Tests."

14. Report on Operation "BACKFIRE," 1:26; "Operation Backfire."

15. Report on Operation "BACKFIRE," 1:26; "Operation Backfire."

16. Group Captain Wilson, "Exploitation of German Scientists," memo, 29 October 1945, CAB file 122/334, TNA. See also Judt and Ciesla, *Technology Transfer*.

17. Cabinet Office to Joint Staff Mission, 12 December 1945, CAB file 122/344, TNA.

18. Cabinet Office to Joint Staff Mission, 12 December 1945, TNA.

19. Jacobsen, *Operation Paperclip*, 176-78, 262; Simpson, *Blowback*, 27-30.

20. Lasby, *Project Paperclip*, 77.

21. Lasby, *Project Paperclip*, 77.

22. Lasby, *Project Paperclip*, 78.

23. Beyerchen, "German Scientists," 291-92; "The Alsos Mission," Atomic Heritage Foundation, accessed 25 September 2015, www.atomicheritage.org/history /alsos-mission; Jacobsen, *Operation Paperclip*, 175-76.

24. "Alsos Mission."

25. "Alsos Mission"; Beyerchen, "German Scientists," 292.

26. Beyerchen, "German Scientists," 292; Jacobsen, *Operation Paperclip*, 145. See also Defense Scientists Immigration Program, "Standard Operation Procedure," 15 March 1958, box 1, DEFSIP Administrative Records, 1958-70, Joint Intelligence Objectives Agency, RG 330, Records of the Secretary of Defense, NARA; Bosquet N. Wev, Captain, USN, "Memorandum for Lieut. General S. J. Chamberlin, Director of Intelligence, GSUSA, Subject: Proposed Presentation to Mr. Hoover Reference Immigration of German Specialists," 7 May 1945, Army-Intelligence Decimal File, 1941-48, box 1001, RG 319, Records of the Army Staff, NARA; and "Scientists and Technicians OMGUS, 1945-46," General Correspondence, 1944-45, box 22, AG 231.2, Records of U.S. Occupation Headquarters, World War II, U.S. Group Control Council, RG 260, Military Agency Records, NARA.

27. Jacobsen, *Operation Paperclip*, 145.

28. Lasby, *Project Paperclip*, 79-80.

29. Joint Intelligence Objectives Agency, "Revised Objective List of German and Austrian Scientists," 2 January 1947, container 82, RG 319, NARA; Joint Chiefs of Staff, Joint Intelligence Objectives Agency, "US-UK Combined Allocation List, January 1951" (revision of previous list dated October 1949), container 81, RG 319, NARA; Beyerchen, "German Scientists," 292.

30. Lasby, *Project Paperclip*, 88; Jacobsen, *Operation Paperclip*, 178-80.

31. Lasby, *Project Paperclip*, 89; Jacobsen, *Operation Paperclip*, 180-81.

32. Jacobsen, *Operation Paperclip*, 191-95; Lasby, *Project Paperclip*, 107; Simpson, *Blowback*, 33.

33. Jacobsen, *Operation Paperclip*, 194, 201-2.

34. Simpson, *Blowback*, 34-35; Neufeld, *Von Braun*, 219.

35. Simpson, *Blowback*, 36.

36. Simpson, *Blowback*, 36; Jacobsen, *Operation Paperclip*, 225, 227; 247-48; Bosquet N. Wev, "Memorandum: Proposed Presentation to Mr. Hoover Reference Immigration of German Specialists," 7 May 1945, box 1001, RG 319, NARA.

37. Simpson, *Blowback*, 36-39; Jacobsen, *Operation Paperclip*, 248; H. Graham Morison, "German Specialists and Scientists in the United States under the Protective Custody of the Joint Intelligence Objectives Agency," 6 November 1947, Army-Intelligence Decimal File, box 1001, RG 319, NARA.

9. Arthur Rudolph

1. Feigin, "Office of Special Investigations," 332, 335, 337. See also Ward, *Dr. Space*, 157; Neufeld, *Von Braun*, 475; and Jacobsen, *Operation Paperclip*, 426-27.

2. Franklin, *American in Exile*, 11.

3. Ward, *Dr. Space*, xi.

4. Franklin, *American in Exile*, 38.

5. FBI report, 11 February 1949, file 77-693, El Paso Field Office, 3. This document is included in FBI, *Arthur Rudolph*, released under the Freedom of Information Act. All FBI documents, unless otherwise noted, come from this published file.

6. Franklin, *American in Exile*, 39.

7. Franklin, *American in Exile*, 7-19, 23-27, 38-54, 58-63; FBI report, 11 February 1949, file 77-693, El Paso Field Office, 3.

8. Franklin, *American in Exile*, 65-66, 70-71, 75-79, 81-82.

9. Franklin, *American in Exile*, 83-85, 88-91, 97; Feigin, "Office of Special Investigations," 331-32.

10. "Arthur Rudolph," Operation Paperclip, accessed 15 December 2016, www .operationpaperclip.info/arthur-rudolph.php; "Operation Backfire."

11. Feigin, "Office of Special Investigations," 332.

12. Feigin, "Office of Special Investigations," 332; "Arthur Rudolph."

13. Feigin, "Office of Special Investigations," 332.

14. The Displaced Persons Act and the Refugee Relief Act were "two of the most far-reaching immigration laws ever enacted by Congress." Their purpose was to

allow the oppressed, including the victims of Nazi persecution and political refugees fleeing from communism, to immigrate to the United States. Between 1948 and 1953 more than six hundred thousand people immigrated to the United States from various countries under these acts. Feigin, "Office of Special Investigations," 1.

15. FBI report, 11 February 1949, file 77-693, El Paso Field Office, 3.

16. FBI report, 11 February 1949, file 77-693, El Paso Field Office, 5.

17. FBI report, 22 September 1951, file BH 105-179; FBI report, 17 April 1962, file 151-13, Tampa Field Office, 1; "Arthur Rudolph"; *Pershing II Weapon System*, TM 9-1425-386-10-1, Department of the Army, June 1986, ch. 2, p. 1, http://pershingmissile .org/PershingDocuments/manuals/TM%209-1425-386-10-1.pdf; Headquarters, Department of the Army, "The Pershing Project Office," https://history.redstone .army.mil/miss-pershing.html. Much of FBI file BH 105-179 has been blacked out.

18. Feigin, "Office of Special Investigations," 332; "Arthur Rudolph."

19. Franklin, *American in Exile*, app. A, "Transcript of U.S. Army Interrogation of Arthur Rudolph in June 1947," 169-85.

20. Franklin, *American in Exile*, app. A, 169-85.

21. SA report, 17 April 1962, file 151-13, Tampa Field Office.

22. SA report, 4 May 1962, file 151-11, San Diego Field Office.

23. SA report, 4 May 1962, file 151-37, Birmingham Field Office.

24. Memorandum from Director, FBI, to SAC, Washington Field, 6 April 1962, 1-2; AIRTEL from SAC, El Paso (151-6) (P) to Director, FBI, 10 April 1962, 1; SA report, Tampa Field Office, 1; SA report, 4 May 1962, file AQ 151-4, Albuquerque Field Office, 1-2; SA report, San Diego Field Office, 1-3; SA report, Birmingham Field Office, 1-6; report, 4 May 1962, file 151-6, El Paso Field Office, 1-2; IC report, 5 May 1962, file BA 151-57, Baltimore Field Office, 1-2; report from an unnamed office, 7 May 1962, file 151-87, Washington DC Field Office, 1-3.

25. Feigin, "Office of Special Investigations," 333.

26. Feigin, "Office of Special Investigations," 333-34; Franklin, *American in Exile*, app. A, 169-85.

27. Feigin, "Office of Special Investigations," 333-34.

28. Feigin, "Office of Special Investigations," 334.

29. Feigin, "Office of Special Investigations," 334.

30. Feigin, "Office of Special Investigations," 334-35; Franklin, *American in Exile*, app. D, "The 'Indictment': Record of Meeting between the OSI and Rudolph's Attorney in September 1983," 353-55.

31. Feigin, "Office of Special Investigations," 334-35; Franklin, *American in Exile*, app. D, 343-47; and app. G, "Agreement between Rudolph and the Justice Department," 353-55.

32. Feigin, "Office of Special Investigations," 335.

33. Feigin, "Office of Special Investigations," 335.

34. Feigin, "Office of Special Investigations," 336.

35. Feigin, "Office of Special Investigations," 336.

36. Feigin, "Office of Special Investigations," 336.

37. Feigin, "Office of Special Investigations," 337.

38. Feigin, "Office of Special Investigations," 337.

39. Feigin, "Office of Special Investigations," 335–38; Franklin, *American in Exile*, app. H, "OSI Letter Which Transmitted 'Evidence' of Rudolph's 'Guilt' to West German Government," 357–59.

40. Feigin, "Office of Special Investigations," 338.

10. Scientists Who Avoided Investigation

1. Reinke, *German Space Policy*, 470.

2. "Wernher von Braun," Famous Scientists: The Art of Genius, accessed 17 December 2015, www.famousscientists.org/wernher-von-braun/; Ward, *Dr. Space*, 10–11; Petersen, *Missiles for the Fatherland*, 30–31; Neufeld, *Von Braun*, 12–24.

3. Ward, *Dr. Space*, 11.

4. Ward, *Dr. Space*, 12; "Wernher von Braun"; Neufeld, *Von Braun*, 25–27.

5. Ward, *Dr. Space*, 12.

6. Ward, *Dr. Space*, 12.

7. Neufeld, *Von Braun*, 25.

8. Neufeld, *Von Braun*, 31.

9. Neufeld, *Von Braun*, 31.

10. Ward, *Dr. Space*, 14–16; Neufeld, *Von Braun*, 37–38.

11. Ward, *Dr. Space*, 15–16.

12. Neufeld, *Von Braun*, 39–44; Ward, *Dr. Space*, 16–17.

13. Ward, *Dr. Space*, 20. For more on Arthur Rudolph, see chapter 9.

14. Ward, *Dr. Space*, 17.

15. Reinke, *German Space Policy*, 23; Ward, *Dr. Space*, 17–18; Neufeld, *Von Braun*, 49. For more on Dornberger, see chapters 8 and 9.

16. Ward, *Dr. Space*, 19–20; Cornwell, *Hitler's Scientists*, 148–51.

17. "An Oral History with Mr. Karl Heimburg and Mr. Bernhard R. Tessmann," interview by Dr. Charles Bolton, 6 March 1992, Huntsville AL, vol. 399, Stennis Space Center History Project, Mississippi Oral History Program, USM, 3–4 (hereafter cited as "Oral History," USM).

18. "Oral History," USM, 4; "Generalmajor Dr. Walter Robert Dornberger," Some of the Prisoners Held At Special Camp 11, accessed 16 December 2015, www.specialcamp11.co.uk/Generalmajor_Dr_Walter_Dornberger.htm.

19. Heike Hasenauer, "Rocket Pioneers," U.S. Army, 6 October 2008, www.army.mil/article/13102/Rocket_pioneers/.

20. "Oral History," USM, 1–3; "Karl L. Heimburg," Public Affairs Office, George C. Marshall Space Flight Center, 27 March 1972, www.nasa.gov/sites/default/files/atoms/files/karl_heimburg_biography.pdf.

21. Hasenauer, "Rocket Pioneers."

22. For more information on Lt. Gen. Walter Dornberger, see chapters 8 and 9.

23. "Oral History," USM, 4–7.

24. Ward, *Dr. Space*, 22.

25. Hasenauer, "Rocket Pioneers."

26. Hasenauer, "Rocket Pioneers"; Jacobsen, *Operation Paperclip*, 12–15; Ward, *Dr. Space*, 22.

27. Hasenauer, "Rocket Pioneers."

28. Jacobsen, *Operation Paperclip*, 32–34; "Bernhard Tessmann," Operation Paperclip, accessed 20 July 2016, www.operationpaperclip.info/bernhard-tessmann.php.

29. McGovern, *Crossbow and Overcast*, 4.

30. McGovern, *Crossbow and Overcast*, 4–6, 108–9, 112, 115–17.

31. McGovern, *Crossbow and Overcast*, 117; Jacobsen, *Operation Paperclip*, 68.

32. Lt. Col. Edmund Tilley, G.S., Special Investigations, Field Information Agency, Technical/"T" Force, 69 H.Q., Control Commission for Germany, BAOH, "List of Documents on Guided Missiles Found at OBERJOCH in June 1947," 19 June 1947, FO 1031/12, TNA.

33. For a more detailed discussion of these events, see Bower, *Paperclip Conspiracy*; McGovern, *Crossbow and Overcast*; and Jacobsen, *Operation Paperclip*.

34. McGovern, *Crossbow and Overcast*, 130, 145.

35. "Oral History," USM, 10.

36. For a more detailed examination of Arthur Rudolph, see chapter 9.

37. For a more detailed explanation of Operations Backfire, Overcast, and Paperclip, see chapter 8.

38. "Oral History," USM, 12–13.

39. "Dr. Wernher von Braun: First Center Director, July 1, 1960–Jan. 27, 1970," MSFC History Office, accessed 21 December 2015, http://history.msfc.nasa.gov/vonbraun/bio.html; "Marshall Space Flight Center," NSL Photography: The Photography of Ned S. Levi, accessed 31 January 2017, www.nslphotography.com/ScienceEngineeringandIndustry/Space-Exploration/Marshall-Space-Flight-Center/i-c4HHvT6.

40. "Dr. Wernher von Braun"; "Marshall History Overview," NASA, accessed December 12, 2015, www.nasa.gov/centers/marshall/history/overview.html.

41. "MSFC Organization Announcement," 5 December 1968, signed Wernher von Braun, Director.

42. Wolfgang Saxon, "Arthur Rudolph," obituary, *New York Times*, 3 January 1996.

43. "Dr. Wernher von Braun."

44. Saxon, "Arthur Rudolph"; "Biography of Wernher von Braun"; "Oral History," USM.

45. Books about these scientists and their experiments include Cornwell, *Hitler's Scientists*; Jacobsen, *Operation Paperclip*; Beyerchen, *Scientists under Hitler*; Weikart, *From Darwin to Hitler*; Weikart, *Hitler's Ethic*; Bergman, *Nazi Darwinian Worldview*; and Lifton, *Nazi Doctors*.

46. Lifton, *Nazi Doctors*, 33–35, 452; Jacobsen, *Operation Paperclip*, 75–77.

47. USHMM, "Portrait of Kurt Blome as a Defendant in the Medical Case Trial at Nuremberg," accessed 31 January 2017, https://collections.ushmm.org/search/catalog/pa1036650; Jacobsen, *Operation Paperclip*, 75–77.

48. United States v. Alfried Krupp et al. (Case 10), 16 August 1947-31 July 1948, "B) Organizations: Summary," Records of the U.S. Nuremberg War Crimes Trials Interrogations, 1946-49, roll 7, M 1019, RG 238, War Crimes Records, NARA, 3-4; Jacobsen, *Operation Paperclip*, 7, 160-61; Bower, *Paperclip Conspiracy*, 294; Lifton, *Nazi Doctors*, 452; Cornwell, *Hitler's Scientists*, 360-61. See also Pozos, "Nazi Hypothermia Research"; and Deichmann, *Biologists under Hitler*.

49. Jacobsen, *Operation Paperclip*, 48, 160-63.

50. Jacobsen, *Operation Paperclip*, 48, 160-65.

51. "Tabun (GA): Nerve Agent," Centers for Disease Control and Prevention, 26 May 2015, www.cdc.gov/niosh/ershdb/emergencyresponsecard_29750004.html.

52. "Facts about Sarin," Centers for Disease Control and Prevention, 20 May 2013, https://emergency.cdc.gov/agent/sarin/basics/facts.asp.

53. Jacobsen, *Operation Paperclip*, 49, 75-76.

54. Jacobsen, *Operation Paperclip*, 75-76.

55. Jacobsen, *Operation Paperclip*, 76-78. See also Capt. Harry K. Lennon, "Preliminary Interrogation Report: Prisoner; Dr. Blome, Kurt," 2 July 1945, RG 153, Records of the Office of the Judge Advocate General, War Crimes Branch, NARA. A copy of this one-page report is also on microfilm, Interrogation Records Prepared for War Crimes Proceedings at Nuremberg, 1945-47, roll 23, M 1270, NARA.

56. Jacobsen, *Operation Paperclip*, 159-65; "Kurt Blome," Operation Paperclip, accessed 23 December 2015, www.operationpaperclip.info/kurt-blome.php.

57. United States of America v. Karl Brandt et al. (Case 1), 21 November 1946-20 August 1947, Records of the United States, Nuremberg Trials, Collection of World War II, RG 238, War Crimes Records, NARA, 6, accessed 23 December 2015, https://www.archives.gov/resea,rch/captured-german-records/microfilm/m887.pdf (site discontinued). See also United States of America v. Karl Brandt et al. (Case 1), 21 November 1946-20 August 1947, roll 28, M 1270; rolls 32 and 37, M 887, Records of U.S. Military Tribunals at Nuremberg, 1945-47, NARA.

58. Jacobsen, *Operation Paperclip*, 160-65.

59. Bower, *Paperclip Conspiracy*, 294; "Kurt Blome"; Jacobsen, *Operation Paperclip*, 292-98, 364.

60. Feigin, "Office of Special Investigations."

BIBLIOGRAPHY

Manuscript and Archival Sources

National Archives and Records Administration (NARA), College Park MD
    M 887, Records of U.S. Military Tribunals at Nuremberg, 1945–47
    M 1270, Interrogation Records Prepared for War Crimes Proceedings at Nuremberg, 1945–47
    RG 153, Records of the Office of the Judge Advocate General
    RG 238, War Crimes Records
    RG 260, Records of U.S. Occupation Headquarters, World War II
    RG 263, Records of the Central Intelligence Agency
    RG 319, Records of the Army Staff
    RG 330, Records of the Secretary of Defense
    RG 391, Records of the Investigative Records Repository
National Archives of the United Kingdom (TNA), Kew, London
    Cabinet (CAB) Files
    Foreign Office (FO) Files
    War Office (WO) Files
University of Southern Mississippi (USM), Hattiesburg
    "An Oral History with Mr. Karl Heimburg and Mr. Bernhard R. Tessmann." Interview by Dr. Charles Bolton. 6 March 1992. Huntsville AL. Vol. 399. Stennis Space Center History Project. Mississippi Oral History Program.

Published Sources

An Act to Amend the Immigration and Nationality Act, H.R. 12509, 95th Congress (1977–78). Congress.gov. Accessed 21 December 2016. www.congress.gov/bill/95th-congress/house-bill/12509.

Allen, Charles R., Jr. "Nazi Criminals Living among Us: The 'Fascist Genocides Who Have Bought Their Way into the United States.'" *Jewish Currents*, January 1963, 3–12.

———. "Nazi War Criminals in Our Midst: From Estonia, Lithuania and Latvia." *Jewish Currents*, March 1963, 3–16.

"Barring Axis Persecutors from the United States: OSI's 'Watch List' Program." *Office of Special Investigations* 54, no. 1 (2006): 19–22.

Beiner, Theresa M. "Due Process for All: Due Process, the Eighth Amendment and

Nazi War Criminals." *Journal of Criminal Law and Criminology* 80, no. 1 (1989): 293–337.

Bergman, Jerry. *Hitler and the Nazi Darwinian Worldview: How the Nazi Eugenic Crusade for a Superior Race Caused the Greatest Holocaust in World History*. Canada: Joshua, 2012.

Bernanos, Georges. *La France contre les robots*. Paris: Livre de Poche, 1999.

Beyerchen, Alan. "German Scientists and Research Institutions in Allied Occupation Policy." *History of Education Society* 22, no. 3 (1982): 289–99.

———. *Scientists under Hitler: Politics and the Physics Community in the Third Reich*. New Haven: Yale University Press, 1977.

Bower, Tom. *The Paperclip Conspiracy: The Battle for the Spoils of Nazi Germany*. London: Joseph, 1987.

Breitmen, Richard. "Tscherim Soobzokov." American University. Accessed 29 January 2017. https://fas.org/sgp/eprint/breitman.pdf.

Breitman, Richard, Norman J. Goda, Timothy Naftali, and Robert Wolfe. *U.S. Intelligence and the Nazis*. New York: Cambridge University Press, 2005.

Brewda, Joseph. "KGB and Mossad Linked to Attempted Murder of Tscherim Soobzokov." *Executive Intelligence Review (EIR)* 12, no. 34 (1985): 55–56.

Butler, Hubert. "The Artukovitch File (1970)." Reproduced in *Archipelago* 1, no. 2 (1997). www.archipelago.org/vol1-2/butler.htm.

Cavanaugh, Thomas A. "Aquinas's Account of Double Effect." Geschke Center, University of San Francisco. 1997. http://repository.usfca.edu/cgi/viewcontent.cgi?article=1027&context=phil.

Clark, Roland. "European Fascists and Local Activists: Romania's Legion of the Archangel Michael (1922–1938)." PhD diss., University of Pittsburgh, 2012.

Cornwell, John. *Hitler's Scientists: Science, War, and the Devil's Pact*. New York: Penguin, 2004.

Cummings, Richard H. *Cold War Radio: The Dangerous History of American Broadcasting in Europe, 1950–1989*. Jefferson NC: McFarland, 2009.

Deichmann, Ute. *Biologists under Hitler*. Translated by Thomas Dunlap. Cambridge MA: Harvard University Press, 1999.

Ezergailis, Andrew. *The Holocaust in Latvia, 1941–1944*. Washington DC: United States Holocaust Memorial Museum, 1996.

FBI (Federal Bureau of Investigations). *Arthur Rudolph: The FBI Files*. BUFILE: 105-11507. N.p.: Filiquarian/Qontro, n.d.

Feigin, Judy. "The Office of Special Investigations: Striving for Accountability in the Aftermath of the Holocaust." Edited by Mark M. Richard, Former Deputy Assistant Attorney General, Department of Justice, Criminal Division. December 2006. www.justice.gov/sites/default/files/criminal/legacy/2011/03/14/12-2008osu-accountability.pdf.

Feis, Adam S. "OSI's Prosecution of World War II Nazi Persecutor Cases." *United States Attorneys' Bulletin* 54, no. 1 (2006): 8–14.

Finkielkraut, Alain. *Remembering in Vain: The Klaus Barbie Trial and Crimes against Humanity*. New York: Columbia University Press, 1992.

Franklin, Thomas. *An American in Exile: The Story of Arthur Rudolph*. Huntsville AL: Kaylor, 1987.

Goda, Norman J. W. "Manhunts: The Official Search for Notorious Nazis." In Breitman et al., *Intelligence and the Nazis*, 419–42.

———. "Nazi Collaborators in the United States: What the FBI Knew." In Breitman et al., *Intelligence and the Nazis*, 227–64.

———. "Tracking the Red Orchestra: Allied Intelligence, Soviet Spies, Nazi Criminals." In Breitman et al., *Intelligence and the Nazis*, 293–316.

Gordon, Gregory S. "OSI's Expanded Jurisdiction under the Intelligence Reform and Terrorism Prevention Act of 2004." *United States Attorney's Bulletin* 54, no. 1 (2006): 24–29.

Hearings before the Subcommittee on Immigration, Citizenship, and International Law of the Committee on the Judiciary House of Representatives, Ninety-Fifth Congress, First Session on Alleged Nazi War Criminals. August 3, 1977. Serial No. 95-39. Vol. 1 of *Alleged Nazi War Criminals*. Washington DC: U.S. Government Printing Office, 1978.

Hearings before the Subcommittee on Immigration, Citizenship, and International Law of the Committee on the Judiciary House of Representatives, Ninety-Fifth Congress, Second Session on Alleged Nazi War Criminals. July 19, 20, 21, 1978. Part 2. Serial No. 39. Vol. 2 of *Alleged Nazi War Criminals*. Washington DC: U.S. Government Printing Office, 1979.

Herzstein, Robert Edwin. *Waldheim: The Missing Years*. New York: Arbor House/Morrow, 1988.

Hinojosa, Michelle. "Summary." 1948 Displaced Persons Act. U.S. Immigration Legislation Online. Accessed 23 December 2016. http://library.uwb.edu/guides/usimmigration/1948_displaced_persons_act.html.

Hunt, Linda. *Secret Agenda: The United States Government, Nazi Scientists, and Project Paperclip, 1945 to 1991*. New York: St. Martin's Press, 1991.

Jacobsen, Annie. *Operation Paperclip: The Secret Intelligence Program That Brought Nazi Scientists to America*. New York: Little, Brown, 2014.

Johnson, Wade. "Summary." 1952 Immigration and Nationality Act, H.R. 13342, 82nd Congress (June 27, 1952). U.S. Immigration Legislation Online. http://library.uwb.edu/static/USimmigration/1952_immigration_and_nationality_act.html.

Judt, Matthias, and Berghard Ciesla, eds. *Technology Transfer Out of Germany after 1945*. Australia: Harwood Academic, 1996.

Kennedy, Michael. "'A Deed Agreeable to God': Andrija Artuković and Croat Ustaše Connections with Ireland." *Irish Studies in International Affairs* 25 (2014): 187–201.

Lasby, Clarence G. *Project Paperclip: German Scientists and the Cold War*. New York: Athenem, 1971.

Legge, Jerome S., Jr. "The Karl Linnas Deportation Case, the Office of Special Investigations, and American Ethnic Politics." *Holocaust and Genocide Studies* 24, no. 1 (2010): 26–55.

Lifton, Robert Jay. *The Nazi Doctors: Medical Killing and the Psychology of Genocide.* New York: Basic Books, 1986.

Maripuu, Meelis. "The Execution of Estonian Jews in the Local Detention Institutions in 1941–1942." In *Estonia, 1940–1945: Reports of the Estonian International Commission for the Investigation of Crimes against Humanity*, edited by Toomas Hiio, Meelis Maripuu, and Indrek Paavlo, 651–60. Tallinn: Estonian Foundation for the Investigation of Crimes against Humanity, 2005.

Mazower, Mark. *Inside Hitler's Greece: The Experience of Occupation, 1941–44.* New Haven: Yale University Press, 1993.

McGovern, James. *Crossbow and Overcast.* London: Hutchinson, 1965.

Morgan, Ted. *Uncertain Hour: The French, the Germans, the Jews, the Klaus Barbie Trial, and the City of Lyon, 1940–1945.* New York: Morrow, 1990.

Naftali, Timothy. "The CIA and Eichmann's Associates." In Breitman et al., *Intelligence and the Nazis*, 337–74.

Nazi War Crimes Disclosure Act. National Archives. www.archives.gov/about/laws /nazi-war-crimes.html.

Neufeld, Michael. *The Rocket and the Reich: Peenemunde and the Coming of the Ballistic Missile Era.* Cambridge MA: Harvard University Press, 1996.

———. *Von Braun: Dreamer of Space, Engineer of War.* New York: Vintage Books, 2008.

Paris, Erna. *Unhealed Wounds: France and the Klaus Barbie Affair.* New York: Grove, 1985.

Petersen, Michael B. *Missiles for the Fatherland: Peenemünde, National Socialism, and the V-2 Missile.* New York: Cambridge University Press, 2009.

Posner, Gerald L., and John Ware. *Mengele: The Complete Story.* New York: Cooper Square Press, 2000.

Pozos, Robert S. "Nazi Hypothermia Research: Should the Data Be Used?" *Military Medical Ethics* 2:437–61. Accessed 20 December 2016. www.valas.fr/IMG/pdf /z-military_ethics.pdf.

Rashke, Richard. *Useful Enemies: John Demjanjuk and America's Open-Door Policy for Nazi War Criminals.* Harrison NY: Delphinium Books, 2013.

Rees, Laurence. *How Mankind Committed the Ultimate Infamy at Auschwitz: A New History.* New York: MJF Books, 2005.

Reinke, Niklas. *The History of German Space Policy: Ideas, Influences, and Interdependence, 1923–2002.* Translated by Barry Smerin and Barbara Wilson. Paris: Beauchesne, 2007.

Rosenbaum, Eli M. "An Introduction to the Work of the Office of Special Investigations." *United States Attorneys' Bulletin* 54, no. 1 (2006): 1–8.

Rosenbaum, Eli M., and William Hoffer. *Betrayal: The Untold Story of the Kurt Waldheim Investigation and Cover-Up.* New York: St. Martin's Press, 1993.

Ruffner, Kevin C. "The Case of Otto Albrecht Alfred von Bolschwing." *Studies in Intelligence* (1998): 61–77.

———. "CIA's Support to the Nazi War Criminal Investigations: A Persistent Emo-

tional Issue." Central Intelligence Agency. 14 April 2007. https://www.cia.gov
/library/center-for-the-study-of-intelligence/csi-publications/csi-studies/studies
/97unclass/naziwar.html.

———. "Kurt Waldheim and the Central Intelligence Agency (U)." *Studies in Intelligence*
(2003): 51–65. http://numbers-stations.com/cia/Studies%20In%20Intelligence
%20Nazi%20-%20Related%20Articles/STUDIES%20IN%20INTELLIGENCE
%20NAZI%20-%20RELATED%20ARTICLES_0018.pdf.

Ryan, Allan A., Jr. "Attitudes toward the Prosecution of Nazi War Criminals in the
United States." In *Contemporary Views on the Holocaust*, edited by R. L. Braham,
201–26. Boston: Kluwer-Nijhoff, 2011.

———. *Klaus Barbie and the United States Government: A Report to the Attorney General of the United States*. Washington DC: Government Printing Office, 1983.

———. *Quiet Neighbors: Prosecuting Nazi War Criminals in America*. San Diego: Harcourt Brace Jovanovich, 1984.

Schiessl, Christoph. "The Search for Nazi Collaborators in the United States." PhD
diss., Wright State University, 2009.

Sher, Neal M., Michael Wolf, Patrick J. Treanor, and Peter R. Black. "In the Matter of
Kurt Waldheim." Office of Special Investigations Criminal Division Report. 9
April 1987. https://ia601409.us.archive.org/10/items/INTHEMATTEROFKURT
WALDHEIM/IN%20THE%20MATTER%20OF%20KURT%20WALDHEIM
.pdf.

Simpson, Christopher. *Blowback: America's Recruitment of Nazis and Its Effects on the
Cold War*. New York: Weidenfeld & Nicolson, 1988.

Spitz, Vivien. *Doctors from Hell: The Horrific Account of Nazi Experiments on Humans*.
Boulder: Sentient, 2005.

Steinacher, Gerald. *Nazis on the Run: How Hitler's Henchmen Fled Justice*. Oxford:
Oxford University Press, 2008.

Tomasevich, Jozo. *War and Revolution in Yugoslavia, 1941–1945*. Stanford: Stanford
University Press, 2002.

The USA PATRIOT Act: Preserving Life and Liberty. Department of Justice. www
.justice.gov/archive/ll/what_is_the_patriot_act.pdf.

U.S. General Accounting Office. *Widespread Conspiracy to Obstruct Probes of Alleged
Nazi War Criminals Not Supported by Available Evidence—Controversy May Continue*. Washington DC: U.S. General Accounting Office, 1978.

"Verfahren wegen Verbrechen in Konzentrationslagern [Proceedings for crimes in
concentration camps]." DöW Dokumentationsarchiv des österreichischen Widerstandes [Documentation Centre of Austrian Resistance]. http://ausstellung
.de.doew.at/b142.html.

Waldheim, Kurt. *Kurt Waldeim's Wartime Years: A Documentation*. Vienna: 1987.

Ward, Bob. *Dr. Space: The Life of Werner Von Braun*. Annapolis: Naval Institute Press,
2009.

Weikart, Richard. *From Darwin to Hitler: Evolutionary Ethics, Eugenics, and Racism
in Germany*. New York: Palgrave Macmillan, 2006.

BIBLIOGRAPHY

———. *Hitler's Ethic: The Nazi Pursuit of Evolutionary Progress.* New York: Palgrave Macmillan, 2009.

Weingert, Peter. "German Eugenics between Science and Politics." *Osiris* 5 (1989): 260–82.

Weiss-Wendt, Anton. *Murder without Hatred: Estonians and the Holocaust.* Syracuse: Syracuse University Press, 2009.

White, Elizabeth B. "Barring Axis Persecutors from the United States: OSI's 'Watch List' Program." *United States Attorneys' Bulletin* 54, no. 1 (2006): 19–22.

Wistrich, Robert S. *Austrians and Jews in the Twentieth Century: From Franz Joseph to Waldheim.* New York: St. Martin's Press, 1992.

INDEX

Department of Special Affairs (DSA), 193–94

Department of State, 13–14, 25–26, 28, 34–35, 37–38, 67–68, 122–23, 163–64, 179–80, 205–6, 211–12, 227, 229, 230, 240

deputy chiefs of staff, 217–18

Diesbach, Julius, 70–71

Displaced Persons Act of 1948 (DPA), 5–6, 18, 195–97, 240, 309n14

Dollfuss, Engelbert, 134–36

Doppelreiter, Franz, 34–35

Dora-Nordhausen, 238, 247–48, 255, 260, 271, 286

Dornberger, Walter, 214–16, 221–22, 235–39, 265, 267, 269–70, 272–75

Dörnten, 212, 272–73

dwarfs, 69–70, 73, 77–80

Eckstein, Alejandro von, 85–86, 87

Egan, Michael J., 27–28

Eichmann, Adolf, 23, 42–43, 87–88, 90, 101, 106–7, 108, 112, 117–18, 119, 122–23, 130, 179

Eilberg, Joshua, 26–27, 28, 30–31, 124–25

Eisenhower, Dwight D., 55, 144, 225, 276

Erskine, David, 55–56

Estonia, 186–87, 188–92, 194–97, 199–200, 203–6; German occupation of, 190, 191–92, 194, 195, 198; Home Guard (Selbstschutz) of, 190, 192; Soviet occupation of, 186–87, 189–90, 199–200, 203–6

Federal Bureau of Investigation (FBI), 10, 12, 25–26, 37, 179, 240–41, 245–47

Fedorenko v. Inus (1981), 203–5

Feigin, Judy, 1

Field Information Agency, Technical, 225–26

Fischer, Georg, 84

Fischer, Maria, 84

Flossenbürg, 6, 8–9

Fort Bliss TX, 226, 240–41, 244, 245, 274–76

France, 24, 107–8, 167, 187–88, 224, 260, 266–67, 270, 271; and Klaus Barbie, 40, 42–55, 60–64, 66–68; and Kurt Waldheim, 140–42, 143–44

Freedom of Information Act, 69–70

French Resistance, 47, 49–51, 52–53, 55

Garmisch Partenkirchen, 215, 239, 244

Garvey, Dale, 53–54

Gehlen, Reinhard, 115–17, 118–19, 130

General Accounting Office (GAO), 20–21, 25–27, 31

Gerhard, Wolfgang, 89–93

Gestapo, 2–3, 23, 138, 167, 238; and Klaus Barbie, 40, 47–48, 50–51, 52, 66–67; and Otto von Bolschwing, 103, 108–9, 113, 128–29

Goggin, Ray F., 115

Greece, 101, 158–61, 205–6

Green, John C., 228

Groves, Leslie, 224–25

Gruber, Karl, 145, 146–147

gypsies, 18, 22–23, 74, 78–79, 157–58, 165, 168, 169, 170

Hardy, Rene, 50–51

Harz Mountains, 272–73, 281

Heidler, Ana Maria, 171

Heimberg, Karl Ludwig, 259–60, 266, 268–71, 275–79, 282–83, 286–87, 288; with army ordnance, 268–69; early years of, 268–69; education of, 268–69; employment of, 266–70; at Mittelwerk, 269 71; at NASA, 276–78; at Peenemünde, 268–69, 270; in postwar period, 275–77; surrender of, 274–76, 282–83; and V-2 rockets, 269–70, 272, 275; during wartime, 268–69, 270–72. *See also* Braun, Wernher Magnus Maximilian von

Heylandt, 234–36

Heymann, Philip, 28–29

Himmler, Heinrich, 73, 104–5, 108, 112–13, 130, 237, 280–81, 282, 285–86

Hitler, Adolf, 41–43, 52, 98, 168–69, 228, 282; and Austria, 134–36, 137–39; and German prewar expansion, 187–88; and Otto von Bolschwing and "Jewish question," 107–10, 112–13, 130; and rocket program, 236–37, 266, 270

Hitler Youth, 41–42